Balkan Genocides

Studies in Genocide: Religion, History, and Human Rights

Series Editor: Alan L. Berger, Raddock Family Eminent Scholar
Chair of Holocaust Studies, Florida Atlantic University

Genocide is a recurring scourge and a crime against humanity, the effects of which are felt globally. Books in this series are original and sophisticated analyses describing, interpreting, and articulating lessons from historical as well as current genocides. Written from a range of scholarly perspectives, the works in this series articulate patterns of genocide and offer suggestions about early warning signs that may help prevent the crime.

Balkan Genocides: Holocaust and Ethnic Cleansing in the Twentieth Century, by Paul Mojzes

Jihad and Genocide, by Richard Rubenstein, President Emeritus and Distinguished Professor of Religion at the University of Bridgeport

Balkan Genocides

Holocaust and Ethnic Cleansing in the Twentieth Century

Paul Mojzes

ROWMAN & LITTLEFIELD PUBLISHERS, INC.
Lanham • Boulder • New York • Toronto • Plymouth, UK

Published by Rowman & Littlefield Publishers, Inc.
A wholly owned subsidiary of The Rowman & Littlefield Publishing Group, Inc.
4501 Forbes Boulevard, Suite 200, Lanham, Maryland 20706
http://www.rowmanlittlefield.com

Estover Road, Plymouth PL6 7PY, United Kingdom

British Library Cataloguing in Publication Information Available

Library of Congress Cataloging-in-Publication Data
Mojzes, Paul.
  Balkan genocides : holocaust and ethnic cleansing in the twentieth century / Paul
Mojzes.
     p. cm. — (Studies in genocide : religion, history, and human rights)
  Includes bibliographical references and index.
  ISBN 978-1-4422-0663-2 (cloth : alk. paper) — ISBN 978-1-4422-0665-6 (electronic)
  1. Genocide—Balkan Peninsula—History. 2. Genocide—Yugoslavia—History.
3. Ethnic conflict—Balkan Peninsula—History. 4. Ethnic conflict—Yugoslavia—
History. 5. World War, 1939–1945—Atrocities—Balkan Peninsula. 6. World War,
1939–1945—Atrocities—Yugoslavia. 7. World War, 1914–1918—Atrocities—Balkan
Peninsula. 8. World War, 1914–1918—Atrocities—Yugoslavia. 9. Yugoslav War,
1991–1995—Atrocities. I. Title.
  DR48.M65 2011
  364.15'1094970904—dc23
                                    2011029338

∞™ The paper used in this publication meets the minimum requirements of American
National Standard for Information Sciences—Permanence of Paper for Printed Library
Materials, ANSI/NISO Z39.48-1992. Printed in the United States of America

To members of my family and millions of
known and unknown victims of the Holocaust
and other Balkan genocides, ethnic cleansing,
and crimes against humanity

Contents

Preface

The idea of researching and writing about the Holocaust, genocides, and ethnic cleansing in the Balkans came late in my scholarly career, despite the fact that they affected me early in life when I lost numerous members of my immediate and wider family to genocidal activity. Early on, I concentrated my scholarship on the life and suffering of the churches in the Balkans, beginning with my doctoral dissertation, "A History of the Congregational and Methodist Churches in Bulgaria and Yugoslavia," completed at Boston University in 1965. Subsequently, I broadened that interest to study the larger field of Eastern European and Soviet-area studies and to include all Christian churches as well as, to some extent, other religious communities. By the 1970s, in my editorial capacity at *The Journal of Ecumenical Studies*, I had come to focus my attention on inter-Christian ecumenism as well as inter-religious dialogue. I was drawn not only into the exploration of the causes of suffering due to interconfessional strife and Communist persecution but also into finding ways of alleviating that suffering. Dialogue seemed to be the most effective way to improve the conflicting situations, and I plunged into promoting Christian-Marxist dialogue, particularly in Eastern Europe. The result was *Christian-Marxist Dialogue in Eastern Europe* (1980), written at a time when it was not at all clear that Marxism was in its twilight as the inspiration and justification for the Communist system that would collapse in Europe by the end of that decade. In the late 1980s, governing circles in Communist-dominated Eastern Europe and the Soviet Union contended that religion was freely practiced, while most religious persons claimed to be persecuted and restricted in their religious liberties. These conflicting claims led me to undertake a region-wide exploration of the issue—a study that I expected would become an eye-opening and comprehensive account of the real situation. But just as I was completing the manuscript, Communism collapsed. Many of the insights that I gained through laborious research soon became fairly widely known facts. The book, published in 1991, ended up being titled *Religious Liberty in Eastern Europe and the USSR: Before and after the Great Transformation.*

In the wake of the fall of Communism in the late 1980s and early 1990s, people were euphoric because it seemed that the former Communist countries would transition to democracy, guaranteeing the human rights and freedoms to which so many had aspired. Soon it would become obvious, however, that there were good reasons for dubbing the time as "post-Communist." It seemed, as Miroslav Volf aptly put it using a New Testament story, that while one "demon" was being driven out, another seven had moved in (see Matthew 12:45ff).[1]

In Yugoslavia, the country of my birth, post-Communist developments turned in directions even more disastrous than in other former Communist countries, leading to its dissolution in the bloodiest conflagration in Europe after World War II. During this time, I received more invitations to speak about the problems in Yugoslavia than I did to speak about the state of religion under Communism and post-Communism. I sensed that those who were reporting on the wars in the Balkans underestimated the role of religion, so I began to explore the role of religion in the area. The result was a book published in 1995, *Yugoslavian Inferno: Ethnoreligious Warfare in the Balkans.*

The remedy for the ethnoreligious conflicts and wars going on in Yugoslavia also seemed to be interreligious dialogue, particularly among Jews, Christians, and Muslims. By this time, I had become involved at the international level in Jewish-Christian-Muslim dialogue through the initiative of my close colleague Leonard Swidler of Temple University. Around the same time, to my surprise, my acquaintance and a fellow Methodist from Yugoslavia, Boris Trajkovski, was elected to the presidency of the Republic of Macedonia. On his invitation I, together with Leonard Swidler, facilitated interreligious dialogue and the formation of the Council for Interreligious Cooperation in Skopje. This council succeeded in making its modest contribution to the peace process, despite Trajkovski's untimely, tragic death in an airplane crash in 2004.

My writing and lecturing on the tragic consequences of the Balkan conflicts led to a surprising invitation from Richard Stockton College of New Jersey to become the Ida E. King Distinguished Visiting Professor of Holocaust and Genocide Studies for the fall semester of 2003. Teaching undergraduate and graduate courses, I came to a deeper awareness of just how frequent and pervasive the genocides, including the Holocaust, were in the Balkans. I also realized how comparatively little they had been studied, despite the huge outburst of books about the wars in the Balkans in the 1990s and despite the ongoing trials of war criminals by the International Criminal Tribunal for the Former Yugoslavia. Having received an invitation to contribute several articles and book chapters to a large study of religious genocide, I focused on a lengthier chapter entitled "The Genocidal 20th Century in the Balkans."[2] The research for that chapter convinced me that there needed to be a book-length study of that topic and that I was the right person to write it, especially because of my predilection not to take an ethnic stance in my analyses but to look for a balanced, comprehensive approach, without claiming to have been among those with direct access to the raw data. Also I realized that while the Holocaust in other parts of Europe had been adequately researched, this was not the case in regard to the Balkans, and that other genocides either were completely unrecognized, even in the Balkans, or were well-known in the Balkans (such as the Jasenovac concentration camp) but practically unknown outside the area.

Thus I aim to process what other researchers, scholars, journalists, and reporters have collected and presented regarding various aspects of the larger topic and to deal comprehensively with the entire dismal picture. In writing this, I am belatedly paying my debt to my ancestors who became victims of the genocidal process; I am doing so without focusing the blame on their particular perpetrators but instead realizing that the unknown perpetrators of these events had fallen prey to genocidal ideologies and demagoguery. Having realized how much of my early education under the Communist system was a biased and distorted account of half-truths, and having seen how the successor elites that took over the former Yugoslavia replaced a Marxist distortion of history with their own equally, if not more, distorted views (which in turn led to additional mutual recriminations and accusations), my deeply held conviction is that the *whole* truth needs to be presented in order to be able to more effectively deal with the dire consequences of past injustices.

In the past, my attempts to be even-handed and impartial resulted in criticism by authors of rival nationalities, who accused me of bias favoring their enemies and of animosity toward their respective sides. This was particularly true of my book *Yugoslavian Inferno*, which Croatian reviewers judged to be anti-Croat, and Serbian reviewers saw as anti-Serbian. I fully expect that a similar response may greet this book, and this would be no surprise because, as Baron d'Estournelles de Constant wrote, in the Balkans, "it is impossible to avoid the reproach of a party, if one does not take sides with it against the others, and conversely."[3]

My graduate students at Richard Stockton College of New Jersey challenged me to present the complex events and processes in the Balkans in the courses on the Holocaust and genocides. They provided the incentive to undertake this project as we realized how neglected is the study of the Holocaust and the genocides in the Balkans. I enjoyed their curiosity and dedication.

I am grateful for the help by my friends Barrie and Betty Eichhorn, who did the bulk of the initial copyediting, and my former colleague in religious studies at Rosemont College, Sarah Spangler, who edited two of the chapters. Also I thank my friend and neighbor, Ilija Šaula, who added diacritical marks on all the Slavic letters, thus contributing to greater accuracy of the text. The editorial staff of Rowman & Littlefield Publishers were invariably helpful. Professor Alan Berger, series editor, took an early interest in this work and encouraged me throughout; I am pleased that we have become friends through this process. Sarah Stanton, acquisition editor, and Jin Yu, editorial assistant, worked with me during the early phases of manuscript preparation; Jehanne Schweitzer, production editor, and Gail Fay, copyeditor, whipped it into its final shape. And foremost I am grateful to my wife, Elizabeth Mojzes, for her inexhaustible patience for my being both present and simultaneously absent during the many months of writing this book.

Initially I planned to provide a few maps to assist the readers in orienting themselves. Modern technology has made this superfluous. Readers can easily locate all of the regions, cities, towns, villages, and rivers mentioned in this book by simply accessing www.google.com/earth or www.maps.google .com, which provide much greater detail than what could be done here.

Pronunciation Guide

SERBO-CROATIAN-BOSNIAN

A, a = car
C, c = cats
Ć, ć = mutual
Č, č = chapter
Dj, dj = ginger
Dž, dž = just
E, e = pen
G, g = go
H, h = loch

I, i = deep
J, j = yard
Lj, lj = million
N, n = no
Nj, nj = new
O, o = dormitory
Š, š = ship
U, u = broom
Ž, ž = treasure

GERMAN

ä = made

ü = Muenster

HUNGARIAN

A, a = awe
C, c = cats
S, s = short

Á, á = master
Sz, sz = sad
Ü, ü = Muenster

ALBANIAN

Ç, ç = change

1

Definitions of Genocide and Ethnic Cleansing

In this chapter I examine the meaning of the key terms *Holocaust, genocide,* and *ethnic cleansing.* The term *Holocaust* has been adequately explained and understood both in the scholarly literature and among the general public. Usually it refers to the deliberate attempt to exterminate Jews under Hitler's Nazi regime; sometimes the definition more broadly includes other victims of Nazism slated for eradication. In this book the first meaning will usually be employed, although at times the broader sense of the word will also be used. The term *genocide* is more controversial; some use the term narrowly and precisely, adhering to the legal and scholarly definitions, while others use *genocide* vaguely and carelessly, as a sweeping charge regarding numerous mass killings. I devote most of this chapter to examining the term *genocide* as it applies to the Balkans (currently, the following countries are included: Albania, Bosnia and Herzegovina, Bulgaria, Croatia, Greece, Kosova, Macedonia, Montenegro, Serbia, Slovenia, and the European part of Turkey). *Ethnic cleansing* came into general use recently despite its more ancient origins, and therefore I also examine and use this term in this and subsequent chapters, especially chapter 4.

If there were "bragging rights" for being a genocidal and ethnic cleansing area, the Balkans could claim championship status. Building on centuries of wars, the occupation by great powers, and insurrections, the twentieth century was ushered in and closed by genocidal practices in the Balkans, with many of those issues still being played out well into the twenty-first century.

Those of us who lived in the Balkans during the twentieth century became aware of the words *genocide* and *ethnic cleansing* only *after experiencing* both of them directly. Neither our formal education nor the informal memo-

1

ries of elders offered clear reasons as to why such outbursts of hatred and great violence occurred between people who had also known times of harmony or at least passive acceptance of each other.

For most people, even for genocide scholars, World War II is the yardstick by which to measure genocide. Engaged in this war were three enormous ideological systems, each governed by strong governments and mighty armed forces: Nazi-dominated Germany, in alliance with Italian Fascists, was engaged in a life-and-death struggle against Marxist-inspired Soviet Communism, which had only temporarily become allied with Western capitalist democracies. Then there were the many smaller national or ethnic groups that got involved in the frequently chaotic violence as the groups shifted from being allies to being enemies and then allies again. Smaller European countries, such as those in the Balkans, were in one way or another enmeshed in this confrontation either by collaboration in a military takeover, or by being trampled under the major powers' brutal occupation. Blood was endlessly spilled. Millions of people died or were displaced, wounded, tortured, imprisoned, raped, burned out of their homes, or robbed of their valuables. Words fail to describe their misery and suffering.

The current prevailing scholarly analysis of these events identifies totalitarian governments as the major culprits. Consequently, scholars of genocide usually blame the powers of the state directed against minorities (e.g., Jews, Roma/Gypsies, Kulaks, Communists, Serbs, Muslims, Armenians). In this thinking, minorities were the scapegoats that needed to be removed, one way or the other, because they stood in the way of the triumphalist ideological worldview of either the German Nazi or Soviet Communist governments. Japan's role in the conquest of much of Asia also neatly fits into this scenario.[1]

The conviction prevailed that genocides were masterminded and ordered by powerful rulers, such as Hitler, Lenin, Stalin, and Mao Zedong.[2] That assumption created the annoying journalistic and later popular notion that all dictators who were ideologically inimical to us, such as Muammar Gaddafi, Idi Amin, Slobodan Milošević, or Saddam Hussein, should be quickly labeled "Hitler." This labeling by torturous analogies was quickly abandoned after the dictator in question was neutralized. However, the label was then readied for the next dictator. If not the rulers, then powerful generals or ministers in government were considered the main culprits of genocide, such as Talaat Pasha, Enver Pasha, and Jemal Pasha, who were the leaders of the Committee of Union and Progress and who dominated politics in Turkey during the Armenian genocide of 1915. Additionally, some hypothesized that German and Austrian diplomats and generals, in a prelude to the Armenian genocides of a subsequent period, provided the main impetus and support for the attempted extermination of the Armenians. In the same manner, Radovan Karadžić and

Ratko Mladić were held, along with Slobodan Milošević, as being mainly responsible for the Bosnian genocides. It is convenient to blame individuals and judicially helpful to consider specific people responsible for the main thrust of genocidal activity. In that way, entire nations or religions are not blamed for being genocidal. But this theory is far from convincing when one looks more carefully at the actual events on the ground.

Norman Naimark dismissed the role of ancient tribal or national conflicts in twentieth-century European genocides. He carried out a comparative study of several major genocides on the continent with the aim of emphasizing the heretofore underexplored role of contemporary political and social reasons for their occurrence. "Ethnic cleansing in former Yugoslavia, from this perspective, is a profoundly modern experience, related to previous instances in the twentieth century but not a product of 'ancient hatreds.'"[3] The advantage of focusing on contemporary causes and culprits suggests that remedies for current problems can be found in the contemporary world. This provides hope that the political will can be found to end them speedily and to prevent them from reoccurring. Consequently, the focus is on those political and related forces that caused the outbreak of ethnic cleansing or genocide, namely, modern nationalism and racism, seeking to block those activities or subsequently put their leaders on trial. However effective this path may be in producing desirable political or military action, it is simplistic for a scholarly analysis to dismiss *all* of the important pre-twentieth-century contributive factors. One of Naimark's weakest arguments is that "racism is a strictly modern product," a belief that he takes from Zygmunt Baumann.[4] Usually the term *modern* applies to the entire time frame starting around the fifteenth century, but these authors focus on more recent roles of social Darwinism, "scientific" disciplines such as eugenics, and technological abilities of modern state bureaucracies that aim to standardize, homogenize, categorize, and control the population. Political elites, supported by the technocrats, scientists, scholars, media, and medical and legal professions, were indeed beneficiaries of and major culprits in the rise of modern nationalism and racism. But their role seems insufficient to explain the broad involvement of populations in the entire range of violence from pogroms to genocides. While it is correct that Nazi racist theories brought some new dimensions to racism, surely racism predates the twentieth century or else African slavery in the New World and the European treatment of colonized people since the "age of discovery" would not have occurred. It is unhistorical to eliminate significant causes of contemporary developments simply because the inclusion of pre-twentieth-century causal factors "encompasses too much chronological territory and too many variations of a similar theme."[5] Certainly it is easier and neater to analyze events of greater proximity, but one should not dismiss influences on people's behavior just because they stem from the distant past. Therefore I reject attempts like Naimark's, to focus only on twentieth-century causality.

Benjamin Kiernan presents another interesting theory focusing upon certain social strata as perpetrators of genocides throughout history.[6] He takes the clue for his book title *Blood and Soil* from the well-known Nazi German slogan "Blut und Boden," which emphasizes kinship and the possession of the land as the stimuli for genocides. Kiernan posits that agriculturists, toilers of the soil, develop a deep affinity for the land that, along with clannish bonds of kinship, makes them perpetual genocidaires. His book is, indeed, a comprehensive history of genocides. However, the agriculturalist interpretation seems forced, artificial, one-dimensional, and ultimately unconvincing, despite the well-known rivalries between urban and rural settlers. While Serb villagers in Bosnia held in contempt the urban-dwelling Muslims and relished the shelling of Sarajevo from the mountains, as I have described elsewhere,[7] this is far from being a sufficient explanatory cause for the carnage between Serbs, Croats, and Bošniak Muslims in Bosnia in the 1990s.

Henry R. Huttenbach[8] has pointed out that the UN (United Nations) convention's description of genocide is a source of some confusion and is not easy to apply. It is hard to delineate precisely when mass violence morphs into genocide. Proving genocide has occurred is extremely difficult as one has to prove intent. "Intention is next to impossible to prove for lack of evidence; genocidists are careful not to leave a paper trail. . . . In most cases of genocide, intent has to be inferred from the radical acts of genocide, which leaves a problem of determining when an instance of mass killing became genocidal."[9]

Huttenbach points out that ethnic genocide is frequently accompanied by culturecide (forced assimilation and destruction of cultural monuments) and gendercide (the systematic targeting of either women or men). Further, he underscores the role of the political, religious, and intellectual elites in spreading extremism and hatred. Historically, these groups, particularly the intellectuals, tended not to condemn the war and ethnic cleansing when the war was going in favor of their ethnic group, but when the tides turned they started speaking out in favor of reconciliation and peace.[10] When hostile ethnoreligious groups inhabit the same territory and claim that it belonged to them in the distant past, the rivalry is greatly intensified to "genocidal proportions" because both groups have collective memories of battles past and realize that losing means they are going to be ethnically cleansed by their rivals; hence, they try to preempt it by becoming perpetrators of ethnic cleansing.[11]

A single cause theory of ethnic cleansing or genocide, especially recent ones, does not suffice as an adequate explanation. There is overwhelming evidence of spontaneous and often widespread hatred among people who had once been neighbors. In addition to whatever greater or smaller roles government played in inciting, allowing, or directing ethnic cleansing and genocide, there is clear evidence of other significant factors, such as the genocidal role played by the army, media, journalists, scholars, teachers, poets, novelists, and artists, as well as major and minor religious leaders. The all-too-willing participation and responsibility of the common people raised for me the question of collective responsibility.[12] Why did people, who often claimed that they had lived peacefully and harmoniously with their neighbors, turn suddenly against them, wishing to eliminate them? It struck me, as a person who was raised in a multinational family that lived in harmony, that another ideology besides the great social ideologies of Fascism, Communism, and democracy provided the main impetus for the outbreaks of extermination. It was ethnonationalism—or, more accurately, national chauvinism, or, in my own terminology, ethnoreligiosity—that seemed to be the illness that had infected many strata of the Balkan population during the twentieth century. They seemed bent on eliminating not only those of other national groups with whom they shared territory but members of their own group who favored co-existence, tolerance, and cooperation. For instance, one member of my wider family, for whom I have little regard, would sometimes burst out in rage over some imagined injustice by persons of another ethnicity and say that he would like to rip their throats out through their anuses (it was expressed in grosser language). Ironically, both of his daughters married men from the ethnic groups that so irritated the father!

A more recent book has brought greater theoretical clarity to my own thinking: Benjamin Lieberman's *Terrible Fate: Ethnic Cleansing in the Making of Modern Europe*.[13] Most authors distinguish between ethnic cleansing and genocide (while others regard ethnic cleansing as a euphemism for genocide), with ethnic cleansing being a softer term used either to connote activities less grievous than genocide or to avoid the more horrid sounding word *genocide*.[14] Lieberman considers pogroms as (usually) the first stage in the removal of a population from an area or from this world, followed by ethnic cleansing and finally by genocide, the most sweeping attempt to completely exterminate a targeted population. He also mentions ethnic war as a fourth stage when two or more ethnic groups try to eliminate each other from a territory that they jointly inhabit. Lieberman then subsumes all three or four stages under the general term *ethnic cleansing* as the main thread of his book.

The word *pogrom*, meaning "riot," is of Russian origin and is usually encountered in the experiences of violent anti-Semitic outbursts in nineteenth- and twentieth-century Russia. Pogrom became a more nuanced term than riot, though they share common elements. A more accurate meaning of pogrom is genocidal massacre, that is, a semi-spontaneous mob attack, an outburst by a more dominant ethnic or religious group over a minority that is usually

scapegoated for an alleged undermining of values that weakens the entire society (such as defense of the country in time of war, spying, cooperating with
the enemy, hoarding of goods or selling at exorbitant prices, and attacking or
murdering innocent members of the majority group). For the purposes of this
book, we'll consider pogroms as being massacres that are not primarily of an
economic nature, for example, when employers organize massacres of strik-
ing workers either by police or by strike-breakers. These pogroms focus on
ethnic or national, religious, and cultural differences, though pogroms sometimes have an exclusively political character. Pogroms sometimes precede
and at other times may be part of a more comprehensive ethnic cleansing.

In its narrower sense, ethnic cleansing—a term that does not (yet) have
legal standing but is clearly understood (in the sense that if you see it happening, you will recognize it)—is an organized campaign to forcibly transfer
a population out of an area. Ethnic cleansing may be planned and ordered by
governing or military authorities, or it may be the result of spontaneous outbursts of fear and rage by neighbors of a different ethnic, religious, or cultural
composition. Often it follows periods of relatively good intergroup relations
that break down with the onset of a crisis, usually during disintegrating or
transitional periods. Ethnic cleansing consists of threats, individual killings,
group violence, arrests, torture, rape, and arson—all leading to spontaneous
flight, forced migrations, or deportation.

We must put to rest the frequent charge that the term *ethnic cleansing* was
originally coined by the Serbs in Bosnia in 1992 and that, therefore, it was a
particularly Serbian activity. The practice of ethnic cleansing is probably as
old as humanity, and there may have been other locations where the term was
already used. Within the Balkan region it was previously used by the early
nineteenth-century reformer of the Serbian literary language Vuk Karadžić
(unrelated to the war criminal Radovan Karadžić), who used the term *cleanse*
(*očistiti*) for the massacre of Turks in Belgrade in 1806.[15] Likewise, Montenegro's prince-bishop Petar Petrović II-Njegoš, who is considered by many as
the greatest poet of the Serbian language, used it in his great epic poem "Gor-
ski vijenac" (Mountain Wreath), published in 1847, to describe the massacre
of Turks and other Muslims (*poturice*—a put-down word for Slavic converts
to Islam) that may have taken place over a century earlier with the intention
of cleansing Montenegro of the Muslim occupiers, whom the prince-bishop
regarded as obstacles for liberation of his country.[16] The poem has inspired,
or at least supported, the attempts by the Balkans' Christian population to rid
themselves of the Muslim presence. A more recent use of the term was more
sinister in that the speaker, a government official, called for ethnic cleansing
to take place. On June 2, 1941, in a speech at Nova Gradiška (in the immediate vicinity of Stara Gradiška, the site of one of the concentration camps in

the Jasenovac complex), Milovan Žanić, chairman of the Legislative Committee of the Independent State of Croatia that drafted laws, said, "This must be the land of the Croats and of no one else, and there are no methods that we Ustaše will shrink from to make this country truly Croatian and to *cleanse* it of the Serbs. We are making no secret of this. This is the policy of our state and when we put it into effect we will be doing what is inscribed in the Ustaša principle."[17] The same man stated that his country "should resort to whatever means necessary to build the Croatian State and cleanse it of Serbs. Destroy them wherever we can."[18]

What some people today consider a case of ethnic cleansing, such as in the two Balkan wars, was regarded by eyewitnesses as policies and acts of extermination for which they did not yet have the right word, genocide, available; today we may identify them as genocides. While there is no sharp delineation between ethnic cleansing and genocide, especially at the end of the spectrum where ethnic cleansing is so violent that it develops into genocide, there is, at the other end of the spectrum, ethnic cleansing that is synonymous with population transfer, expulsion, forcible deportation, or purging the unwanted "traitors" or "enemies" from other ethnic groups—even members of one's own ethnic group who are too friendly with or supportive of the unwanted groups. The key distinction is intent: in ethnic cleansing the intent is less than extermination of the victim group, while in genocide it entails the group's destruction. Of course, intent is more easily recognized theoretically than in real life. Someone may, in a rhetorical overstatement, say, "Let's kill them all" but not really mean it, while others may never explicitly call for it but actually plan for a "final solution."

However, there is consensus that genocide is the most awful stage of ethnic cleansing in the wider sense of the term, namely, a planned, conscious, often government-conducted attempt at exterminating, eradicating, and, if possible, making a group vanish from the face of the earth—a true final solution to the alleged problems caused by the targeted group's presence among the rest of the population. The UN Convention on the Prevention and Punishment of the Crime of Genocide of 1948 remains the official definition of genocide, despite the fact that it has been criticized as being both too narrow (e.g., it does not include politicide) and too broad (it stipulates genocide even when the actions are carried out against a part of the group, though it is not clear how small or large that part ought to be). Some have argued (e.g., Israel Charny) that the intentional killing of even one member of a group with the intent to exterminate him or her already qualifies as genocide, but that seems so inclusive that it makes genocide an ever-present experience both in time and in place. If genocide is to be found everywhere, it loses its horrendous character and inhibits us from wanting to prevent it.

The UN Convention on the Prevention and Punishment of the Crime of Genocide provides the following definition:

> Article II: In the present Convention, genocide means any of the following acts committed with intent to destroy, in whole or in part, a national, ethnical, racial or religious group, as such:
>
> (a) Killing members of the group;
> (b) Causing serious bodily or mental harm to members of the group;
> (c) Deliberately inflicting on the group conditions of life calculated to bring about its physical destruction in whole or in part;
> (d) Imposing measures intended to prevent births within the group;
> (e) Forcibly transferring children of the group to another group.
>
> Article III: The following acts shall be punishable:
> Genocide;
> Conspiracy to commit genocide;
> Direct and public incitement to commit genocide;
> Attempt to commit genocide;
> Complicity in genocide.

Huttenbach observes that while the preceding definition was adopted by subsequent tribunals that tried war crimes and genocides, those same tribunals all found the definition inadequate and confusing, and thus they interpreted, amended, and supplemented the definition as they saw fit.[19] The basic disagreement is between what Huttenbach calls the "literalists" and "generalists," namely, those who try to apply the UN convention's language strictly in the narrowest sense of the words and those who apply it as a general principle that needs to be used more flexibly in concrete situations. The difference between the literalists and generalists may explain the difficulties in judging, for instance, whether, when, and where the breakout of violence in the various Balkan wars crossed into genocidal intent and genocidal action. What may appear to observers or victims as a case of genocide is hard to prove legally as the intent is more difficult to demonstrate in a court of law. Usually those who commit genocide are careful to avoid the "smoking gun" or "paper trail" and the thin line between mass killing and genocide turns out to be arbitrary.[20]

Robert Gellately and Benjamin Kierman point to the difficulties with the UN convention's definition in determining *intent* to destroy a group and the meaning of the words "as such." From a legal perspective, genocidal intent also applies to acts of destruction that are not the specific goal but the predictable outcomes or by-products of a policy, which could have been avoided by a change in that policy. In international law, then, "genocide describes *both* deliberate mass extermination campaigns specifically motivated by fear or hatred of a victim group, . . . *and* destruction of human groups pursued for more indirect or political purposes. . ."[21] The authors also point out that "as such" may apply to the group, meaning destruction of the communal group as a group, or it may apply to members of the group when one is killed because he or she is a member of such a group.[22]

A very large number of scholars have pointed out that there is a nexus between war and genocide, as genocides most often take place during wars, or that genocides are a kind of war. Huttenbach notes, "Because of the nature of its violence, genocide should be understood as lying within the parameters of war, both as a precipitator of war and as an offspring of war."[23] But it is clear that not every war includes genocide. The first war of the dismemberment of Yugoslavia, the brief war in 1991 in Slovenia, did not contain genocidal or ethnic cleansing elements. On the other hand, genocides may take place (or may be claimed to be taking place) when an area is not in a state of war. In 1986 or even earlier, leaders of the Serbian Orthodox Church and some Serbian nationalists claimed that genocide was being carried out by Kosovo Albanians on Kosovo's Serbian population—at least thirteen years before a war broke out in that province of Serbia. This particular case illustrates the impressionistic and arbitrary character of claims of genocide. What seemed to be a case of genocide to the leaders of the Serbian Orthodox Church and many Serbs of Kosovo, the American scholar Michael Sells dismissed (perhaps prematurely) as a Serbian nationalist claim of "genocide" fabricated to pursue policies that would later end in real genocides against Muslims, both Bosnian and Albanian, in the 1990s.[24]

Ethnic or religious war is a case of violent confrontation between two or more groups, usually sharing a territory, conducted in order to determine who owns the land exclusively and whose group is to dominate the historical processes determining the future. The wars in Bosnia in the 1990s may be a good example of ethnic, or, more accurately, ethnoreligious, warfare in which ethnic cleansing in the narrower sense was attempted with partial success and in which genocide may have taken place.[25]

Beyond establishing the classification of ethnic cleansing, Benjamin Kiernan's far more important contribution is that he related ethnic cleansing to the process of nation-building out of which modern Europe was created. His starting point is the decline of the multiethnic and multireligious empires, such as the Hapsburg, Ottoman, and Russian empires (as he focuses more on Eastern Europe, thus bypassing the Western European empires that until the emergence of Nazi Germany had not focused on ethnic cleansing), followed by the rise of modern nationalism, which started in Western Europe and slowly spread to Eastern and Southern Europe with devastating impacts. As the various peoples of these empires became aware of their ethnic, linguistic, religious, cultural, literary, and historical identities, they developed, usually under the prompting of the intellectuals, a desire for people of their own kind to live in increasingly homogenous homelands. They began a struggle for liberation from what they perceived as the yoke of the empire. Most of this process began early in the nineteenth century, but the process hasn't ended yet as the Nazi and Communist empires interrupted the process of separating themselves from each other and delineating where the borders between these new nation-states ought to be. "The first wave of modern European ethnic cleansing emerged along the borders of the empires that no longer exist: the Ottoman and Russian empires."[26] I would have added the Hapsburg Empire to the above two and emphasized that these empires were frequently at war with each other over the terrain where future ethnic cleansing would take place. In the Balkans these wars also caused a series of uprisings against the empires: rebellions in Serbia in 1804 and 1815–1817, the Greek War of Independence in 1821–1830, the Bosnian-Herzegovinian rebellion in 1875, the Bulgarian rebellion in 1876, and the rebellions on the island of Crete in 1866–1867 and 1896–1897.[27] All of these rebellions contained a strong ethnic component and aimed at national liberation from the imperialism.

It was in these rebellions that the desire to remove the Turks and their converts out of the midst of the majority population (whom the Muslims merely regarded as *raya*, or the servile masses) was manifested. At first this desire arose among the intellectuals, many of whom had received their education in the learning centers in Western Europe where they became imbued by the ideas of the French Revolution that were conducive to nation-building. Teachers, poets, novelists, priests, cartographers, and historians rushed into action, reminiscent of what happened as a prelude to the outbreak of the wars of Yugoslavia's disintegration in the 1980s,[28] and urged people to throw off the imperial domination and create—or, better yet, re-create—former pre-Ottoman or pre-Hapsburg feudal states based on their alleged ethnic identity. The peasantry, which was by far the largest segment of the population, was much slower to arrive to this awareness, but they too responded, as their oppression, taxation, and suffering from foreign overlords was extremely burdensome. The rebellions were put down by the Ottoman Turks with much bloodshed and repression—actions that later stimulated equally bloody revenge when the tables were turned. For this turning of tables the Balkan people eagerly awaited and prepared themselves politically and militarily.

While most of the ethnic Christian groups increasingly turned against the Muslims, they also turned against each other. The Ottoman principle of governing included the division of the population into *millets* based on religious identification. There were Muslim, Jewish, Eastern Orthodox, Armenian, and

Roman Catholic *millets*. The vast majority of the Ottoman Empire's Christian population was Orthodox, and it was juridically under the limited dominion of the Greek Orthodox Patriarch of Constantinople (Istanbul). Greek bishops and priests had been given privileged positions that were increasingly being resented by the non–Greek Orthodox people, and thus interethnic rivalries and antagonisms emerged within this *millet*.

Of all the empires, the Ottoman Empire had the longest and most pronounced decline, which was exploited by its rivals as well as the subject people whose grievances became more pronounced as the hope for throwing off the imperial yoke became more visible, perhaps with the assistance of another empire. The varied populations' mutual contempt for each other became more pronounced. Religion sometimes "united" the empire's populations, but it more often divided them; their religious identities usually did not include knowing the beliefs and moral rules of the others' respective faiths. So, "the breakdown of imperial power on the edge of the empire in a region with divided population" would promote future outbreaks of ethnic cleansing.[29]

The two Serbian rebellions of 1804 and 1815–1817 did not lead to outright ethnic cleansing. They were directed toward the abuses of the corrupt local Turkish warlords and landlords supported by the *jannisaries* (elite Ottoman troops consisting of formerly Christian children converted to Islam). Both rebellions caused massive Turkish retributions but provided increasing local self-government and semiautonomy for the Serbs on part of the territory to which they aspired.

By 1876 the rebellion in Bulgaria became even more ethnically charged. The rebellion was unsuccessful and provoked much bloodshed, particularly by the actions of the *Bashi-Bazouks*, the Turkish irregulars. Most of them were local Turks, Pomaks or Circassian Muslims who were known personally by the Bulgarian villagers whose lives they took on "the field of skulls and bones."[30] To this the Bulgarians responded by seeking the complete expulsion of Muslims. As the Bulgarians were unable to carry it out by themselves, they sought the assistance of the Russian tsar.

The Russo-Turkish war of 1877–1878 did lead to the eventual independence of Bulgaria. At first the Russian army pushed the Turks almost to Constantinople (Istanbul); then they retreated but finally ended the war victoriously. With each drive of the respective armies, the targeted population fled in panic, emptying villages and towns as the well-founded fear of massacres drove people into desperate columns of refugees that clogged the roads for weeks. Again the main culprits of massacres and arsons were the *Bashi-Bazouks*, but the local Bulgarian bands, called *komitadji*, were responsible for ethnic cleansing of the Muslims. Indeed, at the end of this war the number of Muslims in Bulgaria was radically reduced.

Lieberman concludes that both the Russian and Ottoman armies caused much destruction and aided in displacing populations. On the local level, grassroots ethnic cleansing took place during the wars. According to Lieberman, the motives for such cleansing were plunder (an important but not determinative motive), increasing mutual antipathy, the rise of Bulgarian national awareness due to better education, religious identification, personal experiences of persecution by Turks, and cycles of revenge due to not merely personal tragedies but collective experiences of ethnoreligious pogroms or massacres and the burning of villages that led to mass flights and expulsions.[31] Farther south and west similar conflicts took place in Greece and on Crete between Greeks and Turks along with Muslim converts, resulting in an analogous mutual hatred and bloodletting and leading to the eventual expulsion of the Muslims.

According to Lieberman,

> Early forms of ethnic cleansing across Eastern Europe and Western Asia began both as government policy and as a grassroots phenomenon. . . . But much of the pressure to expel neighbors of a different ethnic or religious identity emerged at a local level. A populist path toward ethnic cleansing was most evident in the Ottoman regions. Violence and mass flight most often took place when Ottoman authority either broke down or confronted major threats. . . . Numerous eyewitnesses to massacres in the wars for Turkey in Europe reported how strikingly ready so many ordinary people were to attack their neighbors, to steal their property, to burn their homes, even to kill them—and to drive away the survivors.[32]

And a further observation by Lieberman holds true,

> While new stories of age-old nationalist hatred constructed by intellectuals, along with the personal experiences of revenge killing and flight, cast entire peoples as national enemies, on an individual level those who were identified as members of an enemy nation might simultaneously be seen as harmless acquaintances or neighbors. This same paradox would remain a key element of ethnic cleansing through the end of the twentieth century.[33]

As is evident from the preceding, I concur with much of Lieberman's findings. My major disagreement with him is that he believes the inception of genocidal inclinations takes place during the collapse of empires. He sees the rule of the empires as far more benevolent and efficacious than I do. I perceive empires, not as associations of diverse peoples under the benevolent rule of an autocrat, but as state structures based on conquest and colonial power, more often than not by brutal capture of the land and the enslavement or servitude of the local population. People of one nation or religion dominated and exploited the subject people. The fact that there had been sometimes long periods without great rebellions does not mean that the population was satisfied with their lot, but that they simply saw no way out of their "destiny." The intellectuals' narratives of past glories and colonial enslavement were often fictitious. The masses of the newly rising nation-states found such warm response because liberation resonated with their experience of oppression. They really did suffer. And they really wanted to be free. The fact that freedom often eluded them in their newly established countries was another matter.

Both the elites and the general population experienced real or imagined threats during the great crises and transitional periods in their collective destinies. These threats were experienced not merely individually but also collectively, in families, clans, villages, regions, and lands. It is immaterial whether the threats were real or imaginary—just observe the behavior of Americans, and, indeed, others, after twenty some terrorists attacked the United States on September 11, 2001. People responded in fear and anger. The natural response is to rally together against the threat. Group solidarity forms almost instantly; human beings still possess the same herding instinct that animals do. The observation that "birds of a feather flock together" does apply to humans as well. Whether such bonding is based on skin color, linguistic affinities, or ethnic bonds, it makes no difference, nor does it make a difference that many of these bonds are artificial constructs. When some Macedonians were attacked by some Albanians, for example, they sought protection and security from other Macedonians, even though not all Albanians attacked them and even though some Macedonians were their enemies. The herding instinct, which seems a defense mechanism, is also closely related to the pack mentality, our recognition that we can assert ourselves and achieve our goals when we act together against those who are in our way, who threaten to obstruct us in achieving our goals. Much has been written about nearly every group having a narrative of victimization—real or imaginary. We seek to find the cause of our victimization and to prevent those who caused it from inflicting more danger. In order to eliminate it, we need force. If we don't have real power, we invent it. The epic folk poetry of the Balkans illustrates how fiction can replace reality in order to provide the psychological satisfaction of not being completely defenseless against oppression. Take the legendary figure of Kraljević Marko (Prince Marko, 1371–1395), who in reality was an Ottoman vassal who died fighting *for* the Turks in Asia Minor but in poetry and folklore was transformed into a mighty warrior *against* the Turks, Albanians, and other Muslims, capable of supernatural feats, giving the captive Slavic population something to dream about when confronted by cruel reality. The study of folk poetry tends to disprove the notion that somehow the colonized population during the time of empires was satisfied until it was artificially stimulated by the elites to turn into bloodthirsty promoters of modern nationalism.[34]

While the interethnic conflicts were escalating in the Balkans in the nineteenth century, the twentieth century would bring about a veritable explosion of ethnic cleansing of genocidal proportions. In the second decade of the twentieth century in the southeastern parts of the Balkans, the two wars named after the peninsula would deliver the earliest European genocides and ethnic wars of the century that totally overshadowed the earlier uprisings and wars of independence.

Jacques Semelin provides socio-psychological analyses of massacres and genocides.[35] He points out that the social and political uses of imaginary constructs based on fear and anxiety are transformed into hatred in order to purify society by removing or destroying allegedly evil-minded "others" who are the source of the troubles that beset society. Semelin provides a comparative study of the Holocaust, the Yugoslav wars of the 1990s, and the Rwandan conflict of 1994 and also provides useful insight into how ordinary people internalize the propagandistic interpretation of the enemy in order to be able to indulge in orgies of violence.[36]

Using the most recent ethnic cleansing and genocidal experiences in the Balkans, Michael Mann presents several factors characterizing ethnic cleansing. I consider all but one of his points as accurately reflecting the Balkan experiences. The point I disagree with is that "murderous ethnical cleansing is modern, because it is the dark side of democracy,"[37] which is contradicted by the evidence provided earlier. Yet Mann disproves the more commonly held notion that democracies do not carry out ethnic cleansings and genocides, only dictatorships do. According to Mann, another factor that leads to violent ethnic cleansing is that ethnic identification replaces arrangements based on social class and channels the resentments into ethnic emotions. The threat of violence increases when movements that claim to be heirs to ancient state structures begin to make claims to overlapping territories and when these claims receive a sympathetic hearing by significant portions of the population. The chance for violence increases when the stronger side believes it has the necessary military prowess to forcefully implement its goals, or else that the minority is backed into a situation in which fighting is better than surrendering. War tends to break out when radicalized factions of the state take advantage of a confused geopolitical situation. Contrary to popular perceptions that ethnic cleansing is conceived and planned by a few despotic leaders, Mann claims that initially, ethnic cleansing is not the intent of the perpetrators. Instead of it being the sinister plot by a few leaders, it is the result of the coalescence of radical governing elites, bands of violent militants that often organize themselves into paramilitary units, and a critical mass of the population that provides support to the elite and the militants. Lastly, Mann states that during ethnic cleansing and genocide, ordinary people become able and willing to commit atrocities against the victims.

Other refinements of the notions of genocide and ethnic cleansing originated from the International Criminal Tribunal for the Former Yugoslavia (ICTY).[38] The very creation of ICTY and its statute, as it was established by the UN Security Council and approved by the UN General Assembly, was a further development of the basic lines established at the Nurenberg International Military Tribunal that tried Nazi leaders for war crimes and crimes against humanity in 1946. Among the important advancements of ICTY rulings are that states must comply with international court orders to arrest and deliver accused perpetrators, that crimes against humanity occur not only in international conflicts but also in internal ones, and that these crimes may be committed both by agents of a state and by insurgents or terrorists. Intent by the perpetrator must exist for a crime against humanity to occur in a systematic and widespread attack against civilians. Specific offenses are enumerated, such as extermination, torture, rape, forced deportation, enslavement, arbitrary imprisonment, and persecution, as well as other inhumane acts, a phrase that provides for future expansion.

Despite the similarities between extermination and genocide, ICTY made a distinction. Extermination is when a mass killing takes place without the clear intent to destroy the entire or part of the group as specified in the UN Genocide Convention. There must be intent to destroy a sizable group of the targeted population in order to consider the action genocide. The court also distinguished between deportation and forcible transportation in that the former means expulsion across international borders whereas the latter takes place within the boundaries of the state. The court also detailed the meaning of torture as an intentional element of a crime against humanity in that it can be either physical or mental violence, aimed at either obtaining information or punishing, humiliating, intimidating, or discriminating against a person in which at least one official person participates within the scope of an armed conflict. ICTY officially added rape to the list of war crimes and crimes against humanity. Rape was specified as a coercive (even threatening force) sexual act with or without actual penetration. Persecution was defined as infringement of fundamental human rights based on religious, racial, ethnic, or cultural grounds or political opinion.

Ethnic cleansing has not yet received clear legal definition. Currently from a legal perspective it is a conglomeration consisting of the categories of war crimes and crimes against humanity, and it may or may not include genocidal massacres and even genocides. Ethnic cleansing, despite its vague legal standing, is generally easier to demonstrate than genocide. Genocide can also be more easily established before the court of public opinion and even history than before a court of law.

While ICTY based its deliberations on the UN Genocide Convention, it added some clarity to aspects of aiding and abetting genocide or being guilty of genocidal acts. Generally, genocide includes the relentless drive to destroy the targeted group and the need for demonstrable direct or indirect evidence that the accused both had knowledge of the murders and was conscious of the intent to commit genocide. The court also decided that even when destruction is intended only against a specified or localized part of a group (such as the 7,000–8,000 Muslim men captured in Srebrenica by the Serb army), it is still to be classified as genocide. ICTY stated, "The killing of all members of the part of a group located within a small geographic area, although resulting in a lesser number of victims, would qualify as genocide if carried out with the intent to destroy the part of the group as such located in this small geographic area."[39] The size of such a group has to be significant enough to have an impact on the entire group and to threaten the physical survival of the group. The court also decided that forcible transfer of a group by itself cannot in itself determine genocidal intent. The court also decided that premeditation does not necessarily mean intentionality in a charge of genocide. And finally the bodily or mental injury need not be irremediable or permanent but must cause "grave and long-term disadvantage to a person's ability to lead a normal and constructive life."[40] The words "normal and constructive life" seem too slippery as a legal concept, though they are understandable in common parlance.

The clarifications and expansion of charges regarding genocide, war crimes, crimes against humanity, and specific subcategories have already been applied by the International Criminal Tribunal for Rwanda and in the drawing up of the Rome Statute of the International Criminal Court in 1998. It is to be expected that they will also be applied in any future court cases regarding war crimes, crimes against humanity, ethnic cleansing, and genocide.

2

The Heritage of Horrors

Writing about the Balkan genocides is different than writing about the Holocaust. Regarding the Holocaust there is a remarkable consensus among scholars of various nationalities about the main outline of events and even most of the details (except issues such as why the Red Army stalled its advance as it approached Warsaw). The research of German scholars does not contradict the findings of American, Israeli, French, British, and other scholars, although there may be differences in emphasis. Only Holocaust deniers, who also come from various national backgrounds, contest that the Holocaust took place, and few consider these deniers trustworthy interpreters of events of that period.

Not so regarding the Balkan genocides. The writers of the histories of the twentieth century (and before) who belong to various nationalities, especially those from the Balkans, have irreconcilable differences, and thus their accounts vary regarding not only what caused this or that event but also how they describe the events themselves. Greeks, Turks, Bulgarians, Albanians, Serbs, and Macedonians have widely divergent interpretations of the early twentieth-century shrinking of the Ottoman Empire and the wars that accompanied this retreat. Serbians, Croatians, Bosniaks,[1] Italians, Hungarians, Bulgarians, Germans, and others have different interpretations of the events of World War II. Moreover, people within the same nation have radically divergent interpretations depending on their ideological commitments. Hence, Serbs of a royalist orientation who admire General Draža Mihailović's Četniks[2] differ in opinion from those who followed the German-installed leader of rump Serbia, Milan Nedić, and both of them would differ even more markedly from Communist Serbs who were members of the Partisan[3] movement. As to the events of the late twentieth century, not only do Serbs, Croats, and Bosniaks of Bosnia and Herzegovina offer very different narratives, but Bosniaks following Alija Izetbegović have an utterly different perspective from those following Fikret Abdić. Serbs who followed Radovan Karadžić have a very different view from the approximately 30,000 Serbs who remained in Sarajevo along with General Jovan Divjak, a Serb who sided with the government of Bosnia and Herzegovina under the leadership of Alija Izetbegović when Sarajevo was pounded by General Ratko Mladić's forces. Serbs who followed Slobodan Milošević have an entirely different perspective from the Serbians who opposed the wars and fled abroad in the tens of thousands so as to avoid serving in the armies that would be sent to Bosnia. And perhaps the most irreconcilable narratives are those of Serbs and Albanians from Kosovo, whose interpretation of the past and present are so contradictory[4] that one would hardly grasp that they are talking about the same place. U.S. congressional delegations went to Kosovo in the early 1980s and noted discrepancies in the stories they heard, and when they returned ten years later, hoping to hear more consistent accounts of events, they found that accounts continued to be divergent regarding what had been happening, what was at stake, and how the conflict might be resolved. If one went to Kosovo today, one might actually find that the differences are even greater than before, as Kosovo is no longer part of Serbia and there is only a token presence of Serbians left in the newly independent state of Kosova.[5]

One of the most contentious issues in these accounts deals with what transpired between Croats and Serbs during World War II, especially in regard to the concentration camp at Jasenovac (see chapter 4). Milan Bulajić, the former director of the Museum of the Victims of Genocide in Belgrade, is one of the main proponents of the claim that the executions at Jasenovac and other activities of the Croat nationalist Ustaše movement[6] carried off a massive genocide of Serbs, Jews, and Roma amounting to hundreds of thousands to over a million victims. He has persistently pushed for international recognition of the massacres as genocidal and has sought to have the contemporary Croat government accept responsibility for the genocide. Frequently Bulajić interprets the events of the 1990s in Croatia and Bosnia as a continuation of those genocidal policies toward Serbs, especially the "Lightning" and "Storm" military offensives that in effect drove all Serbs out of the regions of Croatia.

On the other hand, a former Ustaša[7] commander of the Jasenovac camp, Dinko Šakić, who had escaped to Argentina after 1945 but was extradited to Croatia for a trial in 1999, defended himself along the lines forwarded by the late president of Croatia, Franjo Tudjman—namely, that Jasenovac is a Serb-Communist myth intended to destroy Croats. At his trial, Šakić showed absolutely no remorse, saying that Jasenovac was not an extermination camp but a work camp where the enemies of the Independent State of Croatia were dealt with humanely and kindly and that, during his command, there had been no killings. Rather, he maintained, the camp was organized against those who were complicit in the Serbian genocidal policies against the Croatian people from 1919 until the establishment of the Independent State of Croatia.[8] Šakić maintained that his conscience was clear before God and that, under similar circumstances, he would do the same now because the biological existence of the Croat people is threatened. He admitted that Jews and Roma were interned on an ethnic basis but stated that internment was only for those Serbs and others who were enemies of the state and were trying to destroy Croatia. Titoist Yugoslavia, as well as the recent wars in the Balkans, were seen by Šakić as evidence that Serbs have continued planning and carrying out genocide over Croats to the time of the 1999 trial.

Šakić was found guilty of war crimes and crimes against humanity and sentenced to twenty years in prison, but to Bulajić that was totally inadequate. He thinks Šakić should have been tried for the crime of genocide[9] and further believes not only that the court proceedings were part of a conspiracy by the Croatian court to deny that genocide was carried out by the regime of the Independent State of Croatia, but also that the present state of Croatia continues to harbor the same intentions toward Serbs.

The contradictory and unresolved viewpoints regarding Balkan genocides can be demonstrated even by the actions or inactions of religious leaders. Until 2009, no Croat Catholic bishop had visited the Jasenovac camp area since 1945, to the great irritation of the Serbs. Finally, Bishop Marin Srakić of Djakovo did visit in 2009. A few months after that visit, the Zagreb archbishop, Cardinal Josip Božanić, visited Jasenovac with some other higher clergy and held a mass in the local Catholic Church. There, the cardinal mentioned the Serb, Jewish, and Roma victims and condemned the Ustaša regime, but he defended the Catholic Church and immediately attacked the Communists who, he said, have been responsible for even greater crimes than those perpetrated at Jasenovac. Thereupon, Cardinal Božanić proceeded to evoke the memory of the Serbs stigmatizing the Croats as a genocidal people and of the Serb aggression against Croatia and Bosnia. He, like so many others, was unable or unwilling to separate these evils so that every remorseful "yes, we did it" was followed by the accusatory "but you did the same or worse."

When I published my book *Yugoslavian Inferno: Ethnoreligious Warfare in the Balkans* in 1994, Croat reviewers accused me of being pro-Serb; Serb reviewers accused me of being pro-Croat. Had the book been reviewed in Bosnia, reviewers would have probably accused me of being anti-Bosniak. From this I conclude that my interpretation was reasonably objective as, indeed, I tried my best to avoid being one-sided. In the Balkans, such objectivity is unwelcome, as the motto seems to be, "If you are not for me, you are against me." Should this book be read by some in the Balkans, I expect a similarly disapproving response, despite my efforts to describe and analyze the developments that brought about these nightmarish "solutions" in the hopes that they might not be repeated in the future.

It is self-evident that genocides do not occur in a vacuum and without causes. In order to get a better understanding of what transpired in the Balkans in the twentieth century, it is helpful to know Balkan history from ancient times. This, of course, is not attempted here. I only point out some moments that prepared the ground for making the nightmares possible; for, as is true of all nightmares, there are previous events that trigger them.

One factor is the heritage of horror. Many are aware of the bloodshed in Homeric ancient Greece, by the Spartans at Thermopolis, by Philip and Alexander of Macedon, and in the Roman conquests. Less well-known by Western readers are Byzantium's wars against the newly established Balkan states of Croatia, Bulgaria/Macedonia, Serbia, and Bosnia, as well as the states' wars among themselves. An example of the kinds of cruelty perpetrated in these wars is the battle in 1014 between the Byzantines under Emperor Basil II and Bulgaro/Macedonians under Tsar Samuel. When the Byzantine army had outflanked, surprised, and defeated the Macedonians in the area of present-day southeastern Republic of Macedonia, they proceeded to blind the entire captured army, leaving only one soldier among every 100 with one eye to lead the other 99 home. To this day, the Macedonian village near where this happened is called Očevad (digging out eyes). People in the Balkans have long memories of gruesome events that serve as reminders of the need for revenge.

Then came the waves of conquests by Romans, Byzantines, Venetians, Crusaders (third and fourth), Hungarians, Austrians, Ottoman Turks, Napoleonic French, Italians, Germans, Soviets, and lastly NATO (North Atlantic Treaty Organization). Empires from outside the region more frequently determined what was happening in the Balkans than the people living there. Foreign occupations definitely crushed the rights and freedoms of those whom they held captive.

Different peoples adjusted differently to conquests. Some resisted, some were subdued, some were converted and assimilated, some suffered inferiority complexes coupled with irrational pride and hubris, and so on.

Take the Albanians, for example. It is possible that they are heirs of Balkan aborigines, perhaps Illyrians, who were apparently driven into the most inhospitable terrain in the Balkans—the present-day location of Albania. Converted first to Christianity, they divided into Orthodox (south) and Catholic (north) branches in the eleventh century, depending on their respective proximities to the capitals of these two branches of Christianity (the rest of the Balkans was equally split between the Orthodox and Catholics, mostly along an east-west line of division). Later they succumbed to the Ottomans and largely converted to Islam (today they are the only European country with a Muslim majority—about 70 percent); the region has also been the home and headquarters of the Bektaši, a very non-legalistic, flexible, and tolerant mystic community that is outwardly Muslim. Tribal organization in Albania retained its influence, ruled by a strict honor code that to the present retains the practice of vendetta.

The Albanians' poverty drove them to seek sustenance where they could find it, and they readily "rented themselves out" to whomever would hire them to help control an area, as they excelled as warriors. Sometimes they fought on the side of the Turkish sultan to control local insurrectionist warlords and landlords; sometimes they fought against the sultan on the side of the warlords. In this task, the Albanians traversed the Balkan Peninsula, often venturing far from home, and if they were not properly paid, they would maraud, plunder, and kill as the need arose.[10] Thus Albanian bandits in the eighteenth and nineteenth century roamed western and central Macedonia and besieged Prilep, Štip, Debar, and Veles (all in the present-day Republic of Macedonia); Kyustendil, Vidin, Nevrokop, and Stara Zagora (in Bulgaria); Soko Banja (Serbia); and Ionannina (Greece).[11] They also migrated frequently in search for more fertile land, commercial opportunities, and guard duties in which they served local notables but were quite willing to change sides if they were not paid the promised fee.

One may not be surprised to find that while a modern scholar may be nonjudgmental about this mode of survival, those whose town or village had been besieged, occupied, destroyed, and devastated by the Albanian bandits did not have a particularly fond view of them. The animosity toward the Albanians by their neighbors, who had formed an alliance against the Ottoman Empire in the First Balkan War, was "natural" because the Albanians were the only Ottoman captives who did not rebel against the Turks. They did not endear themselves to any of their neighbors. It did not matter to them that the Albanian Muslims figured they were better off under the Turks than they would be under the rising new "Christian" states. Given what transpired in the First Balkan War, it is clear that they were right. However, Albanian cooperation with the Turks earned them the reputation of being outposts of conquest-oriented Islam among the Christian states of the Balkans.

I was born in Osijek, Croatia (then the Kingdom of Yugoslavia) in 1936, but later my family moved to Novi Sad, the capital of Vojvodina (in Serbia), which at that time in 1941 was under Hungarian control. After World War

II, as a young boy in the 1950s, I visited Osijek on several occasions, staying with my aunt's family for summer vacations. A pleasant city stretched out along the Drava River, Osijek was inhabited primarily by Croatians, though Serbs, Germans, Hungarians, Jews, and others also lived there. It has a beautiful, dominating Catholic cathedral, a number of other Catholic churches, and much smaller Lutheran, Orthodox, Pentecostal, Baptist, and Jewish places of worship. The city, like all the other cities of the northern tier of the former Yugoslavia, has a distinct Austrian architectural design. I visited Osijek in 1995 when it was still threatened by a Serbian invasion and had been bombed by artillery attacks that pockmarked houses and pavement—it was a city besieged and gripped by a fear rooted in the awareness of what had happened to neighboring Vukovar, which Serb forces thoroughly destroyed and then took from the Croats, massacring much of the Croat population.

My next visit to Osijek took place in the spring 2005 when I was invited to teach at the Evangelical Theological School. Peace had come, the city had been fixed up, and a new pedestrian bridge had been erected next to the bank that had once been under Serbian control—it was a pleasant stay, except that I had to be careful to use the Croat rather than Serbian version of what I consider a common language. As a gift from the faculty and students, I received a beautiful folio book of the city that included the history of Osijek. To my utter astonishment, I discovered from the old engravings pictured in the book that Osijek had been an Ottoman Turkish fortification in the fifteenth century and that it had brimmed with eight to ten mosques but did not have a single church in sight. None of these mosques survived after the Turks had been defeated by the armies of the Hapsburg prince, Eugene of Savoy. There is no mention in the book of how and when the mosques were destroyed. One can imagine the retreating Turkish army having vacated the city, but what happened to the rest of the Muslim population? Were they massacred? Expelled? Left on their own, fearing revenge? Was it gradual or instant? Not a word was mentioned about their fate in this book.

What we do know is that after the Hapsburg victories over the Ottomans in Hungary, Slavonia, and Vojvodina, the territories were suddenly emptied of Turks and other Muslim populations and repopulated, under the orders of Empress Maria Theresa and her heirs, with Hungarians, Germans, Croats, Serbs, Czechs, Slovaks, Ruthenians, Romanians, Jews, Gypsies, and many others.[12] This means that the population again became overwhelmingly Christian of various denominations, with hardly any Turks left (in fact, I had never met a Turk prior to coming to the United States). Obviously ethnic cleansing took place. Was there similar ethnic cleansing when the Ottomans took over the area from the Serbs, Croats, Hungarians, and Austrians several centuries earlier? Or were the Ottomans so tolerant that they merely added a superstructure comprised of occupying Turks to the admixture and then proceeded to convert to Islam whoever was willing to accept the new faith? The non-Muslim Balkan peoples treated Turks and their converts with antagonism, and not without some reason.

Subsequent to the Ottoman takeover of the area, the population structure of many cities changed. New immigrants moved in; others emigrated because they felt pressured or threatened, much like many Germans did after World War II when they were under threat of being expelled, interned in concentration camps, or killed outright or by hunger and disease (practices that the Nazi Germans had perpetrated upon other populations). Novi Sad, the city in which I grew up, was at one point one-third Hungarian, one-third Serb, and the rest German and other minorities. Sixty years later it is four times as large but is now predominantly Serbian in composition, including a large number of Serb immigrants from Bosnia, Herzegovina, Krajina (Croatia), Dalmatia, Montenegro, and Kosovo. This influx of immigrants was due to yet other ethnic cleansings resulting from the violence of World War II and the wars of the 1990s. Some came on their own because of economic opportunities; others were expelled by political, economic, and military pressure and were relocated by the government.

All of these examples of conquests and liberations profoundly traumatized the population and left a legacy of horror. It should not be surprising that among the people are those all too willing to settle old accounts, even when those who caused the traumas are no longer around. Any "other" will do.

3

Balkan Wars 1912–1913

An Unrecognized Genocide

The first European genocide of the twentieth century took place during the Balkan wars of 1912–1913; it is a heretofore unrecognized genocide. My aim is to raise awareness that genocide took place during these wars, pointing out that these wars occurred prior to the Armenian genocide and may have had a causal connection with the Armenian genocide. The Ottoman government may have drawn the (erroneous) lesson from the Balkan wars that to forestall losses of its territory and its own Turkish population like that which was sustained in the Balkan wars, the Ottoman government should carry out a preemptive genocide of the Armenians. The accuracy of my hunch needs to be explored by others more familiar with the Armenian genocide.

Unsurprisingly, an Internet search for "genocide during the First Balkan War" or "genocide during the Second Balkan War" does not yield a single entry; the word *genocide* had not been coined when these wars were fought. Yet a search for "Armenian genocide" yields many entries even though it too occurred prior to the coining of the word. There are several reasons for the discrepancy. The post-genocide Armenian diaspora settled in the West and was united in pressing their case, and the genocide against Armenians was carried out by a large empire, the Ottoman Empire, against one of its subject people. The Balkan wars, however, were a case of mutual genocide by the participant nations; therefore, none dared press their case before the world of public opinion for fear that their own genocidal activity would be exposed. Also, the genocides during the First Balkan War (1912–1913) and the Second Balkan War (1913), were quickly overshadowed by the outbreak of World War I (1914)—a calamity of much greater scope and import. An additional reason may be that the people in the Balkans had been so severely brutalized

25

in the many previous wars and occupations that large-scale massacres of the populations had become an ordinary fact of life.

Books on the Balkan wars don't mention genocide. Here are three examples. A Serbian account of the wars, *Dnevnik pobeda*,[1] provides some grisly details of the savage nature and enormous human losses of the final stage of the liberation of the Balkans from Ottoman rule, including accounts of the burning of entire villages, of officers, soldiers, and paramilitaries raping local women and meting out military (in)justice on the spot to captured inhabitants of other ethnicities. But despite very vivid accounts of the utter brutality of the battles, these accounts romantically revel in the swift, though costly, victories, showing only a glimmer of awareness of the bitter defeat the enemy experienced. Nor do recent histories interpret these events as being genocidal in nature.

In *The Balkan Wars*,[2] André Gerolymatos provides a fairly detailed account of the military strategies of the armies, but he clearly points out that military occupation of a territory meant determining ethnonational borders for the future, only occasionally hinting at civilian losses. In *The Balkans*,[3] Misha Glenny correctly uses the word *inferno* to describe the First Balkan War (and the second was no different) and cites some extremely powerful contemporary accounts of the massacres of civilians that were published soon after the wars. In his opinion, the four "new" countries that fought the Ottomans were overcome by nationalist fever and greedily overreached in their claims for territories. Glenny's picturesque statement "possession would count for all of the law"[4] was used to describe the Greeks reaching Salonika just hours prior to the Bulgarian forces. This statement could easily be applied to other conquests as well, yet he does not see genocide taking place amidst the mayhem.

While general opinion holds that the Armenian genocide (1915–1923)[5] is the earliest genocide of the twentieth century, this is not the case. It was preceded by German colonial forces' genocide against the Herero in southwest and east Africa in 1902 and then, as will be demonstrated here, by the Balkan genocides of 1912–1913. All the main stipulations of the UN Convention on the Prevention and Punishment of the Crime of Genocide are evident in the Balkan wars, namely, that "there was intent to destroy, in whole or in part, a national, ethnical, racial or religious group."[6]

The brief facts of the Balkan wars are as follows: the Ottoman Turkish Empire had been receding from its maximal expansion in Europe for several centuries. During the nineteenth century, several formerly occupied peoples rebelled and succeeded in establishing independent states, namely, Serbia, Greece, Montenegro, and Bulgaria, as well as Romania to the north. Turkey succeeded in holding on to the lands of Albania, Kosovo, Macedonia, and

Thrace. The first constitutional monarchy, prompted by the Young Turk rebellion, promised equal treatment to all nationalities within their defined borders, but that hope quickly vanished due to an ascending Turkish majoritarian oppression. All the while the newly established Balkan countries burned with the bright flames of a reawakened national consciousness, yearning to reestablish themselves on the territories that their predecessor states held during the pre-Ottoman Middle Ages. The problem was that these state territories overlapped, each having expanded and contracted during different centuries.

While Serbia, Greece, Montenegro, and Bulgaria each nourished their separate ambitions, they were united in a single goal—to drive out the Turks from the Balkans. A series of secret bilateral political and military agreements among them led to the outbreak of the First Balkan War in October of 1912 in which the four allies—Montenegro, Bulgaria, Greece, and Serbia—attacked the Ottomans and in bold military attacks drove the Turks practically to the gates of Constantinople (Istanbul). The war ended in May 1913 with a treaty at the Conference of London, but the territorial ambitions of several of the victorious states, particularly Bulgaria, were left unsatisfied as the allies had not clearly demarcated who would get what. Each army rushed to conquer and claim as much land as possible for its country. This quickly led to the outbreak of the Second Balkan War in June 1913, with Bulgaria attacking the Serbs and Greeks. It was a fateful mistake for Bulgaria because Turkey and Romania decided to take advantage of the vulnerability of the Bulgarian forces being stretched out too thinly on several fronts. Needless to say, Bulgaria became the big loser. Bulgaria was forced to sue for peace, and by August 1913, the Treaty of Bucharest established a considerably smaller Bulgaria, with Serbia and Greece dividing a goodly part of Macedonia; Greece and Turkey divided Thrace, and Romania received Dobrudja. Prior to the outbreak of the Balkan wars, the Albanians rebelled against the Ottomans without wishing to sever links with Constantinople (Istanbul). The London Conference awarded the Albanians a country with somewhat undefined borders, to the chagrin of Montenegro, Serbia, and Greece.

Most history books of the Balkan wars provide the details of the interplay between the great powers (the Ottomans, Austria-Hungary, Russia, France, England, and Germany) and the nascent Balkan states. They trace the battles and borders in the swiftly changing situation but devote very little attention to the manner in which the war was carried out between the various intermingled ethnic groups in these newly liberated/conquered territories. The historians from the Balkan countries tend to write narratives justifying the liberation, and they count the casualties inflicted by their "heroic" armies, glorying that the Turks were finally removed as overlords and complaining that other conquered lands "rightly and historically" should be theirs. Only the 1913

Carnegie Endowment Inquiry[7] concentrates on the horrible ethnic cleansing—by means of massacres, torture, rapes, deportations, and forcible ethnic
absorptions—that took place during these wars, acts that were truly genocidal
in nature as defined by the aforementioned UN convention on genocide and
the legal clarification and expansion of the term by the International Criminal
Tribunal for the Former Yugoslavia (ICTY). The Carnegie Commission demonstrates in great detail that all the belligerents violated *every* article of the
Second Hague Conference of 1907, "The Convention Concerning the Laws
and Customs of Land Warfare," to which all the countries involved in the two
Balkan wars were signatories.[8]

Baron d'Estournelles de Constant points to the "excess of horrors" in these
wars

> carried out not only by armies but by mobilized gangs, and in reality by the
> medley of nations; local populations being "divided into as many fragments as
> there are nations fighting each other and wanting to substitute one for another.
> . . . This is the reason why so much blood was spilt in these wars. The worst
> atrocities were not due to regular soldiers. . . . The populations themselves killed
> each other."[9]

He points out in the conclusion of the study that "every clause of international
law relative to war on land and to the treatment of the wounded, has been
violated by *all* the belligerents."[10] The commission also points to the moral
consequences of the war since "the many crimes [were] as disastrous for their
authors as for their victims and their respective countries. We are shown millions of human beings systematically degraded by their own doing, corrupted
by their own violence . . . by showing us how the generations of tomorrow
are corrupted by the heritage of their forefathers."[11]

In this way, the Carnegie Commission not only describes the genocide
but also makes the prophetic prediction of its consequences in the area, for
the remainder of the century. The Carnegie Commission concludes that the
Second Balkan War was the bloodier of the two and that

> it was the beginning of other wars, or rather of a continuous war, the worst of
> all, a war of religion, of reprisals, of race, a war of one people against another,
> of man against man and brother against brother. It has become a competition, as
> to who can best dispossess and 'denationalize' his neighbor.[12]

> The real culprits in this long list of executions, assassinations, drownings,
> burnings, massacres and atrocities furnished by our report, are not, we repeat,
> the Balkan peoples. . . . The true culprits are those who mislead public opinion
> and take advantage of the people's ignorance to raise disquieting rumors and
> sound the alarm bell, inciting their country and consequently other countries

into enmity. The real culprits are those who sacrifice the general interest to their own personal interest which they so little understand, and who hold up to their own country a sterile policy of conflict and reprisals.[13]

While the commission does not use the word *genocide*, the ethnic cleansing, war crimes, and crimes against humanity all contain characteristics of genocide in that the actions aim at permanently removing entire ethnic and ethnoreligious groups from areas that the governing political and military elites of the participating countries intended to claim as their own. The intention to drive out all ethnic groups but one's own did not prevail in every territory (e.g., Albanians were not driven out of Kosovo and Macedonia), but in areas that were closer to the future borders between the Balkan states, ethnic cleansing was carried out in earnest. As Benjamin Lieberman states, "the First Balkan War was a conflict by and against civilians,"[14] and it was simultaneously a war of liberation of the Balkan nations from Ottoman occupation.

Here are the commission's own words regarding what they believed to be the common feature of the behavior in the Balkan wars:

War is waged not only by the armies but by the people themselves. The local population is fragmented into parts nationality, and these fight each other to eliminate the "other" from "their" territory. This is why these wars are so sanguinary, why they produce such a great loss of men and end in the annihilation of the population and the ruin of whole regions. We have repeatedly been able to show that the worst atrocities were not due to the excesses of the regular soldiery, nor can they always be laid to the role of the volunteer, the Bashi-Bazouk. The populations mutually slaughtered each other and pursued with a ferocity heightened by mutual knowledge and the old resentments and hatreds they cherished.

The first consequence of this fact is that the object of these armed conflicts, overt or covert, clearly conceived or vaguely felt, but always and everywhere the same, was the complete extermination of an alien population. In some cases this object expressed itself in the form of an implacable and categorical "order"—to kill the whole male population of the occupied regions. . . . Here the intention is clearly to spare only those no longer capable of carrying on the race and those still young enough to lose their nationality through reeducation as a Greek.[15]

The authors proceed to say that it was the same with the Turks, but the Slavs (Bulgarians and Serbians) may have been "a trifle less barbarous"—a claim not borne out by their own data—suggesting that "it does not follow that there was no intention of conquering the territory without maintaining an alien population there."[16] Turkish and Greek populations suffered from Bulgarians. Bulgarian populations suffered from Turkish, Greek, and Serbians.

Albanian, Turkish, and Bulgarian/Macedonian populations suffered from Serbians, and so forth. Soldiers' letters to their friends and families testify in gruesome detail about the suffering. A Serbian soldier referring to some Albanian villages wrote, "There is nothing but corpses, dust and ashes. There are villages of 100, 150, 200 houses, where there is no longer a single man, literally *not one*."[17] Just as there is evidence that Serbian and Montenegrin officials ordered their troops to systematically burn all the villages in a region, an Arab Christian soldier who fought in the Turkish army testified that orders were given to proceed with the destruction systematically. The writers of the Carnegie report add, "It would be too much to assume that the outrages committed on women were the realization of an 'order.'"[18] Clearly, the Carnegie Commission was not yet capable of conceiving what came to be documented in the genocides of the late twentieth century—that the raping of women can be ordered and can become a pattern for carrying out genocide and ethnic cleansing.

A "necessary correlative" to the gruesome extermination noted by the Carnegie Commission was the flight of the targeted population both prior to and after the military onslaught: "Since the population of the countries about to be occupied knew, by tradition, instinct, and experience, what they had to expect . . . they did not wait for their arrival, but fled."[19] The occupying armies, finding empty or half-empty villages, simply set them on fire whether or not there were people in them. Sometimes they purposively collected the captured population into a mosque or church and then blew it up or set it on fire—a practice that would be repeated during the genocides of World War II and the wars of Yugoslavia's disintegration in the 1990s. Hundreds of thousands of emigrants fled into total uncertainty, many dying of hunger and exposure; sometimes they were caught up in the paths of the contending armies, at which point some refugees set upon other fleeing populations in anger and revenge—all of this creating a vortex of horror and inhumanity.

> The Turks are fleeing the Christians, the Bulgarians before the Greeks, the Albanians before the Servians [sic]; and if emigration is not so general as between the Servians and the Bulgarians, the reason is that these two nations have not, so to speak, encountered on their own soil, while soil coveted by each, namely Macedonia, they regarded already as peopled by men of their own race. . . . The means employed by the Greek against the Bulgarian, by the Turk against the Slav, by the Servian against the Albanian, is no longer extermination or emigration; it is an indirect method which must, however, lead to the same end, that of conversion and assimilation.[20]

There are detailed reports of the Greeks' systematic massacre of Turks in the First Balkan War, and the captured correspondence of Greek soldiers testifies to a similarly systematic killing of Bulgarians and Macedonian Slavs in the second war. Some soldiers were shocked by their own gruesomeness, and others were proud of it, in a matter-of-fact sort of way. Bulgarians dealt with Turks and Greeks similarly. What is puzzling is that sometimes the Greeks would arm local Turks to help them slaughter as many Bulgarians as possible; other times the Bulgarians would get the assistance of local Turks in killing Greeks.[21]

There are only two numerically large religions in the southeastern part of the Balkans: Christian Orthodoxy and Islam. The Bulgarians, Greeks, Montenegrins, Romanians, and Serbs are all Orthodox, while the Turks, most of the Albanians, some of the Bulgarians and Macedonians, and the Serbs of the Sandžak in Novi Pazar are Muslim. While the Turks succeeded in converting and even Turkicizing (i.e., converting and assimilating) former Christian populations, the victorious Balkan allies thought they were entirely justified in reconverting these Muslims back to Christianity by persuasion or by force. Particularly drastic was the case of the Pomaks of Bulgaria and eastern Macedonia. They were of Slavic stock, but the Bulgarian authority, with the active complicity of the Bulgarian Orthodox bishops and lower clergy, baptized them into the Bulgarian Orthodox Church, gave them Bulgarian Christian names and baptismal certificates, and then tragicomically sprinkled them with holy water with one hand and forced them to bite a piece of pork sausage with the other, thus violating a Qur'anic injunction against pork.[22] This was done despite the solemn promises made by the Bulgarians at the treaties of Constantinople (1912) and Bucharest (1913) that everyone's religious convictions and liberty would be respected and defended.

The First Balkan War unexpectedly led to the quick rout and retreat of the Turkish armies. The defeated and disarmed Turkish soldiers who surrendered were slaughtered, as were civilian Turks; Turks whose ancestors settled in these regions centuries ago were ethnically cleansed, often after torture and mutilation. Not only were ethnic Turks targeted; vengeance was directed toward all Muslims, who were frequently regarded by the Balkan population as *poturice* (those who became Turks by conversion to Islam). Christians of all nationalities turned against the Muslims, against whom they had a grudge not only for being their political overlords who bossed them and taxed them but also for being the landowners who exploited them. The Muslims' villages were burned; they were robbed and killed, raped and tortured, resulting in "unmeasured suffering," according to the Carnegie Commission.[23] Leon Trotsky and Western war correspondents reported on Serbian and Montenegrin assaults, particularly by irregular bands, against Albanian villages and populations in Kosovo and other areas where the population was mixed.[24] "As many as 20,000 Albanians may have been killed and tens of thousands fled."[25] The Serbian and Montenegrin armies and paramilitaries intended to change the ethnic composition of Kosovo by cleansing it of Albanians. The regular army was restrained in its destructiveness against the Albanians, but the reservists and paramilitary bands were unimaginably cruel. While one may dismiss these excesses as not having been authorized by commanding officers, Trotsky, who at the time was a war correspondent for a Kiev newspaper, noted that Serbia's King Peter I, on a tour inspecting the battlefields, remarked that Albanians are not worth the ammunition but should be clubbed to death.[26] In 1913 in an area that Greeks and Albanians had jointly inhabited—called Northern Epirus by Greeks and Chamëria by Albanians—Greeks sought to ethnically cleanse Albanians. Some of the Muslim Albanians were apparently not entirely clear whether they were Albanians or Turks and voluntarily fled to Istanbul and other Turkish areas.[27] Still others fled to what became Albania.

The commission also notes that public opinion in the Balkans does not condemn excesses committed by Christians against Muslims. "The burning of villages and the exodus of the defeated population is a normal and traditional incident in all Balkan wars and insurrections. It is the habit of these peoples. What they have suffered themselves, they inflict in turn upon others."[28] Prophetic words, indeed, as the practice of burning and expelling continued during Word War II and the wars of the 1990s.

Coercion was not restricted to Christian-Muslim relations; there were also a lot of intra-Orthodox issues. For a long time, the Greek clergy had not only dominated the ecumenical patriarchate in Constantinople/Istanbul but were also appointed to many leading clerical posts throughout the Balkans. This was often resented by both the lower clergy and the people, because the liturgy was frequently delivered in Greek. When the Bulgarians created the autonomous exarchate, it was not recognized by the patriarchate of Constantinople (Istanbul), and there was a steady tug-of-war between those who were forced to remain loyal to the patriarchal church or to the exarchal church. On top of that, the Serbian archbishop also desired to extend his influence in all lands where Serbs dwelled, and he asserted that Macedonia should be under his jurisdiction. Thus a fierce ecclesiastical conflict arose that was generally settled by whichever army controlled a city or village. The corresponding clergy would take over no matter how much opposition there may have been by the resident priest or people. One should recall that in the Ottoman Empire, which was organized along religious lines (*millet*), the ecclesiastical jurisdiction also included juridical and even political authority and thus the priests and bishops exercised power, sometimes with a gun in their hand. This merging of ecclesial and administrative powers occasionally led to bloodshed and expulsions. It wasn't only Turks who would kill a dangerous or insurrectionist bishop or priest; during the Balkan wars, this happened even among the coreligionists of a different ethnicity. Hence, church structure was affected, as the Orthodox Church is organized along ethnoreligious lines.

During the Second Balkan War, the ethnic cleansing between Greeks and Bulgarians frequently resulted in the murder of the local priest along with other prominent (as well as ordinary) villagers of the other ethnic group. For instance, in Serres, the Greek archbishop's militia was armed by priests and sent to "hunt down" the Bulgarian population in the town and surrounding villages. Bulgarian men were taken to the bishop's palace where they were questioned in a "kangaroo court" presided over by a priest, and after their money was confiscated (plunder often being the real reason behind the religious persecutions), they were executed—their main offense being their nationality.[29] From the perspective of many Greeks, including the hierarchs, the Bulgarians were not Christians in *their* sense of the word.[30]

During the First Balkan War, the Bulgarian army advanced close to Constantinople (Istanbul) and occupied Edirne (Adrianople). While the contemporary European newspaper reports probably exaggerated the horrors, the Carnegie Commission provides ample details of the suffering and plunder of the defeated population, which the commission ascribes more to the local Greek population (and to a lesser degree the Jewish and Armenian) than to the regular Bulgarian army.[31] However, the report by a Russian official who was in Edirne (Adrianople) at the time of the Bulgarian conquest and talked to many eyewitnesses painted a very distressing picture of the atrocities committed by Bulgarian gendarmes and soldiers (with the knowledge of their commanding officers): plunder, rape, torture, burning—every conceivable inhumanity including murder, predominantly of Turks but also of Jews and Greeks. Of the 15,000 captured Turkish soldiers and 5,000 civilians captured, only 10,000 were alive by the time they were to be deported to Bulgaria. The commanding General Veltchev condoned the plunder and desecration of mosques (Bulgarian soldiers urinated from minarets and "uttered vulgar indecencies about Mahomet" and "said openly—and the remark appears to harmonize with the serious views of his government—that Bulgaria had no need either of Greeks or Moslems, and that they would take advantage of the first opportunity to wipe out the whole Greek and Mussulman population."[32]) In the Second Balkan War, the Turks retook Edirne and other territory in Thrace. Before the reconquest, Thrace had been a no-man's-land and local Turks and Turkish prisoners used the opportunity to arm themselves. They then exacted vengeance upon the Bulgarians, this time with the help of the local Greek population that preferred the Muslim Turks over the Christian Orthodox Bulgarians (in one place, the Greeks helped the Turks tie the Bulgarians' hands with cords).[33]

In Thrace, the Bulgarians and Turks exterminated each other amid mutual sacrilege. Bulgarians desecrated mosques by spreading dung on the floor, used them as ammunition depots, tore up copies of the Qur'an, razed mosques and schools to the ground, destroyed cemeteries, and so forth. When the Turks reoccupied the territories, they destroyed Bulgarian villages, desecrated churches, tore up copies of the Gospel and other church books, and sometimes killed people in the churches.[34] One account states that in Has-Keui, "the men were shut up in the church . . . all the women were collected in a spacious barn and the soldiers banqueted for twenty-four hours, outraging all the women from eight to seventy-five years of age."[35]

Thus during the First Balkan War, according to Lieberman, "of all agents of terror, bands of irregulars prompted the greatest fear" and yet these "bands of irregulars had strong connection both to military authorities and local communities."[36] Accumulated historic grievances; ancient and recent national animosities; the fear of reprisals for earlier violence; "a sense that those under attack do not deserve the protection afforded by conventional rules of conduct"[37] and a heritage of resolving issues by violent means (abuse begets abuse both in families and in societies); a life of such pervasive poverty that justified brigandage, looting, and robbing; great uncertainties as to how the fighting would end—all these were motives for the gruesome behavior of the people.

During the Second Balkan War, the ethnic cleansing became even more pronounced because the victors had not yet achieved their goals of unifying the territory to which they aspired and had not yet homogenized the population in the area under their control in order to feel more secure in their territorial claims. Former allies turned as savagely against each other as they had against their common enemy, the Ottomans. Now there was clearer "evidence of official intent to expel civilians."[38] Lieberman reports that the "British Vice Consul Heard concluded that 'the wholesale extermination of the Bulgarian population has been carried out on a systematic plan by the Greek troops, with the assistance of organized bands of Antartes [irregulars].'"[39]

In Serres the Greeks carried out a genocide of the Bulgarians, but in Doxato it was Bulgarians who exterminated the Greeks, with the assistance of the local Turks and Bulgarian Muslims.[40] The Carnegie Commission concluded that while the Bulgarians burned down 4,000 Greek homes in Serres, in northwestern Macedonia the "Greeks burned one hundred and sixty Bulgarian villages and at least 16,000 Bulgarian homes."[41] In Demir-Hissar, the Greek-Bulgarian genocide was mutual, as the fighting favored first one side, then the other. The Greek bishop had been the leader of the local armed Greeks, so the Bulgarians mutilated his body, either while he was still alive or after he died.[42] In Nigrita, the Greeks destroyed the Bulgarians and then killed the Muslims for staying neutral during the fight.[43]

Strumica (contemporary Macedonia) during the First Balkan War was occupied by all three allied armies simultaneously. Turks of the city and environs were plundered and killed. A Serbian officer presided over a "trial" at which a simple question was asked—"Is the Turk a good or bad man?"—and nine out of ten villagers said bad. With no further investigation, the person on trial was executed. Some believe that 3,000–4,000 Muslims were killed in Strumica. Then the Serbians withdrew and the Bulgarians and local guerilla bands took over. They ordered the Muslim population to assemble in the mosque, robbed them, and then executed the wealthier Turkish villagers. In the Second Balkan War, the Bulgarians withdrew and the Greeks temporarily took control of the area. Seeing that they could not hold the area, the Greek and Muslim populations were forced to move to Kukush, where they were promised settlement in homes and farms that Greeks had previously cleansed of all Bulgarians. Then the Greeks set their own homes in Strumica on fire. Strumica finally passed to Serb control.[44] The Serbs undertook a policy of forced assimilation of the local population as Serbs, about which more will be said below.

Turkish nationalism increased markedly after their defeats in the First Balkan War. If Turks reoccupied an area previously occupied by Bulgarians or Greeks, they usually massacred the male populations of Bulgarians or Greeks as revenge for what happened to them when the Greeks or Bulgarians drove the Turks out. By 1913, the Turks were engaged in massive reprisals and vengeance against not only Bulgarians, Macedonians, and Greeks but also Armenians.

In each of these massacres, the women were raped, including young girls and pregnant women. The militaries of all nationalities, regular and irregular, raped the women and frequently slaughtered them, but always the women of the other ethnic groups. The concept of genocidal rape had not yet come into existence—it would be in Bosnia and Herzegovina in the 1990s where specific attention would be paid to genocidal rape, as opposed to wartime rape. The Carnegie Commission's report is replete with very specific references to "outrages" of women in practically every village and town affected by these wars. In addition to rape, there was the frequent butchering and death of the women, from children aged eight to old women aged eighty. It is my distinct impression that genocidal rape may have been more widespread during these two Balkan wars than in the wars of the 1990s, despite the fact that the latter received a lot of publicity, while those of a hundred years ago received practically none. Here is a quote from the previously mentioned report by the Russian official who was present at the Bulgarian conquest:

What the women of Adrianople had to endure is beyond the imagination.

> Outrages were committed against Greek, Jewish and even Armenian women, despite the Armenians' devotion to the Bulgarian cause. Naturally the worst violence was devoted to the Turkish women. Respect was shown neither for rank nor age. Among the women violated there were as many girls of tender years as aged women. Many of these girls are now actually with child. All those who could afford to do so have gone to hide their shame in remote regions. Many have lost their reason. Most keep silent about their misfortune, for reasons easy to understand.[45]

The Bulgarians were neither better nor worse than the other nations' soldiers and officers who often mass-raped women for days on end and threatened to kill anyone who attempted to interfere. Obviously, they feared no reprimand. There were neither disciplinary measures nor trials against the rapists. Some reports suggest that if a village's women were hidden or had escaped, the men were sexually violated instead.

"The Macedonian question" lay at the center of the Bulgarian-Greek-Serbian claims. This area contained an ethnically mixed population of not only these three groups but also Turks, Vlachs (Romanians), Albanians, Jews, and Roma (Gypsies). The Bulgarians thought of the area as western Bulgaria; to the Greeks, it was northern Greece; and to the Serbs, it was southern Serbia. The Carnegie Commission's conviction was that the Slavic majority of that area was Bulgarian, though in subsequent years it became clear that those in the area have a sufficiently strong sense of their own ethnic identity to consider themselves none of the three. But during the Balkan wars, all three countries tried to convince the Macedonians that they were Bulgarians, Greeks, or Serbians, respectively. In order to do this, each country used "extermination, emigration, assimilation"—which is the title of one of the report's chapters.

The Carnegie Commission's conviction that most Macedonians were Bulgarians might have been based on the Bulgarian government's greater willingness to cooperate with the commission, which the Serbs and Greeks largely refused to do. The commission believed that the Bulgarians had been less barbaric in Macedonia because they felt most of the indigenous population was of their own Bulgarian ethnicity. Nevertheless, the Carnegie Commission does describe the forced conversion of most ethnic Bulgarian Muslims (Pomaks). The Pomaks were also drafted into the army and frequently, with the help of the local Turkish Muslim population, massacred Greeks. Macedonian insurgents and the Bulgarian army carried out mass murders of Greeks in places like Akangeli and Doxato, but they did greater damage to the majority Turkish population in a number of Balkan cities. They were mercilessly killed or exiled, many choosing to be evacuated to Asia Minor by way of Salonika. The appendices of the Carnegie Commission's report more clearly implicate Bulgarians in these massacres than the analytic and descriptive text of the report. In some places, local Armenians initiated massacres of the Turks.[46] It may be useful for some researchers to see whether such events contributed to the later Armenian genocide by the Turks.

The Greeks apparently detested the Bulgarians (or the indigenous Slavic population) and considered them less than human—"bears" they called them—and used systematic and inhumane methods of assimilation and extermination. Salonika had a mixed population and was a particularly contested city, initially occupied by both Greek and Bulgarian armies, but the Greek army attacked and prevailed. The captured soldiers, Bulgarian clergy, teachers, and notables were tortured and exiled to some Aegean islands or even killed.[47] In Salonika, Edessa/Vodena, Castoria, and many of the villages of southwestern Macedonia that came under Greek occupation, people were persecuted not for what they may have done but for simply regarding themselves Bulgarians. The slogan was "If you want to be free, be Greek," and "the people were made to say that they had been Greeks from the most ancient times, but had called themselves Bulgarians under the influence of Bulgarian propaganda"[48] or the fear of Komitadjis. Everything written in Slavic script was erased, the property of Slavs was confiscated, their schools were closed, and their language was suppressed (Slavs were regarded as Bulgarophone Greeks who had to be reeducated into the use of Greek). Slavic churches were closed or taken over by the Greek clergy. Most of the Bulgarian higher clergy were expatriated to Bulgaria, though some were murdered (e.g., Archimandrite Eulogios). Local priests were forced to assert they were Greeks, conduct services in Greek, and profess loyalty to the patriarchal Greek Orthodox Church. Particularly ironic was the covering with dung and burning of images of Saints Cyril and Methodius, the apostles to the Slavs,[49] oblivious to the fact that they had been Greek brothers from Salonika! (The Carnegie Commission noted that the Jewish population of Salonika also began to be persecuted by the Greek administration.[50]) Thus all vestiges of Bulgarian and Slavic Macedonia had been suppressed in Greece, beginning during the Balkan wars and continuing to the present.[51]

The terror was similar, though not as drastic in the conflict between Serbians and Bulgarians, in the second war. Bulgarians were "pillaging houses, stealing money and outraging women." And "the same methods were employed by the Servian invaders towards the Bulgarian population."[52] Based on the extent of the dominion of some Middle Age Serbian rulers such as Dušan the Mighty, whose capital was Skopje (in Macedonia), and the birthplace of the legendary Serb hero Prince Mark (Kraljević Marko), which was Prilep (also in Macedonia), Serbian propaganda asserted that Macedonians are actually Serbs rather than Bulgarians, and the Serbs undertook a very aggressive campaign of Serbianizing the local population. They did not carry out massacres, except against local Turks and Albanian insurrectionists, but they coerced Macedonians to declare themselves Serbians. On the one hand, the Serbs claimed that they had liberated their ancient homeland; on the other, they behaved as colonial rulers. Macedonians were basically given an option to declare themselves Serbs and remain unmolested or to die (less frequently) or be exiled to Bulgaria (more frequently). The Carnegie Commission called it "assimilation through terror."[53] Six archbishops and bishops of the Bulgarian Orthodox Church did not succumb to pressures and were exiled to Bulgaria.[54] Priests and parishioners were forced to renounce the Bulgarian exarchate and come under the jurisdiction of the Serbian Orthodox Church. Local schools were closed and Serbian schools multiplied. People were forced to change their surnames by adding the typical Serbian ending of *ić* (e.g., Kalajlijev became Kalajlijević, Temkov became Temković). In one instance, villagers were exiting their Orthodox church after the liturgy and found a table on which there was a piece of paper and a revolver. The message was clear: sign and declare yourself a Serb, or die. All villagers signed.[55] But there were many more horrendous Serbian massacres of both Turks and Macedonians/Bulgarians, as well as Albanians, in cities like Skopje, Veles, Prilep, Ohrid, Kruševo, Monastir/Bitola, Kumanovo, Gostivar, and Tetovo. Many were carried out by legalized brigands belonging to the "Black Hand" (Crna Ruka), a secret Serbian society that was particularly sinister.

Occasionally the opposition to Serbianization grew to the point of resistance and even insurrection. In the Bitola region in August and September 1913, the Orthodox considered seeking union with the Catholic Church in order to preserve their nationality.[56] This was not done, but around Ohrid, Struga, and Debar there was a short attempt at insurrection and talk of organizing an autonomous Macedonian government.[57] But the Serbian government put down that insurrection as it did insurrections around Prizren and Djakovo in Kosovo. The latter two resulted in the flight of some 25,000 Albanians. Many insurrectionists were shot, and a number of Macedonian and Albanian villages were burned down.

Compared to the Greek persecution of Bulgarians and Macedonians, the Serbs were relatively more tolerant because of the common Slavic heritage. That did not stop the Serbians and Bulgarians from being fierce rivals and engaging in several wars during the nineteenth and twentieth centuries. I think the most gruesome propaganda was the Greek program that produced visual placards with pictures of Greek volunteers gouging out the eyes of Bulgarian soldiers (as a reprise of Byzantine emperor Basil II's defeat of Tsar Samuel in 1014, in which every 99 captured Bulgarian/Macedonian soldiers were blinded and every 100th was left with one eye in order to lead the others home) or tearing a Bulgarian's face with their teeth. It is interesting that the Greek intolerance of their allegedly more primitive neighbors to the north was not racist in the classical sense of the word. If Bulgarians, Macedonians, Albanian, or even Turks were willing to accept being Greek, they were usually spared further persecution. It appears that the ancient Greek tradition of Hellenizing "barbarians" still resonated in the minds of many modern Greeks.

What were the Carnegie Commission's conclusions? As mentioned earlier, the word *genocide* had not yet been invented when the Balkan wars of 1912–1913 occurred. Members of the Carnegie Commission did not go to the Balkans to carry out their investigation because they had clear knowledge of the extent of the massacres and mutual extermination of populations; as of the report's writing in 1913, that knowledge had not been clearly grasped in Europe. However, the commission's field observations in the Balkans clearly led them to conclude that what took place is what today we would not hesitate to call genocide.

"From first to last, in both wars, the fighting was desperate as though extermination were the end sought. . . . There is evidence to show that in some cases these acts were committed by soldiers acting under orders."[58] The commission called it "the most uncalled for and brutal war of modern times,"[59] not realizing that in a very short time an incident in Sarajevo, also in the Balkans, would spark a much greater war that would overshadow the Balkan wars to such a degree that the world would never have a chance to fully recognize what had transpired during those wars.

> When a band of soldiers or *comitadjis* [Macedonian brigands], either under orders or, as was many times the case, under the impulse of hatred, greed, and lust, surrounded and attacked a village, the very doors of Hell seem to be opened. No language can describe the tortures and griefs which followed.[60]

> It is still more horrible that when the battle is over, any prisoners that are made are not kept; it is preferred to make an end of them.[61]

The appendices, which run about 120 pages of single-space, small font,[62] itemize the horrors in a way that makes for very difficult reading, and yet the report is more often than not written in a nonemotional, simple, factual language. The Carnegie Commission reports only a segment of what transpired in all areas of hostility, and yet it is these "qualitative" reports and interviews that make a compelling case that genocide took place.

The figures of the dead, wounded, and exiled are quite incomplete. The report estimates there were 200,000 Turkish refugees, and it also suggests that the Turks had no means to estimate the number of Turks killed.[63] Over

135,000 Bulgarians (probably including Macedonians) became fugitives from Greek-occupied territory alone.[64]

The Carnegie Commission makes some devastating conclusions regarding the role of religion, noting that the teaching of righteousness and charity are an exception, not the rule: "The Church [meaning all religious institutions] does not systematically teach either morals or religion; its bishops and priests are the employes [sic] of the State and they are propagandists of nationality. Conversion with them means a change from one nationality to another whether accomplished by persuasion or force. Religious convictions or faith have nothing to do with it."[65]

The costs of the genocides impacted not only the populations who lived in the affected areas at the time of these wars but also future generations. Prophetically, the commission wrote about "the reflex psychological effect of these crimes against justice and humanity" that has been absorbed into the body politic of these nations, like a virus that threatens the very life of these nations. "Here we can focus the whole matter—the fearful economic waste, the untimely death of no small part of the population, a volume of terror and pain which can be only partially, at least, conceived and estimated, and the collective national consciousness of *greater crimes than history has recorded*. This is a fearful legacy to be left to future generations."[66]

And, indeed, in the collective memory of the Balkan nations, as well as in the awareness of nations that are regarded as great powers or as the "international community," is the knowledge that the outside world soon forgets, but the children and grandchildren do not. These descendents often reenact the genocidal destructions that have been enacted by their ancestors, or if their people were the victims of genocidal onslaught, they often decide that their time has come to destroy whichever neighbors they can. The old game of the abused becoming the abusers plays itself out not only in individual lives but also in the collective. What the Ottomans or Hapsburgs visited on the Balkan nations, the Balkans mercilessly duplicated when their own moment had come. What happened in 1912–1913 was clearly an omen of the later Balkan genocides in the same century.

The Balkan wars' genocides were carried out with impunity. Did these wars also give implicit "permission" to solve problems with genocide, since the culprits for the genocides in the first two Balkan wars went unpunished?

EPILOGUE: WORLD WAR I AS THE THIRD BALKAN WAR

World War I is inextricably linked with the Balkans in the minds of most people worldwide through the assassination of the Hapsburg archduke Ferdinand in Sarajevo by a young Serb. This event is cited as the immediate cause of the outbreak of hostilities that would claim the lives of about 15 million people in the largest world conflagration up to that point. However, our focus will shift farther east and south of Sarajevo.

In connection with the events in the Balkans during World War I, much has been written about the heroism of the engaged armies, troop movements, maneuvers and battles under excruciating conditions, the retreat of the Serbian army through Albania in the middle of a winter with huge losses in men and animals, the drawn-out battles on the Thessalonica front, and the ultimate liberation of the occupied territories. Human losses have been described as staggering, on the battlefields, in bombardments, and from the contagious diseases that decimated the population (scarlet fever, typhoid fever, small pox, cholera, and diarrhea being the major plagues).

At the same time, there has been insufficient examination of the genocidal elements of World War I (though I do not attempt to explore that issue here). However, claiming that every aspect of suffering of one's own people was genocide leads to absurdities. For instance, Serbian scholar Isidor Djuković argues that Serb POWs (prisoners of war) and civilians who were in Austro-Hungarian internment camps beginning in 1914 were the first Serbian victims of genocide in the twentieth century.[67] That assertion is entirely unsubstantiated and unsupportable. Djuković details the number of interned and their severe suffering and states that the goal of these imprisonments and tortures was to exterminate the Serbs—all the Serbs—so the Hapsburgs could open their desired Drang nach Osten (Push to the East). Djuković's claim is rhetorical overkill and does not serve the case of other, more verifiable claims of genocide of the Serbs. There is already a danger of over-utilization of the word, and this is one instance of it.

Having said that, there is one aspect of World War I that can been seen as genocide, namely, the Bulgarian occupation of Serbian and Macedonian lands, which could be considered (at least nominally) as the Third Balkan War.

Briefly, after the assassination of the archduke, Austria-Hungary issued an ultimatum to Serbia, parts of which no sovereign country could accept, and the Austro-Hungarian monarchy declared war on Serbia in 1914. The first two major attacks by the Hapsburgs, who had been joined by the German Reich, were successfully repulsed by the Serbs. However in 1915, Bulgaria was avidly courted by both the Central Powers and the Entente and joined the Central Powers because they promised Bulgaria all the lands it aspired to but lost in the Second Balkan War. So in 1915, a third major offensive against Serbia began.

This great offensive against Serbia caused a retreat toward Kosovo and Albania, not only by the Serbian army but also by a huge portion of the civilian population, who feared relocation to camps in Hapsburg territories (already practiced by Hungarian troops) and, more so, what the Bulgarians would do to them if captured. Unsubstantiated statements have been made that Austro-Hungarian troops carried out genocide against the Serbian people.[68] In addition to retreating in the bitter winter of 1915, the Serbs faced Albanian inhabitants who were very hostile toward them. In 1913, Albanians in Kosovo had rebelled against their new Serb overlords, and the Serb army and irregulars had carried out vicious reprisals.[69] Now it was the Albanians' turn to take advantage of the Serbian predicament, and they continued the cycle of revenge with killing and looting. Not all who attempted escape to the Adriatic Sea via the inhospitable Albanian mountains lived to be transferred by Allied ships to the Greek island of Corfu. Those who did were eventually transferred to the newly established Allied front at Salonika and eventually, by 1918, returned victorious to their native land. Serbian rhetoric called this period their Calvary/Golgotha and Resurrection, taking inspiration from the early Christian narrative to which rhetoric they would return in the wars of the 1990s.

The outbreak of World War I so soon after suffering an ignominious defeat in the Second Balkans War afforded the Bulgarian government an opportunity to achieve its designs for a Great Bulgaria. The government joined the Hapsburg Empire, Germany, and Turkey fighting against Great Britain, France, Russia, Romania, and Serbia, the latter being the main reason for entering the war. The Bulgarian army occupied eastern Serbia and most of Macedonia during the period of 1915–1918. In and of itself, no matter how brutal the warfare, this occupation would not normally have merited mention here. However the brutality of the Bulgarian army, the irregulars (Komitadji), and the later civil administration had all the features of ethnic cleansing. Anyone unwilling to submit him- or herself to the occupiers and become Bulgarian was tortured, raped, interned, and killed in particularly gruesome manners, some of which were recorded photographically.[70]

Two chapters in the volume *Golgota i vaskrs Srbije 1915–1918* are devoted to reports of the Bulgarian atrocities. One was the Inter-Allied Commission especially established for the examination of violations of the Hague Conventions and of general international law.[71] This document summarizes the violations of the Hague Conventions, the massacre of the civilian population, torture, rape, internment, punitive economic expropriation, requisitions, and various taxes, plunder, forced labor, destruction, arson, and other actions aimed at destroying the Serbian presence in the newly occupied territories. The aim of the Bulgarian government was to create pure Bulgarian territories by denationalizing the Serbs and Macedonians.

In the immediate after-war period of December 1918 and January 1919, an American journalist, William A. Drayton of Union Club, New York, did a thorough examination of the Bulgarian war crimes in the territories that the Bulgarians had occupied. He described this data vividly in his report.[72] Here it suffices to quote at length some of Drayton's concluding remarks:

> I think I brought to light that the Bulgarians indisputably carried out bestiality most repugnant and of most inhumane nature. Barbarian attitude toward the civilian population, male or female, old or young, torture, plunder, blackmail, brigandage, killings and sadism permeate the statements that we collected.
>
> We are especially stressing that nowhere was there even a trace of investigation. Bulgarians killed and tortured without mercy whomever they wanted whenever they wanted. They did all this not because they were challenged. They did it systematically and persistently throughout full three years. I am not saying that every crime was carried out by a command, but I assert that organized mass killings took place and that this terror, as such was inspired by Bulgarian leaders and approved by the entire nation, with the clear goal of Bulgarization of the land by exterminating the population. Their victims were even old people, unable to be soldiers, women, and children.[73]

"In eastern Serbia whole towns were deserted as Bulgarians approached. The earlier Austrian invasion left the town of Nis in southeastern Serbia crowded with refugees, but the town emptied out as the Bulgarians neared," reported British travelers Alice and Claude Askew.[74] The high probability that civilians would be either forcibly Bulgarianized or killed caused them to flee, thereby assisting the perpetrators in their goal of having an ethnically standardized territory consistent with their national dreams and aspirations.

Ultimately, the Bulgarians had to give up this plan because their army was defeated and the armistice signed on September 30, 1918, forcing Bulgaria to give up all its conquered territory. However, the dream was not abandoned but rather shelved until 1941, when Bulgaria once more occupied the lands it believed were rightfully its own.

If the members of these international commissions and international travelers and journalists were reporting the truth, then it appears that ethnic cleansing (at a minimum) and genocide (at the maximum) did take place between 1915 and 1918, carried out by Bulgarians on Serbs and Macedonians.

THE GREEK-TURKISH WARS

The Greek-Turkish wars of the 1920s came as a sequel to World War I, with the Greeks hoping to recapture their ancient Asia Minor homeland. All the fighting had clear earmarks of ethnic cleansing and perhaps genocidal massacres, but it took place in Anatolia (Asia Minor) and therefore does not belong in the scope of this book. What is relevant to the Balkan ethnic cleansing is that based on the Treaty of Lausanne in 1923, a forcible exchange of population resulted in 350,000 Turks being expelled from Greece and 1.3 million Greeks being expelled from Turkey.[75] A by-product of these exchanges was that Turkey was willing to accept Muslims from the Balkans. Allegedly these were "Turkish Muslims," but in reality many Bosnian, Serbian, and Montenegrin Slavic, as well as Albanian Muslims, migrated to Turkey. The Muslims of the Balkans felt severe pressure in their newly independent Christian countries and thus migrated. While many of the migrations were not forcible deportations, Albanian scholars maintain that the Greek government and voluntary bands under the pretext of implementing the Treaty of Lausanne did use force and deception to expel the Cham Albanians from lands (Epirus or Chamëria) that were claimed by both Greece and Albania.[76] Here the story replicates the attempts by the other Balkan people to extricate themselves from living intermingled, resulting in ethnic cleansing by whoever was more powerful and more violent in a given area.

4

Multiple Genocides of World War II

Western Balkans

The material about the ethnic cleansing, genocide, and Holocaust that occurred during World War II is so extensive that it seems wise to divide it into three chapters. In this chapter I make some general remarks about genocidal issues of World War II, then analyze events in Croatia, including the role of the Catholic Church, the Italian occupational policies, Slovenia, and Bosnia and Herzegovina, with the exception of Serb Četnik exterminations of Muslims and Croats in Bosnia and Herzegovina, which I discuss in chapter 5.

The popular awareness is that the great human losses of the Holocaust occurred mostly in central and northeast Europe (Germany, Holland, Poland, and the Soviet Union, especially in the Ukraine), Czechoslovakia, and Hungary. However, human losses in the Balkans were also catastrophic, and the killings were at least as gruesome as in the areas that are better known to the academic and general public. Beginning in 1941, after countless bloodbaths occurred, "the most terrible bloodbath in all of Balkan history" took place.[1] There are several reasons for the mind-boggling scope of the tragedy in the Balkans. First, the Balkans, and particularly Yugoslavia, was divvied up by not one, but four occupying forces. Several quisling governments functioning as Nazi German and Fascist Italian protégés tried to establish their authority with much brutality. Armed resistance was waged against both the foreign occupying powers and their puppet governments. On top of the guerilla activity, a full-fledged civil war raged along both ideological and nationalistic lines. Finally, the Balkans' genocide victims were not only Jews and Roma (Gypsies) but also the contending ethnic groups, particularly the Serbs. Croats and Bosnian Muslims were also massacred by Četniks and Partisans. "German aggression triggered a war of nations."[2] With regard to the genocides, no

45

simple categorization of these events is possible, as in many cases the extermination was directed not simply against one group but against two, three,
or more. Analysts of each nation exclusively stress the victimization of their
own group, while denying, overlooking, or diminishing the genocide or ethnic cleansing of others. Jewish authors, for instance, tend to focus on the extermination of Jews, overlooking the genocide of the Serbs, who often died at
their side. Serbs tend to focus on the genocide of Serbs, paying scant attention
to that of Jews and Roma or to crimes they themselves perpetrated against
others. In April 1942, a German commander reported "[a] senseless slaughter
of the Serbian population in Bosnia." The same would have applied to Croatia
as the Ustaše and other chauvinistic Croats saw the war as an opportunity
to remove the "enemy" Serbs from their midst. The ethnic hatred was often
coupled with ideological enmity against Communists (which was heartily
reciprocated). Often both Jews and Serbs were given the double designation
of "Judeo-Communists" and "Serbian Communist bands," respectively. The
Ustaše wanted to purge their territory, "to clean off the poisonous damagers
and insatiable parasites—Jews, Communists, and Freemasons—from their
national and state body."[3] Prompted by the Nazis, the Jews and possibly the
Roma (regarding the latter, the intent is less clear) were slated for near total
extermination due to Nazi racist policies.

PRELIMINARY PHILOSOPHICAL AND THEOLOGICAL CONCERNS

For the former Yugoslavia, Jasenovac is a symbol subsuming all the horrendous genocidal actions that transpired primarily against Serbs, Jews, and
Roma but also against the political enemies of the Nezavisna Država Hrvatska
(NDH), that is, the Independent State of Croatia—the Nazi puppet state that
organized the genocide. Using the name Jasenovac as a symbol, many Serbs
overreached by rejecting the very idea of an independent Croatian state and
regarded all who favored the idea—including the Roman Catholic Church
and the Vatican, which provided support to that state—as being guilty of the
genocide. Unsurprisingly, most Croats and the Catholic Church have been
unwilling to own up to such broadly drawn-up charges and have attempted
to restrict the impact of these allegations. In their zeal for self-defense, the
Catholic Church and many Croats have found themselves accused of being
Holocaust deniers or genocide deniers, as they fall way short of acknowledg-
ing responsibility where it would be morally appropriate to do so.

   As a preliminary issue, we need to address how scholars and clergy have
intentionally manipulated the research of genocides for political, economic,
or other advantage, and how this manipulation not only warps the sanctity of

our memory of past victims but also thwarts our ability to improve the future, which can only be accomplished in good conscience by the pursuit of truth and justice.

After World War II, the issue of Jasenovac had been a constant subtext in Serb-Croat relationships. This is the most likely reason why Josip Broz Tito's Yugoslav government did not play up the role of Jasenovac as was done with other European extermination camps. Tito's government attempted to allow the wounds to heal and the peoples of Yugoslavia to forge the "brotherhood and unity," which the Communist slogan so strenuously attempted to imprint in people's minds. After Tito's death, interethnic relationships deteriorated until they finally reached a feverish and even genocidal pitch in the 1990s. Serb intellectuals, writers, journalists, and politicians started blaming Tito's government for a deliberate suffocation of the truth about Jasenovac, allegedly to protect the perpetrators. Vuk Drašković, a Serb author, wrote *Nož* (Knife),[4] which uses extraordinarily powerful images of the killings of Serbs (but also of Serb reprisals) by Herzegovinian Muslim Ustaše, in which Jasenovac appears marginally but clearly as a symbol of evil that has not been avenged adequately. Many Serb leaders maintained that justice could not be carried out as long as the truth was suppressed. Many Croat and Muslim leaders either failed to respond or counterattacked by blaming Serbs for the extermination of Croats (as well as other anti-Communist forces) at the end of World War II (described in chapter 7). There were accusations and counteraccusations and while elements of the truth did reach the light of day, no peaceful means was found to deal with the truth; it led to another series of Balkan wars in the 1990s that had genocidal characteristics. These wars inflamed the discussion of what transpired during World War II, filling it with new acrimony and hate. An instance of this can be found in a series of five conferences that were initiated in 1997. The first was in New York in 1997, followed by one in Banja Luka, Bosnia, in 2000; a third in Jerusalem in 2002; and a fourth and fifth again in Banja Luka in 2007 and 2011. Even though the participants of these conferences were heavily Serbian, with a much smaller number of Jews and an even smaller number of others, the proceedings of the conferences are a living example of the severe tensions regarding the claims and counterclaims about the nature and extent of the genocide that occurred in the Balkans.[5]

It is a natural human characteristic to care about the successes and painful experiences that befall one's own group. Thus it is not surprising that it is usually members of the victimized group in both natural and human disasters that research, write about, and distribute information about the suffering that was experienced. Even before the term *genocide* was invented by Raphael Lemkin, people sought to have the tragedies experienced by their group more widely known. Therefore, it is not surprising that more historical accounts of genocide are often written by the members of the victimized groups, unless the group is comprised of barely literate or illiterate victims. The case of the Roma is an example. Their suffering during World War II has usually been written about by outside scholars and journalists, while little has been recorded by the Roma themselves. Perhaps for that reason, less is known by the general public about their suffering than about the groups who have a well-educated population that can speak for themselves as well as document their case. Hence, we know more about the suffering of Jews than of Roma during the Holocaust in Yugoslavia. It stands to reason, then, that Armenian scholars, journalists, politicians, and others wrote about the Armenian genocide of 1915 (as well as earlier massacres in 1894–1896 and 1908); Jews wrote voluminously about the Holocaust concerning the roughly 6 million exterminated under Hitler; Russians wrote about the Gulag; Germans wrote about the expulsion of the German population from Eastern Europe after World War II; and so forth.

However, what comes naturally is not necessarily also good. There are problems when we write about our own group. It is hard not to be overly subjective and motivated by revenge, attempt to calculate war reparations, to gain advantage in the present and the future for the losses of the past, obtain military and propaganda advances in later conflicts, and propagate many other mixed or even outright base motives. In situations where the extermination was not one-sided, there is a pronounced tendency to catalogue, describe, and even maximize the destruction caused by the enemy while minimizing and even overlooking entirely the killings and destruction caused by one's own group. In the Balkans every group has claimed not only that it was victimized but also that genocide was carried out against them.

The meaning of the term *ethnic cleansing* has been raised. Is it simply a euphemism for genocide, as some have claimed, or is it a more limited notion than genocide, as I have claimed?[6] My view is that "every genocide is ethnic cleansing, [but] not every ethnic cleansing is genocide."[7] It seems to me that a coercive but nonviolent exchange of population on a small scale, which has happened numerous times during the twentieth century, is ethnic cleansing but it is not genocide. While scholars and lawyers may disagree about the extent of genocides in Bosnia and Herzegovina in the 1990s, hardly anyone denies the widespread ethnic cleansing.

As one may expect, persons from within the victim group tend to consider a greater number of incidents as genocidal and frequently exaggerate the number of victims and the horror of these events. These individuals are the maximizers, about whom Peter Brock writes that they mastered "the technique of multiplication and extrapolation used to arrive at exaggerated and routinely inflated body counts."[8] On the other hand, the *genocidaires*, or even later generations of groups accused of having committed genocides, frequently either completely deny or at least decrease the numbers of victims and the severity of the destruction. They may be called minimizers. Regarding the number of their victims in World War II, the Serbs were maximizers, while regarding casualties that they inflicted in the wars of the 1990s, they were minimizers. The exact opposite was the case with Croats. Perhaps the clearest example of this maximizer-minimizer dichotomy relates to the killings in the extermination camp of Jasenovac: Serb author Velimir Terzić[9] claimed that at least a million Serbs were killed, whereas Croatia's president, Franjo Tudjman, enthusiastically cited Serbian Četnik war crimes but ardently reduced the number of Serbian victims by the Ustaše.[10] Two serious scholars, one a Serb, Bogoljub Kočović, and the other a Croat, Vladimir Žerjavić, have come to a near consensus, with Kočović estimating Yugoslavia's total real casualties at 1,014,000 and Žerjavić at 1,027,000.[11] In absolute numbers, the incomplete estimate of lives lost and the percentage of victims in the corresponding ethnic group would be as follows:

- o 487,000 Serbs (6.9 percent)
- o 207,000 Croats (5.4 percent)
- o 86,000 Muslims (6.8 percent)
- o 60,000 Jews (77.9 percent)
- o 27,000 Roma (31.4 percent)

However, these figures do not distinguish where or how the individuals died, whether in battles, concentration camps, prisons, executions, disease, or other causes.[12]

I do not intend to get into the numbers game, though numbers do give some indication of the scope of the tragedy. Establishing a generally dependable figure for all genocides based on scholarly criteria, including the one at Jasenovac, is desirable and would be useful for purposes of truth and justice. Using the numbers game as a political bludgeon and propaganda weapon to humiliate and oppress, is unethical. By deliberately exaggerating or underestimating we are playing dangerous games with the horrendous reality of genocide or ethnic cleansing. In the case of exaggeration, we are at least symbolically destroying additional, though illusory, members of the victim group. By reducing the numbers, we are denying the very real suffering, torture, and deaths that did occur, pretending that these people never lived. The effect is destroying them twice—once when they died and again by eliminating them and their memory.

The act of maximizing or minimizing the number of victims means claiming a half-truth. Perhaps the number was grossly exaggerated and by reducing it, the half-truth exaggerates in one direction. And vice versa, by increasing the number that had been underestimated, the half-truth exaggerates in the other direction. However, it is a generally accepted insight that two half-truths do not make a whole truth but lead into total error. An example of the harm a half-truth may cause can even be found in scholarly publications when an author, presumably well-meaning, accepts too wide a spectrum of estimated victims,[13] which may lead the thoughtful reader to wonder about the accuracy of other, perhaps more reliable data. Claiming a half-truth may also mislead an entire generation of students who may not inquire further but take these data as being true. *For all the above reasons, we must decisively say "no" to both the deniers and fabricators of the genocide in Jasenovac and other similar cases.*

When such a casual attitude toward truth is the result of estimates by survivors soon after the slaughter, it may be psychologically understandable that these individuals are in a state of shock and are not objective observers, having been surrounded by staggering numbers of exterminated friends and neighbors and often having barely survived intended murder themselves. It is even understandable psychologically (though it is certainly not the work of a healthy, normal mind) when the perpetrators inflate the numbers of those they have destroyed and boast about it. It is even a forgivable sin (but a sin nevertheless) when politicians, for allegedly greater purposes of raison d'etat, use figures loosely for their own advantage. We know that politics is the art of the possible, and many a politician has bent the truth to gain an advantage, such as larger reparations claims, more advantageous borders, a more favorable peace treaty, and so forth.

However, there are two groups for whom the maximizing or minimizing of genocide numbers is unforgivable: scholars and clergy. When scholars and clergy misrepresent genocides (and for that matter other claims), it is particularly dangerous, even demonic, because people tend to trust them more than politicians, journalists, lawyers, the military, and members of many other professions.

The very reason for the existence of scholars is to seek the truth in their various branches of intellectual inquiry. They are usually not under the same political exigencies as politicians (though they are not immune from political pressures and ideological seduction) and generally are given more time and resources (such as access to materials, documents, and archives as well as linguistic training) to research and establish the truth—perhaps not the Absolute Truth, but the regular, down-to-earth, commonly understood truth. The national origin, religion, or citizenship of the scholar should not matter (though in the past, it tended to matter very much). By discovering data, using critical thinking, debating, discussing, and cooperating with other scholars, the scholar seeks to establish the hard facts, as fairly and objectively as humanly possible.

Since utter objectivity is impossible to human beings—though many scholars falsely claim that they possess it—the scholar must clearly divulge her or his biases, which every human being has by the very fact of being human. We all see and hear the world through a particular filter, through our own set of eyes and ears. When a scholar's natural inclinations and biases are admitted openly, then the readers/listeners can take precaution to interpret what the scholar says. Most people would understand, for instance, that a Chinese scholar may perceive the facts differently than a Japanese scholar. But it would be unforgivable for a Japanese scholar to claim that the genocide in Nanking and other parts of China did not occur in the winter of 1937. The same applies to Serbian and Croatian scholars—as well as Jewish, German, Slovenian, Bošniak, Italian, American, and others—commenting on what transpired in the Balkans (and specifically in the territory of the former Yugoslavia) during World War II. Is it completely unrealistic to look forward to the day when one would find reliable, non-propagandistic books about the genocides committed in the Balkans, written by a variety of scholars, perhaps working together in establishing the facts?

Up until now, the clergy of all major faiths in the Balkans tended to see themselves as shepherds/pastors of their flock. And who will blame a shepherd for being a defender of his flock against the threats of wild beasts? But the clergy are not merely shepherds; they also consider themselves agents or messengers of God. In this second task, they may fail miserably because they frequently interpret God as favoring their own nation, when that may not be so. The clergy claimed (and still claim), "Gott mit uns," "Bog čuva Srbe," "Bog čuva Hrvate,"[14] and similar sentiments. Greatly neglected are the divine calls for justice, righteousness, truth, mercy, forgiveness, reconciliation, peacefulness, concern for the other—and, at least in Christianity, the mandate to "love one's enemies."[15]

Just as the UN Convention on the Prevention of the Crime of Genocide includes *intention* as a crucial element in determining whether certain actions are genocidal, the same should and must apply to scholars and clergy. What is the *intention*, motivation, or purpose of the author or speaker? If it is to manipulate the readers, to obtain propaganda advantages, to gain financial or material rewards, to humiliate a perceived enemy, to claim a territory for otherwise insufficient reasons, to settle ancient accounts, to sow hatred, to spread fear among the population for the purpose of organizing them to attack, and a myriad of other reasons, then the individual is clearly abusing scholarship and the preaching of God's word.

A somewhat more complicated issue is whether it is justifiable to manipulate the data for revenge. If the result of scholars' labor is that the perpetrators of recent genocides are punished, then there is a certain satisfaction that they got what they deserved. The problem is that in the efforts to avenge the deaths of the victims, the avenging side often kills indiscriminately many innocent victims of the other side. Mahatma Gandhi has clearly warned the world that pursuing an "eye for an eye" policy ends in blinding the whole world. That is surely what happened with regard to wars in the Balkans, more than once, including the most recent events at the end of the twentieth century.

Only by establishing the truth about events through historical, theological, psychological, sociological, archeological, judicial, and any other dependable means can we actually obtain justice.[16] Obtaining justice satisfies our desire or even our presumed need for revenge, and it does so in a way that is less likely to ignite a future round of genocides.

Based on truth and justice, it is possible to undertake the arduous task of genuine forgiveness and reconciliation, which I contend is a nearly superhuman feat, yet absolutely necessary for lasting peace. The ability to forgive and secure reconciliation with our enemies is a divine gift available to us, if we are willing to receive it. The memorial to the victims of Fascism in Novi Sad on the banks of the Danube River where many hundreds were killed in the winter of 1942, reads, "Sećanje je spomenik tvrdji od kamena. Ako smo ljudi oprostiti moramo, zaboraviti ne smemo" (Remembrance is a memorial harder than stone. If we are people we must forgive, but must not forget).[17]

GENOCIDE IN THE "INDEPENDENT STATE OF CROATIA"

During World War II, the Nazis permitted the establishment of a puppet state, ironically named the "Independent State" of Croatia, governed as a dictatorship by a Fascist terrorist group named Ustaše (Insurrectionists). They were extreme, right-wing anti-Semites and anti-Serbs presenting themselves ideologically as ultra-Catholics. The total extermination of Jews and Roma was a plausible goal. However, Serbs were too numerous for the same fate, so Milan Budak, the Croat minister of education, repeated the famous formula uttered twenty to thirty years earlier in regard to dealing with the Muslims on the territory of Yugoslavia: "Kill a third, expel a third, and convert a third." Indeed, all three methods were enthusiastically and mercilessly pursued, seeking to *čistimo* (we are cleansing) the land of Serbs. It took Ante Pavelić's Ustaša Croatian government much less time than it took Hitler to move from discrimination, isolation, pogroms, and ethnic cleansing to genocide. Perhaps it was because the path had already been marked by the Nazis. The Croatian government began as soon as they took power in April 1941.

Slavko Goldštajn, a noted Jewish-Croatian anti-Fascist historian and publicist, has pointed out that Ante Pavelić, a Croat lawyer from Herzegovina, and his Ustaše supporters had already planned the genocide for years while his small band of followers trained for a takeover of Croatia in camps in Italy and Hungary before the outbreak of World War II. One of Pavelić's propagandists, Mijo Babić, had written in 1932,

> When blood starts to spill it will gush in streams . . . the blood of the enemy will turn into gushes and rivers, and bombs will scatter their bones like the wind scatters the husks of wheat, . . . every Ustasha is poised . . . to thrust himself upon the enemy, with his body and soul, to kill and destroy it . . . the dedication, revolvers, bombs, and sharp knives of the Croatian Ustashe, who will cleanse and cut whatever is rotten from the healthy body of the Croatian people.[18]

As for Ustaše, "wherever he gets, the Serbs he captures, he erases everywhere even the last trace of their existence."[19] Hitler's plenipotentiary in Zagreb during most of the war, Glaise von Horstenau, stated, "Pavelić trod back on the soil of his homeland in April 1941, intent on no less . . . to annihilate by sword and fire, the 1,800,000 Orthodox Christians living mixed with the country's four million Croats and 700,000 Muslims."[20] And a leading Ustaša ideologist, Dr. Mladen Iveković, stated that he believes no Croat state can survive unless "we make efforts to have the Serbs disappear from our lands."[21] Both Hitler and von Ribbentrop gave to Pavelić explicit support for the deportation of Serbs to Serbia and his intolerant national policy, on June 6, 1941. Dido Kvaternik, the chief of security services of Croatia, who had been sent to Germany to study such methods of intolerance, came back with ideas of concentration and death camps.[22] But, of course, mass killing of Serbs had already begun in April of 1941. The pupil was as eager as the master.

There was a reason for implementing these genocidal intentions in phases. These phases were not put into operation uniformly because different parts of Yugoslavia and Croatia had been under different occupational regimes and the target groups varied. The exceptions were the Jews and Roma, who were persecuted in all regions, and the Serbs, who were the target group only in Croatia, Bosnia and Herzegovina, Vojvodina, and Kosovo.

Phase 1 was the registration of all Jews and the immediate arrests of prominent and younger Jews, Serbs, and Communists with concomitant plunder of businesses and homes. The wealthier Jews were evacuated to provide lodging for the officers of the invading armies and their collaborators. At first, the plunder was not state organized but carried out by greedy individuals, both foreign and domestic; soon, however, it became government sponsored. The German occupational authorities initiated the collection of an exorbitant "voluntary contribution" from the Jewish communities, especially in large cities, to be paid in currency, gold, jewelry or real estate. Once the contribution was paid, Jews would allegedly be permitted to carry on. Following these "collections," members of the target group were ordered to vacate entire areas of the city in the shortest possible time so that people had to leave behind most of their possessions and property.

Initially, the people arrested were not usually detained very long before being released. The goal was to give the impression that after enduring some harassment, they would be safe and, therefore, would not attempt to flee. A smaller number of those arrested were taken to the two concentration camps set up soon after the takeover, where most of them were murdered (see the information about the Koprivnica, Jadovno, and Pag camps later in this chapter).

Phase 2 began with an extraordinary legal decree issued by Ante Pavelić on June 26, 1941. This decree declared the Jews collectively guilty of disturbing the peace and of controlling the supply of essential goods on the market, and as a result, they were to be summarily deported to open-air collection centers. The Jews, and other anti-Fascists, were declared "unsuitable persons" who could be interned with no further explanation, trial, or judgment by the sole authority of the Ustaše. Germany's attack upon the Soviet Union in June 1941, in which the Independent State of Croatia was Germany's ally, caused more intense clashes with Communists and anti-Fascists. The result was a far more systematic roundup of the target groups for purposes of extermination in the concentration camps, especially the one in Jasenovac. This was the most intensive period of arrests and deportations with the main purpose of extermination, and it resulted in the largest number of killed. This phase lasted until the summer of 1942.

A short period of relative quiet ensued, followed by phase 3, which began in May 1943 and lasted till the end of the war in May 1945. At Germany's request, the final roundup of the remaining Jews took place with the purpose of delivering them to the extermination camps in Poland and Germany.

The Drive for an Ethnically Pure Croatian State

Nazi racist ideas infected the extremist nationalists of many countries, and the Ustaša movement in Croatia became obsessed with cleansing Croatia of those whom they considered their ethnic rivals, particularly Serbs, Jews, and Roma. Building on politics of the Croatian Party of Rights and the ideas of Ante Starčević, a nineteenth-century Croat ideologue, Ante Pavelić spearheaded the Ustaše movement, which was based on the racist ideas of Croat superiority and Serb inferiority, and he did so while he and many of his followers were still in exile in Italy and Hungary due to their terrorist activities. The Ustaše movement's aim was to destroy the Yugoslav state in order to create a Croatian state. The outbreak of World War II and the rise of Nazism and Fascism were conducive to the fulfillment of his ambitions when Yugoslavia collapsed under the attack of the Axis powers on April 6, 1941. On April 14, 1941, Pavelić declared himself the Poglavnik, or head (more or less the same title as Führer or Duce), of the Independent State of Croatia, a country that only a few governments recognized. The Ustaše targeted their hatred at Jews, whom they believed to be biologically different (and intent on taking over the world); the Roma, whom they simply considered subhuman; and the Serbs, whom they considered culturally and even biologically inferior to Croats and alleged oppressors of the Croats, threatening their very survival.

Soon after taking power, between March of 1941 and October 1942, the Ustaše passed a total of seventeen laws and decrees,[23] mostly against the Jews—such as the one that limited citizenship to Aryans (Ustaša ideologues claimed that Croats were descended from Goths rather than Slavs, thus an Aryan race), the Law on the Protection of Aryan Blood and Honor of the Croatian People—and on April 30, they created the Race Policy Committee to "regulate the domain of racial biology, race policy, and racial hygiene or eugenics."[24] The persecution of Jews began in the city of Osijek, where it was initiated by an aggressive German minority and then quickly adopted by Pavelić's government. Andrija Artuković, minister of the interior, was the government's most outspoken anti-Semite who vigorously promoted anti-Jewish policies stating that "actions of cleansing were necessary" and justified, not merely "from moral, religious, and social viewpoints, but also from a folk-political view because international Jewry is united with international communism and free masonry, having attempted and to this day still attempting to destroy the Croatian people."[25] Desire to nationalize and loot Jewish property was also a powerful factor in promulgating anti-Jewish legislation.

The arrests, deportations to concentration camps or exile, killings, arson, looting, and so on began almost immediately upon the arrival of Ustaše from abroad. They were quickly joined by local extremists. However, they never became a majority movement but always remained a fanatical minority that had grabbed dictatorial powers with the support of the Nazi Germany and Fascist Italy. Soon their actions became so inhumane that even their Italian and German allies recoiled. The Ustaše's extermination policies became catastrophic for the Serbian, Jewish, and Roma populations. The latter two were smaller in size, and the Ustaše, mostly under Nazi influence, intended to eliminate them completely. Due to the Ustaše's inordinate hatred of the Serbs (who may have constituted 25 percent of the total population), the previously mentioned one-third formula was applied, as verbalized by the minister of education and respect for God, Milan Budak. However, the formula was not applied evenly—many more were exterminated than were converted or deported.

Jasenovac, a Symbol and the Largest Extermination
Camp in Southeastern Europe

The Hall of Silence at the U.S. Holocaust Memorial Museum in Washington, DC, contains the names of the main extermination camps, such as Auschwitz, Chelmno, Majdanek, Sobibor, and Treblinka as well as Jasenovac. The first five are all in the territory of Poland and are well-known to the general public; Jasenovac is the least well-known in the West. It was the largest extermination camp in terms of area in all of Europe, and it was not under the direct command of Nazi Germans nor was it staffed by them.[26] For Serbs, it has the same significance as Auschwitz has for Jews.

Jasenovac has become the most contentiously debated issue. It is the subject of intensely emotional claims and counterclaims by Serb and Croat authors, politicians, and common people. Being the most powerful symbol of the genocide in the Balkans, it contributed to the outbreak of the wars of the 1990s. Some Serb authors contend that between 600,000 and 1 million Serbs were *killed* by Ustaše, and some more broadly accuse Croats and the Catholic Church for the functioning of Jasenovac and other death camps. At the same time, some Croat authors insist that Jasenovac was merely a work camp in which no more than 40,000 or 60,000 inmates *died*.

Jasenovac was not the earliest of the approximately twenty-four concentration camps functioning in NDH; that distinction belongs to either the camp Danica in Koprivnica or Jadovno near Gospić in Lika, both of which were established in April 1941. The camp at Stara Gradiška probably operated the longest, having been established later in April 1941 and ceasing its operation on April 23, 1945, when Partisan units freed the prisoners. The main camp of Jasenovac was liberated on May 2, 1945. On April 22, 1945, two large groups of the remaining inmates, assuming that they would all be liquidated, attempted a breakout. Most of them lost their lives in the attempt (only 91 out of over 1,100 survived).

The Jasenovac concentration camp was not a single site but a complex of five camps near the town of Jasenovac north of the Sava River. It consisted of Jasenovac I (Krapje), Jasenovac II (Bročice), Jasenovac III (Ciglana, the brick factory), Jasenovac IV (Kožara, a leather shop in the town of Jasenovac), and Jasenovac V (Stara Gradiška),[27] as well as a number of execution places such as Donja Gradina and Uštica (south of the Sava, in the territory of Bosnia). During certain periods the camps at Djakovo and Lepoglava also belonged to the command structure of Jasenovac. Thus, Jasenovac was a complex of camps, the total area of which varied from around 60 square miles to around 130 square miles depending on which camps were included under Jasenovac's central command during certain time periods.

The total number of inmates that could be accommodated in the complex was about 7,000 but usually there were no more than 4,000 at a given time. This meant that killings took place very quickly most of the time, in order to eliminate the surplus created by the constant arrival of new inmates.[28] The legal basis for concentration camps was established by the decree of Ante Pavelić and Mirko Puk on December 25, 1941—decree number CDXXIX-2101-Z-1941, The Decree of Undesirable Persons Threatening Public Order and Security. The internment could last three months to three years, but those inmates who were given the three-year sentence were often executed immediately upon arrival at the camp. The overall chief of all camps was Eugen Dido Kvaternik. The commander of the Jasenovac camps was Vjekoslav Luburić Maks, who planned the camp while still an emigrant in Italy. In October 1941, he went on a ten-day tour of the German concentration camps to gather new ideas. It should be emphasized however, that the Jasenovac camp was not under any direct German influence or oversight; it was an entirely Croat Ustaša enterprise. Luburić's deputy was Ivica Matković, but Ljubo Miloš, Miroslav Filipović-Majstorović, and Hinko Dominik Picilli were the other commanding officers of the camp. They seemed to compete to see who could be more sadistic and bloodthirsty by personally torturing and killing the inmates.

The most intense exterminations took place during the years 1941 and 1942, while during 1943 and the first half of 1944 killings slowed down some, only to pick up in intensity in the second half of 1944 and 1945. When it became obvious that the Allies were winning the war, the Ustaše tried to cover up their crimes by liquidating the remaining "enemies," exhuming the bodies from mass graves, burning the evidence, mining most of the camp buildings, and thoroughly destroying all the written evidence.[29]

The number of people who were killed in the Jasenovac complex is wildly contested, with estimates ranging from 20,000 to a million[30] and the most frequent range being from 50,000 to 700,000. Vladimir Žerjavić estimates the total number of killed at 70,000, of whom 45,000 to 52,000 were Serbs; 12,000 were Croats and Muslims; 13,000 were Jews; and 10,000 were Roma.[31] However, I tentatively adopt 77,000 to 79,000 as the most realistic, historically based figure,[32] of whom 69,842 individuals were documented by name in the registry of the Jasenovac museum in 2006.[33] Dragan Cvetković, a historian working at the Museum of Genocide Victims in Belgrade, estimates between 122,300 and 130,100 victims, of whom 77,000–81,000 were Serbs; 18,000–19,000 were Jews; 18,000–20,000 were Roma; 7,000–7,500 were Croats; 1,300–1,500 were Muslims; and 1,000–1,200 were of other or unknown nationalities.[34] The approximate gender ratio was 60 percent male and 40 percent female. There were special camps for children up to the age of fourteen, where a very large number of children were killed. While some maintain that the Ustaše created Jasenovac for the opponents of the regime regardless of their nationality, this is patently false. The camp was established before armed resistance to the Ustaše began. While, indeed, a number of people were in the camp because they were considered political enemies (such as Communists, anti-Fascists, or members of the Partisan guerillas), ethnicity clearly was the main criterion, with Serbs, Jews, and Roma, including infants, being deported to the camp simply on the basis of who they were rather than what they did.

One of the many disagreements about the camps is whether they were labor camps or death camps. Slavko Goldstein answers this by stating that they were both, as well as transit camps, because about 10,000 were moved to forced labor in the villages of the Požega area; 6,000 to the Daruvar area; and more than 10,000 to Germany.[35] In Jasenovac I and II, the Ustaše killed all inmates. Jasenovac III was at first a work camp, but when there were more than 5,000 inmates there, the surplus were killed. Jasenovac IV was mostly a work camp, while Stara Gradiška (Jasenovac V) started as a work camp for political opponents of the regime but turned into a death camp when Jews from Jasenovac and Serbs from the insurrectionist areas were deported to it en masse.[36]

Regardless of the shifting policies, the vast majority of the inmates did not leave the camp alive. Some of the organizers were sent to a smaller camp in Germany to learn how to organize a camp, but as the Ustaše's camps became much larger with a high level of new inmates, they killed the excess with methods that horrified even some Nazi German observers. Compared to the Nazi camps, the Jasenovac camps' methods of extermination were more personal and less industrial (no gas chambers)—the most mechanized killing, aside from deliberate starvation and disease, was throwing live victims into the huge furnace at the brick factory. The Croatian State Commission for Establishing Crimes of Occupying Forces and Their Assistants completed its report on December 15, 1945. They based much of their work on the eyewitness report of sixty-two survivors that summarized some twenty-three major ways of mass killings.[37]

Some of the methods of extermination were as follows:

1. killing by starvation
2. death by infection or infestation
3. stabbing by knives or pointed objects (e.g., stabbing pregnant women in the womb)
4. nailing to a tree
5. torture (e.g., cutting off breasts or limbs, gouging out eyeballs)
6. drowning

7. throwing into the furnace
8. hanging
9. shooting with firearms
10. slaughter by cutting throats
11. smashing heads with mallets or hammers
12. smashing children against walls or impaling them on a bayonet[38]

Ustaše camp guards often ordered inmates to carry out the killing and torture. For instance, some of the Roma inmates were ordered not only to be grave diggers for the mass executions but also to rape and slaughter those marked for execution. Sometimes Roma prisoners were required to slaughter other Roma, and then the remaining Roma would be killed by the guards.

Among his many eyewitness accounts from Jasenovac, Cadik I. Danon Braco, a survivor, describes how a Serb inmate who tried to escape was tied to a post and beaten to death by the other Serbs confined to the same barracks. Danon tells of a young Serb who said, "'I had to. What else could I have done?' In each of these barracks there are Ustashi spies who will inform the guards whenever a prisoner tries to escape. The reprisal would be ten to twenty inmates executed."[39] The foreman of the Jewish barracks told Danon that he too would have felt constrained to order the same execution to save other inmates. Danon then writes, "For a while I reflected upon this incident and realized that the Ustashi authorities of the Independent State of Croatia had supremely perfected their criminal system of annihilation to the paint [sic] where even we ourselves had to kill each other. They had this achieved [sic] the embodiment of evil while vile informers, as always and everywhere, carry on their work."[40]

The suffering of the inmates is almost indescribable, as were other circumstances where the commandants and the guards were given free reign to exercise their sadistic and pathological inclinations. Sometimes guards held competitions to see who would kill more people, more gruesomely in the shortest time. In narratives of genocide, there are frequent claims that the cruelty displayed in Jasenovac exceeds all other throughout history anywhere in the world. While I am not making such an unverifiable claim, it is noteworthy that even Nazi officers were shocked at the physical brutality displayed by the perpetrators in Jasenovac as they tended to forego the more mechanized or automated forms of extermination for the very personal and direct sadistic torture and killing.

Other Ustaše Camps

There were over thirty concentration camps in the territory of the Independent State of Croatia,[41] not all of them death camps. (This is not an attempt to provide comprehensive coverage, but a sufficiently wide sample is provided here in order to give an adequate picture of the scope of genocidal activities.) The very first death camp was established during the second phase of persecution in the late spring and early summer of 1941. The Jadovno camp was intended as an extermination camp. It was established sometime between April 11 and April 15, 1941, when Ustaše trucked several hundred internees to Gospić, a site intended almost entirely for exterminations. Gospić is located on Mt. Velebit at a site nearly 4,000 feet in elevation in Lika near the Adriatic coast. There are deep gorges and pits (some over 300 feet deep) that served as the mass dumping areas, avoiding the need to dig individual graves. Many of the victims were not even registered in the camp as they were taken directly to the edge of the ravines where they were sometimes shot but more often slaughtered with knives and blunt objects; sometimes they were simply pushed into the ravine with their hands tied by wire and then hand grenades were lobbed in to finish them off. Of course, many did not die right away; crying and moaning could be heard for days. Sometimes the Ustaše would throw dogs into the pit to feed on the dead and wounded.

In Jadovno the Ustaše killed 38,010 Serbs; 1,998 Jews; and 88 Croats and a few "others" for a total of 40,123.[42] Serb authors tend to focus on Serb victims; Jewish sources on Jewish losses. A Serb eyewitness claims that the Jews were the first ones to be thrown into the gorges, followed by Serbs.[43] Over a thousand children and 55 Orthodox priests were killed. All of this was accomplished in 122 days, which means that on average 329 people were killed each day. Other sources state that as many as 10,000, including several hundred Jews, were killed in Jadovno,[44] while still other sources claim there were 68,000 victims of which up to 2,500 were Jews. On August 21, the Ustaše closed the camp and transferred the remaining Croats to other camps, while the Jews and Serbs were liquidated. The Jadovno site was insufficiently explored until recently due to the deep gorges where the bodies were disposed and the fact that some of the gorges had been sealed off with concrete (apparently by the Yugoslav Communist government after World War II). Additional sites with skeletal remains were located in the 1980s.[45]

At the former furniture factory Danica in the village of Drnje near Koprivnica, the Ustaše established a camp on April 29, 1941. The majority of inmates were Serbs, followed by Jews and Croats. The camp was closed in July 1941, but during its existence it was inhabited, on average, by 3,000 inmates (once expanding to as many as 9,000); the number was controlled by the occasional release of inmates or, much more often, with their deaths by execution, beating, hunger, and brutal labor. At the camp's closing, all the surviving Serbs and Jews were transported to Jadovno and executed, while Croats were taken to Stara Gradiška and Jasenovac, where most of them perished.[46]

On the Adriatic island of Pag, the Ustaše established two camps on June 25, 1941, despite the fact that the island was under Italian occupation (Zone II). This means that the Italian administration was aware of what was transpiring in the Ustaše camps, but did not intervene. One camp was in Slano (for men) and the other in Metajna (for women and children). In Slano, the Jews were strictly separated from the Serbs and anti-Fascist Croat internees. The barracks were unfinished and without a roof so that the victims slept on the stone floor, and many under open skies. Twelve hours of hard labor daily was accompanied by torture, hunger, and disease. The internees were executed at the nearby place named Furnaža or taken in boats to the Pag Channel and dumped into the sea with rocks around their necks. Sometimes the camp administrators played a cruel joke on the inmates by telling them they were being released when in fact they were being taken to their deaths.[47]

In Metanja, women were frequently raped and then killed by being disemboweled and having their breasts cut off. Some exhumed bodies of women were found with their belly sewn shut with wire; inside was a several-month-old infant, who died buried in his mother's body.[48] A Croat Catholic priest came on Sundays to say the mass and to rape the women. Ustaše guards would brag to locals in taverns that after the initial three to four victims, it is easy and exciting to kill.

The Ustaše withdrew from Pag on August 19, 1941, having killed many of the inmates and taking some with them to other camps in Croatia, mainly Jadovno, Kruščica, and Jasenovac. The total number of victims is unknown because upon the Ustaše departure (on September 22, 1941), the Italian garrison was ordered to exhume the bodies and to cremate them in order to prevent the potential spread of disease. No material evidence remained, but two Italian physicians who served in their armies described the gruesome exhumation in some detail.[49]

Lobograd near Zlatar-Bistrica used to be a home for the elderly. It was vacated in September 1941 in order to receive 1,300 mostly Jewish and some Serbian women, many transferred from the Bosnia camp in Kruščica. Typhoid fever raged, and the Ustaše tortured, killed, and raped inmates. The camp was closed in the fall 1942 with the Jewish women transported to Auschwitz, younger Serb women to Germany for forced labor, and older Serb women to Serbia.[50]

The camp in Djakovo near Osijek was unusual in that the Ustaše and German authorities in Osijek ordered the Jewish community to find a location for Jewish women whom they planned to expel from Osijek. Under great pressure, the community found a place, and 1,830 Jewish and about 50 Serb women were deported to the camp, which was to be self-administered and supplied. Matters worked relatively well until the Ustaše added 1,200 inmates from Stara Gradiška. These women had been infected with small pox and typhoid, which rapidly spread through the entire camp and killed five to six women daily. The camp was then taken over by Ustaša commanders and rape and torture were added to the inhumane conditions. In June 1942, the camp was closed with 2,400 deportations to Jasenovac and over 500 buried in Djakovo.[51]

Tenje was a satellite community of Osijek that became the sole ghetto in Croatia. Osijek Jews had been ordered to build the hamlet to which about 3,000 Jews from Osijek and the region of Slavonia were deported, starting in June 1942. On August 15, an SS officer arrived and organized the transport of about 700 children and 300 adults, who were sent to their death in Auschwitz the very next day. On August 18, a second transport was sent to Jasenovac; on August 22 the remainder were dispatched, with some taken to immediate extermination, probably in Gradina near Jasenovac, while others were sent to Auschwitz. Of about 3,000 Osijek Jews who were deported in 1942, only about 10 returned from Jasenovac and Auschwitz.[52]

When Germans took over all territories formerly held by Italians in 1943, they examined the records in Croatia and concluded that it was not Judenrein (cleansed of Jews) as they expected. This was partly because the Ustaše had given "honorary Aryan" status to rich Jews who could pay for this privilege. Additionally, those Jews who married Gentiles were exempt from deportation, and it seems that an unusually large number of Ustaše leaders had married Jewish women, including Pavelić himself.[53]

Marko Attila Hoare helpfully concludes that the Ustaše genocide of Serbs was different from their attempted extermination of Jews and Roma, though there were similarities. The Ustaše's alliance with Nazi Germany necessitated incorporating themselves into the Holocaust master plan at Hitler's insistence. Their rivalry with the Serbs escalated into hatred as the sizable Serb presence in Croatia and Bosnia clashed with their aspiration of an ethnically pure Croat state. Seeing that they could not numerically kill all Serbs, the Ustaše settled on two additional modes of ethnic cleansing—deportation and assimilation through conversion—both likewise of genocidal nature.[54] The "Croatization" of Serbs was attempted mostly through Catholic proselytism and unsuccessful attempts to create a Croatian Orthodox Church.

The Role of Catholic Clergy, or "Always Croats! Always Catholics! God and Croats!"[55]

When I wrote my 1995 book *Yugoslavian Inferno: Ethnoreligious Warfare in the Balkans*, I had to make an effort to persuade the publisher to use the word *ethnoreligious* rather than *ethnic and religious* or *ethno-religious*. I insisted on the single word in order to indicate just how intertwined these two concepts were during the Balkan wars of the 1990s. In investigating the genocides of World War II, I find it even more necessary to use *ethnoreligious* as a single word. Often, when Croat Catholic priests in the past (and even in the present) spoke or wrote, it was not clear whether he was more a Croat to whom Catholicism seemed a useful instrument to assert Croatian interests, or whether he was a Catholic Croat who so desired the victory of Catholicism over Orthodoxy and Judaism that he was willing to accept Serbs and Jews as Croats, provided they convert to Catholicism. One may wonder whether such a priest weighed these factors or whether he even knew that Croat and Catholic are not synonyms. Additionally, many Croat Catholic clergy and believers had an ardent desire to bring the Orthodox believers back into the fold of the papal church, sometimes letting these Serbs live because by becoming Catholic, they also became Croats. Allegedly 200,000 Serbs were converted to Catholicism,[56] most of them temporarily. Conversion was sometimes for the benefit (and salvation) of the victims' souls, but such rebaptized Serbs might be killed anyway, frequently in the very church where they had just become Catholics. Often, Croat hatred of Serbs was so great that their Serb bodies had to perish, while their "Catholic" souls had just been saved. Orthodox priests and bishops, as well as churches, were the particular target of the murderers who seemed to relish torturing Orthodox clergymen prior to terminating their lives.

It is important to distinguish between the Ustaša state authority's desire to convert the Orthodox to Catholicism and the Catholic Church hierarchy's handling of those conversions. Although historians like Vladimir Dedijer make sweeping allegations that the Roman Catholic Church, including the papacy, nurtured centuries-long hatred of Serbs and wished to exterminate them if they were unsuccessful at converting them to Catholicism,[57] this is a vast exaggeration.

The first governmental legal order about conversion was issued on May 3, 1941, very soon after the establishment of the new state. Most researchers state that the Catholic Church gladly followed this law and facilitated the mass conversion of Serbs, who did so obviously not out of conviction but out of fear that otherwise they would not survive. Croatian Catholic representatives and scholars are now countering by saying that actually this law was the clearest example of the disagreement between the new state and the Catholic Church and that generally the Catholic Church permitted only individual cases of conversion based upon clear proof of voluntary decision making and instruction in the faith.[58]

Of the ten Orthodox bishops who resided on the territory of NDH in 1941, Metropolitan Bishop Petar of Sarajevo, Bishop Platon of Banja Luka, and

Bishop Sava of Karlovac were tortured and killed. Metropolitan Bishop Dositej of Zagreb reached Serbia, but he died soon afterward from his traumas. One hundred and eighty-seven Orthodox priests were killed, along with thirty monks, plus several hundred priests were exiled.[59] Vladimir Umeljić itemizes the names and the specifics of the destiny of the bishops and thirty-one priests.[60]

It is well documented that there were quite a few fanaticized Catholic priests so enthused by the declaration of the independence of Croatia that they joined the Ustaše, not only blessing and supporting their gruesome work, but even joining in the killing. Clearly the hierarchs were not in complete control of every priest. Some of the hierarchs were enthusiastic supporters of the new order. One of the most conspicuous of these priests, the Franciscan Miroslav Filipović later nicknamed Majstorović (as in master killer), became for a period of time the commander of the Jasenovac camp. He and similar priests were defrocked when their misdeeds became public.[61] Once again we look to Umeljić and Dedijer, who provide extensive lists of Catholic priests who propagated forcible proselytism or killing of Serbs.[62]

The broader question about the complicity of the hierarchy and Vatican bureaucracy, including Pope Pius XII, is harder to establish. For the vast majority of Serb investigators, their guilt and responsibility is clear; these investigators insist that not only did the hierarch tacitly accept the genocide and forced proselytism carried out under unstable wartime conditions but they were also the instigators and promoters, as they saw this as a golden opportunity to "heal" the thousand-year-old schism. From the pro-Ustaša Catholic clerical point of view, God, in his providence, had blessed the Croats doubly by both granting them their long-desired independence and giving them another chance to be the *antemurales Christianis*, incorporating all the Orthodox in their territory into the Mother Church, for which they expected gratefulness and commendation from the Holy Father.

The evidence is contradictory. There are orders by Archbishop Alojzije Stepinac that Orthodox are to be permitted conversion, but only if the conversion is clearly voluntary or is done to save someone's life. Yet other bishops gloried in the rapid increase of Catholics and newspapers reported about "The Return to the Faith of their Grandfathers."[63] Documents exist detailing the release of individuals from concentration camps under the condition that they go back to their home and immediately get baptized as Roman Catholics. It would not be surprising that even thoughtful Catholic priests would find themselves in a quandary when handed such documents.

But what do we make of the seemingly cordial receptions of Ustaše and German Nazi high officers by Catholic hierarchs? What do we make of the Croatian Bishops Conference's strong recommendation that Pius XII grant an audience to Ante Pavelić, who had been sentenced twice in absentia for treason and murder prior to becoming the head of the Croatian state? Archbishop Ivan Šarić of Sarajevo seemed to be an enthusiastic supporter of the Ustaše, whereas Bishop Alojzije Mišić of Mostar condemned their crimes, stating, "The Holy Church will not accept the confession of all those who against God's laws are killing and sin against human life, as well as those who deliberately are destroying or taking the property of others, nor can it nor will it forgive their sins."[64] As the case of Bishop Mišić and the few other clergy who refused to bless the murderous mayhem shows, it was possible to not support the killings without risking harm to themselves. The Ustaše were so eager to portray themselves as utterly loyal Catholics that the hierarchs could have safely played a far more moderating and pacifying role than most of them did. It seems that for many of them, nationalistic feelings as Croats prevailed over religious feelings as Catholics—unless one is willing to maintain that the Catholic Church was so eager for worldly power that it condoned all methods of expanding its influence over people and lands. The Franciscan friar Marko Oršolić has severely criticized the Croat nationalist priests, not only for their excesses and belated, lukewarm distancing from these genocidal crimes, but also for their unrepentant attitude toward the acceptance of the compatibility of National Socialism and Fascism with Christian teachings.[65] Among Muslim, Orthodox, and Protestant clergy there were also Nazi sympathizers and collaborators, but regretfully only few repented openly and boldly on behalf of their communities for the sins and crimes of this period—unless it was to condemn the rival ethnoreligious communities.

GENOCIDAL ASPECTS OF ITALIAN OCCUPATIONAL AUTHORITIES IN YUGOSLAV LANDS

Since Nazi Germany and Fascist Italy as well as Bulgaria and Hungary were members of the Axis, one might assume that when these countries simultaneously attacked and partitioned Yugoslavia, they displayed similar genocidal policies. But this assumption is contradicted by the fact that Jews, as well as Serbs, eagerly sought to migrate to territories held by the Italians because of a fairly widely held conviction that the chances of survival under Italian military or civilian rule were vastly superior to the chances under either the Germans or NDH, that is, the Ustaše. Indeed, many Jewish survivors expressed gratefulness that they or members of their families succeeded in reaching the Italian occupational zone, as the Italians did not display special genocidal intentions toward Jews in the manner that Germans and Croats did.[66]

The scope of the Italian occupation of the Balkans was considerable. It included the southwestern part of Slovenia, the entire Dalmatian coastline (including the islands in the Adriatic), a second military zone in the Dalmatian hinterland (in which control was uneasily and unevenly shared with NDH), all of Montenegro, most of Kosovo and eastern Macedonia (the latter two having been incorporated into "old" Albania, which the Italians controlled since 1938), and western Greece. Italy considered the Mediterranean and the Balkans as its *spazio vitale* (living space) in which their "race" had a natural right to resurrect the Roman Empire.

A number of Holocaust scholars have pictured the Italians as benevolent, even friendly, to Jews and others. Jacques Sabille explains that the Italian attitude toward Jews was actually formulated in response to the bestiality that the Croat Ustaše manifested toward Jews and Serbs immediately upon the outbreak of the war. He writes, "The Italian troops immediately and spontaneously reacted against this bestiality. There was no time for orders to have arrived from above. The Italian officers and men, singly and in groups, did all that was possible to take the Jews out of the terror zones and hide them in safe places in parts annexed by Italy, or in Italy itself."[67]

Though these deeds are corroborated by numerous eyewitness accounts, Sabille maintains there are few written records as the soldiers' actions were illegal, albeit noble and ethical. Jews allegedly enjoyed equal rights and complete liberty. Italian diplomatic and military authorities allegedly opposed or sabotaged German and Croat policies and resisted Nazi and Ustaše pressure to deliver the Jews and the Serbs to the extermination camps. The Italians insisted that a time-consuming census of the interned population should take place so that they could determine who was an Italian Jew, who was a citizen of the annexed territories, who had come as a refugee to these zones, and so forth.

These were all delaying tactics with the ultimate aim of providing humane protection to all segments of population under Italian rule. In order to counter German pressures, the Italians established a concentration camp on the island of Rab (Arbe in Italian) between May and August 1943, the alleged purpose of which was to keep the Jews from being deported to the death camps in Poland. Most of these inmates were permitted to transfer themselves individually to Italy or hide or join the Partisans.[68]

The first hypothesis to explain Italy's protection of the Jews was that until Italy's surrender to the Allies on September 8, 1943, no Jews were handed over to the Germans or other local authorities, because of the underlying humanitarian qualities that characterize the Italian civilization. The flaw in this hypothesis is that at Rab, in addition to about 2,650 Jews there were about 13,000 Slovenians (and some Croats) in a separate camp. These prisoners were brought to Rab before the Jews and were treated so atrociously that about 4,400 of them died.[69] The food, water, and lodging conditions in both camps were horrendous.

The second variant of this theme suggests that Italian armed forces and civil authorities in the annexed lands did all in their power to provide as much protection to Jews and Serbs as was possible in these trying war years. The claim is that Italians are good people with an ancient Christian civilization and that only a racial theory promoted by Mussolini messed up an otherwise honorable record.[70]

Davide Rodogno, having thoroughly researched and analyzed the numerous military and civilian records, concludes that these two theories are not sustainable. He states that "the belief that the Italian government stopped deporting Jews as soon as it realized that deportation meant extermination is mistaken."[71] According to Rodogno, the annexed territories were to be the testing ground for applying anti-Semitic laws of the "new order" that would subsequently be implemented in Italy. "The anti-Semitic laws were applied with special harshness in the province of Fiume [Rijeka] to both Jewish natives and Jewish refugees. For the Italian authorities knew that expulsion to Croatia amounted to the issue of a death sentence."[72] But expel they did, not only Jews but other refugees as well, from all three Italian prefectures in Dalmatia, escorting them to the frontier and refusing them reentry.

The Italians considered the NDH as a client state over which they were hoping to exert influence; this seems to have been agreed upon between Hitler and Mussolini. However, Rodogno maintains that Germany sabotaged the agreement and exerted a commanding influence in both Slovenia and Croatia, much to the Italians' chagrin. The Italians witnessed much violence and terror by the Ustaše against both Jews and Serbs. And the Germans supported the Ustaše, particularly in regard to the Jews so that the Italians compared this behavior to the "darkest Middle Ages." Particularly astonishing to the Italians was that among the leaders and propagators of the tortures and slaughter were Croat Catholic priests.[73] This put the Italian commanders into a quandary as to how they should respond to the horrendous behavior of their allies. While some Italian officers and soldiers did carry out missions of mercy, the official position was that Italian soldiers were not to protect the persecuted civilians. For instance, on the island of Pag, the Ustaše established a concentration camp for Serbs and Jews where they murdered the inmates on a regular basis. The commanders of the Italian garrison stationed nearby did not permit any intervention.[74] When the Ustaše withdrew from the island, the Italian soldiers had to sanitize the site, that is, remove all evidence of the murders. In reports of the Italian military regiments, estimates of the casualties of Ustaše genocides indicate that the Italians were very much aware of the staggering numbers of the victims. The Italians' concern was that the activities of the

Ustaše would drive the Serbian population to join the Partisans rather than the Četniks, who many times cooperated with the Italians in fighting the Partisans. Hence, their main concern was not so much a general humanitarian concern as it was a strategic concern regarding how to govern the annexed territories more effectively with the support of the local population. The government in Rome, including Mussolini, was fully informed on most aspects of the genocidal activities, including a report by a deputy commander of the Marche Division to the Gabinetto Armistizio-Pace (Armistice-Peace Cabinet) that said, "Famished [Serbian] women in the prison at Gacko were offered their spit-roasted children to eat."[75] Full knowledge of the atrocities did not rupture the intergovernmental relations with the Axis powers, which were more exasperated by their rivalries in regard to spheres of interest than revulsion of their genocidal intensions. According to Rodogno, "Although some divisional or regimental commanders did take sporadic and isolated action to protect civilians, in general Italian soldiers watched the massacres in frozen immobility."[76] The brutality, especially the outrages against women and children, clearly caused distress among many soldiers, but the Italians had discovered that the horrors they witnessed were not mere excesses of the criminal element among the Ustaše but were ordered in writing by the Croat government to annihilate the "Serbian race." While the hearts of individual Italian men may have been touched by the suffering, the Italian ambassador to Zagreb, Rafaelle Casertano, urged that Italian empathy (he called it pietism) must cease and no further assistance must be given either to Jews or Serbs.[77] Rodogno concludes, "At no time did occupation policy have 'humanitarian' aims, and its purpose was never to 'save' Orthodox Christians or Jews from Ustasha persecution."[78] Italians were more concerned that handing over Jews to the Germans or Croatians would have a damaging effect on their reputation and their ability to govern the annexed territories; their actions were not motivated by an ethical concern that turning them over would mean extermination. By the middle of 1942, they were fully aware of Germany's Final Solution.[79] "Indeed, Jews were often refused entry, expelled, interned or consigned to the government authorities of the occupied territories because they were refugees, and not simply because of 'racial' discrimination."[80]

Restrictive measures were applied to Jews who sought to enter the annexed territories or to move to Italy, as "consular visas" were no longer issued to foreigners of the "Jewish race." Similarly, people who sought to join family members in Italy were rejected. Foreign Jews who hailed from countries that had anti-Jewish racist laws were routinely prevented from entering Italy.[81] About 800 Jews who tried to enter Fiume (Rijeka) were expelled between July 1941 and May 1942, while the local Jews were interned. Similar actions took place in the Italian prefectures of Dalmatia, that is, Sušak and Split. Governor Giuseppe Bastianini intended to rid Dalmatia of all of its small Jewish communities and applied Italian anti-Semitic laws to them, denying them ration cards and interning about 2,000 in the concentration camp at Ugliano. The Italian authorities were fully aware that turning them over to the Croats amounted to a death sentence because it was known that in August 1942, the Croats and Germans signed a treaty whereby Croatia would deliver all of its remaining Jews to Germany. Jews were desperate to avoid this fate. Through exorbitant bribes, some were able to secure the services of Croatian sailors who helped them illegally cross the Adriatic to the Italian coast.

The German and Croatian governments exerted strong pressure on the Italians to surrender at least those Jews that had sought refuge in the Italian zone, but the Italians refused to comply—mostly in order to assert their independence. Confronted with the argument that all Jews are enemies of the Axis and spies for the Allies and hence need to be exterminated, by 1943 the Italians interned at the camp on the island of Rab about 2,260 Jews from the Italian-occupied zones 2 and 3 in the Italian annexed territories. This was not conceived as a rescue operation but as a way to resist German interference.[82] Luca Pietromarchi wrote shortly before Italy's surrender,

> We should disassociate ourselves from the Germans in order not to be blamed, even indirectly, for the acts committed by the Germans. The remaining Italian zones should be administered according to humanitarian principles, leaving the best possible memory of us behind. Also in regard to German conceptions, so different from the Italian ones, we should comply with the rules laid down by the law of war and with humanitarian principles.[83]

On March 1, 1942, General Mario Roatta, commander of the Second Italian Army, issued Circular 3c with instructions to implement a policy of repression, including mass internment and scorched-earth measures, which he advocated as a colonial policy. This policy led to de-Balkanization and ethnic cleansing of the Balkan people, who were clearly regarded as inferior races. This later led to Italian colonization, as well as policies of Italianizing the population. The measures included in the circular included the evacuation of entire villages and regions and the taking of hostages, as well as summary executions of rebels. The circular stated, "Seize normally as hostages those persons suspected of sympathizing with the Partisans, but in case of necessity, even other persons. Pay attention to select hostages from every social strata of the population. They will answer with their life for every attempt made against the Italian soldier, in the locality of their origin, in the event the guilty ones cannot be found."[84] In Circular 4, Roatta stated that "rebels must not be treated according to the formula *tooth for a tooth*, but that of a *head for a tooth*."[85]

Severe repression was carried out in Slovenia and Montenegro. General Mario Robotti carried out these policies "with maximum energy and without pity" in Slovenia, where he complained subsequently that not enough people were killed. His orders were to shoot on the spot anyone who committed hostile acts against Italian authority, to destroy the buildings of those who aided the rebels, and to shoot all able bodied-men who simply found themselves without good reason in a combat zone or in isolated localities.[86] By the end of June 1942, the Italians had destroyed 104 villages, whereas the Germans had only destroyed 16. Some of the Italian commanders justified these actions using the same measures as their adversaries. One of the functionaries, Giacomo Zanussi, stated, "What can be seen, I must confess with sadness, will be that by dint of being in the midst of Balkans we [ourselves] have ended being Balkanized, and thus doing sometimes what they do habitually, surely not worse, that being totally impossible."[87] As the war continued, both the Italian military and civilian position in Slovenia hardened. The high commissioner, Emilio Grazioli, wrote to the minister of the interior on August 24, 1942, "The problem of the Slovene population can be resolved in the following manner: (1) destroying it; (2) transferring [sic] it; (3) eliminating the dissident elements, [by] carrying out hard policy, but one with justice and an approach so as to create the basis for an . . . assimilation."[88] Here we have an expression by a high government official of the *intent* to destroy, remove, transfer, or assimilate an entire ethic group, which would indicate genocidal intent. At a meeting in Gorizia on July 31, 1942, Mussolini considered mass deportation of the Slovene population.[89]

In Montenegro, at first, the Italian authorities seemed to try to use soft measures to incorporate Montenegro into the Italian sphere through one of several political approaches. The Italians were completely surprised when suddenly on July 13, 1941, a mass rebellion of Montenegrins broke out that drove out the Italian army from all but a few city garrisons. The revolt was subsequently suppressed; however, the Montenegrin population continued to engage in various guerilla activities against the Italians. The Italian command vacillated between taking a soft position of general amnesty to all but the leaders of the rebellion and implementing harsh retaliatory measures. The protagonists favoring the harsh measures prevailed toward the end of the war, which meant summary executions, taking and killing of hostages, and burning of villages and homes. Yet the rebellion could not be put down.

The Italians had their own internment camps. Around 25,000 people from the province of Ljubljana, 6,000–8,000 from the province of Fiume (Rijeka), and an additional 2,000 from Dalmatia had been interned between November 1941 and May 1942 alone.[90] However, most of the documents regarding these camps have been destroyed so that often not much more than the name of a camp is known.[91] Some were camps for POWs; others were for civilians. For Yugoslavia, the number of internees is about 100,000 to 150,000 while the figures for Albania, Greece, and Macedonia are even less certain. In an official note to the Italian government, the Vatican had complained that about 30,000 inmates in Slovenia lived under dreadful conditions, to which General Roatta claimed that less than 20,000 were interned and of these 6,577 were in the camp at the island of Rab, where he claimed the number of inmates never exceeded 10,500.[92]

Prior to the establishment of the concentration camp on Rab, the Italians opened a camp in Kraljevica, Dalmatia, to which about 1,250 Jews were consigned. Mostly they were assigned to the hard physical labor of working on roads and in stone quarries. In June and July 1943, the inmates were transferred to the island of Rab. A concentration camp had been established in June 1942 to which the Italian government sent about 13,000 Slovenes and 2,650 Jews, who were strictly separated from each other; the Slovenes were treated worse than the Jews.[93] About 4,400 internees died in this camp. The numerous elderly and children frequently became sick and died. When Italy capitulated, some of the inmates jumped the Italian guards and took their weapons and with the help of the Partisans, all Slovenes and about 2,000 Jews were transferred to liberated territories. Those able to fight joined the Partisans, and the others were distributed throughout the region where the local population took care of them. Regretfully, many were killed when the German army carried out a counteroffensive. About 300 elderly and sick Jews decided to remain on Rab and they were subsequently captured and deported to Auschwitz by the German army that landed on the island in March 1944. Other Jews who had been arrested in various Dalmatian cities were taken either to Jasenovac or to the fairgrounds in Zemun near Belgrade, where practically none survived.[94]

Italy's surrender in 1943 quickly led to the capitulation of Italian forces in the Balkans. Since the armistice of September 8, 1943, was announced suddenly, the announcement did not reach most of the Italian commanders in the Balkans right away. Once received, the information did not clarify what the commanders should do and whether they were now at war with Germany. The Germans suffered no such uncertainties. They rushed to occupy all territories that were held by the Italians and treated them as enemy combatants, fighting against those who chose to resist, capturing them, executing them, taking them to internment in Germany, and so forth. Sometimes the Italians were attacked simultaneously by their former allies and their former enemies. Some of the Italian forces joined Partisan units; others sought to withdraw to Italy any way they could. The result was chaotic as well as tragic since many of them lost lives after the unconditional surrender. The resistance fighters against Fascism and Nazism benefited from this precipitous collapse as they came into possession of an enormous cache of arms and equipment that increased their effectiveness. This surrender of the Italian governing structures prevented further escalation of the repressive measures of Circular 3c that had been implemented in the first half of 1943.[95]

What was good news for the Allies and all those who resisted the forces of occupation was not necessarily good news for those who tried to save themselves from extermination, especially the Jews. While the Italian policies toward the Jews were inconsistent and ranged from benevolent to repressive, that was not the case with the Germans and Croatian Ustaše. After September 8, 1943, all Jews and many Serbs who had been relatively safe found themselves hunted down. The Jews were delivered to the extermination camps in Poland or Germany,[96] while the Serbs were left to the mercies of NDH, which had declared war on Italy when Italy surrendered.

The documents detailing the behavior of the Italians show no evidence of a clearly genocidal intent or practice, except in the above-mentioned memo by High Commissioner Emilio Grazioli; nonetheless, they are culpable of having clear knowledge of both the Final Solution and the Ustaše genocides and of responding either passively or militarily, aiding their allies until they surrendered to the Allies on September 8, 1943. At the same time, it does need to be acknowledged that the Italians' positive reputation was deserved. If the desperate Jewish and Serbian refugees could make it to the Italian territories or Italy proper, they had a much better chance of survival. It is also true that individual Italian officials as well as ordinary soldiers often assisted such refugees, some because of true humanitarian sentiments, others because of hefty bribes by refugees who still had some financial means.

Rodogno concludes,

> While it is true that the Italians interned thousands of Jews rather than hand them over to the Germans, they nevertheless expelled a large number or turned them back at the borders in all the occupied territories. There were indeed "good Italians" who rescued persecuted Jews and persons of other faiths and nationalities, but I do not believe the thesis that Italians as a whole were *brava gente* who refused to give the Jews over to the Germans for humanitarian reasons. Citing individual acts in order to claim that humanitarianism is inherent to the Italian national character, asserting that it would be intrinsically impossible for Italians to harm Jews voluntarily, is to make claims that have no basis in fact.[97]

This statement is equally applicable to the Italian attitude toward the Balkan people, whom they considered culturally inferior and expendable in the pursuit of Italian *spazio vitale*—not unlike the German pursuit of Lebensraum.

SLOVENIA

Slovenia was partitioned between a German-annexed northern part and an Italian-annexed southern part. Seemingly both intended to change the population structure and Germanize or Italianize it. Hitler ordered the German occupiers, "Machen Sie mir dieses Land wider Deutsch!" (Make this land German again for me).[98] The Slovenian language was forbidden to be taught and spoken. A German minority had lived in a Slovenia enclave for about 800 years when the Italians asked for their relocation so they could populate the area with Italians. The Germans agreed and moved these people to a part of the country where Slovenes had lived prior to their being expelled and taken north of Berlin to be used as forced labor until the end of the war. The SS deported from their zone about 585,000 (or 73 percent) of the population, with the intention of Germanizing one-half of those who remained (the ones they deemed it possible to naturalize) and deporting the others to Germany; still others sought refuge in Serbia. In 1942, a year after the implementation of the order, the process had to be stopped because of the massive resistance by the Slovenian population. Afterward, Hitler and Himler agreed that the Partisan resistance fighters were to be exterminated along with the Jews. The result was that about 55,000 Slovenes were killed and 340,000 were arrested, but no one was ever punished for it.[99] This forcible deportation was ethnic cleansing according to the UN Genocide Convention's definition.

The fate of the Slovenes under Italian control has been described in the previous section.

BOSNIA AND HERZEGOVINA

Bosnia and Herzegovina (B&H) had a very complex ethnic makeup. There were three major ethnic groups (Muslims, Serbs, and Croats) and Jewish and Roma minorities, as well as several occupying armies (German, Italian, NDH Ustaše, and Domobran [Home Guard]), plus two main guerilla forces (Serbian Četniks and multiethnic Partisans). Describing and analyzing what transpired in B&H during the four war years is difficult because of the diverse ethnic makeup. Due to B&H's central location within Yugoslavia, its ethnic diversity, and the above mentioned plurality of armies and guerillas, the conflicts were bloodier (just as they would be again fifty years later) than elsewhere. But as can be expected, there is no consensus as to which nationality suffered more. Noel Malcolm states, "Altogether 75,000 Bosnian Muslims are thought to have died in the war; at 8.1 percent of their total population, this was a higher proportion than that suffered by the Serbs (7.3), or by any other people except the Jews and the Gypsies. Muslims had fought on all sides—Ustasha, German, Chetnik, Partisan—and had been killed by all sides."[100] However, Aleksa Djilas presents a different estimate. According to him, in a population of 2.8 million, the human losses were 400,000 and "every sixth Serb, eighth Croat and twelfth Muslim" perished.[101] A. Djilas attributes the shift in the ethnographic structure of Bosnia to the greater losses by Serbs than by Muslims. While it is true that the Serb Četniks and Partisans, whose composition was predominantly Serb, killed a very large number of Muslims and Croats, the very fact that B&H was part and parcel of NDH meant that the preponderant state and military power was with those who had allied themselves with Germany, meaning mostly Croats and Muslims. It is impossible to adjudicate what proportion of all those who were killed in B&H was due to *politicide* or ethnic cleansing or simply casualties of a civil cum international military conflict. But it is already evident from the discussion of what transpired in NDH (into which B&H had been incorporated) that the most victimized groups were Serbs, Jews, and Roma, who were slated for ethnic cleansing and genocide as the Ustaše government wanted to make B&H an integral part of the purely Croat territory. Četniks and Partisans also carried out gruesome massacres, and at the end of the war, the winning Partisans executed most of those whom they considered "enemies of the people."

The Bosnian Croat population largely welcomed the creation of NDH under whose government they aspired to live. Upon the quick collapse of the Yugoslav Royal Army, the Croats and significant segments of the Muslim population—whom the Croats courted by calling them "the flowers of the nation" and "the purest Croats but of the Muslim faith"—joyously welcomed the arrival of the German and Croatian forces. Soon the Italian army also arrived, and while they were regarded as allies, the Croats hoped for sovereignty over all of B&H. The Italians were almost uniformly perceived as the least barbarous and aggressive, but they departed early, leaving the Serbs to their main enemies, the Croats and those Muslims who were pro-Croat. For Jews, Nazi Germans were the main source of threat, though the Ustaše willingly killed, incarcerated in concentration camps, or delivered to the Nazis all the Jews they could apprehend.

We have already covered the fate of the Serbs who lived near Jasenovac, both in the Serbian Krajina of Croatia and in the Bosnian Krajina, which also had a large Serb populace. Until relatively recently, little was researched and written about the killing of Serbs and Jews in the area of Sanski Most. As in other cases, the estimates vary but about 7,000 Serbs were rounded up (Jews represented a small minority of perhaps sixty-five persons, mostly residing in the town of Sanski Most), of which about 5,500 were killed on a hill named "Šušnjar." The killings were genocidal in nature not only based on the evidence of lost lives but also supported by the previous threats by Ustaše representative Dr. Viktor Gutić from Zagreb, who stated, "I have issued drastic orders for their complete extermination. Do not be weak toward any of them, bear in mind that they were our grave-diggers and destroy them wherever you can."[102]

No concentration camps were established in this territory; there were only short-range incarcerations in prisons, municipality buildings, schools, store houses, attics, and cellars or subsequent deportations to Jasenovac and other camps in Croatia proper. But this meant that the Serbian population was either massacred on the spot in their own villages or were marched to other collection points for large-scale massacres. Sometimes the arrested would be released only to be later rearrested and executed. Some Serbs, fearing extermination, fled to Serbia, leaving practically all their possessions behind; at times, they were required to assign all their property in perpetuity to the Ustaše. There was often discussion among the villagers as to what they should do. The younger tended to advocate resistance or flight into the forest, but the elders, fearing large-scale retaliation, prevailed in convincing the majority to stay. They believed their neighbors, with whom they thought they had good relations, would not allow them to be killed. In that assumption they were wrong; many who voluntarily registered with the new authorities never came back. Many Serb houses were burned down as were entire Serb villages.

The Germans and Ustaše wrought horrible vengeance for every one of their rank who was wounded or killed. The killing of a German or Ustaše soldier immediately led to the execution of hostages or mass slaughter of the largely innocent population, predominantly men between sixteen and sixty, but also women, children, and the aged. In one particularly gruesome case, on May 9, 1941, about thirty Serbian men were executed by shooting and their dead bodies were hung in the park and the streets of Sanski Most to intimidate Serbs and Jews.[103] Many photographs of the hangings have been preserved.

In B&H, the single worst genocidal massacre of 2,862 (others estimate 4,000–5,500)[104] happened on St. Elijah's holy day on August 2–3, 1941. It was preceded by mass arrests at the end of July; the Ustaše then marched these people to the various execution spots around Sanski Most. The victims were taken to Šušnjar where two pits about three meters wide, forty meters long, and two meters deep had been dug by the victims themselves. There they were killed over a period of three days with any imaginable weapon or tool ranging from machine guns to picks, axes, and knives. According to local legend, blood oozed out of these mass graves for months, turning the soil to reddish clay.

The word was spread that those who converted to Roman Catholicism would be spared, and hundreds of surviving women and children sought to save their lives by converting. The Orthodox priests had been exiled or imprisoned, and the Catholic priests carried out the instructions after the applicants allegedly filled forms on which they stated that their conversion was voluntary. Some Serbs chose to die rather than convert; others caved in temporarily to save their lives. They were told they would now become good Catholic Croats. There is no evidence that the higher clergy investigated or spoke out about these abuses.[105]

The massacres and attempts of ethnic cleansing by Serb Četniks will be described in chapter 5.

The Fate of Jews in Bosnia and Herzegovina

Prior to the outbreak of World War II, about 14,000 Jews lived in B&H, predominantly in cities, with the largest concentration in Sarajevo. The Sarajevo Jewish community was one of the most prominent Sephardic Jewish communities, with a number of synagogues and a Jewish museum and library that contained some of the most valuable medieval manuscripts, including the famous illuminated Sarajevo *Haggadah* manuscript brought from Spain after the expulsion of the Jews in 1492. Out of those 14,000 it is estimated that about 12,000 perished, 11,000 of them in concentration camps.

The only concentration camp in B&H was in Krušćica. The victims were taken to camps in Croatia proper, particularly Jasenovac (for which one of the major extermination grounds was in Gradina, on the Bosnian side of the Sava River), while others to the Sajmište fairgrounds in Zemun.

The German army and the Ustaše marched into Sarajevo on April 15, 1941. The very next day, the largest synagogue was looted and vandalized beyond use and the same happened to the other synagogues in town. In contrast to other parts of the Independent State of Croatia, the mass arrest of B&H Jews did not take place immediately, but started in September 1941. In contrast to the measures against the Serbs, the actions against the Jews may be considered mild,[106] though all of the restrictive legislation passed by the Ustaša parliament in Zagreb was also applicable and used in B&H. This included looting, forced labor, and killing of hostages, but seemingly the main motivation was for the German and Ustaše officers to move into Jewish houses and apartments.

On September 3 the Ustaše conducted their first mass roundup, targeting Jews who lived in the more desirable locations, followed by another wave of expulsions several days later. The healthy and the sick, the old and the young were all cruelly evacuated and taken to the village of Krušćica about ten miles from the town of Travnik, the only formal concentration camp in B&H. To this location were also relocated about a thousand Jews, mostly women, who had been on the island of Pag in the Adriatic, along with Jews from Germany and other German-occupied territories who had sought refuge in Bosnia along with the Sarajevo Jews—a total of about 3,000 people, mostly Jews. Beatings, very meager food rations, and the rape of women and girls were normal activities. At the end of September, the inmates were relocated, men to Jasenovac and women to Lobograd.[107]

The German army decided to get into the action of expropriating Jewish houses, so the Gestapo started arresting Jews and taking them into the former military barracks in Sarajevo—the men into the prison cells and the women and children into the stables. Some of the women and children were released, and since there were no suitable dwellings, they were placed into synagogues and the bombed-out building of the Jewish humanitarian association Benevolencia. Their situation was so miserable that some may have requested to be taken to the camps in Croatia where they imagined the situation was better. It was not. The camps in Croatia had no space for them, so these poor people were transported back and forth in freezing weather and without food. Finally, those that survived this torture were taken to Djakovo and Stara Gradiška camps where they were greeted with an outbreak of typhoid fever.

On October 16 and 17 another wave of arrests followed, and these people were all transferred to camps in Croatia on October 26 and 27. The largest mass arrest was carried out by the Ustaše on November 15 and 16, and these people, about 3,000 of them, were almost immediately transported to Jasenovac.

By August 1942 over 8,500 Sarajevo Jews were sent to camps. Only Jews who lived on the outskirts had not yet been rounded up, but their time also came. They were collected and sent directly to Auschwitz on August 24, 1942—only about 120 Jews who had skills, usually medical, needed by the rest of the community remained behind.[108]

In Bijeljina, the local Volksdeutsche were in charge of arresting groups of Jewish men and locking them in the synagogue where they beat and tortured them. Groups of local Volksdeutsche and German officers and soldiers raped Jewish women, some of whom were taken to local pubs and raped. In the end, the Germans rounded up all the remaining Jews and sent them to camps.

In Brčko, in addition to about 150 local Jews, there were also about 200 Austrian Jews who hoped to save themselves from the Nazis. But the Ustaše were headed by a particularly sadistic killer, Vjećeslav Montani, who led the internment of all Jews. They started killing Jews in December, mostly by taking them to the Sava River during very severe weather to kill them. About 340 Jews perished, mostly by having their heads bashed in with hammers and hatchets; their bodies were then tossed into the river.[109]

In Bugojno, where there were few Jews, the Ustaše apprehended twelve Jews, cut their throats, and then pushed them into a deep ravine containing the bodies of nearly 2,000 Serbs who had suffered the same fate.

Francetić's "Black Legion" Ustaša unit arrived in Rogatica in February 1942, and they promptly tied up about 25 Jews with wire, tortured them, and then slit their throats. In Tuzla, there was a somewhat larger Jewish community of over 300 Jews, of which 261 were sent to camps where they lost their lives. A group of Jewish physicians and medical personnel and their patients were arrested on April 22, 1944, by members of the predominantly Bosnian Muslim (commanding officers were German) SS "Handžar" division, who slit the throats of about 50 Jews. Between April 1 and May 6, the Black Legion played the main role in torturing and abusing Jews of Vlasenica. They took all Jews to a ravine, raped some of the women, cut the throats of both the men and women, and then pushed 57 of them into the ravine.[110]

These are but illustrative cases of the enormous losses of human life in B&H—Jewish, Roma, Serb, Croat, and Muslim. Tito's attempts to carry out swift and merciless revenge against collaborators were followed by a joint multiethnic cooperation to build a "New Yugoslavia," which at first succeeded but ultimately did not. Four decades later, the pain and suffering from World War II was reawakened, leading to an upsurge of hatred based on each ethnicity's desire to defend themselves or avenge their loved ones. Another round of Balkan wars, ethnic cleansing, and genocide took place, with the people of B&H being cast into another inferno.

5

Multiple Genocides of World War II

Northeastern and Central Balkans

In this chapter, I cover the events of World War II as they affected the regions of Bačka, Baranja, Banat, Serbia, Montenegro, Albania, and Kosovo. I also cover the fate of Jewish POWs in German camps and the Serbian Četnik massacres in Bosnia and Herzegovina. Not included is Srem (Srijem), as it was part of the Independent State of Croatia during World War II (see chapter 4). Bačka and Baranja were under Hungarian occupation, Serbia and Banat under German (parts of Serbia under Bulgarian occupation), and Kosovo under Italian, German, and Bulgarian occupation. The fate of Jewish-Yugoslav POWs and Roma is also included in this chapter.

BELGRADE AND SERBIA PROPER

Belgrade was and is the capital of Serbia (and for years doubled as the capital of Yugoslavia). I use the words *Serbia proper* to designate those parts of Serbia that are south of the Sava and Danube rivers extending to Macedonia but not including Kosovo. Belgrade and Serbia proper (other than the relatively small parts that had been occupied by Bulgaria, which are discussed at the end of this section) were under German military occupation and administration. A Serb puppet regime headed by General Milan Nedić collaborated with the Germans in controlling the territory and getting rid of unwanted Jews, Gypsies, and political enemies. The region of Banat in the Vojvodina to the northeast of Belgrade was also an administrative unit of Serbia in which a large number of Volksdeutsche, the German minority in Banat, cooperated closely with the occupational authority.

Serbs make up the majority of the population of Serbia proper, though there are also minorities such as Albanians, Roma, Germans, and Serbs of the Muslim faith. The German racist policies throughout Europe were naturally implemented in Serbia as well; hence, I start with the destruction of the Jews. Out of a total of about 11,150 Jews in the territory of Serbia, 7,700 lived in Belgrade. To this number were added 2,100 Jews who had been deported to Belgrade from Banat. In addition, there were 1,300 German Jews who had fled from other German-occupied territories and were caught in Serbia (the vast majority of them ordered to reside in the town of Šabac).

In Banat, Hitler and the Gestapo had the enthusiastic support of a sizable segment of the large German minority. During the war, this German minority practically ruled the region and enthusiastically plundered Jewish properties. With much merriment, some of these Volksdeutsche ridiculed and tortured Jews, coming up with various demeaning and painful ways to exacerbate the forcible labor to which they were subjected at a moment's notice by any German soldier or local guard member or a simple bully.[1] One such "game" was to arrange mock executions or hangings of victims who were later actually shot or hung. No mass murders seem to have taken place in Banat itself because the German authorities decided to deport all Jews to Belgrade. In the night between August 14 and 15, 1941, all Banat Jews were arrested. The Jews from Veliki Bečkerek (later renamed Zrenjanin), Crnja, and Jaša Tomić were held briefly in Veliki Bečkerek; those of Novi Bečej, Novi Kneževac, and Velika Kikinda were held in Novi Bečej; and the Jews of Pančevo and the vicinity were immediately transferred to nearby Belgrade. Of course, they were plundered of all of their valuables and clothing. The Veliki Bečkerek group was taken by train to Belgrade on August 18, and those of Novi Bečej by boats on September 20. A total of about 2,500 Jews were deported to Belgrade, and at first all were released utterly impoverished to the care of the Belgrade Jewish community; soon thereafter the men were rearrested and taken to camps at Topovske šupe (Canon sheds) and Banjica.[2]

Immediately upon their military takeover of Serbia by early May 1941, the German Military Command imposed forced labor on Jewish males as well as exorbitant punitive taxes and restrictive decrees.[3] At first the German repression specifically targeted Jews (and to a lesser degree Gypsies), based on racial grounds, and involved relatively few outright killings. But after the Communist Party of Yugoslavia called for resistance against Germans upon Germany's declaration of war against the Soviet Union on June 22, 1941, Germany shifted its propaganda against Jews from racial to allegedly ideological and political grounds through a constant association of Jews and Communists in the press and in announcements of executions and arrests. In June and July the first Yugoslavian attacks upon Nazi troops took place, which immediately resulted in a new German army policy: for every killed German soldier, 100 hostages would be executed; for every wounded German soldier, 50 hostages would be executed.[4] While the intention was to threaten the entire population, in fact at first the executions concentrated on the male Jews who had already been registered and collected into labor camps, especially in the Banjica military barracks and Topovske šupe on the outskirts of Belgrade. The policy worked well in that the general population was under the impression that many Serb hostages were being shot along with Jews, while the Germans had a ready-made excuse to dramatically reduce the number of Jews.

The camp at Banjice located in the Dedinje section of Belgrade was established on June 22, 1941. Part of the camp was under the Serbian collaborationist government's administration and was intended for political prisoners, but the Gestapo administered the other part with tens of thousands of inmates, among whom were also some women and children. Serbs, Jews, and Gypsies were rapidly delivered to the camp and many equally rapidly shot, mostly at Jajinci, Marinkova Bara, and the Jewish Cemetery, as well as at the Sajmište fairgrounds in Zemun. It is estimated that some 68,000 corpses were cremated toward the end of the war, but about 1,400 were discovered.[5]

While the Gestapo carefully registered most of the inmates and activities in Banjica, that was not the case with Topovske šupe, which was the first extermination camp for Jewish men and was established around August 20, 1941. At first the Jews from Banat were interned there and then afterward all Jewish males fourteen years and older, which culminated in the last and most massive internment on October 18, 1941. The conditions were horrendous and the camp was guarded by Nedić's gendarmes, collaborationist Serbs, who, according to Jennie Lebel, often exceeded the cruelty of the German police.[6] In order to threaten the inmates, the gendarmes carried out public hangings of those who attempted to flee. Topovske šupe became a reservoir of ready-made hostages for execution whenever the Nazis wanted to retaliate, so that daily between 150 and 400 mostly Jewish inmates were shot. Men were regularly taken to Jajinci, Jabuka, and elsewhere for execution, but it was usually under the pretext of being taken to Austria to work on farms where their treatment and food would be good; thus, men often volunteered for this transfer. The camps were not large enough for all the Jews, and therefore inmates had to be exterminated so that new ones could be brought to the camps.

By September 1941 it became obvious to the Germans that transferring Jews to Romania or Poland to allegedly prevent them from conspiring and propagandizing against the government was not efficient enough, and therefore Adolph Eichman recommended to the German command that the Jews be shot. The number of surviving Jewish males had already been reduced to about 4,000, of which about 500 were needed to prepare the Sajmište fairgrounds as a concentration camp for the women and children; the others were systematically shot along with a certain number of Gypsies who had been earmarked for digging mass graves, collecting the clothing of the victims, burying the dead after execution, and then usually being executed themselves to reduce the number of witnesses. By the end of October nearly all Jewish men and the majority of interned Gypsies had perished. A German officer noted that Jews and Gypsies behaved differently as they were being shot. The Jews went to death very composed, standing erect (or at attention), whereas the Gypsies wailed and cried and constantly moved, some of them even jumping into the grave hoping to fake death. The same commander stated that the German soldiers were not troubled by the executions, except perhaps at night when they reflected about the events of the day.[7]

The execution of the men took place in four major installments, with more frequent killings of smaller numbers interspersed between the middle of September 1941, October 9 and 11, and November 1. In each case, the men were told that they were being relocated to better labor conditions in Austria but in fact were taken to Jabuka near Kovin in Banat or to the outskirts of a shooting range near Belgrade on the road to Niš.

Less than a month after the liquidation of most of the Jewish men, all Jewish women and children, a total of about 7,500 from Belgrade, Banat, Šabac, Niš, Kragujevac, Kosovska Mitrovica, Novi Pazar, and other cities were delivered to the Sajmište fairgrounds on the left bank of the Sava River across from Belgrade.[8] About 600 Roma (Gypsies) were also interned and lived even more miserably than the Jews, but most of them were released after six weeks. The Jews were not released, except for about ten women married to Christians. Several fair pavilions, including the largest one (in which about 5,000 people were located) were "prepared" for these inmates, but the living conditions were dreadful. Due to previous bombings, most of the glass had been shattered, and rain, wind, snow, and ice made life in the overcrowded pavilions unbearable. People froze (the winter of 1942 was one of the coldest on record), endured flu epidemics, lay on wet straw or just bare boards, and had totally inadequate food. The SS camp leadership supplied provisions for the guards but left the administration of the camp to the Jews themselves without even basic supplies. Children suffered dreadfully because their mothers were unable to provide them with food and heat. Any attempts to communicate with the outside world were strictly punished, usually by being shot in front of the other inmates as a warning.

At the end of February 1942, the camp administrators began the process of destroying all the Jewish inmates. For this process, a very large hermetically sealed truck was brought in from Berlin, which could take 100 people (standing room only). At first the administrators sought volunteers, promising resettlement to much better locations and displaying a certain amount of courtesy and kindness (the driver even gave children candies and held them in his arms!). The Jews were told to mark all of their belongings and to place them in an open truck that always left the camp behind the big gray vehicle. Full of hope, the victims left, not realizing that they would not arrive alive at their destination. That vehicle[9] was later named *dušegupka* (soulkiller), as the carbon monoxide from the truck's exhaust was pumped straight into the interior and all died. The trucks crossed to the Belgrade side of the river and then headed to Avala Hill on the outskirts of the city, where groups of Roma had already dug mass graves into which the dead bodies were dumped. This happened almost daily except for Sundays and holy days, with the last transport delivering its dead on May 10, 1942. Soon thereafter it was possible for an SS leader to report to the German commander of Serbia, "The Jewish question, as well as the Gypsy question, has been completely solved. Serbia is the only land in which the question of Jews and Gypsies had been solved,"[10] and the general reported to Berlin "Serbien ist Judenrein."

The claim was not literally correct. Out of about 16,000 Jews living in Serbia, 14,500—or 83 percent—were murdered.[11] Those not killed included Jews married to Gentiles, many of whom survived the war; those who had joined the Partisans or fled abroad; the several hundred Jews in the Jewish and other hospitals in the city, both as patients and as medical personnel; those in insane asylums; and those who were hiding with Serbian families. Hiding Jews was, as elsewhere in the domains of the Third Reich, punishable by death of the entire family who dared to take Jews in. Those who were hidden in towns were at greater risk because there was always a chance that someone who was cooperating with the Nazis or their quislings would report them; Jews were more effectively hidden in the mountains of Serbia where the Germans and their collaborators rarely ventured, and usually when they did, people were warned and often both the Jews and many local Serbs would hide out for months in inclement weather. These were, indeed, righteous gentiles who were later honored by Yad Vashem.[12]

Nevertheless the Nazis and their collaborators continued the hunt for the remaining Jews. By March 19, 1942, the patients, medical personnel, and their families were all arrested—as many as 7,000–8,000—and were told that they would be relocated to Poland. The *dušegupka* truck pulled up to the hospital entrance and twice a day took groups to unknown locations, but the passengers were never heard from again. The last such transport left on March 22.[13] Smaller groups were rounded up subsequently and in July and November 1942 were shot in Deliblato.

In the interior of Serbia there were two major concentration camps. One was ironically called "Red Cross" because it was near a Red Cross building

in Niš in the southeast of Serbia; the other camp was in Šabac in the northwest of Serbia. Jews from smaller towns in Serbia were taken to the nearest
of these camps.

The Red Cross camp in Niš was operated by the Gestapo. In the middle
of October all Jews were brought to this camp—about 200–300 local
people and a certain number of emigrant Jews—and other transports of
Jews from the interior kept arriving. The executions of adult males started
in November, and the first mass execution took place in February 1942 on
a hill named Bubanj (Drum). During the second mass execution, a larger
number of Serbs and the remaining Jews were shot. Roma were again used
for the gruesome work of digging mass graves. The women and children
were taken in the spring of 1942 to Sajmište, where they shared the fate of
the others in the gas trucks. The last mass shooting in Niš took place on
October 17, 1943, when the last eighteen Jews were executed. As a result,
there were practically no Jews left in Niš.

Prior to World War II, there were very few Jews (actually only about 60)
in the town of Šabac, due west from Belgrade. In 1939, about 1,300 Jews
(mostly from Germany, Austria, and Czechoslovakia) were added to this
number. Usually referred to as the Kladovo Transport, this group of Jews
sailed east (toward the Black Sea) in the hope of eventually getting into Palestine. However, they came to a permanent halt in their journey at Šabac, as
their application for visas for Palestine had been rejected. The local population accepted these travelers warmly, but in August 1941 a common tragedy
befell both hosts and guests. The Germans imprisoned all Jews, about 1,200,
in a camp in the town. As the resistance against the occupying forces grew,
the Germans started executing hostages, both Serbs and Jews. A drastic order
was issued on September 24, 1941: all males between the ages of fourteen
and seventy were to gather—about 5,000 local Serbs and about 1,100 Jews.
This huge column of people was ordered to run to a village where they stayed
for two days without food. Then the prisoners began the "bloody march" in
which they had to run twenty-three kilometers (about fifteen miles). Anyone
who lagged behind or fell was shot. A week later they were returned to the
camp in Šabac, from which some Serbs were gradually released while others
were shot. Then on October 12 and 13, all Jewish males, about 400 of them,
and about 160 Roma were taken to the village of Zastavica and shot.[14] They
were plundered before and after the shooting. As always, gold teeth were ex-
tracted, fingers were cut off in order to take the rings, pockets were emptied,
and body cavities searched.

The women and children from Šabac were taken to Sajmište in January
1942, and there they all lost their lives between March and May. It is said that
only two women survived out of the initial 1,200 Jews imprisoned at Šabac.

Jews who were being discovered after 1942 were mostly taken to the Banjica camp in Belgrade and shot at Jajinci. The inmate logs of the Banjica camp indicate that 455 Jews were inmates and without exception were executed.

After the Jewish women had been eliminated from Sajmište, the camp was used for the internment of "Communists," that is, those who participated, or were alleged to have taken part, in the resistance movement. It became such a hellish place that some compared it to Jasenovac and some of the worst German extermination camps. Of over 92,000 inmates, 47,000 were killed, and others were sent to forced labor in Germany and Norway. It was to Sajmište that the Nazis brought Jews whom they had captured after the surrender of Italy. Such was a group of Jews from Split, Croatia. Beginning on November 6, 1943, the men of this group suffered the horrible fate of exhuming bodies from mass graves in Jajinci in order to cremate them. It is estimated that 68,000 corpses were burned. None of the 180 Split Jews were ever heard from again.

Lastly, in June 1944 a group of about 120 Jews from Montenegro and 400 from Priština in Kosovo were brought to Sajmište. A few were killed in the camp but most were taken to Bergen-Belsen, as the Germans were gradually forced to withdraw. Out of about 500 who were taken to Bergen-Belsen, it is estimated that only about 100 survived.[15]

A very large number of Serbs were killed by the Nazis and their collaborators. There is a great deal of information about that fact. Here it suffices to use a German source, *Vernichtungskrieg: Verbrechen der Wehrmacht 1941–1944*,[16] which provides a wealth of documentary and photographic sources itemizing the major massacres of Serbs, Jews, and Roma, while focusing on the Serbs. Beginning on April 6, 1941, the damage started with the massive bombing of Belgrade, a city that wasn't even protected by antiaircraft defense. There had been no declaration of war. About 50,000 people died, more than in the bombing of Warsaw, Coventry, and Rotterdam combined.[17] Sporadic resistance against the Nazis began early. This resulted in immediate draconian retaliatory measures of public hangings and executions by the Nazis, with the intent of terrorizing the population into submission. Instead, the resistance increased, both by Communists led by Tito and by the nationalist Četniks led by General Draža Mihailović. The more widespread the resistance became, the more extensive were the punishments. The Germans zeroed in on the Communists and Jews for propaganda purposes, hoping to pacify the population, but soon began with massacres of not only those who were in some vague way involved in resistance but also the civilian population, mostly men between the ages of fourteen and sixty.

They began with the above-mentioned bloody march in the vicinity of Šabac, where they established an open-air concentration camp in Jarak, with

25,000 Serbs, Gypsies, and Jews from which they took large groups of people and shot them at will. In two other cities massacres took place. On October 15, 1941, at Kraljevo, the Germans executed 300 people because German soldiers were being shot at from some homes. The next day they killed 1,736 men and 29 "Communist" women.[18] Just a few days later in Kragujevac 2,300 civilians were executed because ten Germans were killed and twenty-six wounded. This massacre became particularly embedded in the memory of all Yugoslavs because an entire graduating high school class, along with the class master, was marched to its death. In just the last three months of 1941, for their losses of 160 dead and 278 wounded, the German army killed between 20,000 and 30,000 local people, mostly civilians.

What do we name these killings? Genocide it was not, because there was no intent to eradicate all Serbian people, though some German army officers told their troops they were taking revenge for the German soldiers killed in Serbia during World War I! It wasn't ethnic cleansing, because there is no evidence that the Germans wanted to remove the Serbs from these locations. The massacres can best be labeled war crimes and crimes against humanity. The massacres took on genocidal characteristics in that the intent was to destroy a part of Serbia's population based on their ethnicity; the Germans executed hostages who themselves were not guilty of any crime. After the end of World War II, in the Serbian collective psyche, the memory of these killings figured strongly in terms of how they dealt with the remaining German minority (see chapter 7) as well as Germany's support of the secession of Slovenia and Croatia in 1991 and the NATO bombardment in 1999.

In the eastern-most sections of Serbia that were under Bulgarian administration, the situation was not much different. In the town of Pirot, there were between 180 and 200 Jews who were immediately registered by the Bulgarians. The able-bodied men were at once sent to hard labor, building roads and such.[19] On March 12, 1943, 188 Jews of Pirot were arrested and then taken via Sofia to the port city of Lom. There they joined the ship transport of Thracian Jews that departed on March 20 and were delivered to Treblinka; only three people succeeded in running away during the trip.[20] The Bulgarians also attempted to convince and pressure the local population to declare themselves Bulgarians rather than Serbs.

BAČKA AND BARANJA UNDER HUNGARIAN OCCUPATION

The region of Bačka is a plain located between the Danube and Tisa rivers south of Hungary. Baranja is a smaller area northwest of Bačka, north of the Drava River and also south of Hungary. Hungary considered these regions part of their southern lands (which, indeed, they were until 1920 when Hungary lost them to Yugoslavia by the Treaty of Trianon). When Hungary joined the Axis powers, it was awarded these two provinces when Yugoslavia was partitioned. Hungarian troops crossed the border on April 12, 1941, but since all Yugoslav armed forces had already withdrawn, the Hungarians occupied the entire area without any resistance. This did not mean that there was no bloodshed. Whether spontaneously or by order, Hungarian soldiers and some of the pro-Fascist local Hungarians went on a rampage, attacking and looting Serbian and Jewish homes, beating up people, and in some cases murdering them. On April 14, as many as 500 Jews and Serbs were bayoneted to death.[21] It seems there were some previously assembled lists of individuals who were to be killed—probably as a means of preventive terror.

Hungarian authorities intended to "rebalance" the ethnic makeup of the population and ordered the expulsion of all non-Hungarians and non-Germans who had moved to the region since Hungary was forced to cede these territories in 1920. Those who were expelled to Serbia were better off, at least for the time being, whereas those Jews and Serbs who were expelled to the Independent State of Croatia were immediately in harm's way. Some were killed in the immediate post-occupation days (according to some, about 3,500 individuals, 25 of whom were Jews)[22] in what can be considered ethnic massacres. During their arrests and incarceration, many were terribly beaten and tortured. Witnesses who survived those tortures, as well as translators and some of the perpetrators captured after the war, provided vivid descriptions of the interrogations, which often ended in death.[23] To deal with those suspected of potentially offering resistance, the Hungarian authorities established temporary concentration camps in Ada, Bačka Topola, Begeč, Odžaci, Stari Bečej, and Subotica. About 2,000 Jews and many Serbs spent from two weeks to two months in these camps. Jews who were not in camps were given forced-labor assignments.

Hungarian anti-Semitic legislation of 1939 was applicable in Bačka and Baranja, but since civil authorities had not yet been firmly established, these laws were applied selectively, thereby placing the Jews into great uncertainty and anxiety. A number of Jews who had migrated to the area were sent to Serbia, where they were interned in the Banjica camp and subsequently shot, or to Croatia, where they were also liquidated. The number who perished in this manner is not known. However, 1941 passed without mass killings, and some people expected that, at least with respect to the treatment of Jews, Hungary would follow a more enlightened policy. This turned out to be a half-truth.

Whether by solely unauthorized decisions of the Hungarian military and civilian leaders who governed the southern and eastern border region, or with the knowledge and consent of at least some of their superiors in Budapest, by

December 1941, preparations were made for massacres of Serbian and Jewish populations in Bačka. At first the plan was to stage a shoot-out (supposedly due to a "rebellion") that would give cover for these sinister plans; then, on January 4, 1942, an actual skirmish broke out between Hungarian troops and a small group of resistance-minded Serbs. Four Hungarian soldiers and gendarmes were killed, providing the excuse for a major massacre that is known as Ratsiya (from the Italian word *razzia*, meaning "raid"). The entire area was placed under marshal law, and local Hungarians were issued weapons to support the police, gendarmes, and soldiers.

The Ratsiya first started in the village of Čurug but was almost immediately expanded to Gospodjinci, Djurdjevo, Šajkaš, Temerin, Titel, and Žabalj. On Orthodox Christmas Eve and Christmas (January 6 and 7, 1942), house to house searches began in Čurug to find "suspicious" people (among them children and infants!) who were taken to storage sheds, township buildings, or schools. Some were released, but approximately 500 to 1,000 people (about 100 of them Jews) were brutally beaten with every conceivable implement and tortured in all manners; some of the women were publicly raped and some children were bashed against the walls. After the attackers had taken all valuables, they killed the victims using machine guns, finishing off those who survived with individual pistol shots. Then the bodies were taken in trucks and dumped into the river Tisa. A similar process took place in Žabalj between January 7 and 9. Twenty-nine Jews from Žabalj and thirty-seven Jews from Temerin were killed, along with hundreds of Serbs.

The massacre in the city of Novi Sad and towns of Stari Bečej and Srbobran took a little longer to organize because the Hungarians intended to kill many more victims. The bloodiest was the Ratsiya in Novi Sad; there are still arguments as to just how many people were killed in the three-day period from January 21 to 23, 1942. The first two days were relatively peaceful—people were arrested on the streets and in their homes and taken for interrogation; many were released, though some people were shot summarily while they were being apprehended, and others were sent to be shot without a trial or inquest. This wasn't satisfactory to the initiators of the Ratsiya so on the evening of January 22, they staged a "real battle" in front of the government building in the city center at which some Hungarian soldiers received fake wounds. The staged attack inflamed the perpetrators, and on the third day nearly indiscriminate killings took place in many locations around the city, on several city streets and squares, in the Orthodox cemetery, at the soccer stadium, and at the beach on the banks of the Danube River, the latter being the location of the most massive massacre. As these were some of the coldest days on record, the river had frozen solid so that German tanks could cross it on ice. Long lines of Jews and "Communists" (the latter mostly

Serbs), including children, were brought by trucks, ordered to strip to their underwear, and then taken to a hole in the ice where they were either shot or simply pushed in (some with hands tied in their back by wire). This lasted all day, until about 4 p.m., when an officer arrived and said that the long line of about 1,000 people should be taken back to the city and released because, as he told them, "all the guilty people have now been executed."[24] As I grew up in Novi Sad, I always heard that 3,000 people were killed during the Ratsiya; this was also the number usually cited in the literature.[25] However, the more realistic estimates of recent studies[26] indicate there were about 870 Jews and 430 Serbs, namely, a total of 1,300.

In Stari Bečej another fake "rebellion" was staged and mass arrests took place on January 26–27. About 200 people, of whom about 100 were Jews, were taken by trucks to the Tisa River and there killed and thrown into the river. (Incidentally, the following spring when the ice thawed, corpses floated down the Tisa and Danube rivers and were never given burials, nor were they individually identified.)

On the bank of the Danube in Novi Sad, a very powerful and appropriate memorial with text in Serbian and Hebrew states, "As people we must forgive but never forget." The names of those who died not only in the Ratsiya but also in the first half of 1942 are chiseled in black marble.

There was another extermination method—forced hard labor. The Hungarian army established militarized labor units, the so-called *munkácsi* (laborers), to which predominantly Jewish males aged twenty-one to forty-eight were drafted, irrespective of their health, and placed under the command of gendarmes and army officers. The commanders were given some latitude in how they treated the conscripted workers, so some camps during certain times had a more tolerable situation than others. Those who were assigned to the Sombor camp and other camps scattered throughout Hungary proper suffered less than those who were sent to the Ukraine to dig trenches for the Hungarian army and those sent to the copper mine in Bor, Serbia. One hard labor camp was in Bačka Topola. There wasn't a great deal of meaningful labor here, so the camp commander forced inmates to move stones from one pile to the other and to perform strenuous exercises—the men ran from one barrack to another for two hours, then jumped like frogs for an additional two hours in over 100 degree (Fahrenheit) weather, leading to exhaustion and death. Approximately 4,000 Bačka and Baranja Jews went to hard labor camps, organized in units of about 200–250 men.

Some 1,500 Bačka Jews became part of the about 10,000 Hungarian Jews sent to the Eastern Front (mostly to Ostrogonsk, Voronyezh, and the Don basin in the Ukraine) on September 19, 1942. They could only take one set of summer clothing, and they could not take any blankets or food with them.

They were housed in barns, animal sheds, ruined homes, or open fields, and the cold Russian winter arrived early. The daily regime was very strict—exhaustive labor, little sleep, beatings, and executions for the most minor infractions, including hanging for hours on posts while the rest of the unit had to stand at attention and watch. Typhoid fever, dysentery, and the freezing weather decimated the men. For instance, out of 124 men, only 6 members of unit 105/III were liberated early in 1943 by the Red Army.[27] Other units were forced to disarm mine fields without any previous training or tools. They were deliberately shot by the soldiers for any or no provocation. The fate of these people was unknown to their families, and for years the families waited to see whether their relatives would return, some assuming that the Soviets took them to Siberia as POWs; according to one estimate only 2 percent of all the Jewish laborers sent to the Eastern Front did return.[28]

On March 19, 1944, the German army carried out a coup d'etat in Hungary and on October 16 installed the Ferenc Szálasi's Arrow Cross Fascist puppet government. The new rulers thought that the Jews had not been dealt with severely enough, so they increased the scope and the intensity of the genocide. The previous Hungarian administrations had not previously been so comprehensive in their genocidal measures. Now the Germans and the Hungarian radical right wing decided to apply the Final Solution to the Jews in Hungarian lands. They issued new decrees and secret measures, indicating the willingness of the new Hungarian government to cooperate with Adolf Eichman's assignment to deliver the Jews to the death camps. The arrests, beatings, torture, and murders became even more extensive. Remnants of the workers' brigades that were retreating from the Ukraine were reorganized, placed under Arrow Cross or SS leaders, and sent on death marches; anyone who could not keep the rapid pace of withdrawal was shot. Those who survived to cross the German border were sent to the various death camps. The camp in Bačka Topola, which had served a variety of purposes since 1941—a camp for the *munkácsi*, for political prisoners, and for holding those to be deported—was now taken over by the SS, who applied the methods they did elsewhere in the Reich. The camp was closed on July 18, 1944, when all but a few inmates were sent to Auschwitz.

The arrests of the remaining Jews of all ages and health conditions began in Novi Sad on April 26. Some 1,900 people were first gathered in the synagogue and then several days later transported to a camp in Subotica, where about 4,000 Jews from other locations in southern and western Bačka were also taken. Curiously, the Subotica Jews, who formed one of the largest Jewish communities (over 3,000 Jews), were not rounded up at first but were confined to a ghetto, which appears to be one of the few Jewish ghettos created in the territory of the former Yugoslavia. Jews from Baranja and western Bačka were taken to the nearby city of Szeged in Hungary. After about twenty days, the inmates of Subotica and Szeged were moved farther north in Hungary to the city of Baja, where a total of about 8,000 Jews from Baranja and western Bačka were gathered into a former factory. As an adequate supply of food could not be obtained, a number of inmates died of hunger. The Subotica Jews were moved to Bácsalmas, where they received the same inhumane treatment.

Now the process of gathering the inmates into transport camps was complete, with about 14,000–15,000 from Bačka, Baranja, and parts of Hungary. The deportation and killing of these people (about four-fifths of them women, the rest children and older people) began. The majority were transported by the German forces to Auschwitz.[29] They left between May 26 and June 25 in the well-known cattle cars or otherwise sealed coaches with about eighty people to a wagon, standing room only. These cattle cars were not opened for days, and they had no food, water, or toilet facilities. Unsurprisingly, during the few instances when the wagons were opened, many corpses were dumped out and crazed people were killed. Local people were not permitted to provide any assistance to the deportees. The story of their fate in the death camp of Auschwitz is well-known to anyone with minimal information about the Holocaust. Out of 1,900 deported Novi Sad Jews, only about 300 survived.[30]

While it is wrong to make comparisons of suffering, surely those who worked in the copper mines of Bor endured one of the most incomprehensible cruelties. About 6,200 Hungarian Jews were delivered to Bor in July 1943, of which about 10 percent were from Bačka. In the mines under SS supervision, prisoners worked twelve-hour shifts in knee-deep water. Others were sent to build a railway or roads on extremely meager rations and were given no rest by their Hungarian guards. Extreme and cruel punishments were meted out for little or no reason, often punishing not only the accused person but also the entire unit.

By the middle of September 1944, the Red Army was advancing closer, and the Germans evacuated the mine.[31] They created two columns of inmates—the first, consisting of 3,600 prisoners, left on September 17; the second, consisting of 2,500 men, left on the 29th. The first column marched an incomprehensively torturous, long route: Bor–Belgrade–Jabuka–Novi Sad–Crvenka–Baja–Szent Királyszabadja, and then on to Buchenwald, Fossenburg, and other camps. A great massacre took place in Crvenka (Bačka) where about 700 inmates were shot. Others were "thinned out" along the road both by their various guards as well as by passing soldiers of other units, who killed them just "for the hell of it." The second group followed a slightly different route and ended up in the German camp at Oranienburg. Out of the group of 2,500, it seems that only a few survived. These people had marched from the middle of September to late October, often without shoes, clothing, water, food, rest, medical assistance, or a touch of human care. Rather, local German and Hungarian populations displayed hatred and contempt, often adding to the misery of the inmates. Those who saw the inmates march through the cities testified they were a frightening sight. Out of about 600 Jews from Bačka, only 9 survived—6 by escaping and 3 who were returnees from the death camps.[32]

THE FATE OF THE YUGOSLAV ARMY'S JEWISH POWS

Some strange anti-intuitive information has emerged from the research of Jennie Lebel. Proportionately the largest percentage of Jews who survived the war had become German POWs after the surrender of the Yugoslav Royal Army. The Yugoslav army surrendered on April 16, 1941. Hundreds of thousands of soldiers and officers became POWs. The surrender was so quick that the Nazis didn't at first know what to do with the POWs and sent them home with the order to report by a given date. Some of the Jews decided not to report, thinking they had a better chance to survive as civilians. Ironically, most of these Jews perished along with the other Jews as described previously. But about 650 Jewish officers and soldiers did report and were taken to the Oflag (officer's camp) and Stalag (soldiers' camp) in Nuremberg. The Germans attempted to separate and distinguish the Jewish POWs from the other Yugoslavs by having them wear a yellow band or star, but there was protest and resistance by the other Yugoslavs (mostly Serbs, because Croats, Hungarians, Bulgarians, and others who served formerly in the Yugoslav army were released by the Germans); two months later, Jews were no longer discriminated against on that basis. Of course, some were murdered and wounded and others committed suicide, especially when they discovered that their families had "moved in an unknown direction," that is, to the death camps, and others were shot by German guards who decided to disobey orders—but most of these Jews survived the war, whether by running away to save themselves or when they were all liberated by the Allies.[33] In this freakish exception to the pattern, the German army more or less followed the Geneva Convention with regard to those countries that had been cosigners of the convention. These prisoners were allowed visits by the Red Cross, correspondence, and even packages from their families—until those families disappeared from the face of the earth.

MONTENEGRO

Montenegro was occupied first by the Italians who supported the establishment of a puppet kingdom of Montenegro; this kingdom was to become a part of the greater Italian Empire. Having been unable to secure anyone willing to be a king, various governors ruled. The Montenegrin Četniks and Partisans together rose to a massive popular rebellion against the Italians, but they soon parted ways. A very chaotic situation prevailed as various Četnik, Partisan, and collaborationist groups made alliances only to betray or double-cross each other, so it is not practical to attempt a summary of the main events here. Croats and Albanians at one point sought to partition Montenegro, but Italians, and then Germans who replaced them, balked. Fighting broke out between Montenegrin Orthodox and Muslim clans, resurrecting old blood feuds (vendettas) that had been practiced among Montenegrins and neighboring Albanians since time immemorial. The brutality of their fighting is proverbial, as is the deep-seated mutual hatred and suspicion.

Only about thirty Jews lived in Montenegro prior to World War II. That number increased when some Jews from Serbia and B&H (Bosnia and Herzegovina) fled to Montenegro. The Italian occupation forces did not harm the local Jews, but they rounded up the refugees and took them to camps in Kavaja and Sijak, in Albania, and subsequently transferred them to camps in Italy.[34]

ALBANIA AND KOSOVO

Albania was invaded by Italy in April 1939 and became an Italian protectorate. In the middle of April 1941, the Germans occupied all of Kosovo but relatively soon turned most of it over to the Italians. Kosovo and a small section of western Macedonia were then incorporated into the protectorate of "Great Albania." The Germans, however, kept a small, northern part of Kosovo for themselves because of the valuable mining region. A sliver of the province was, along with Macedonia, annexed to Bulgaria.

Prior to the outbreak of the war, a very small number of Jews, fewer than 500, lived in Kosovo and fewer yet in Albania. During the war the Jewish community became enlarged by Jews from Serbia who fled to Kosovo. The rumor that the Italians and Albanians treated the Jews better than the Germans turned out, on the whole, to be correct. In 1941 and 1942, Jews from northern Serbia (mostly Belgrade) and from Macedonia, as well as Jewish refugees from Germany, Austria, and Poland, arrived in Priština, Prizren, and Uroševac in the Italian-controlled section, where they were basically safe. About 150 of them were "preventively" arrested, and simultaneously the Italian administration told the leaders of the Priština Jewish community to organize their transfer to Berat in Albania, where the Jews were distributed among local families and were given a chance to work and earn some money in order to survive. Jennie Lebel wrote that the Albanian population, which hardly had any previous contacts with Jews (as there were only about 200 in all of Albania prior to the war), were not infected by anti-Semitism and treated the newcomers well, while the Italian administration did not harass them.[35]

The Germans, of course, were different, as they showed no mercy toward Jews. All Jews of Novi Pazar and Kosovska Mitrovica were rounded up on March 2, 1942, and delivered to Belgrade, where the men were taken to the concentration camps and were killed in Bubanj and the women and children were taken to the Zemun fairgrounds and systematically gassed in the *dušegupka* trucks (see earlier description).

Then the Italian authorities interned Jews in a camp in Priština. The Jews feared that they would be turned over to the Germans, but the Italian commander gave his word that this would never happen. However, on March 14, 1942, the Italian army blockaded the city and the camp and arrested the Jews. Some of these Jews were turned over to the Germans, who took them to be gassed at the Sajmište camp in Zemun. Others were taken to the camp in Berat, Albania.[36] The population of Albania was more protective of the Jews than the Kosovar Albanians were. Even so, there were some cases of cruelties against Jews in Albania. Sometimes the smugglers, seeing that some Jews had jewelry and money on them, simply robbed them and killed them. When Italy surrendered and all the Italian concentration camps were dissolved, the population of Albania continued to protect and hide the Jews or take them to the ports on the Adriatic Sea from which they could travel to Italy.[37] Those inmates who were able to fight joined the Albanian resistance units, while others hid out in the more remote Albanian villages until the end of the war.[38]

Being "better than Germans" apparently does not mean that the Italians were consistently good to Jews. As seen previously regarding the Jews from Priština, the Italians "had no particular qualms over delivering up the Jews."[39] When Italy surrendered to the Allies and Germany took over all territories formerly held by Italy, things changed dramatically. Claims have been made that Kosovar Albanians continued to protect the Jews, but the protection and assistance the Jews received in Kosovo had been more due to the Italian administration than to the local population. The Kosovar Albanians were less hospitable to Jews, as they tended to be more unfriendly to any outsider given their bitter historical experience. Thus, from the time Germans re-occupied Kosovo after the surrender of the Italian army in 1943 and until the end of the war, any Jews captured in Kosovo, Montenegro, and Albania became part of the Final Solution. Enthusiastically supporting the Germans, Kosovar Albanian leaders, as well as the general population (with notable exceptions) participated in the looting and beating of Jews. Discrimination was widely practiced, so that most Albanians felt they had a "license to kill" Jews, Serbs, and others.[40] The short-lived Skenderbeg SS Division, formed in February

1944, cooperated with the Nazi Germans by arresting 280 Jews and delivering them to the Nazis for a journey of no return. This division was better known for its lawlessness of murdering, raping, and looting in mostly Serb neighborhoods than for assisting the Germans in the war effort.[41]

Albanians of Kosovo welcomed the defeat and partitioning of Yugoslavia enthusiastically, as their dream to live in a Great Albania had finally happened—with the help of Fascist Italy and Nazi Germany. To them it was not important who was helping them reunite with Albania. In Kosovo the Albanian-Serbian relationships had always been a zero sum game, and this was now their opportunity to get rid of the Serbs, as well as others; Kosovar Albanians desired to live in an ethnically homogeneous environment. They wanted revenge against the harsh rule of the Serbs after their bitter experiences during the Balkan Wars, during World War I, and under the Kingdom of Yugoslavia. Albanians and Serbs may have lived next to each other peacefully in certain places and certain times, but more often than not they were engaged in a series of retributions for harsh treatments suffered when the "other" was in charge. Between 1941 and 1945, up to 100,000 Serbs and Montenegrins were killed or expelled from Kosovo.

The number of Serbs who have been ethnically cleansed (killed or deported) is a matter of contentious debate between Albanian and Serb sources. The range is 30,000–100,000 expelled and 3,000–10,000 killed. The Belgrade authorities of the time counted about 70,000 Serb refugees from Kosovo.[42] According to Tim Judah, Carlo Umilta (the Italian civil commissioner for Kosovo), who was an eyewitness, wrote, "The Albanians are out to exterminate the Slavs . . . not a single house has a roof; everything has been burned down. . . . There are headless bodies of men and women strewn on the ground."[43] During the first German and then the Italian occupation of Kosovo, local Albanians had been more restrained in their attacks on the Serbs, but after the Italians surrendered in 1943, the local Albanian authorities, who had been given more local self-governing power, increased their attempts at ethnic cleansing of the Serbs. The actual numbers of exiled and killed Serbs and Montenegrins, especially those who settled in Kosovo after World War I, will never be known. Recent Serbian studies have itemized, for every year from 1941 to 1945, the very large number of Slavic villages that were destroyed or eradicated and the thousands who were tortured and killed in gruesome ways—women who had been raped, schools that were destroyed, churches and cultural monuments torn down, cemeteries plowed over, wells poisoned—all with the apparent aim of eradicating evidence of Serb and Montenegrin presence in Kosovo.[44] But those claims will need to be further scrutinized.

The Kosovar Albanians had such abiding hatred for the Serbs that there was practically no response to invitations by Partisans to join the resistance against the Nazis or Italians. After the war, Kosovar Albanians were treated harshly by the new Yugoslav government because they were regarded as Nazi and Fascist collaborators and were therefore suspected of being enemies of the new socialist order. By the middle of 1945, Kosovar Albanian forces were defeated; however, both armed and passive resistance against reincorporation into Yugoslavia continued. Sporadic fighting with rebel bands lasted until 1948. The new Communist Yugoslav government prohibited the return of 50,000–70,000 deported Serbs and Montenegrins to their homesteads in Kosovo in the hope that the cycle of revenge would be terminated. That turned out to be a vain hope. One consequence of the ethnic cleansing was that the demographic picture was strongly tilted toward a considerable ethnic Albanian numerical prevalence. Forty to fifty years later this tilt led to unrest and war that ended with almost the total ethnic removal of Serbs and Montenegrins from Kosovo.

MASSACRES AND ETHNIC CLEANSING BY ČETNIKS

At the beginning of the war, the Četniks under the leadership of General Draža Mihailović were officially the continuation of the Yugoslav Royal Army; however, these forces were composed almost solely of Serb officers, soldiers as well as volunteers. They were usually referred to as Četnik units. At first they fought against the occupying forces, but as the war got increasingly complicated they focused on fighting the Partisans and, of course, the Croat Ustaše and Domobrans, while increasingly making accommodations for the Germans and Italians. According to David MacDonald, it "was clear from wartime accounts, the Četniks were willing to side with the Germans if it could mean the destruction of the Partisans."[45] Seeing how the Serb populations in Croatia and B&H were slaughtered in astronomic numbers, the Četniks increased their attacks against Croats and Muslims, believing that they all supported the Independent State of Croatia. Many Serbs joined the Četniks in self-defense. As the ferocity of the fighting increased, the Četnik leadership increasingly dreamed about a postwar "Great Serbia" that would be homogenous, ethnically cleansed of non-Serbs, "alien elements." In their military activities they committed massacre, arson, rape, looting, and other types of war crimes. The Partisans as well as the Ustaše started accusing them of "genocide"—accusations that have been frequently and indiscriminately charged on all sides even though the word wasn't coined yet.

The Četniks did fight for the Serbian cause, and because they had allegiance to the king (who was a Serb), they were bitterly opposed to the Communists, as they dreaded the spread of Bolshevik ideology and power. This ideological stance elicited for them the support of a fair number of Orthodox priests, some of whom joined them with weapons in their hands. In December 1941 Draža Mihailović issued "Instructions" that can readily be interpreted as favoring an ethnically clear Serb territory as the foundation for any post–World War II arrangements.

The relevant parts of the "Instructions" state the Četnik mission:

o The creation of a "Great Yugoslavia" within which there will be a "Great Serbia" with an ethnically clean Serbia, Montenegro, B&H, and Vojvodina.

o The cleansing of all national minorities and antistate elements from the state.

o The cleansing of the Muslim population from the Sandžak (southwest Serbia) and of both Muslims and Croats from B&H.

o The settlement of cleansed areas of minorities by Serbs and Montenegrins.[46]

Concomitant with the "Instructions," a scorched-earth practice commenced when they overran Croat and Muslim villages in B&H. "During the operation we carried out the complete annihilation of the Moslem inhabitants, without regard to their sex and age. . . . The whole population has been annihilated. The morale of our units was very high,"[47] reported a Četnik commander, Pavle Djurišić, on February 13, 1943, saying his troops killed 9,200 Muslims in response to the "Instruction" by Mihailović.

Viewing the Muslims as allies of the Ustaše, the Četniks, and in certain instances even the Partisans, attacked the Muslim population of B&H and Montenegro. In Foča, a town on the Drina River, several thousand Muslims (mostly civilian) were massacred. General Mihailović, the most important Četnik commander, admitted at his trial in 1946 that Četniks were eager to cleanse the Muslims; they regarded these attacks as acts of revenge for the Muslim killings of Serbs.

Bosnian Muslims had three options, as they were not welcomed by the Četniks. Many of them joined the Ustaša or Domobran forces as the Croat government courted the Muslims, calling them the "flower of the Croat nation." Many Muslims concluded that their interests would be best protected if they allied themselves with Hitler and Pavelić. Others, a smaller number at first, joined the Partisans—not trusting either the Ustaše or the Četniks—and many of them became convinced Communists who, after the liberation of Yugoslavia, played a significant role in the Communist leadership. The third option was to protect themselves by creating local defense units. Germans convinced those choosing the third option that they would be best defended by the creation of two SS mountain divisions, Handžar (scimitar) and Kama (dagger), under the direct leadership of German commanders and in German uniforms but wearing Muslim fezzes and other Muslim insignia. These units were created under the direct influence of Grand Mufti of Jerusalem Hajji Amin el-Hussain.[48]

It isn't easy to sort out whether Četniks attacked the Muslims first and then the Muslims retaliated, or the other way around. Conspiracy theories are always rife in the Balkans. Some blame the Ustaše, saying that purely Croat Ustaše units carried out massacres of Serbian villages wearing the distinctly Muslim fez and calling each other Muslim names. Others say that many Muslims joined the Ustaše and in that capacity carried out attacks. Also debatable is whether the Četnik massacres were retaliatory in nature or whether they initiated the cycle of death.

Regardless of who started the killing, Četnik groups carried out horrendous massacres of Muslims. After the Italians withdrew from eastern Bosnia, the Četniks entered the town of Foča between December 5 and 20, 1941, and killed 300 Muslims in the city and several hundred in the neighboring boroughs of Goražde (1,370), Fojnica, Čajnice (418), and Divin (423). From December 30 to January 26, 1942, Četniks occupied Goražde and slaughtered 1,370 Muslims and Catholics and burned many neighboring villages to the ground. It is claimed that 7,000 were killed between Foča and Ustiprača, with daily killings on the bridges over the Drina and about 20,000 thrown into the river. On August 15, 1942, Četniks again took Foča and killed another 300. For Višegrad and vicinity there is a list of about ten villages with the approximate number of victims based on the recollections of survivors.[49] Četniks killed 1,492 Muslims in Plevlje and 314 in Prozor and vicinity. The total estimate of Muslims killed by Četniks is between 80,000 and 100,000, most likely about 86,000.[50]

Dragan Cvetković, in an analytic study based on existing statistical data that are neither fully reliable nor complete, but are the best available, states that Četniks were responsible for 65.89 percent of the losses of Bosnian Muslims.[51] In Foča the Četniks were responsible for 89.52 percent of Muslim executions, "which clearly indicates their desire to eliminate them from the territory of the borough."[52] In Srebrenica, Muslims account for 95.74 percent of all people killed by Četniks.[53] Cvetković attributes these massacres to retaliation due to the threat to the biological existence of the Serb people in the territory of Croatia, to which B&H belonged.

Did the Četniks carry out genocide of Muslims during World War II? The intent existed, judging from Mihailović's "Instruction," but the fighting fluctuated and was so complex that some units may have carried out massacres one day and been massacred the next day. Surely they wanted to "cleanse" certain territories of Muslims, but they did not have the military might and the backing of the Yugoslav royal government in exile in London. General Mihailović swore allegiance to that government, and that government did not order such actions. It is clear, however, that Četniks are guilty of war crimes, crimes against humanity, massacres, and ethnic cleansing. Equating Ustaše and Četnik crimes does not stand critical scrutiny. According to MacDonald's research, "there were clear qualitative differences between the Allied-backed Četnik monarchists with their small-scale massacres, and the Nazi-backed Ustaša with their Croatian-run concentration camps."[54]

GENOCIDE AGAINST ROMA (GYPSIES)

Gypsies are mentioned as the target for extermination in nearly all documents and studies. And yet, very little concrete information and data are known. The reason is not that somehow Roma escaped the genocidal intentions of all Nazi allies, but that the Roma did not have the educational and institutional framework to collect the information and to share it with the world. Historically the most discriminated against and demeaned of all ethnic groups in Europe, Gypsies were generally denied the opportunities to receive the skills by which to record and propagate the injustices done to them both in the past and during World War II.

If the number of victims from all ethnic groups is highly contested (given a general admission that it is most unlikely that the exact number will ever be known), the number of Roma victims is even more so. What is known is that the racist laws that had been introduced in the various parts of the Balkans under Nazi influence included Gypsies among the groups who were exempt from the legal protection given to the majority population. They were not merely second-class citizens; they were at the bottom of the social stratification—outcasts. In Serbia, the law stipulated that they had to wear an armband with the word Zigeuner (German for Gypsies). Streetcars and buses had signs forbidding Jews and Gypsies to ride. Gypsies' presumed Aryan descent did not provide protection.[55] In NDH (Nezavisna Država Hrvatska), a legal decree of December 25, 1941, stipulated that people who were unsuitable and murderous should be taken to concentration camps, and this clearly applied also to Roma.

One of the few Roma scholars is Dragoljub Acković, M.A. He states that one of the reasons for our ignorance regarding the extent of Roma extermination is not only that many of the documents about the camps had been destroyed prior to the end of the war; Roma were so undervalued as human beings that often they were not even recorded in the camp registry but simply brought to the camps and exterminated.[56] Gypsies' attempts in B&H to disguise themselves as Muslims (they followed all three main religions—Orthodoxy, Catholicism, and Islam) were countermanded in Sarajevo by an announcement forbidding them to wear fezzes and Muslim folk costumes instead of their more typical Roma folk costume. Generally, most Roma had a hard time disguising themselves because they were darker skinned than the surrounding population. The targeting of Roma was clearly a racist act, and there is little doubt of the Nazi and Fascist intent to get rid of them since both regimes perceived the Roma as they did the Jews: as populations polluting the European racial pool.

As an illustration of the losses, Acković estimates the massacre of Gypsies in Serbia as follows: in Leskovac, 250 Roma were liquidated; in Niš, 380; in Kraljevo, 80; at a camp in Batajnica, more than 500; and in the Banjica camp near Belgrade, 5,000–7,000. In Croatia, the order was to arrest all the Roma wherever they were found. A total of 5,541 Roma children died in Croatia.[57] For Jasenovac, Acković estimates 80,000 Roma victims, although the number is very likely lower. In NDH alone, out of the approximately 17,000 Roma, 12,240 were murdered.[58] While for other ethnic groups the number of men liquidated vastly outnumbered the losses of women, this was not the case with Roma, among whom (similar to the Jews) about half of the victims were women. Cvetković's estimate that 18,000–20,000 Roma were killed in Jasenovac is perhaps the most realistic number. Damir Mirković estimates 27,000 Roma were exterminated at Jasenovac, which would represent 34.2 percent of their total population.[59] All studies agree that there are simply no dependable records showing numbers of Roma exterminated on the entire Balkan Peninsula.

Roma were frequently exploited prior to their extermination. They were forced to perform many "dirty" jobs, the worst being to unload the dead from the gas truck or collect them throughout the camps, to dig the mass graves, to sometimes watch the mass executions at these graves, and to cover the bodies; then they were shot in order to remove the witnesses. This exploitation was done on the assumption that Roma have no moral qualms about performing such odious work, when actually, they were just hoping to somehow survive the mass murder. One gets the impression that the local populations generally thought of the Gypsies as a pesky nuisance, an irritant, and were accepting, perhaps even gladly, of the Nazi approach to solving that problem. The interethnic relations between the multiplicity of ethnic groups in the Balkans varied from intolerance to tolerance and back, but all of them invariably were intolerant toward the Roma. Gypsies were used as entertainers, primarily musicians, and they were treated deplorably, as problematic troublemakers. As we know, the Nazis and their allies saw themselves as problem solvers.

Since the Nazis didn't finish the job, various neo-Nazi groups presently continue the persecution, and they are not alone.

6

Multiple Genocides of World War II

Southeastern Balkans

BULGARIAN JEWS NOT DEPORTED TO DEATH CAMPS

The government and people of Bulgaria have received recognition and praise for having resisted Nazi pressure to deliver their Jewish population to the death camps, though they did deliver the Jewish populations of Macedonia, Thrace, and eastern Serbia, which came under their control (as described in this chapter). Although the 48,000–50,000 Jews of Bulgaria, which constituted less than 1 percent of Bulgaria's total population, avoided deportation, they suffered all the other anti-Semitic restrictions and indignities typical of Nazi-inspired Europe.

The government of Bulgaria, headed by King Boris III, succumbed to Hitler's pressure to join the Axis in early March 1941, when Hitler promised Bulgaria the annexation of the aforementioned regions of the Balkans. The Bulgarians already considered these regions an integral part of their country that had been, in their view, illegally awarded to other states after World War I. Prior to joining the Axis powers, however, and as early as the middle of 1940, Bulgaria had adopted anti-Semitic laws in the parliament under the influence of pro-German government ministers, some of whom had gone to Germany to learn anti-Jewish measures from the masters. Particularly sweeping was the bill For the Defense of the People, which targeted the well-integrated, mostly ancient Romaniot and Sephardic Jewish population. It has been said that in Bulgaria, the general population had not developed virulent anti-Semitism because the Jews spoke Bulgarian, tended to be secularized, and were generally not economically better off than most of the population. The For the Defense of the People legislation stipulated that anyone who had at least one Jewish parent would be classified as a Jew and that Jews would be stripped of their Bulgarian citizenship, would not be allowed to hold public office, would have to wear yellow stars, would have to change their names if they were Bulgarian-sounding, would not be allowed to practice certain professions or serve in the army, would not be able to intermarry or cohabitate with non-Jews, and would be allowed only limited enrollment at universities. After 1941, forced labor units were organized for all Jewish males between the ages of twenty and forty. The Commissariat for Jewish Affairs was established, headed by Alexander Belev, a well-known anti-Semite. Then, in May of 1942, about 20,000 Jews from Sofia were expelled from the city and placed in various camps throughout the country.[1]

In January of 1943, the Nazi government dispatched representatives to Sofia to plan, in cooperation with Bulgarian government officials, particularly Peter Gabrovski and Belev, the deportation of all Jews from Bulgarian territory. The agreement was secret, but fortunately it was leaked and opposition to its implementation was formed. Heading the opposition was a vice president of the parliament, Dimiter Peshev (who is the real hero of this story), who collected signatures of forty-two deputies and exerted pressure on the government.[2] Two metropolitan bishops of the Bulgarian Orthodox Church, Stephan and Kiril, also opposed the plan. Stephan said that if the deportation process began, he would open all the churches as places for Jews to take refuge, and Kiril stated that he would lie down on the train tracks to prevent the deportation. The Holy Synod of the Bulgarian Orthodox Church devoted several sessions to discuss how to help the Jews. The two prelates intervened on their behalf, especially for converted Jews, by speaking to numerous government officials on several occasions, and their moral standing in the community gave weight to their intercessions. The bishops and even individual clergy, such as Rev. Boris Kharalampiev of Pazardzhik, also defended their local Jews. Both clergy and bishops issued baptismal certificates to Jews with the intention of protecting them.[3] Such courageous resistance influenced King Boris III to resist Hitler's personal pressures on him. Boris told Hitler that his country needed Jewish labor for road building and maintenance, convincing Hitler that the deportation should be delayed, and this ultimately saved the Bulgarian Jews. Nazis continued to pressure the government, but the resistance lasted long enough that when it became evident that the Axis powers would lose the war, the Bulgarians joined the Allies after Soviet troops entered Bulgaria on September 8, 1944. Just prior to that, the Bulgarian government had abrogated all anti-Jewish legislation and had abolished the Commissariat for Jewish Affairs.

Contradictory information exists about the treatment of Jews by the Bulgarian government. Some say that the treatment of Jews was harsh and cruel, and that the government applied its racist legislation strictly; others, including many Bulgarian Jewish survivors, praise the humanitarian attitude of many government representatives who did not apply the laws strictly and acknowledge the kindness shown by Bulgarian peasants and the general population to those who were resettled in various villages instead of being sent to camps. Despite contradictory accounts of these events, and granting that ambiguities always remain, it is appropriate to celebrate that, for whatever reason, approximately 50,000 Jews had the good fortune of avoiding the destiny that was otherwise common to the rest of Balkan Jewry.

MACEDONIA

Starting on April 18, 1941, Bulgaria occupied the section of Macedonia that had once been a part of Yugoslavia[4] (the eastern part of Macedonia was occupied by Italy and had been annexed to its puppet state, Great Albania, which also included Kosovo) and Thrace. Prior to the Bulgarian occupation, Macedonia had been part of Yugoslavia, and Thrace had been part of Greece. In these "newly liberated territories"—which the Bulgarians had held for a short time during the First Balkan War and World War I and to which Bulgaria aspired as integral parts of their state territory—the policy toward the Jews was altogether different from that applied in Bulgaria proper. Unlike non-Jewish Macedonians who were granted Bulgarian citizenship, Jews were not given the protection of citizenship, although they were truly indigenous to the area, their ancestors (called Romanioti) having settled in the area during the Roman times or even earlier, long before the Slavs migrated there. Other Jews (called Sephards) had arrived later as part of the dispersion of Jews from Spain and Portugal caused by the Inquisition.

During World War II, there were over 8,000 Jews in Macedonia, a small portion having arrived recently as refugees from Serbia after the Nazis took Belgrade and started rounding up Jews. Some of these refugees were returned to Serbia, where they suffered the fate of the rest of the Jewish population. Another small number continued the flight westward toward Italian-held territories in Albania, where some found refuge among locals who had rarely, if ever, met any Jews; others headed to Italy where the Italians provided them better protection and conditions than they would have had in Albania. Still others, particularly the young, joined the Partisan resistance movement in which many perished but some survived until the end of the war.

The Jews were an urban population. In Macedonia they lived predominantly in Skopje, Štip, and Bitola, with only a few living in other municipalities. That made it easier for the Bulgarian administration to apply the many discriminatory anti-Semitic laws that were passed by the pro-German Bulgarian government. The Law for the Protection of the Nation issued on January 21, 1941—prior to the Bulgarian entry into the war against Yugoslavia—contained severe anti-Jewish measures.[5] So did subsequent legislation and decrees of both the king and various ministries, all of which applied to Jews living in Macedonia and Thrace as well. Jewish properties were expropriated, and Jews were forbidden to marry or date non-Jews; were under constant police surveillance; could not own cultural, medical, tourist, or entertainment enterprises; were double-taxed; were forbidden to have Slavic names; could not serve in the armed forces, except in special labor units (*trudovachki druzhini*); and as of September 29, 1942, had to wear a yellow star on their left sleeve.[6] These were all preliminary measures singling out Jews for severe repressive measures, a prelude to genocide, but even in the early stages of persecution, these measures threatened the biological survival of the Jewish people.[7] Alexander Belev, the Bulgarian government's chief of the Department for Jewish Questions who had received his racist training in Germany, was not merely proactive in the passage of anti-Jewish measures; he actively participated in the deportation of Jews, orchestrating, for example, the deportation of many on four ships from the port of Lom on the Danube to Vienna and on to Treblinka.[8]

In November 1941, all newcomer Jews were required to register with the police, and about fifty of them were immediately handed over to German authorities and taken to the camp Jajinci near Belgrade, where they were executed. By the end of 1942, the Bulgarian and German governments engaged in intensive negotiations toward the Final Solution of the Jewish problem, and the Bulgarian government promised to deliver all Jews from the newly liberated territories, haggling only about the amount the Germans would pay per person. The Department of Jewish Affairs within the Ministry of Foreign Affairs carried out a census of Jews, counting 7,762 in the country, a number that grew to about 8,000 with the arrival of Jews from other parts of Yugoslavia who had fled into Bulgaria hoping that the Bulgarians would be more tolerant.[9]

On February 23, 1943, a secret agreement was signed between the Bulgarian and German governments to deport as many as 20,000 Jews. Due to pressure exerted on him by Metropolitan Bishop Stephan and the parliamentary deputy Dimitar Peshev, King Boris III convinced the Germans that the Jews of Bulgaria were needed for forced labor, and thus "only" 7,122 Macedonian Jews and 4,221 Thracian Jews were deported to extermination camps.[10] Representatives of the Bulgarian government justified the deportations by stating that the Jews negatively affected the population in these territories by spreading false information. Insisting that Bulgarians are the "most tolerant of peoples," the Bulgarian government argued that they needed to get rid of the Jews in order to defend themselves.[11] Their "self-defense" was so efficient that 97 percent of the Jews who lived in Macedonia were deported to their death—an extermination of truly genocidal proportions.

The process went as follows: On March 10 and 11, 1943, the cities of Skopje, Bitola, and Štip were blockaded, and the Bulgarian police and army collected all Jews, telling them to take their valuables (which were promptly looted) with them. The Bitola and Štip Jews were taken to railroad stations and sent to Skopje, where they joined the Skopje Jews who had been interned in the "Monopol" State Tobacco Factory, adjacent to the railway. They were crammed into rooms for days at a time, 300–500 persons per room, with no food, heat, or hygienic facilities. Three transports were organized. The first transport left March 22, 1943, and arrived in Treblinka on March 28, having been escorted by Bulgarian police across the border to Serbia and then turned over to German Gestapo squadrons who delivered them to their final destination. The second transport left Skopje on March 25 and arrived in Treblinka on March 31; the last transport left on March 29 and arrived on April 5. It is said that not a single one of the persons taken in these transports survived the gassing at Treblinka; hence, no one can tell the story.[12]

During this time, due to a shortage of medical doctors and pharmacists in Bulgaria, the authorities singled out Jewish doctors and pharmacists for release and assignment throughout Bulgarian-held territories. They—along with those who joined the national liberation movement, the Partisans—were among the lucky ones who survived. A small number of children also survived, as they were "adopted" or hidden by "righteous Gentiles."[13] Sadly, according to Jennie Lebel, much of the local population seemed to be either passive or even antagonistic toward their Jewish neighbors before they were taken; some collaborated with the Bulgarian or German authorities, betraying the Jews' whereabouts or hideouts.[14]

GREECE UNDER GERMAN, ITALIAN, AND BULGARIAN OCCUPATION

In April 1941, while Axis powers were attacking and partitioning Yugoslavia, Greece was being overrun by Germans, Italians, and Bulgarians. The Germans occupied Thessaly, western Thrace, and the island of Crete. The Bulgarians were rewarded for joining the Axis by getting eastern Thrace and the Ionians Islands as territories, while Italy, after the initial embarrassment of having been decisively rebuffed by the Greek army in 1940, was rewarded in 1941 by getting central Greece, including Athens.

The single-minded obsession with Jewish destruction was most clearly manifested in the German zone in which Thessaloniki, better known as

Salonika, was located. Of the about 70,000 Jews in Greece, 46,000–50,000 lived in Salonika. In the nineteenth century, the city apparently had a Jewish majority—perhaps the only city in the world where Jews were in that position. But after the retreat of the Ottomans in the First Balkan War, the number of Jews dwindled from 80,000 to about 50,000, while the number of Greeks increased. Salonika remained, however, the city with the largest Sephardic Jewish population in the world.

The German administration immediately began to introduce anti-Jewish measures. In the winter of 1941–1942, hunger affected the Greek population because the German army exported nearly all the food to Germany and also held some for its own use. At the same time, an epidemic of spotted typhoid broke out, which temporarily delayed German deportation plans. But, by the summer of 1942, measures aimed at deportation began in earnest. After registering all Jews, the Germans formed three ghettos in Salonika, the poorest of which was located near the train station and became the starting point for deporting Jews to Auschwitz. Between the beginning of the process in February and the middle of May 1943, 42,830 Jews were dispatched on the 1,000 mile trip to Auschwitz. The first transport was sent on March 15, with 2,800 people; by the end of March, the number of people sent was 13,435, and by the middle of May, Salonika was all but emptied of Jews.[15]

Attempts made by Italy and Spain to save some of Salonika's Jews met with limited success, as they managed to save under a thousand people. The most successful escape involved several hundred Jews who made it to the Italian zone, but Rodogno hastens to note that the Italian archives indicate that Italy helped these Jews for economic and political reasons, not humanitarian ones.[16] Nora Levin describes the perfidious methods the Germans used to trick this large Jewish community into passivity, such as promising relocation to Krakow, Poland. To convince the Jews to cooperate, Germans gave the Jews Polish paper money, allowed them to take certain belongings, showed them beautiful picture postcards allegedly sent by the early deportees, and even coerced their main rabbi, whom they had incarcerated in Vienna, to urge the Jews to comply with German requests for the sake of preserving their own lives. A group of over 300 Jews were shipped to Bergen-Belsen in August 1943; the others all ended up in Auschwitz, from which very few returned.

The Bulgarians took the Thracian Jews from the towns of Ksanti, Drama, Serres, Demir-Hisar, and Djumurdzhina to the port city of Lom on the Danube to be part of the same transport as the Jews from Bulgarian-occupied Pirot in Serbia. From Lom, they were transported by boat to Vienna, accompanied by Bulgarian and German police, and from there they were moved by train to Treblinka, where they met the same fate as those sent to Auschwitz.[17] According to some accounts, one of the four transport boats was so overloaded that police attached a barge and transferred all able-bodied men to it; then the barge was deliberately sunk. This version was never carefully investigated because it ultimately did not matter whether people died on the way to Treblinka or when they got there. Only a few Jewish women from Pirot succeeded in escaping from the transport prior to being loaded on the boats; they were the sole survivors of these roundups.

The Italian administration resisted German pressure to establish a uniform policy toward Jews. They refused to implement the obligatory wearing of yellow badges. Thus Jews shared the destiny of the Greek population and were not targeted by the Italians for arrest and deportation. All of this changed with Italy's surrender in September 1943. The German army quickly occupied all formerly Italian-held territory in the Balkans and at once proceeded to finish the Final Solution. In very quick order, about half of approximately 3,500 Athenian Jews perished in transports that were organized between April and June of 1944. Around the same time, over 5,000 Jews from Arta, Corfu, Ioannia, Kana, Kastoria, and Preveza were deported to death camps in "the East."[18] Other Jews survived either with the help of the Red Cross or with the assistance of Greeks, while some survived by joining the Greek resistance movement, the National Liberation Front. Still others survived because they had intermarried with non-Jews.

In the middle of June, 1,800 Jews from Corfu and 250 from Crete were forcibly transferred to the gas chambers. The last transport of 1,200 Jews from the island of Rhodes arrived in Auschwitz on August 17, 1944.

The fact that these transports were sent so late in the war demonstrates the fanaticism of the architects of the Final Solution. By this time, transportation systems were already burdened to the utmost due to the retreat of the German army and its allies and to the increased fighting, yet they still found boats, trucks, and trains to take these poor civilian victims to their executioners. Levin estimates that out of 60,000 Greek Jews, only 1,475 survived the war.[19] The Jewish community website of Salonika provides a different set of figures—it states that out of 77,371 Jews, 10,226 survived.[20] Levin also reports a story from the town of Volo in Thessaly where Greek Orthodox Metropolitan Bishop Joachim helped Jews flee so that only 130 of the 822 Jews perished.

The ethnic Greek population also sustained enormous losses. Several hundred thousand (some sources state that in Athens alone there were 300,000) died of starvation during the winter of 1941–1942. Tens of thousands died in reprisals as the Greek resistance increased their activity in 1942 and 1943. It is estimated that of the total Greeks killed, the Germans executed 21,000; the Bulgarians, 40,000; and the Italians, 9,000.

The Bulgarians were the worst of the Greek oppressors. The two countries continued to claim territories adjacent to each other. The Bulgarians formally

annexed eastern Thrace and continued the practice of ethnic cleansing that had
been carried out during the two Balkan wars earlier in the century (see chapter
3). While trying to Bulgarianize the local population (some of whom may have
had Bulgarian ethnic roots), the Bulgarians encountered resistance and then expelled or killed many Greeks. By late 1941, over 100,000 Greeks were expelled
from Thrace. As a result of the pressures, a Greek rebellion against Bulgarians
took place in Drama on September 28, 1941, which the Bulgarians put down by
killing about 3,000 Drama inhabitants and, in the subsequent weeks, by killing
an additional 15,000 in the vicinity and surrounding villages. The Bulgarians
clearly carried out ethnic cleansing in Thrace and east-central Macedonia.

The Germans carried out several massacres of the Greek population in response to activities of Greek Partisans. On December 13, 1942, the German
army executed all 696 of Kalvryta's males, completely destroyed the town,
and then killed an additional 600 people in nearby villages. Furthermore, on
August 16, 1943, the Germans murdered 317 people, including 74 children
up to the age of ten, in Kommeno.[21]

Of course, a large number of Greeks also died fighting with each other as
members of two main guerilla groups—one, a right-wing, pro-Fascist group
(EDES), and the other, a left-wing, pro-Communist group (EAM-ELAS).
This fighting was a prelude to what would later become the civil war in
Greece after World War II ended. The right-wing EDES group, under the
leadership of General Napoleon Zervas, carried out ethnic cleansing and massacres in villages that were contested by Albanians and Greeks for decades,
if not centuries, and that Albania wanted to annex with the assistance of Italy
and Germany. The Greeks attacked the region of Chamëria on June 27, 1944,
killing 2,877 people, raping 475 women, and destroying 68 villages.[22] In 1944
and 1945, the Greek nationalist forces of EDES drove out about 20,000 Muslim Cham Albanians into Albania and ethnically cleansed the contested territory of Northern Epirus/Chamëria.[23] Only some Christian Chams remained in
Chamëria, but they were being successfully Hellenized.

The Greek Red Cross has estimated that there were 11,456 Greek internees
as a result of the occupation of Greece, but a figure of 20,000 would not be
an exaggeration and would include both concentration camps and prisons.
One can conclude that what happened to the population in Greece (except for
their Jewish citizens) falls short of genocide. Germans and Italians committed
war crimes and crimes against humanity (particularly the deaths caused by
the famine) with sporadic massacres. The temporary Bulgarian expulsion of
many Greeks did have all the characteristics of ethnic cleansing, but Greece
repossessed Thrace and Greek Macedonia, and the Greeks resettled those
regions after 1944. From that point on, the Slavic and Albanian minority of
Greece was pressured by Hellenizing policies of the Greek governments.

7

Retaliatory Genocides against Wartime Enemies

Those who hoped that the end of World War II would bring an end to the carnage were wrong. May 8, 1945, was for many people, the beginning of payback time for the incalculable suffering that they and their people endured as a result of the Nazis and their collaborators. Since the revenge took place at the very beginning of a rigid Bolshevik-style dictatorship established by Josip Broz Tito, no one in Yugoslavia even dared to talk about it, much less research and write about it. Those who committed these crimes were certainly not going to publicize them except to say that justice was being carried out against the enemies and their traitorous supporters. This is not the place to investigate the adequacy of the system of justice (it wasn't justice, though some people did receive retribution); I focus on what happened to the ethnic Germans, Hungarians, and Italians who lived in the Yugoslav lands, many of them descendants of people who settled there even before the Slavs arrived. I look at the destiny of the captured POWs and the families of those who collaborated with the occupying forces. I do not cover revenge against the Bulgarians because their troops quickly withdrew from Yugoslav lands after they switched sides, with their army joining the Yugoslav People's Army and the Red Army in chasing out the Axis forces. Yugoslavia and Bulgaria were part of the Soviet Bloc for a short time; hence, little or no hostile action was directed toward them.[1]

GENOCIDE OF YUGOSLAVIA'S ETHNIC GERMANS

The vast majority of people in the Balkans and beyond, with the exception of a minority of Germans, are unaware that genocide was perpetrated on

Yugoslavia's German minority in the immediate post–World War II period. Of the victors who were aware of the revenge murders, few in the Balkans regretted the mass killings or the massive deportation of Germans after World War II. Fewer still have called it what it was, namely, genocide. This is probably because people from the Nazi-occupied countries, as well as the Allies in general, felt little sympathy for the German population and regarded the Germans collectively as being guilty for the Hitlerite *magnum crimen*. Yet, there is nothing in the definition of genocide and its longer formulation in the UN Genocide Convention that says a process is not genocide if it is somehow "deserved" by the culpability of some of the members of the group that is slated for extermination and/or deportation.

At the outbreak of World War II, Yugoslavia had the largest ethnic German population among the Balkan countries,[2] numbering approximately 540,000.[3] German-speaking people had lived in Slovenia the longest. A Germanic population had lived in Lower Styria since 1147 and by 1910 numbered 74,000, while Germanic people from Carinthia and eastern Tyrol to Dolenjsko (Kočevje) arrived there around 1330 and numbered 18,000 at the end of World War I.[4] Slovenia had been part of the Hapsburg Empire for about eight centuries. The German population often belonged to the bureaucracy, professions, and commerce that exercised control over the Slovenes, and they carried out a policy of Germanization that eventually led to great resentment by the local population.

Hapsburg rulers—particularly Emperor Karl VI, Empress Maria Theresa, and her son Joseph II—encouraged German populations from Swabia,[5] the Palatinate, Hessen, and Black Forest to settle in the Danubian region of Bačka, Banat, Srem, Baranja, and Slavonia. Those formerly Hungarian areas were left nearly empty when the Turks retreated. The first Swabian migrants arrived as early as 1689, with more arriving in 1712 and in three larger waves: 1722–1726, 1763–1773, and 1782–1787.[6] Fewer Germans settled in Bosnia after the occupation of Bosnia and Herzegovina by the Hapsburg Monarchy late in the nineteenth century. Elsewhere their numbers were negligible. These German settlers were considered Volksdeutsche, in contrast to Germans living in areas with German majorities. Most Germans in the Danubian region were farmers, craftsmen, owners of factories, or merchants. Frequently they were the most prosperous, best organized, and most industrious segment of the total population inhabiting the area. Prior to World War II, it was estimated that they comprised between 530,000 and 650,000 (or 541,000 by other counts) or about 5 percent of the total population of the Yugoslav lands. However, they were concentrated in the northeastern and north-central parts of Yugoslavia, where they made up to 30 percent of the population between the two world wars. They often lived in purely ethnic German villages or constituted a fairly large segment of town and city populations, as in Novi Sad and Osijek. It is important to stress that in their self-understanding, these Germans were not migrant ethnic minorities. They had been living in ethnically compact villages, towns, or districts where they were clearly a majority and created a distinct cultural group usually called Donauschwaben (Danubian Swabians).[7]

On the eve of World War II, many of these Volksdeutsche became attracted to Hitler's idea of a German Reich that would incorporate them into an empire that controlled all of Europe. Many cooperated, not merely ideologically but actively, undermining Yugoslavia as a fifth column, encouraging its capitulation.[8] Even some of the ethnic German clergy became enthusiastic admirers of the Nazi ideology, thereby subsequently inflicting harm on their community.[9] The role of the Schwäbisch-Deutscher Kulturbund or simply Kulturbund was controversial. Some regarded it simply as the cultural association of Germans, while their enemies considered it a dangerous outpost of German imperialism and collaborators in the Nazi war effort. A large number of the Germans in Yugoslavia were nonpolitical, while a small minority were Communists who joined Tito's Partisan movement. During the Nazi occupation of Yugoslavia, many local Germans served the German authorities in various ways, sometimes exceeding in barbarity the regular Wehrmacht (German army). About 80,000 served in the German army while 25,000 of these joined the Waffen SS Division called Prinz Eugen formed by local Germans to fight the Partisans.[10] Survivors claim that they formed these units to protect their dwellings from the attacks by the Partisans, whose incursions they describe in gruesome ways and maintain that even during World War II, the extermination of Germans had begun. In many ways it is not surprising that the Germans became generally hated by most of the Slavic population of Yugoslavia, as they were throughout most of Europe.

After the German army and its allies retreated from Yugoslavia in late 1944 and early 1945, and under the impact of the Partisan insurrectionists and the advancing Red Army, approximately 215,000–245,000 Germans were evacuated.[11] They were not permitted to return to Yugoslavia. Given the post–World War II conditions, it is doubtful that they would have wanted to. It is estimated that 80,000–105,000 Volksdeutsche had joined the German, Hungarian, or Croatian armies, of whom 13,000 were killed in action. The rest were evacuated from Yugoslavia, with the exception of 70,000 who became POWs (according to other reports, 80,000 were captured).[12] Already in 1941, slightly more than 18,000 Germans were transferred to Germany, followed in 1943 by another 20,000.[13] About 200,000 to 250,000 civilians remained in the country at the end of the war.[14]

Generally, Yugoslav sources tend to be silent about what happened to the Germans or claim that the remaining Germans were treated humanely until they emigrated of their own free will. Emigrant German sources document the horrible persecutions with statements by survivors and studies by circles of émigrés regarding the fate that befell the Danubian Swabians. They treat the genocide with no reference to the context. According to these German sources, the evil Titoist Communists attacked an innocent autochthonous German population simply because as Slavs they hated Germans; they also needed to expropriate German property as the basis for the collectivization and nationalization needed to establish a socialist economy. These German sources do not mention Nazi war crimes, crimes against humanity, and genocides of anyone, as if the entire revenge process happened without provocation. These views are unhistorical and unsustainable. While these German sources are impressively thorough and reflect humanitarian concern for the extermination of their own people, they accept no responsibility for the genocide and destruction that was carried out by the Nazi German war machine and their allies, something I consider immoral on the part of the Working Groups (Arbeitskreis). Such ethical blindness causes the reader to wonder whether other parts of the report are, perhaps, also tainted.

There is no explicit written order by Tito or the Politburo of the Communist Party of Yugoslavia to destroy Yugoslavia's ethnic Germans. But there are scattered references by highly placed Communist leaders that affirm their conviction that the German population had been uniformly traitorous in sympathizing with the Nazis and that there was no longer a place for them in the Yugoslav community of nations. Instead, they should be punished collectively as "the enemies of the people." The few Yugoslav authorities who deal with this subject matter occasionally use the term *repatriation* to describe punishing or deporting the Germans, but here this term is incorrect. These people had not lived in Germany or Austria, so *repatriation* clearly referred to expulsion or deportation. After the second session of AVNOJ (Anti-Fascist Council of the People's Liberation of Yugoslavia) in November 1943, there was talk of expelling Germans from all of Yugoslavia. Already, at the fourth session of AVNOJ on November 21, 1944, a decision was made to confiscate the property of all Germans, with three exceptions: (1) those who had joined the Partisans against the occupying forces, (2) those who were in mixed marriages with one of the south Slavic nationalities, or (3) those who had been assimilated into the Serbs, Croats, or Slovenes. The rest of the Germans also lost their Yugoslav citizenship and the right to vote.[15] Dieter Blumenwitz cites top Communist leaders such as Rodoljub Čolaković, Boris Kidrič, Edvard Kardelj, and Milovan Djilas, who intimated that the Germans must be removed from Yugoslavia. Several transports were organized to expel the Germans to Austria immediately at the end of the war, but these transports were returned by either the Soviet or British authorities.[16] In 1946, the Yugoslav government made three diplomatic requests to Allied governments regarding the expulsion of Germans and delivered those requests to the American Embassy, but no response was ever given, making the Western governments culpable through their silence. On March 29, 1945, the Anti-Fascist Assembly of the People's Liberation of Serbia confirmed the view of the Main People's Liberation Committee of Vojvodina with the declaration, "In regard to the German population, which, as one, served German Fascism and which no longer deserves a place in our country."[17]

The Yugoslav parliament made the decision of the second session of AVNOJ retroactive, thus providing the legal basis for the ethnic cleansing of Germans. Of course, the brutal manner in which the genocide took place was not specified by law but was left in the hands of the (often less rather than more) organized Partisan forces. Later, responsibility was turned over to the militia and civil authorities, many of whom were recruited from the population that had suffered most under the Nazis during the war. They now exacted the most horrifying excesses, resulting in the massacre of thousands and thousands of captured soldiers and civilians. Those who had been brutalized by the Nazis and Fascists thought it was their turn to exact vengeance in a similar way.

All the preceding documents clearly indicate Yugoslav *intention*, a necessary precondition for genocide. What remains is to point out the physical facts of genocide against Germans, all of which were present to an overwhelming degree.

Approximately 200,000 German civilians and about 70,000 POWs came under the authority of the Yugoslav Liberation Army (of the approximately 150,000 German soldiers who were on Yugoslav territory on May 8, 1945, when Germany surrendered unconditionally). They seemed to have laid down their arms, and then most withdrew to Austria in a desperate attempt to surrender to the British forces rather than Yugoslavs.

The sequence of events leading to genocide was as follows. In the fall of 1944, prior to the liberation of the northwestern parts of Yugoslavia, massacres of the approximately 2,000 "intellectuals," that is, presumed leaders of the various German communities, took place. This was consistent with the Communist revolutionary doctrine of eliminating the potential resistance by those segments of the population that are most likely not to sympathize with a Communist revolution (a similar action was, of course, undertaken against other real and presumed opponents of the new regime). About 10,000 Germans were killed during the "bloody fall" of 1944,[18] which turned out to be a mass slaughter of both the guilty and innocents who were in any way associated with the Axis regime. The genocide was intensified once the first concentration and extermination camps were set up in late October and November 1944. Around Christmas of 1944, about 12,000 (8,000 women and 4,000 men) were deported to forced labor camps in the Soviet Union, where 2,000 died; others were released, mostly to the German Democratic Republic. About 8,000 Germans who were in mixed marriages or who fought on the side of the Partisans were either released or not interned, but the other 170,000 were interned.[19] It is estimated that between 20,000 and 70,000 innocent people were killed,[20] but the most precise figure seems to be 51,000 children, women, and men died in the camps between 1945 and 1948 (a period of about three and a half years). Only a few of these individuals were regarded as war criminals. In round figures, the total number of exterminated is 64,000, with 40,000 being recorded by name and surname.[21] Another estimate is that 166,970 were interned in camps, of whom 48,447 were exterminated.[22] The claims vary as to how many died in camps. According to some German sources, as many as 210,000 died. About 6,500 Volksdeutsche were formally accused of collaboration with the Nazis, but only 163 were tried for war crimes. Yugoslav sources emphasize the number of Germans released and state that 74,554 German POWs were "repatriated" (more accurately deported, but many left gladly) by 1949, with 1,024 kept as war criminals. Of these, 507 were amnestied and repatriated by the end of 1951, and 75 were executed or died in prison.[23]

Far more drastic was the measure placing nearly all German nationals into concentration camps, initially not distinguishing between those who actively cooperated with the Nazis and everyone else. The remaining German population was driven under appalling conditions to these camps, which were usually located in formerly ethnic German villages, some of which were nearly empty after the retreat of the German armies. Other camps were located in abandoned factories or warehouses that were in or near larger cities. There were two types of camps: labor camps and general camps. The latter were intended to be extermination or liquidation camps. Women with children under fourteen, older people, and those too sick to work were taken there. Conditions in these camps were calculated to cause the death of as many as possible. None of them had gas chambers—death was by beating, torture, and execution, and more commonly by malnutrition, hunger, and contagious disease, such as typhoid and diarrhea. Of course, many never made it into camps; they were killed on the spot or tortured to death in local, make-shift torture chambers or in the woods or fields.

There was a distinction between regions in the handling of ethnic Germans; treatment differed from Slovenia to Slavonia of Croatia, to the Vojvodina region of Serbia. Germans received the harshest treatment in the Vojvodina region of Serbia, where they had been most numerous. Slovenia was liberated in the spring of 1945. The German army and its allied forces—the Croatian Ustaše and Domobrans, the Serbian and Montenegrin Četniks, as well as the Slovenian White Guards and their Domobran units—attempted to surrender to the British forces in Austria. They either were captured by the Partisans while still in Slovenia or were delivered back to the Partisans by the British after they surrendered. The Partisans carried out huge massacres (as described later). A Slovene Parliamentary Investigative Commission of these killings was established in 1995. They reported the existence of many mass graves at Kočevski Rog, Teharje, Brežica, Težno, Gutenhag, St. Haynrih, Pohorje, Strnišće, Brežar, Tepanje, and Zančan, and in the vicinity of Celje.[24] The commission assigned the responsibility for these killings to the Communist Party of Slovenia; the Slovenian OZNA, or Department for the Protection of the People (secret service); and the Second Department of KNOJ, or the Corps of People's Defense of Yugoslavia (Partisan forces). It is assumed that the general directive came from the top Communist Party leadership in Belgrade (Tito, Kardelj, and Aleksandar Ranković), but the details and location were left to the Slovenian Communists.[25] About 7,000 ethnic Germans were also killed—most by summary execution on the spot (or in nearby less public sites), others in extermination camps established after the massacres in places such as Strnišće, Težno, and Teharje near Celje. (The Nazis erected Teharje as a camp during the war; later it became a camp for German POWs and the Slovenian White Guard. After World War II, Teharje was reputedly one the most torturous military camps.) The camps in Slovenia were closed in 1945 and in early 1946, and the remaining Germans were put into cattle trains (who says we don't learn from each other?!) and shipped to Austria.

In Vojvodina (Serbia) and Slavonia (Croatia), the number of Germans was much larger and the process of deportation was consequently more drawn out. Some of the camps were opened in November or December 1944 and were not closed until 1948.

The best known of these camps follow; extermination camps are in italics[26]:

In Banat: Kovin, Nemačka Crnja, Pančevo, Omoljica, Veliko Plandište, Kikinda, Vršac, Veliki Bečkerek (current name Zrenjanin), Bela Crkva, Banatski Karlovac, Mramorak, *Knićanin* (11,000), and *Molin* (3,000). Camps were in forty-two locations.[27]

In Bačka: *Bački Jarak* (the earliest liquidation camp; 7,000), Brestovac, Jabuka, Bačka Palanka, Bačko Dobro Polje, Novi Sad, Apatin, Sekič, Subotica, Vrbas, Odžaci, Filipovo (later named Bački Gračac), Padinska Skela, *Gakovo* (8,500), and *Kruševlje* (3,000);[28] a total of twenty-eight camps.

In Srem: Indjija, Zemun/Novi Grad, *Sremska Mitrovica* (2,000); a total of six camps.

In Slavonia: Josipovac, Velika Pisanica, Tenje by Osijek, *Krndija* (500) and *Valpovo* (1,100); a total of five camps.

In Baranja: Podunavlje and two other camps for a total of three.

There were also camps in Belgrade and the copper mine Bor, Serbia.

From the widespread distribution of these camps and the coordinated time frame of the activities against the Germans, it is clear that these were not spontaneous local actions but were ordered by the central government in Belgrade. Local governments implemented the actions readily and enthusiastically because of the local people's great desire for retribution. German-owned real estate and farmlands were expropriated by the government, and the families of the Partisans who fought in the liberation struggle and who had lived in very impoverished parts of the country were resettled there. Germans' personal property was looted or collected into special warehouses; from here it was distributed to those who had demonstrated need. Here too one sees parallels with the Nazis' treatment of the Jews.

A typical roundup proceeded as follows: German nationals were collected, usually in a warehouse, by Partisan armed units and then marched to one of the villages that had been turned into a concentration camp. Small children were not made to walk, but were placed into horse-drawn carriages. While some Yugoslav authors point out that the villages did not have barbed wire as in Nazi camps, the villages were still carefully guarded, first by Partisan units and later by the militia (police). When someone came too close to the edge of the village, a "warning" shot was fired, followed by shots aimed to kill. Adults received no food at all during their first week or so in the camp; later, they received such meager rations that many, especially the elderly, died of hunger, cold, and disease. Adults were forced to labor in the fields. A terrible fate was reserved for about 30,000 (or 12,000?) younger and middle-aged women and men, who were taken to the Soviet Union (Siberia) as slave laborers where about 16,000 (2,000) died.[29] Parents were mercilessly separated from their children and other members of their families, usually never to see them again, even if some of them survived.

Some children were left to fend for themselves, and many of them died miserable deaths from cold, hunger, disease, and neglect. Others were murdered outright by sadistic commanders or guards. Special children's camps or areas in larger camps were established, seemingly to speed up their deaths. Some children were taken to orphanages, where they were deliberately denationalized to the point where most of them had no recollection of their ethnic and family origins. These orphanages "educated" children to be loyal to the Communist system and leadership. This denationalization process is defined as genocidal in the UN Genocide Convention and is sharply criticized by the German authors of the studies.[30] It should be stated that the conditions in Yugoslavia after World War II were generally horrendous. The lack of food, clothing, medical care, and adequate living conditions were experienced not only by the camp and orphanage inmates but also by much of the population, who had lived in similar conditions for the duration of the war. Putting the German children in orphanages with Yugoslav children indicates the perpetrators were not pure racists. They were willing to assimilate the German children into the majority population. Yet paradoxically, most of the organizers of these destructive measures were rabid anti-German nationalists.

The treatment of the German minority in Yugoslavia between 1944 and 1948 resembles the sadistic barbarities of other genocides. That treatment improved only slightly between 1948 and the late 1950s. Interestingly, German authors of genocide studies of the German population make no parallels to the German treatment of Jews, Roma, Soviet POWs, and the myriad others who were tortured and killed in Nazi concentration camps. From reading their literature, it seems that the horrors against Germans were unprecedented. Of course, it is unwise to compare suffering, but it is also unwise to not see the causal relationship between the genocide of ethnic Germans and the genocides carried out by other ethnic Germans (sometimes the same people were perpetrators and victims, but they were a minority).

The list of woes endured by the German minority is endless;[31] it includes beating with chains, sticks, and planks; knocking out teeth; bashing in heads; cutting off various body parts; and carving up or crushing bodies. Raping women could be especially hurtful in that some of the victims killed their own children in despair, and then committed suicide. Transport into the camp was either by foot or in cattle trains. In the camps themselves, fifteen to twenty people were placed into a room that rarely had beds; usually the inmates slept on a thin layer of straw that was not changed for several years, or they slept directly on the floor with no covers. Since the camps were established in the winter of 1944–1945, a huge number of people simply froze to death. German medical inmates in the camps had no medicine to use to treat illnesses, and frequently, they themselves contracted diseases such as typhoid and died. Those who escaped in order to beg in nearby villages were usually executed.

Bodies of the dead were often lying in the streets for days. They were collected, either by one-wheel pushcarts or by horse-drawn carriages, and then piled up, often naked, and buried in common pits without funeral services. German clergy inmates were usually not allowed to provide pastoral or liturgical services but were often the special target for torture by the antireligious Communist guards. When some of the camps were closed, the surviving inmates were taken to other camps. When death did not occur fast enough, attempts were made to deport the inmates.

Two kinds of escapes were distinguished by the inmates: "black" and "white" escapes. Black escapes were desperate attempts to flee, usually across the border into Austria, Hungary, or Romania. If the inmate was successful, revenge was sometimes taken on the family of the escapee and family members were executed; if the inmate was caught, he or she was usually beaten and then executed. White escapes were tacitly approved by the camp's authorities, hoping to simply get rid of the problem. There were cases where groups of escapees were captured and returned to Yugoslavia; other times Yugoslav and Hungarian border guards exchanged fire and in the crossfire, shot the hapless escapees, as neither side wanted them.[32]

An interesting anomaly occurred in regard to the role of the Soviet troops. The Soviet Red Army had a bad reputation for their treatment of not only the German population but also the liberated allies. They reportedly raped women indiscriminately, stole personal property, and destroyed buildings—all in a drunken, lawless, hate-filled binge. And, indeed, the authors of *Genocid nad nemačkom manjinom u Jugoslaviji 1944–1948* and *Verbrechen an den Deutschen in Jugoslawien 1944–1948* state that Soviet soldiers raped German women and that the Partisans sometimes arranged it for them. But, surprisingly, the testimony of survivors often credits Soviet officers and soldiers as being more orderly and restrained than the Partisans, claiming they intervened on behalf of Germans who were being massacred. When Soviet officers appeared, they often provided for improved conditions in the camps and a more controlled behavior by the guards. Ironically, sometimes the Germans shared the fate of many imprisoned White Russians who had settled in Yugoslavia after the 1917 Bolshevik Revolution.[33] Many of the Partisan guards drank excessively, especially on weekends, and then carried out uncontrolled brutalities.

The suffering of ethnic Germans did not cease after the concentration camps were disbanded. Generally they were not permitted to return to their native villages but were allowed to go to larger cities. Therefore, many had to take three-year assignments to work in difficult and undesirable locations for minimal remuneration and slightly improved living conditions compared to the camps. By the 1950s, they could individually apply for permission to emigrate (most of them to Austria and West Germany) and, upon paying a fee, were able to emigrate. In Germany and Austria, they were gradually resettled from camps to private dwellings and began to link up with each other. They formed associations of Danubian Germans who sought to reconstruct their history and seek remedies for their suffering.

After the outbreak of Yugoslavia's conflict with the Soviet Bloc nations in 1948, Yugoslavia sought to establish better relationships with the West, including West Germany (German Federal Republic). Government officials realized that such relationships would be greatly facilitated by the release of the Volksdeutsche, so they gradually began to release them from the camps and permitted them to emigrate. While they had not exactly been exiled, the Volksdeutsche had suffered much in the camps and had been deprived of their human rights and property; upon their release, most knew they had to leave the lands where their ancestors had lived for more than 200 years. By 1951, 41,769 Volksdeutsche had been deported to Austria and Germany. There were only 60,536 Germans left in Yugoslavia by 1953. In 1961, only 20,015 remained. By 1970, only 12,785 remained, and this figure dropped to 8,712 in 1981 and 5,387 in 1991.[34] The Yugoslav German population went from over 530,000 to a little over 5,000 in about forty-five years. That is a 99 percent reduction! Of the German population that had remained in Yugoslavia in 1944, approximately one in four had died in the camps.

Who is responsible for this genocide? As noted previously regarding the intentionality of the genocide, despite the fact that no document has been uncovered that links the massacres to Tito's direct order, it was Tito's Communist regime all the way to the top that was responsible. The genocide was carried out in the midst of hatred toward all things German, not merely all things Nazi. In the popular mind, it is simply too easy to transfer guilt from a part of the group to the entire group—thus leading to collective guilt. But the same applies to the perpetrators of the retaliatory genocide; it was certainly not *all* Yugoslavs nor *all* Yugoslav Communists who were perpetrators. Seven specific groups of perpetrators can be distinguished.

1. Vigilante groups. Some of the guerrilla Partisans joined spontaneously to harm and kill groups of Germans (similar to lynching). This happened immediately upon liberation, particularly in ethnically mixed towns and villages. Hungarians, Croats, and Serbs who were suspected of having collaborated with the occupying forces were included, as were those who were simply too well to do and were assumed to be enemies of the new regime.
2. Individuals. At times individuals motivated by a vendetta or interpersonal conflict used the postwar chaos to eliminate their rivals.
3. Local People's Liberation Committees. Local outfits interpreted the decisions by AVNOJ to mean that Germans were tagged as "people's enemies," "collaborators of the occupiers," and "Fascists," and therefore, it was justifiable to take extra-legal measures to kill them.

4. People's courts. The primary purpose of "people's courts," as with other kangaroo courts, was to exact retribution and to eliminate potential enemies. These courts mostly operated immediately after the war.

5. Partisan military courts. Upon seizing or liberating a territory, the Partisan units would quickly establish a court-martial to which they brought well-known public figures among the Germans (and others) and either shot them or imprisoned them.

6. OZNA (Odeljenje za Zaštitu Naroda—Department for the Defense of the People). OZNA was the secret service, which was led by the most prominent Communist Party leaders, especially Ranković. Well organized along hierarchical lines from the central to the local branches, OZNA was the instrument for taking and keeping power in the hands of the Communist Party and functioned as the most efficient apparatus for repression, being feared by enemies as well as friends.

7. Special mobile units of commandos. These units terrorized the population through quick strikes at ethnic, political, and economic leaders of the former regimes, leaving the population leaderless, except for the Communists.[35]

While individual responsibility is the most important factor, and while survivors were sometimes able to name the perpetrators, particularly commanders of camps,[36] no one was ever tried or disciplined for this crime of genocide against the Germans. But as the crime of genocide does not expire, some may still be brought to justice. There is, however, a total lack of will to do so. The Associations of Danubian Germans in Germany collected the data on the genocide, disseminated the information about it, and made some people of Yugoslavia in the post-Communist period cognizant of the events, demanding rehabilitation and symbolic compensation from the successor states of Yugoslavia (all but Macedonia)—but that is all that has been done.

A Serbian author, Zoran Janjetović, argues that what happened to the Danubian Swabians was not genocide but ethnic cleansing. While he admits that the Yugoslav government did intend to get rid of the German population, he says the government did not specify how it would get rid of them.[37] Presumably the Yugoslavs intended to deport them rather than kill them. When they did not succeed in deporting the Germans, they held them under such conditions that huge numbers of them died and thus avoided deliberately exterminating them. This argument seems to be pure casuistry because the result was the same, and the motivation surely was to entirely eliminate a large population from their historical residence.

No court ever deliberated whether or not this was a case of genocide, but from a historical perspective, a genocide of Yugoslavia's Germans did take place. A careful legal examination of the facts leads me to agree with Dieter Blumenwitz. Genocide was carried out against this ethnic and cultural group from October/November 1944 (as the war neared its end in the Balkans) to 1948. It was carried out by various means: mass executions, torture, severe bodily and mental harm, internment in extermination and concentration camps, and expulsion (ethnic cleansing). Article II (e) of the UN Genocide Convention was also violated by the forcible assimilation of some of the German children.[38]

One may summarize this genocidal episode in the words of Carl Savich:

> In 1944, the Communist regime under Josip Broz Tito issued a decree that stripped the ethnic Germans in Yugoslavia of citizenship, took away their property, and rescinded their voting rights. This was rationalized as collective punishment for German atrocities and murders committed against Yugoslavs. German property was allocated to migrants from Bosnia-Hercegovina, Croatia, and Montenegro, who settled the region. This was merely a continuation of the cycle of collective punishment, punishing innocent civilians apprehended at random for the alleged crimes of individuals, real and imagined.[39]

Yugoslavia was ethnically cleansed of Germans just in time for the next wave of ethnic cleansing to begin. Surely it was an act of collective revenge that swept the guilty and the innocent in a wave of retaliatory genocide, about which very little has been written, whether or not many Germans deserved the harsh treatment. The concern about this genocide has been expressed primarily by the families of those who were treated without empathy. Ultimately, the blame goes back to Hitler and the Nazi leadership, as Nazi-sponsored genocides were so brutal that little or no sympathy could be felt for any German, even for those who had nothing to do with Nazi atrocities. Tragically, some of the former victims now became unacknowledged perpetrators.[40]

MASSACRES OF HUNGARIANS

The Hungarian population in Vojvodina also suffered major retributions for the Razzia (*racija*, or massacre) that had been carried out in southern Bačka in January 1942 (see chapter 6). In the fall of 1944, many Hungarians (along with Germans)—again, the innocent along with the guilty—were massacred. Hungarian sources claim that about 10,000 Hungarians were eliminated, mostly men between ages eighteen and fifty. This figure is probably too high.[41] Authors who play the numbers game often have an agenda to increase enmity between the different ethnic groups. Therefore, authors commenting on the numbers of Hungarians killed usually add increments of

10,000, raising the number to 20,000, 30,000 (one of 35,000), 40,000, and all the way up to 50,000 victims. The author who started publicizing the massacres of Hungarians was Tibor Cseres,[42] whose work is a combination of journalism, collections of anecdotes, eyewitness accounts, second-hand and hearsay accounts, and a very evident irredentist aim for Hungary to reclaim Vojvodina. He initially gathered information based on accounts by two Bačka Hungarian Catholic priests, Márton Szücs and József Kovács. Cseres expanded those reports, claiming that 34,491 were killed in the fall of 1944, and subsequently raised the figure to over 40,000 along with about 27,000 Hungarians who left Vojvodina.[43] Most other accounts of these massacres seem to be based almost verbatim on Cseres; to these authors, it is practically self-evident that genocide of Hungarians occurred in the fall of 1944, though Cseres himself more accurately uses the terms *blood feud* or *vendetta* to describe the process.

As in the case of German self-justification, the Hungarian sources maintain that during World War II, the Hungarian authorities did not commit massacres of Serbians and Jews. They merely carried out judicially justified executions of Serbian criminal bands. Only occasionally did they exceed appropriate punishment of those who threatened the "new" law and order of a restored domain unjustly taken away by the punitive Treaty of Trianon in 1920.

Among the Slavic Communists, there were those who not only wanted revenge but also wished to prevent any future claims on Vojvodina by Hungarians and Germans. To that end, they urged either an exchange of populations with Hungary or the voluntary migration of Vojvodina's Hungarians back to Hungary. Even in those chaotic days there is no evidence that there was a plan or policy to eliminate the Hungarians from Vojvodina. In villages like Čurug, where the Hungarian Fascists behaved with much hostility toward the local Serbs, the entire Hungarian population of the village moved out,[44] though it is not clear whether they fled or were driven out. Local Serbs of Bačka appear to have been less harsh in their reprisals against the Hungarians than those Partisan troops that had been more clearly traumatized by their own wartime losses. Soviet Red Army officers appear to have been a restraining influence, although in the fall of 1944, both the Red Army and the Partisans sustained huge losses fighting the retreating Nazi armies.

Butchering, torture, summary executions, rape, and plunder were all part of the massacres. They constituted war crimes but were not genocidal in character. The shame is that no one was ever held accountable or punished for these crimes and that there has been a conspiracy of silence based on fear and intimidation. Neither representatives of Communist Hungary nor Yugoslavia dared to lift the veil of this cover-up. It is regrettable that now in the post-Communist period, the examination of these events by Hungarian authors is tainted by anti-Communism, anti-Serbianism, and the desire to restore losses of Hungarian territory to pre-Trianon borders.

ETHNIC CLEANSING OF ITALIANS

The Italian and Slavic population lived intermingled along the Dalmatian Littoral for well over a millennium. The history of the eastern shore of the Adriatic Sea is too complex to be summarized here, but during the centuries of Venetian supremacy, the Italian population, particularly in the northeast Adriatic region, lived in towns and cities while the Slavic population (Slovene, Croat, Serb, and Montenegrin) mostly lived in villages and the hinterland. After the unification of Italy in the second half of the nineteenth century, the Italians were hoping to get rid of the Hapsburg rule and lay claim to much of the eastern shore of the Adriatic; however, the Slavic population also aspired to the Istrian and Dalmatian shore. Italy was on the "wrong" side of World War I, and the newly established Kingdom of Serbs, Croats, and Slovenes was awarded most of the Dalmatian coast, with the exception of Istria. A proto-Fascist military venture in the early 1920s paid off, and Italy was awarded the land north of Rijeka (Fiume) and Zadar (Zara). When World War II broke out, Mussolini's imperialistic designs on the Balkans brought the Italian army and administration to a very extensive area (see chapter 4). Italy, like Hungary and Bulgaria, chose badly and was forced to surrender to the Allies in 1943.

The tables turned. The Italian army and administration were left to fend for themselves, becoming a target to just about everyone: the Germans, the Ustaše, the Četniks, the Partisans, the Greeks, and, of course, the British and the Americans. The Axis powers had lost the war, and the Partisans, now already configured into the Yugoslav Liberation Army, sought to regain not only those lands that were within the realm of the Kingdom of Yugoslavia, but additional territories in which there were large Slovenian or Croatian populations living alongside or intermingled with Italians. Many Italians feared revenge by the Yugoslav population and began moving out, either on their own or through pressure to leave. Unfortunately, from the perspective of the Partisan guerillas, *all* Italians were Fascist and executions of Italians began, at first sporadically and then on a more consistent basis.

After World War II, most Italians thought it "politically incorrect" to avoid defending anything that was related to their Fascist past.[45] The Italian journalist Arrigo Petacco was one of the first to describe the destiny of these Italians. Regretfully, his book is replete with factual errors and is written so impressionistically and with an obvious irredentist agenda that it is difficult to judge whether the claims are realistic or vastly overblown. At one time, the Yugoslav Communist government would have energetically disclaimed the content of a book like this. Nonetheless, as a clearer and more complex picture of the behavior of Partisans emerges (Petacco calls them "Slavic hordes"), it is likely that among the overblown claims there are some realistic ones. Basically, the Partisans did to the Italian soldiers and population what some of the more brutal Italian units (like the Black Shirts) did to the Yugoslavs. Petacco claims that because the revenge was disproportionately harsh, it proves that there was a genocidal intention by the Partisan leadership. Proportionality is hard to judge in such complex warfare. In any case, people were tortured, summarily shot, raped, and forcibly deported. At times the description of the way the Italians were treated resembles the descriptions of war crimes and crimes against humanity presented in previous chapters. The massacres most frequently consisted of shooting or slaughtering Italians and throwing them into the plentiful mountain pits and gorges caused by the karst nature of the terrain along the Dalmatian coast.[46]

Petacco claims, without providing any documentation, that 20,000 Italians were expelled from Istria, followed by an exodus of 34,000 from the zone B area—the area around Trieste that had been assigned to Yugoslav control—and 30,000 from Pula (Pola), from which they fled in panic when the city was awarded to Yugoslavia. He concludes that about 350,000 Italians left lands that became part of Yugoslavia at the end of the war.[47]

Petacco claims that both genocide and ethnic cleansing of Italians took place; he, like so many authors writing about Balkan events, seems to use the words interchangeably. To his credit, Petacco more frequently uses the term *ethnic cleansing*. I see no proof of genocidal intent, because the Yugoslavs did welcome Communist Italians to stay or even emigrate from Italy in order to help build socialism. But, as was the case in almost every Balkan conflict of the twentieth century, the purpose was to lay claim to land on the basis of the numerical preponderance of an ethnic group. Just as Italians had tried to remove Slovenians to empty parts of Slovenia so they could annex it to Italy, the Yugoslavs tried to remove the Italian minority so they could prove that the land belonged to them. It was ethnic cleansing.

BLEIBURG AND THE FATE OF USTAŠE AND OTHER MILITARIES COLLABORATING WITH THE AXIS

At the formal end of World War II, there were wholesale massacres of military units belonging to the various Yugoslav nationalities who were allies of and collaborators with Germany and Italy. While I could have easily placed this discussion in the chapter on World War II, I placed it here because these events did take place after May 8, 1945, which is generally accepted as V-E Day, the formal surrender of Germany to the Allies. However, the very last European battle of World War II fought by large contingents of organized armies was fought in Slovenia on May 14 and 15 and is directly linked with the events that will be described here.

Many current Croatian and Slovenian nationalists have accused Serbs as being the perpetrators of the mass executions of POWs who fell into the hands of the Partisans. They describe it as a simple genocide of Croats and Slovenes by Serbs. However, this is a falsification of events. Tens of thousands of soldiers and civilians—their numbers being hotly contested—were retreating from Yugoslavian territory toward Klagenfurt in Austria in the hope of surrendering to the British. They reportedly consisted of about 8,000 Slovenian White Guards; 1,500 Montenegrin Četniks and Serbian Zbor; and about 20,000 Croat Ustaše and Domobrans (a fourth of them Muslims). There were also a large number of Germans and small number of White Russian Cossacks that fought on the side of the Axis.[48] The retreating soldiers of varied ethnic compositions were accompanied by some of their family members, all in desperate flight because they feared retaliation by the Partisans. In addition, the executors were not just Serbs; some of the identified units that carried out massacres were Slovenian Partisans. The majority of the other Partisan units may have been of the Serb nationality but they, too, were multiethnic. The main force that chased the Axis collaborators across northern Croatia and Slovenia and into Austria was the Third Yugoslav Army[49] under the leadership of General Kosta Nadj (who was of Hungarian descent and lived most of his life in Croatia). That force included the Eleventh Dalmatian Assault Brigade, which was multiethnic. To describe these events as a Serb genocide of Croats simply does not square with the facts.

The Yugoslav Liberation Army,[50] having been assisted by the Americans and the British and in close cooperation with the Red Army, pushed northward and westward. The remaining columns of Germans and their allies were withdrawing, nay, fleeing toward Austria by way of Dravograd, Celje, and Maribor in an attempt to surrender to the Western Allies; they assumed neither the Red Army nor the Partisans would show them much mercy. The Croatian historian Zdravko Dizdar undertook a lengthy analysis of these events, on which the following description of events relies.[51]

Even though it was increasingly obvious that Germany would soon capitulate, the head of the Independent State of Croatia, Ante Pavelić, and his government made very inadequate projections regarding what would happen to his armies and followers. On the day Germany surrendered, Pavelić left Zagreb with his government and gave orders that this huge mass of humanity,

the soldiers still being under command and armed, should march to Austria
and surrender to the British. Apparently, the Croatian leadership was under
the very irrational expectation that when Germany surrendered, the Western
Allies would go to war against the Soviets, arming the Croats so that they
could retake Croatia and liberate it from the prospective Communist control.
They were unaware that the British apparently made an agreement that all
Axis-allied troops from Yugoslavia would be turned over to Tito's forces,
which, indeed, they were. The Yugoslav army sent most of its forces into
the chase and encircled columns of enemy soldiers several miles long. The
Germans surrendered on May 8, making the destiny of the others very pre-
carious. The Yugoslav army blocked several of the routes of escape, so the
main group fled in the direction of Celje, Maribor, and Dravograd, hoping to
reach Klagenfurt, Austria. Once surrounded by the Partisans, they attempted
to fight their way through the encirclement in what is called the Battle of
Poljana (near the village of Prevalje, Slovenia) on May 14. The casualties
were not particularly high—about 300 dead and 250 wounded Ustaše and
about 100 dead and wounded on the Partisan side. The British arrived at the
small Austrian border town of Bleiburg a mere three hours before the Yugoslav army got there, but that was enough time to establish their presence.
The Croat generals refused to surrender to the Yugoslav army, but the British
lived up to their agreement and ordered the Croats and others to surrender on
May 15. A few Croat and other units attempted to flee and fight their way
into the interior of Austria, but the vast majority turned over their weapons
to the British. A few days later the British handed them over to the Yugoslav
army, having tricked the anti-Titoist troops along with their dependents into
believing that they were being taken to Allied camps in Italy.[52]

Initially it was believed that the massacre took place right there at Bleiburg. Dizdar disproves this by pointing out that only individual shootings
took place in Bleiburg and that the captured soldiers were taken to temporary
camps. The problem was that some of the temporary camps were already
filled with 40,000 or more German POWs for whom there was no food or
facilities. Now suddenly, tens (or even hundreds) of thousands of collaborat-
ing people fell in Partisan hands, as well. The Partisans tried to return them
to Croatia and elsewhere in the country. What happened to those people is a
matter of much debate. Retribution and hatred would play a big role in the
ensuing events.

David Bruce MacDonald summarizes the numerical estimates: "Judah
put the number of killed between 20,000 and 40,000, Anzulović at 50,000,
Jelavić between 40,000 and 100,000, 'including civilians' and Tanner at
somewhere between 200,000 suggested by 'Croatian nationalists' and the
30,000 suggested by 'others.'"[53] MacDonald also reports that Jasper Ridley

estimated that between 20,000 and 23,000 were massacred, but that the Partisans did release a number of the younger POWs.[54] Damir Mirković reports the estimates by the Partisan leaders, saying that Milovan Djilas gives a figure of 30,000 while Vladimir Dedijer says 50,000.[55] Further, Mirković reports that Croat authors provide much higher estimates, such as 100,000 Croatian soldiers and civilians; 500,000 Catholic and Muslim Croats (estimate by Ivo Omerčanin); 150,000 soldiers and 300,000 civilians (Stjepan Hefer); 400,000 (Mislav Ježić); or over a million killed and exiled (George Prpić). Some of these Croat authors claim that Bleiburg had 15,000 people killed each day, making it worse than Auschwitz, which had 6,000. Franjo Tudjman's estimate is 35,000 to 50,000, as he and several Croat scholars tried to even out the numbers of Jasenovac and Bleiburg victims.[56] Vladimir Žerjavić provides a breakdown of 45,000–55,000 Croatians and Muslims killed; 1,500–3,100 of Serbian Ljotić's policemen, medic volunteers, and Montenegrin Četniks; and 8,000 Slovenian White Guards, for a total of 54,500–55,000. Žerjavić made an earlier estimate that 60,000–70,000 total were killed, which also equals his estimate with the Jasenovac victims.[57] Dizdar mentions several sets of figures—first, 125,000–185,000 soldiers, a figure he then reduces to 110,000, of which 60,000 were Croats, 40,000 were Germans, and 10,000 were Četniks, plus several thousand civilians—but concedes that one cannot be sure about numbers.[58]

On May 8, 1945 (V Day or V-E Day), Tito gave the order that all armed enemies immediately surrender themselves and their weapons, or they would be "treated without mercy." Another similar message was sent on May 13. On May 14, there was a report in the Zagreb *Vjesnik* newspaper that 10,000 Ustaše had been killed in "battles" in two days.[59] Having been informed that mass killings of the captives began in Celje, against his instructions, Tito sent a telegram to all commanders strictly ordering them not to liquidate the prisoners but take them to camps where they would be interrogated to flush out the war criminals who would then be tried.[60] Despite this order, killings continued and nobody was ever punished for it. Sometimes people were killed individually, sometimes in groups (such as the killing of 200 Ustaše by a Serbian division)—sometimes the killing lasted for days on end. The first killing fields were near Maribor and Celje. Many of the collaborationist forces and families were killed in the next few days, but many were still being killed as late as 1947. Members of the SS Prinz Eugen Division, which were mostly Volksdeutsche and some Croats, were all liquidated.

One of the huge massacres took place in Kočevski Rog in Slovenia. The Fourth Yugoslav Army had received prisoners from the British and first took them, along with those whom they had captured, to camps at Kranj and St. Vid near Ljubljana and from there to Kočevski Rog for liquidation. Kočevski Rog is a mostly uninhabited karst mountain region with many caves, pits, and gorges. These POWs and members of their families were brought there to be shot and thrown into the pits that were later cemented over. Only recently have the pits been partially excavated to find evidence of the mass murders. One former Partisan estimated that 30,000 were killed in various locations there. Excavations undertaken in the last ten to fifteen years indicate that the concealed mass graves in Macesnova Gorica contained mostly Slovene Home Guardsmen; the graves in Pod Kremnom contained Croats, Serbs, and Montenegrin collaborationists; and the graves at still other sites contained mostly Italian or German troops. The discovery of mass graves continues. In late summer of 2010 at Prevalje, another mass grave of about 700 was discovered.[61]

Concentration camps were established in Sent Vid, Škofja Loka, and Slovenj-Gradec, in addition to Maribor, Celje, and Kranj. By May 28, the government decided that most Domobrans could be released as there was little evidence that they were war criminals. Then the government decided to disperse all the remaining collaborationist forces throughout Yugoslavia. This became what many Croats call *križni putovi* (roads of the cross) or *putovi smrti* (roads of death).[62] Some were marched around with no food or drink. Others were taken around in boarded-up trains for weeks, from one end of the country to the other, with the dead bodies being removed from time to time. Some were even taken to Siberia or Greece. Most were dispatched to various parts of Yugoslavia. In Croatia, twelve permanent concentration camps were established, but the largest were in Vojvodina, in which about 110,000 inmates were imprisoned.[63] There they suffered the kind of torture that paralleled the crimes in Ustaše camps during World War II. Revenge produced a rough sort of justice, though it did not always get meted out to the right people.

Contrary to the Geneva Convention on the treatment of POWs, mass executions were carried out by various units of the Second, Third, and Fourth Yugoslav Army. There were special structures within the Yugoslav army responsible for this process. One of them was KNOJ (Korpus Narodne Odbrane Jugoslavije—Corps of People's Defense of Yugoslavia). It was a special unit of the armed forces for the liquidation of the "enemies of the people" (with or without orders), and it is now known that the Slovene KNOJ was responsible for the liquidation of some of their captives. The other was OZNA (Odelenje za Zaštitu Naroda—Department for the Protection of the People), which was the secret service department that investigated and decided the fate of suspects. They had a reputation for handing out death sentences; very few who were investigated were ever found not guilty and released.

It is unlikely that the actual number of the dead will ever be accurately established. Nor will the number of sites where mass killings took place be known—

there are simply too many of them already discovered to be listed. So far there seems to be well over 500. The post–World War II Yugoslav government forbade any mention of Bleiburg or Kočevski Rog. The killing fields, such as Macesnova Gorica, Pod Krenom, Ruganski Klanci, Dvojno Brezo, and Težno, were taboo topics as well. Only in the 1980s did people start pointing out sites of mass graves, such as the Huda Jama mine by Laško, Slovenia, or a dam in Gornji Hrašćani in Croatia;[64] up until then, these sites were only rumors. Survivors started sharing their memories, and the sites with their grisly remnants began to be excavated. Very quickly this process became politicized, as the wars of the 1990s needed not only hardware but also propaganda as ammunition. From the perspective of Croatian nationalists, the "Bleiburg" massacres were a convenient counterargument to Serb propaganda about Jasenovac. The competition of victimology continues, and charges and countercharges are hurled less to honor the victims, particularly the guilty ones (for among the killed in Bleiburg and other slaughter places there were also murderers, torturers, arsonists, rapists, and looters), than to bludgeon the other ethnic groups and stimulate the desire for another cycle of revenge killings. To repeat what I wrote in regard to Serbian, Jewish, Roma, and other victims of the Ustaša regime, *those who intentionally enlarge the number of victims are "killing" fictional members of a group that their enemies did not exterminate. Those who intentionally deny or diminish the scope of the extermination are killing them twice by attempting to destroy even their memory, in addition to the actual lives that were lost or traumatized.* The same would be true for Četnik victims, and it applies equally to the victims of the Partisans.

Cadik I. Danon Braco, a former Jewish inmate of Jasenovac who joined the Partisans in September of 1942, provides an example of the emotional state of people who apprehended the collaborationist forces. He describes how he and his fellow members of the Twelfth Slavonian Proletarian and Elite Brigade, along with other Partisan units and the British army, captured and disarmed the fleeing Ustaše and others near Bleiburg in Austria, on May 15, 1945. He does not describe what happened to the POWs, but he does describe his psychological state of mind. During the event, he disregarded the command of his officer and rushed to disarm the Ustaše and specifically sought the Jasenovac Ustaše regiment. Here is what went through his mind:

> I remembered my father, whom the Ustaše killed bestially in the camp.
>
> I remembered my uncle Gedaja, who had died of hunger in the camp.
>
> I remembered the column of Serb villagers at the camp's gate, and how the Ustaše had seized children, and that red faced Ustaša who had twirled the baby round and threw him to the ground next to his mother. The picture of the broken baby's skull was still vivid in my mind.

I remembered the Ustaša sergeant, who after slaughtering the tired camp inmate, licked the blood from his dagger.

I remembered the terrible smell of human flesh which went out with the smoke from the brick kiln chimney and I remembered poor Morde.

I remembered the slaughtered rabbi and the bloody "talet" on the floor.

The reminiscences were emerging and with them the tears. . . . I decided firmly to find the criminals from the camp who committed all that. I remembered them well, and their faces were haunting me in my dreams. Walking fast, I started toward the immense mass [of surrendering Ustaše]. . . . I felt a superhuman force, nothing could stop me.[65]

How many thousands of Partisans of any ethnicity, who had similar or worse experiences with the captured enemy, would have eagerly, even gladly, wiped out the sources of their own, their family's, and their people's suffering? It probably did not take much convincing by the commanding officers that it was best to simply wipe out this potential source of future opposition to the new order, perhaps using more expeditious methods than they had suffered. I don't mean to justify the extermination, but to describe the frame of mind of the Partisans who had to fight and sustain losses, even after the Third Reich had surrendered. This may shed some light on their mental disposition after four years of inflicted horrors. They reckoned that their time had come to square the accounts. Thus evil evokes evil in response.

Was it genocide? No, if one applies literally the genocide convention. But it was politicide. The killing was intended, but it was not on the basis of race, ethnicity, culture, or religion; it was based on ideology and political convictions. The victims were regarded as traitors and betrayers of their country. To the victims, it wouldn't matter what we call the revenge killings because it was a frenzied, horrific slaughter of vengeance that was unnecessary. The war was over and the POWs should have been placed in camps and de-politicized, while the war criminals should have been tried. The reign of terror that ensued after the end of the war was a direct result of the hatred and desire for revenge against real or alleged collaborators with the Nazis. It was also fed by the Communists' plan to get rid of potential opponents in order to completely take over the governing of Yugoslavia. Having imposed a Communist dictatorship, the new ruling class imposed a conspiracy of silence. Only after the collapse of Communism was the silence broken. Unfortunately, the demise of Communism also brought about the unraveling of the governing arrangement. New conflicts broke out that were the shadows of the tragedy of World War II, and a new series of ethnic cleansing and genocide struck the Balkans. Many more mass killings filled the mass graves.

8

Ethnic Cleansing during Yugoslavia's Wars of Disintegration in the 1990s

In December 1995, I returned from a visit to Sarajevo via Zagreb and walked through the open market with a Bosnian Muslim acquaintance. We saw a man selling butcher knives. The Bosnian asked the seller what the knives were for. He replied matter-of-factly, "To cut Serb throats."

The Balkan wars of the 1990s brought the last European genocide of the twentieth century, but they were also a reprise of the first European genocides of the twentieth century (chapter 3). They were the "most catastrophic event in Europe since the Holocaust."[1]

The phrase *ethnic cleansing* (as seen in chapter 1), was not invented during the fall of Yugoslavia,[2] as was proclaimed by most journalists, but it was certainly popularized and made a household word. There had been ethnic cleansing before the Serbs allegedly invented it in the 1990s, just as there had been genocides prior to Raphael Lemkin's invention of the word. Yet, for most readers the word *genocide* is inextricably related to what they saw on their TVs and read in their newspapers and periodicals or on the Internet about the wars in Croatia, Kosovo, and Bosnia and Herzegovina in the 1990s.

Actually the renewed use of the phrase *ethnic cleansing* occurred prior to the outbreak of the wars of the 1990s. Back in the 1960s and 1970s the phrase was used by the Serbian Orthodox Church to describe the campaign by Kosovo Albanians to dramatically reduce the number of Serbs in the province that the Church and the Serbian people consider to be the cradle of their culture. The Serbian Orthodox Church complained that pressures of various kinds, including killing and rape, were used to oust Serbs from Kosovo and that it was done with the silent complicity of the Yugoslav Communist government.

THE CONTEXT

The Communists of Yugoslavia, under the undisputed leadership of Josip Broz Tito, re-created Yugoslavia after World War II on a different basis than it had during the Kingdom of Yugoslavia. Taking their clues from the Soviet Union's 1936 constitution, they organized a federal state out of the multiethnic mix of inhabitants of the land, creating six republics (Bosnia and Herzegovina, Croatia, Macedonia, Montenegro, Serbia, and Slovenia) with two autonomous provinces established within Serbia as a concession to their multiethnic makeup (Kosovo and Metohija and Vojvodina).[3] There had been no negotiations to determine the administrative borders of these republics and provinces after World War II—they were quickly and unilaterally decided by the Communist Party leadership, headed by Tito, without opposition. The Communists of the different ethnic groups did not oppose the delineation of the internal borders because they all understood that Yugoslavia was to be a centralized state—a "dictatorship of the proletariat"—in which the Communist Party's Central Committee and Politburo, or more precisely Tito himself, would make the decisions and the rest of the people would implement them. Hence, the borders had little significance. Only as decentralization and subsequent democratization crept in from the 1960s onward would voices be raised about issues affecting the well-being of this or that republic or this or that nation or nationality.[4]

Ethnic tensions, some of which existed all along but were repressed due to Communist policies claiming there had been reconciliation, started becoming more evident in the late 1960s. They were increasingly surfacing because, on one hand, the regime liberalized and became less repressive and, on the other hand, economic inequalities had become more obvious, causing more open conflicts about the distribution of resources, the investment policies of industrialization, the gradual introduction of a limited market economy, and the difficulties of the repayment of loans that the government secured from both West and East. After the 1980 death of the only quintessential Yugoslav, Marshall Tito, slow recognition set in that the rest of the Communist leaders had retained their ethnic identities and that the ethnicity of Tito's successor would matter both to his own nationality and to the others.

Since the disintegration of Yugoslavia in Europe's first wars after World War II amidst charges of genocide, ethnic cleansing, and foreign interventions, there were many who claimed that Yugoslavia was an artificial creation bound to fail from its inception in 1919, and that its nationalities never really got along. This is a retroactive abuse of history, as nearly all of us who lived there can testify. While there may not have been universal contentment with Yugoslavia, especially by émigré groups, there was an unusually high level of acceptance, satisfaction, and pride in being Yugoslavs. Yugoslavia was one of the few Communist countries to which people from other (mostly Communist or Third World) countries fled for asylum. There were good neighbor relations among the members of various nationalities, who often lived in mixed neighborhoods, attended the same schools, played on the same sports clubs, dated, and married each other.

What was remarkable about Yugoslavia's sense of unity is that it took place relatively soon after the horrors of World War II. A unique opportunity arose to suggest to the war-exhausted and traumatized population that a new Socialist revolution provided a chance for an entirely new beginning in interethnic relationships, the opportunity to build a new Socialist homeland for these multiethnic communities, and that this relationship was characterized by brotherhood and unity (*bratstvo i jedinstvo*), a slogan vigorously promoted by the Communists and widely accepted by the population.

There are claims, usually by Serbs, that Tito (who was of Croat/Slovenian descent) deliberately suppressed the evidence of the genocides of Serbs and that it was this repression that exploded when Tito died and Communism started crumbling. This is not true. To the contrary, the accounts of the genocides were rehearsed so often in the immediate aftermath of the war (in schools, universities, media, films, etc.), that many (including me) thought that people would never let it happen again. So, when the nationalist incidents began in the late 1970s and continued during the 1980s, fear gripped the hearts of both old and young. When people respond in fear, they frequently act irrationally and resort to the herd instinct, each seeking security from the threat of others by flocking to their own kind.

In retrospect, there seems to have been an undercurrent of repressed awareness that former rivals or enemies often continue to be enemies. People were able to enjoy the friendship and amity of good neighborliness (called *komšiluk*, which was still functioning in many villages and towns, though disappearing in the rapid urbanization of the country).

So, how did the most democratic of Europe's Communist countries fail so catastrophically?[5]

It is not easy to sort out the mutually exclusive claims blaming this or that side or person for what ensued in the aftermath of Tito's death. Some might go back—way back—to the inception of the country, claiming it was placed on unhealthy foundations from the very beginning. But one does not have to go back to Adam and Eve or to the Big Bang to explain the subsequent chain of events. One must go back, however, to the foreign occupation, civil war, war crimes, ethnic and ideological cleansings, Holocaust, and genocides of World War II. Some claim that Tito was too eager to resolve the ethnic hatred without allowing sufficient time for the wounds to heal, for the mangled corpses to be unearthed and reburied, for people to grieve, for culprits to be punished. Some even impute anti-Serbian designs on the part of Tito to cover up Ustaša crimes, blaming him for never having visited Jasenovac. I do not find this convincing. In the utterly chaotic situation at the end of World War II, it made sense to look to the future, rather than to the past as the Balkan people tended to do, and to promote future aspirations of good neighborly conduct and to rebuild the devastated economy as a way of putting to rest the hatred, fear, and suffering.

However, for all his attempts and some accomplishments, Tito and the Communist Party did not succeed in solving the ethnic question. According to Milan Kučan, the first president of a newly independent Slovenia, Tito's failure in this regard was the reason for the breakup of Yugoslavia.[6] The breakup of Yugoslavia did not take place nonviolently, as it did in Czechoslovakia, or with relatively mild violence, as in the Soviet Union, due to various factors, the most important being the resuscitation of memories of the unhealed ethnoreligious and ideological wounds of World War II. The Communist dictatorship used repression to deal with opposition, dissent, and unrest, thereby bringing about an appearance that the wounds had healed when they were actually covered up superficially. As the political, social, and economic crisis deepened after the "Old Man"[7] died, the structures failed and the leaders who replaced him were unable to find a nonviolent resolution. The political, social, and economic crisis increasingly took on an ethnoreligious cloak.

Much controversy was created over whether the wars of the 1990s were wars of foreign aggression (one constituent state or republic of Yugoslavia—namely, Serbia—attacking other sovereign republics, namely, Croatia or Bosnia and Herzegovina) or civil wars breaking out in the process of partitioning Yugoslavia. I reject both of these formulas as too simplistic, in favor of seeing the wars of dismemberment as distinct but connected wars, each having a different nature. Lurking behind most of the wars (except in Slovenia and Macedonia) was the "Serbian question." The Serbs comprised the largest ethno-nation, with 3 of its 8 million individuals living outside the Republic of Serbia, while living within its own borders were the two largest non-Slavic ethnic minorities, the Albanians and Hungarians, along with many other minorities. How could this ethno-nation protect its people if Yugoslavia were to fall apart?

The new Balkan wars were as follows:

1. War for the independence of Slovenia (1991).
Basically, this was a war by the federal government and a few units of its armed forces (JNA, or Jugoslovenska Narodna Armija) against the Slovenian federal unit, which had taken steps to secede. The war began on June 25,

1991, and lasted a mere ten days. The poorly trained recruits of the con-scripted federal army were routed by the mostly volunteer territorial units of the Slovene National Guard. About a hundred people died, some of them innocents who died in the cross fire. The federal army withdrew, and the government in Belgrade, by this time dominated by Slobodan Milošević, allowed Slovenia's secession because Slovenia's population was rather homogenous, living in uncontested territory. No ethnic cleansing or genocide took place in this war.

2. War over Croatia with the attempt of partitioning Croatia between Croats, who sought independence, and Croatia's Serbs, who wanted to become autonomous or to secede from Croatia and annex themselves to Serbia (1991–1996).

There are disagreements as to which of the sporadic violent events should be considered the beginning of the war, but most frequently, June 25, 1991, is regarded as its beginning, just a few hours after the Slovenian conflict broke out. The war lasted till 1996 with periods of ceasefire; the last part of Serb-occupied territory was returned to Croatia in 1998. It was a very bloody and protracted war with many instances of ethnic cleansing and genocide at first, mostly by Serbs over Croats and then vice versa; this will be discussed in chapter 9.[8] About 10,000 died; even more were wounded. Great degrees of physical destruction occurred and hundreds of thousands were displaced, many never to return to their dwellings. The war began as an insurrection of the Serbian minority, which was subsequently supported by the Yugoslav army and Serb paramilitaries against a secessionist government of Croatia.

3. War to dismember and partition Bosnia and Herzegovina (B&H) or to preserve its integrity as an independent country (1992–1995).

This was by far the bloodiest conflict with the largest number of casualties, due to the very complex historical background and ethnoreligious mix of the population. The war began in early April 1992 and formally ended with the Dayton Agreement and the Paris Peace Treaty of December 15, 1995.

Out of a population of about 4 million, approximately 100,000 to 200,000 people were killed. About half of the population became displaced either internally or to other former Yugoslav republics or else abroad. It was in B&H that the most sizable and horrific ethnic cleansing, genocidal massacres, and genocidal rapes took place. Of the three major ethnoreligious populations—Muslim Bosniaks, Orthodox Serbs, and Catholic Croats—it was the Serbs who, with generous assistance from Serbia proper and the JNA, acted most aggressively and destructively. As I discuss in chapter 10, the other two groups also perpetrated war crimes and carried out ethnic cleansing. The first stage was an attack by the Yugoslav army against the newly formed B&H government, which turned into an interethnic war with complex international ramifications.

4. War over Kosovo (1998–1999).
The Kosovo crisis had been the earliest cause of the subsequent wars and ended as the last major war of Yugoslavia's disintegration. This was a war between the rebel KLA (Kosovo Liberation Army—Ustria Çlirimtare ë Kosovës, or UÇK in Albanian) against the Serbian military and paramilitaries. The situation was dramatically altered by a seventy-eight-day bombardment (March 24 to June 10, 1999) by NATO on the territory of the entire Republic of Serbia and Montenegro, then still being called Yugoslavia. Ethnic cleansing was perhaps the most prominent feature of the war because it was a war over who would rule this province populated by Serbs and Albanians. An Albanian demographic explosion and a Serb exodus had taken place that tilted the ratio to at least 9:1 in favor of the ethnic Albanians. At first it was claimed that 100,000 Albanians were killed and 2 million were either exiled to Albania, Macedonia, or Montenegro or internally displaced, but these numbers, like many of the other estimates, were vastly exaggerated, as will be seen in chapter 11. After Kosovo was taken over by NATO ("the international community"), the vast majority of its Albanian population returned. They then vengefully carried out ethnic cleansing of Serbs, Roma, Bosniaks, Turks, and other ethnic minorities. Contrary to the UN's idealistically espoused desire for Kosovo to be multiethnic, it had become nearly homogenously Albanian. Serb fears that they would one day be ethnically cleansed from Kosovo came to pass.

5. War in Macedonia (2001), a low-intensity civil war caused by the insurrection of an ethnic Albanian guerilla force (see chapter 13).
This war was settled with the assistance of the international community after about a hundred casualties and small-scale localized ethnic cleansing.

The upshot of these wars, and the myriad negotiations by both domestic and international players, was that Yugoslavia fell apart into seven distinct, independent states along the lines of Tito's imposed republican or provincial boundaries: Slovenia, Croatia, B&H, Macedonia, Serbia, Montenegro, and Kosovo.

CONTENTIOUS ANALYTICAL ISSUES

The fall of Yugoslavia took place in front of TV and radio audiences all over the world, with daily journalistic reports and analyses. It resulted in a veritable library of scholarly and eyewitness accounts, including some by major diplomatic and military figures, providing a detailed account of the fighting and profiles of the domestic and international protagonists, many of whom had become household names. Hence, there is no need to narrate chronologically the events of the war here, though there are disputes as to who or what was at fault, who started the hostility in this or that location, and who were the victims, the perpetrators, or the bystanders. The following issues about the wars are vigorously disputed:

1. Were the reasons complex or simple?

The answer to this (and some of the other questions discussed here) provides issues for scholarly interpretation as well as fodder for political manipulation. Those who criticize the claim that the reasons for these wars were complex feel that the protagonists of complexity were motivated by the political aim of discouraging or preventing international intervention. Why should one send foreign armies into a domestic quagmire?

Those who criticize the theory of simple causes suspect that its protagonists used the theory to encourage foreign military intervention by claiming that there were clear cases of expansionist aggression by perpetrators against victims. The favorite claim is that the war was Serbian aggression against non-Serbs. Another variant of the theory is that the war was fundamentalist Muslim aggression against Orthodox Christians. The first claim aimed at involving the West; the second aimed at involving either Russia or "Christian Europe."

The problem with the simple cause theory is that it is too simplistic. Balkan history and developments cannot be said to have just one or two explanations, no matter how advantageous that might be for some ulterior purpose.

2. Were the wars caused by ancient hatreds or by contemporary political ambitions of leaders?

The problem presented by this question is similar to the one just discussed. At the time of the conflicts, those who argued that the wars of the 1990s were the continuation of ancient hatreds and rivalries were accused of discouraging the international community from getting involved, as it would be useless to try to solve ancient tribal rivalries. Those who argued that the conflict was of recent origin, based on contemporary political ambitions of power-hungry leaders bent on manipulating the fears of common people, were accused of deliberately oversimplifying in order to facilitate the decision by world powers to get involved militarily.

I see no reason for an either-or case despite some able scholars opting for the second theory.[9] Both are correct. Those who argue that Serbs and Croats did not fight until recent times or that the Ottoman Turks were relatively tolerant of their Christian subjects—at least compared to the prevalent contemporaneous practice of tolerance in Europe—miss the point. The point is that two major "geological fault lines" run through the Balkans. These are particularly severe in the very places where the wars of the 1990s took place. The first fault line occurred with the Great Schism between Eastern and Western Christianity, producing two great Christian Churches, each claiming to be the one true holy and apostolic Church of Christ with the other being so wrong that its members were to be enticed to convert to the True Church. This schism split the Balkans in half, with Bulgarians, Macedonians, Montenegrins, and Serbs adhering to the Byzantine Orthodox tradition centered in Constantinople, while the Croats and Slovenes adhered to the Roman Catholic Church. The line ran smack through Bosnia so that some Bosnians adhered to the Catholic Church and others to the Orthodox Church. A complicating factor in Bosnia was the establishment of a Bosnian church that tried to steer between the two great traditions and was therefore accused, inaccurately in the opinion of recent scholarship, of being of the heretical Bogumil sect. Thus while members of these two churches did not go to war against each other for religious reasons, they surely harbored animosities and rivalries, often stoked by outside powers. They would not have even understood each other's liturgical languages—Latin in Catholic churches and Old Slavonic in the Orthodox.

An additional great rift occurred with the arrival of Islam via the Ottoman Turkish conquests. Certain Bosnian Muslim scholars have attempted to show that Islam started to spread in the Balkans prior to the arrival of Ottoman Turkish armies.[10] Regardless of the accuracy of that claim, the decisive moment occurred with the expansion of the Ottoman Empire into the European heartland from the fourteenth to the twentieth century, which resulted in numerous conversions to Islam. For our purpose it is not important whether the Muslim view of Islam's superiority as divine revelation caused people freely to convert or whether the conversions took place due to coercion or bribery—the promise of economic and other advantages for those who became Muslims. The fact is that the Muslim converts shared many of the advantages that the colonial rulers enjoyed, even when there was tension between the ethnic Turks, who settled in the Balkans as exponents of the empire, and the native converts.[11] The converts were able to communicate with the Turks, had at least rudimentary understanding of Arabic as used in the mosques, were mostly urban dwellers, and had a superior education. The Christian masses, both Orthodox and Catholic, were generally limited to working the fields or tending sheep, thus living in the countryside, being vastly exploited (not in the least by Muslim tax collectors), so that even in this respect people were being pitted against each other. According to Matija

Mažuranić's travelogue from Bosnia in 1840, "All Muslims viscerally hated all Christians. This in itself, thought Matija, wouldn't be so bad if only the Christians were more amicable among themselves. Christians detested each other as if they had nothing in common."[12] Most of the Christian clergy were illiterate; the masses lived in poverty, misery, and ignorance. One of the most odious taxes was *devshirme*, or tax in blood, which was the Muslim practice of raiding Christian villages and abducting young, healthy boys, who were carried to Istanbul and educated as Muslim *janissaries*, an elite imperial fighting force. Some Muslim scholars describe the process benignly, saying that it shows just how tolerant Muslims were, as some of these boys rose to great prominence, even to the post of grand vizier, who actually ran the affairs of the state. But they overlook the fact that for most parents, this was the most cruel act of all since the majority of them never saw their children again and didn't know whether they were alive or dead. Even if the Muslim overlords may have been relatively tolerant, the fact is they were feudal overlords while the Christians were serfs, and by shari'ah law the Christians were a distinctly lower class of population. Some Christian travelers to Bosnia in the nineteenth century noted how abusive and arrogant the Bosnian Muslims were toward the Christians. One should not dismiss the claim of "ancient hatred" based on the absence of numerous uprisings. Illiterate, beaten-down people do not rebel too often—Christians were not content in the empire. The fear of Ottoman reprisals caused great migrations of Serbs to lands now called Krajina, in Croatia, and Bosnia, as well as the great migration of Serbs under Patriarch Arsenije III Čarnojević from Kosovo and southern Serbia to Hungarian lands in 1690. Fear of the Ottomans also led to the phenomenon of *hajduci* and *uskoci*, groups of outlaws viewed as brigands and marauders by the Turks and as freedom fighters by the Christian population.

There are many examples showing that the conflict between Muslims and Christians is not just of recent origin. The enmity was inflamed by the few Balkan Christian students who had gone during the nineteenth century to study at European universities, then returned with modern nationalism from the West, which surely accelerated the conflict, resulting in Christians' strong desire to liberate themselves from "the Turkish yoke." The Muslim converts had ambiguous feelings regarding this process: some opposed it, sensing that they would lose their privileged position, if not their lives; others shared the desire to get rid of the Ottoman overlords. The Muslim converts had not yet begun to create their own Muslim national identity, and at first there were expectations that they would be reconverted to their ancestral faith. By and large that did not happen, and only gradually did those in Bosnia congeal into a distinct national consciousness, first under the awkward designation as Muslims, and then as Bosniaks. But the Christian population considered them a foreign body politick among them, a fifth column that at any moment might be willing to betray their neighbors. This fear of betrayal was reinforced during World War II when some Muslims of B&H formed the SS Handžar and SS Kama division and the Kosovar Muslims formed the SS Skenderbeg division. Thus, the argument that the Balkan population, at least its Slavic segment, lived in harmony and friendship until the nineteenth and twentieth centuries is not convincing.

On the other hand, it is altogether clear that the rise of nationalism and the establishment of nation-states on the territory of former empires led to a frantic desire to reestablish former medieval states at their maximum borders, and this inevitably led to acrimonious conflicts and eventually wars of territorial expansion. These wars always left some of the states aggrieved, hoping for rectification of injustices. A sense of victimization had been nurtured by just about all of the nationalities. Waiting for the earliest opportunity to retrieve what the states felt belonged to them, they seized the opportunity when Yugoslavia slid into the crisis of the 1980s.

Just because the role of both ancient rivalries and contemporary factors complicates the analysis, it does not have to lead to analysis paralysis. The UN and other segments of the international community could get involved to stop the carnage despite its deep roots and contemporary criminal political actions. Complicating the issues is the fact that the great powers' attitudes toward the Balkans in the 1990s were more similar to their positions in 1914; namely, each had its own national interests and sympathies in the foreground, and the powers did not act jointly toward the resolution of the Balkan conundrum.

3. Were they wars of foreign aggression or civil wars?
Most writers from Croatia and Bosnia, as well as Western analysts, consider these wars as being Serbian aggression aimed at creating a Great Serbia. Thus, Serbia invaded the territories of other independent states, especially after some of them had been given recognition by foreign countries such as Germany, the Vatican, Austria, and then others. Obviously, in the case of an aggression of one state against other(s), the UN and other international bodies such as the European Union, as well as individual states, may feel obliged to come to the defense of the invaded state. However, there was another issue fueling this crisis.

Numerous wars have been fought over union versus secession (including the American Civil War). From Serbia's and Montenegro's perspective, first two and then an additional two of the six republics sought to illegally secede. Serbs felt they would be the greatest losers in the secession, because a considerable number of them lived in Croatia (12–20 percent) and in B&H (about

33 percent) and smaller numbers in Macedonia and Slovenia. From the Serb perspective, *if* the other republics were to be allowed to secede, the territories predominantly populated by Serbs (such as the Krajina and sections of western and eastern Slavonia in Croatia, and large sections of B&H) should have the same right to secede and to annex themselves to Serbia so that Serbs could live in one state. When the non-Serb politicians in Croatia and B&H decided to prevent this partition, a civil war broke out, as the Serbs feared they would be the victims of a genocide similar to the one that occurred during World War II. To prevent this from happening, they engaged in preemptive military action. Had the international community forced Slovenia and Croatia and subsequently B&H to guarantee minority rights prior to having their right to self-determination confirmed with international recognition, it is possible that the Serb population living in the other republics would not have responded militarily to the propaganda emanating from Milošević, Babić, Martić, Karadžić, Mladić, and other Serb chauvinist leaders.

Again elements of *both* views are correct; that is, the wars had both foreign and internal causes. While the federal authorities were divided in regard to how to deal with the Yugoslav crisis, some units of the JNA experienced mass desertions of non-Serbs and quickly turned into a predominantly Serb military force; these army units sought to prevent secession. At first they maintained that they were inserting themselves in the middle of local skirmishes and battles,[13] but soon they sided with the Serb local forces. Thus the war had characteristics of both a civil war and a war of foreign aggression because the Serbian political leadership, particularly Milošević, supported the Serb nationalists militarily and economically and inflamed the Serbs to fight the others. No doubt, soldiers from Serbia fought on various battlefields in Croatia and B&H against the local Croats and Bosniaks. Yet there are also testimonies of refugees and survivors stating they were familiar with those who attacked, detained, tortured, raped and killed them. Occasionally, these neighbors and classmates gave a helping hand in times of trouble,[14] but others uncannily turned into brutal, merciless war criminals who pretended not to recognize and did not acknowledge their former friends and cynically inflicted heinous harm upon them.

In B&H, Serbs fought Muslims, Serbs fought Croats, Croats fought Muslims, and Muslims fought Muslims (in the Bihać area). There were Serbian regulars and irregulars, and the same was true of Croats and Muslims. Many Serbs stayed in the besieged Sarajevo, which was being targeted by the Serbs encircling the city. Some Serbs fought as part of the Bosnian government army, which was predominantly made up of Muslims and minority Croats; one Serb served as a general of that army. A Croat serving with Serb forces was tried in The Hague on charges of war crimes that he committed on non-Serbs. In addition to emigrants who returned to fight on their respective ethnic side, foreign volunteers or mercenaries from Russia, the Muslim countries, Greece, Germany, and the United States all got involved, adding to the complexities and ambiguities of these Balkan wars.

The conclusion is that these were civil wars as well as wars of aggression.

4. Were the wars caused by an intra-Yugoslav crisis or by foreign meddling? Even before the war broke out and in the early stages of the war, the Serb public was convinced that Islamic or Western, specifically German, Vatican, or American CIA conspiracies, promoted Yugoslavia's disintegration. Serbian Orientalist-turned-diplomat Dimitrije Tanasković and political scientist Miroslav Jevtić claimed they had evidence of a so-called *zelena transferzala* (green bridgehead)—a planned Islamic fundamentalist expansion from Teheran and Ankara via Tirana and Sarajevo into the heart of Europe, with the long-range plan of converting the Balkans and all of Europe to Islam. According to Tanasković and Jevtić, the Serbs were the bulwark of Christianity, fighting (again, as at Kosovo) to keep the Muslim hordes from overrunning Christian lands. They were puzzled that the West did not recognize the danger and did not value Serbian sacrifices but felt that belatedly the West might recognize its misreading of history.

Another theory is that after the fall of Communism, the West no longer needed Yugoslavia as a strategic country that defied the Soviet Union and decided to break it up in order to gain greater benefit from a fractured rather than unified Balkans (*divide et impera*). This conspiratorial theory has several variants. Some argue that since Germany gave the earliest and strongest support to secessionist Slovenia and Croatia, the old Germanic *drang nach Osten* (push to the East) was revived and the ancient sympathies of the Western Slavs for Austria and Germany had been rekindled. German diplomatic recognition of an independent Slovenia and Croatia seemed to give validity to this assertion.

Others maintain that the wars were a Vatican/Catholic plot. They claim the Vatican had never really given up on its aspiration to absorb the Eastern Orthodox Christians, either by fake ecumenical unity or by cunning, and implemented tactics of forcible expansion of territory or conversion of population. The third variant implicates the Americans, either by plotting "in some dark room in the CIA" (as more than one person told me in a conversation) or by American multinational corporations seeking to destroy competition and gain markets in a mangled, cut-up Yugoslavia.

When I wrote my book *Yugoslavian Inferno*, I was convinced that the responsibility for the wars of the 1990s lay squarely on actors from within Yugoslavia rather than on the accursed foreigners. True, many if not all wars and occupations were caused by people from outside the region—Romans, Byzantines, Franks, Mongols, Venetians, Hungarians, Austrian Hapsburgs, Napoleonic French, Italians, Germans, and Soviets—but this time it was a locally brewed brouhaha. As I saw it, the foreigners were a passive factor in the sense that they did not know how to effectively deal with the crisis, and sometimes they made a bad situation worse through their ineptitude and disagreements (see, for instance, David Owen blaming Bill Clinton for messing up near-accomplished deals with interventionist ideas that countered the negotiated arrangements[15]).

Though it looked at first like a clear either-or decision as to the question of intra-Yugoslav versus foreign meddling, subsequently I realized that it is another both-and case. This fact most clearly dawned on me while I was reading Warren Zimmerman's book *Origins of a Catastrophe*.[16] Zimmerman followed Lawrence Eagleburger as American ambassador to Yugoslavia. Both were capable diplomats who liked Yugoslavia and its people. Eagleburger and Zimmerman stated that the American position was for Yugoslavia to remain a united country. Zimmerman faulted the German government for rushing to recognize the secessionist states without any guarantees that the international community would protect the rights of minorities; without these constitutional guarantees, it is not surprising that the Serbs were fearful of their destiny in these lands. However, Secretary of State James Baker, Eagleburger, and Zimmerman all played into the hands of those who promoted disintegration. Zimmerman traveled around Yugoslavia, meeting the various political actors (e.g., he was playing tennis with Franjo Tudjman, giving him assurances of Western protection) and seemingly encouraging their activities. Then he told Yugoslav federal officials that the United States was standing behind them, *but* they were not to use military power in order to save the federation; if they did, the United States would intervene. That is tantamount to someone telling Abraham Lincoln that he should save the Union but do so without using the Union's army!

The preceding is just one instance of foreign meddling. Yugoslavs themselves caused the demise of their country, but foreign influence was definitely a contributing factor. Foreign powers were even more decisively present in the 1999 Kosovo war. And in all the wars of the 1990s, no small role was played by émigré circles of all ethnicities, who not only propagandized on behalf of their ethnic group and advocated confrontation but also sent significant financial and military aid and personally volunteered their services in the various military units that crisscrossed the land. They were allowed to do so by the international community.

5. Were these national or ethnic wars?
When I initially wrote that the war between Serbs and Croats reminded me less of a war between two European nations, as bloody as those were, and

more of a tribal war between Tutsis and Hutus, my Croat and Serb friends took offense, saying that theirs are ancient nations with great cultural histories. Obviously, I offended their self-image, which looks better from within a country than outside. Many foreign war correspondents got the impression that these were tribal ethnic conflicts, and one very competent political scientist, Lenard Cohen, described it as the war between "tribal Gods."[17]

James Ridgeway and Jasminka Udovički provide a strong counterargument to the claim that the wars were ethnic in nature.[18] They argue that, perhaps with some delay, the Balkan people also became nations, though at the end of the twentieth century people referred to them again as merely ethnic groups. The main reason for the wars was the Balkan peoples' sense of nationalism, or even "ultranationalism," which had been held in check by Tito. According to Ridgeway and Udovički, Milošević very subtly and in a Machiavellian maneuver appealed not to Serbian ethnic pride or identity but to "their real grievances and then conjured up others that began to appear real only after endless repetition. His focus, however, had never been on ethnicity, but on national injury and injustice."[19] Franjo Tudjman likewise offers a restored "thousand-year-old" Croat nationhood that expressed itself as an aspiration even in the guise of the Fascist Independent State of Croatia, and said it was going to liberate them from the alleged Serb dominance. Thus, at least some of the nations (the term used for majorities, whereas minorities are called "nationalities") of the former Yugoslavia had a raison d'etat for fighting these wars.

These are strong arguments with truth in them; however, here again I opt for a both-and solution rather than either-or as offered by Ridgeway and Udovički. A mature nation, even if dominated by a majority national group, would find a way to acknowledge other citizens of that nation-state as members of the community. During the process of disintegration in the former Yugoslavia—which was a multiethnic/multinational state where for a while the vast majority of its citizens got along reasonably well— it was not merely the national interest of Serbs, Croats, Slovenes, and others at stake, but their ethnic identity, which determined who may live and who may die. The identity issue was even more pronounced in B&H because of the composition of its population. It was (and still is) a matter of considerable debate who exactly was a real Bosnian or Herzegovinian. In the wars of the 1990s, people were killed because of their ethnic identity, even if they were barely aware of it themselves. Ridgeway and Udovički implicitly concede this point by naming their book *Yugoslavia's Ethnic Nightmare.*

6. Were these religious or secular wars?
All the religious leaders I have interviewed or whose declarations I have read are united in stating that the 1990s Balkans wars were not religious. Many

scholars agree. The first book written on the wars, Misha Glenny's *The Fall of Yugoslavia*,[20] describes the early stages of the war, including the destruction of sacred objects such as cemeteries, churches, mosques, and monasteries but does not intimate a religious component of the war. But religious leaders, while denying that their own religion played a role, nevertheless assert that other religions did contribute to the wars. Allegedly the others, by the nature of their ecclesiology, do not distinguish clearly between the people and their religion but provide religious cover or sanctification of the wars.

Many people contend that these were religious wars because, allegedly, religion causes most if not all wars. That view is so patently false that it does not deserve a rebuttal. More serious arguments for the religious nature of these wars have been made by several scholars, in particular by Michael Sells;[21] others generally build on Sells's thesis. Sells does not provide an evenhanded exploration of the role of the various religions but critically targets the role of the Serbian Orthodox Church, focusing particularly on the interpretation of the epic poetry about the Battle of Kosovo and on "The Mountain Wreath" of the Montenegrin Bishop Petar Petrović II-Njegoš. Sells coined the term *Christoslavic* to allege a uniquely Serbian identification with the crucifixion and resurrection of Jesus Christ.[22] He also points out that many Serbs believe that Christianity is the natural religion of the Serbs and that conversion to Islam is not only abandonment of the "faith of the fathers" but also an act of national betrayal that ought to be punished even belatedly.

Mitja Velikonja[23] provides a very thorough historical and sociological analysis of the mythological and religious factors leading to the war in Bosnia and, by extension, in Croatia. More recently Garry Phillips[24] took Sells's thesis and developed it into a literary analysis of religious texts. Focusing on the term *Christoslavism*, a term virtually unheard of in the Balkans, Phillips provides some chilling verses of "The Mountain Wreath" by Bishop Njegoš, describing the genocidal massacres of Muslim converts. Phillips assigns major culpability to erroneous readings of the Holy Scriptures. I do not contest that a literal (mis)interpretation of the biblical stories may seem to provide justification for carrying out ethnic cleansing and genocide of enemies, but there was so little biblical literacy among the Serbs (and others) in the Balkans that it seems absurd to consider it a major ingredient in the genocidal mix—at most it was a minor addition to more important ingredients.

All adversaries in the conflicts of the 1990s made use of religion. In 1990, for example, on the streets of Zagreb, the capital of Croatia, stickers were displayed on most store windows in center city stating "Bog čuva Hrvate" (God protects Croats). On TV one could see Serb tanks with a similar graffiti, "Bog čuva Srbe" (God protects Serbs), and the ancient Orthodox symbol of a cross with four *S* letters (in Cyrillic, the letter *S* is written like a *C* in the

Latin alphabet) standing for "Samo sloga Srbina spašava" (Only unity will save the Serbs). A closer investigation reveals not only numerous instances of marginal religious components but also organized and explicit complicity in blessing weapons, supporting the war aims, and even advocating resistance to peace overtures until the war aims of one's side were accomplished. Some of the clergy and theology students participated in battles with weapons in their arms.[25] Certain political leaders sought to consult their religious leaders on the military and political decisions (e.g., Radovan Karadžić claims to have consulted with the Serbian Orthodox bishops in all matters[26]), while others sought photo opportunities with religious leaders, which the latter naively accepted, thinking it was a way for the churches to reenter public life (e.g., Franjo Tudjman with Cardinal Franjo Kuharić).

It is difficult to conceive that authentically religious people would promote and participate in the inhumanities perpetrated in these wars. In fact, it is difficult to imagine nonreligious people doing so, though religious people have frequently claimed a higher level of morality for themselves. My contention is that these were religious wars fought by irreligious people. This is a paradox rather than contradiction. They were not classical religious wars; they were not fought over theology. No explicit efforts were made to convert people from one religion to another as in World War II, although there have been cases where people did declare that they had converted, and they were released from captivity.

The wars did have something to do with the formation of Yugoslavia as a multiethnic/multireligious community of peoples who, during the Communist period, were under massive pressure to become atheists and who succumbed to this pressure, but to different degrees. Prior to the wars, 56 percent of the Croats retained their Catholic affiliation (considerably fewer Slovenians did so), 20 percent of Bosniak Muslims retained their religious practices, and only 17 percent of Serbs and Montenegrins did so. The Communist regime had pushed all religious institutions to the margins, causing them to lose their place in public life.

What happened in the transition from Communism to post-Communism was that religious communities were given religious liberties—not equally, however, as the larger historical communities were provided not just equality but privilege, while the smaller and newer religious communities experienced various degrees of restrictions. Many people sought a spiritual dimension to their lives, and with the increasing insecurities created by the crisis and impending war, they sought refuge and security in their religious communities. In some cases the transformation from Communism to post-Communism created a veritable rush back to the religion of their ancestors.

In the Balkans, as in much of Eastern Europe, there is a very specific form of religiosity that I call ethnoreligiosity, deliberately not separating the words *ethnic* and *religious* or hyphenating them as is customary. Ethnoreligiosity is a specific symbiotic merger of one's ethnic and religious heritage as a means of providing a sense of personal and collective identity. In Yugoslavia, they were no longer "new Socialist men and women" or the citizens of a maverick nonaligned country that was inextricably linked with the name of Tito as soon as someone mentioned Yugoslavia. If they weren't that, what were they?

The great transformation from Communism to post-Communism in the late 1980s and early 1990s was the first revolution that looked sideways and backward instead of forward. Sideways, it looked to the West, where most people seemed to live in freedom with a high living standard, and Yugoslavs associated this with the fruits of democracy. People were less interested in democracy per se than in the consumer products that seemed to be available in abundance. They knew that democracy provides greater personal rights such as free travel, free press, and choice of political parties, but it is questionable whether they were socially prepared for the compromises and the wheeling and dealing associated with democratic governance. Yes, they wanted democracy, but they didn't know what it was as they had no substantive historical experience with it.

Looking back was easier and more comfortable, as it meant rediscovering a latent identity, namely, who they and their ancestors used to be. Their mythohistory—that is, history not as a critical social science or humanistic study but as a mythical construct of the past that highlighted the glorious moments, even including the national crucibles—focused on their collective ethnic identity. Looking back meant discovering who they were and who were "their own" people upon whom they could rely when troubles came.

The fall of Communism resulted in a quest for identity. Most of the inhabitants of the land of the southern Slavs were Slavic (with significant non-Slavic minorities). In the Middle Ages, prior to conquests by Westerners and Ottoman Turks, there were states (not conterminous) during which one or the other country expanded its borders at the expense of its neighbors. Rising nationalism of the nineteenth and twentieth centuries prodded each nation to restore a "great nation"—Great Bulgaria, Great Macedonia, Great Serbia, Great Croatia, Great Albania, Great Greece, Great Hungary, and so on.[27] However, there was simply not enough land to accommodate all that greatness!

Tito's formula was *bratstvo-jedinstvo* (brotherhood and unity) of nations and the creation of a Socialist identity rather than forging a synthetic Yugoslav nationality. Relatively few declared themselves as being of Yugoslav nationality; mostly it was those who somehow felt they did not clearly fit into the established national categories. When the ardor for Socialism waned in the 1970s and 1980s and then collapsed by the end of the 1980s, the question "If not Socialist, what?" brought the answer "Serb," "Croat," "Slovenian,"

Macedonian," "Albanian," and so on. Those of Muslim heritage in Bosnia who had not yet embraced the word *Bosniak* called themselves "Muslim" (clearly distinguished from Albanian Muslims or Macedonian Muslims or Montenegrin Muslims).

This ethnic stratification inevitably led to rivalry, as each nation felt that its neighbors stood in the way of claiming its rightful place under the sun. Neighboring nations/ethnicities were experienced as a threat. The result was a nationalist flight, "Svoji k svojim" or "Svaki svome" (Each to his own). The herd instinct, which is as powerful among people as it is among animals, signaled that safety could be found among one's own people when one's own identity came under threat.

When the "other" is somehow distinctly different in language, in skin color, or even in hair and eye color, those outward markings may suffice to show who is "mine" and who is "theirs." But, how does one know who is their own and who isn't when people look alike and speak alike? For the major ethnic groups in the former Yugoslavia, one of the few real identity markers was religion, no matter how neglected or repressed it had been. The ethnoreligious identity had rarely been displayed assertively. Hence the role of religion was camouflaged.[28] Religion was rarely a choice, regardless of whether one attended public worship or knew religious teachings, because in the Balkans, as in many other European countries, a collective notion of religion prevails. As an example, a friend, who is a well-known poet in Skopje, Macedonia, once stated, "I am an atheist but I am a Macedonian Orthodox atheist." The same is true of innumerable people to whom religion hadn't played a very important role until the 1980s and then suddenly became cognizant of this formerly implicit identity. Now, when they became threatened, particularly if they might be killed on account of this identity, many people (for instance Ratko Mladić) embraced it explicitly and even aggressively, using religious symbolism in their acts of violence against those not of their own ethnoreligious identity.

This led to a more rapid restoration of religion to public prominence after years of Communist oppression and decline. The by and large unsophisticated religious leaders almost instinctively resorted to the age-old claim to be defenders of the nation. Enough people accepted those claims. This probably would not have sufficed had not the more experienced and clever political leaders realized that they could manipulate both the leaders and the religious populace for their own aims. Some of the leaders were particularly brazen in this process (e.g., the aforementioned Radovan Karadžić), some were genuine in their religious stance (e.g., Alia Izetbegović), and some did not resort to make-believe religiosity of their own (e.g., Slobodan Milošević). As Ambassador Jakob Finci, the leader of the Jewish community of Bosnia stated, a confusion of competencies between religious leaders and politicians gradually took place. Religious leaders became spokesmen for their ethnoreligious group while politicians preached lofty ideas. Many religious leaders distinguished themselves as becoming vociferous advocates in defense of "their people" within their "historic" hearths (hardly anyone uses hearths any longer, but hearths are ever present in political and religious discourse!) rather than just members of their religious institution.[29] Politicians, on the other hand, preach about peace, progress, and recently, even dialogue.

The reasons for the outbreak of the wars in the former Yugoslavia are very complex, and "a well-developed appreciation for nuance would generally reject an either/or approach, which in itself denies ambiguity and complexity."[30] Additionally, the causes of these wars were contemporary economic, social, religious, and political *as well as* ancient hatreds. Reluctantly, I concluded in 1993, in spite of my pacifist convictions, that military intervention was necessary to stop the carnage and might coerce the combatants to negotiate not just a fake cease-fire, of which there were many, but a genuine halt to the war in Bosnia, which did take place in the form of the Dayton Agreement in November 1995.

The wars of the 1990s were rife with ambiguities and ironies. One need almost always say, "On one side this, but on the other side that." Usually, those who believe there is no clear-cut right and wrong side in these wars are accused of moral relativism. The reader should be forewarned that some of the events and many, if not most, of the numbers of killed, wounded, and raped are imprecise and highly contentious. The numbers are provided in this book as a signpost regarding the scale of destruction. However, not only were the estimates often and consciously inflated or covered up but the discrepancies in estimates are astonishingly large. In addition, the losses sustained by one side were sometimes credited to another, thus reversing culpability. Peter Brock, an American journalist, wrote an important though controversial book attempting to unmask the role of propaganda in determining the culprit, assigning the blame, or warping the numbers.[31] He is one of the few Western journalists convinced that the Serbs were disproportionately maligned while the Croats and Bosniaks were mistakenly cast in the role of victims. He blames "pack journalism" and the lack of objectivity for misleading Western public opinion into making the Serbs scapegoats for the wars and becoming conduits for the Bosniak and Croat propaganda.

Despite ambiguities, I contend that it is still possible to adjudicate blame and responsibility, but not in a definitive manner. To paraphrase Reinhold Niebuhr, even though all had sinned, not all are equally guilty! In the chapters that follow, I shall try to be nuanced in my assessment of who are the major culprits for the genocides at the end of the twentieth century.

The central concern of the following chapters is whether planned genocides took place (including ethnic cleansing, genocidal rape, and massacres) or whether they were ordinary war crimes that are part of most wars. I start with Croatia, then B&H, followed by Kosovo, and finally Macedonia. As the brief war in Slovenia did not have genocidal characteristics, it will not be covered.

9

War in Croatia

Slobodan Milošević was the first of the Communist politicians to realize that Tito's death had left a leadership vacuum, so in the mid-1980s he attempted to seize power and become Tito's successor. Had he done so sooner, he may have succeeded, but by the mid-1980s, the Communist rulers in the various republics were unwilling to yield their own power bases. Milošević's maneuvers provoked resistance, particularly in Slovenia and Croatia. The more the reawakened Serbian nationalism led by Milošević threatened the nationalist forces in Slovenia and Croatia, the more they distanced themselves from Belgrade and set out on a road that would eventually bring them independence. The Serbs in Croatia vividly remembered what happened to them under the Independent State of Croatia during World War II and responded with understandable concern, especially as Serb politicians and Orthodox churchmen stoked this memory with the dramatic excavations of World War II mass graves during the 1980s. The fact that the right wing of the Croatian nationalists resorted to slogans and images of the Ustaše reinforced the fear.

Of all the areas in Croatia where the Serbs where in majority, the area known as Krajina (former military border region along the Hapsburg and Ottoman empires)—where most of the slaughter of Serbs took place during World War II—naturally felt most threatened. Having a century-old military tradition and having noticed that the Croats had begun a process of replacing ethnic Serb policemen, bureaucrats, and teachers with Croats, the Serbs there decided to resort to preemptive measures.[1] The tensions escalated, increasing the fear as well as the determination of each side not to "lose out." The Krajina Serbs began their "log revolution" in 1990. They barricaded roads with felled trees, logs, and rocks, disrupting traffic and often shooting at Croat trucks and cars. Due to the unusual geographic shape of Croatia, this threatened to cut Croatia in two. As long as the victims could be named, many said it wasn't war yet. The logic of the developments clearly favored an outbreak of war because there were no Vaclav Havels or Mihail Gorbachevs among the Yugoslav leaders who could appeal to higher values or preside over a peaceful breakup.

OVERVIEW OF THE WAR

The war in Croatia lasted from 1991 to 1995, but the last segments of Croat territory in eastern Slavonia were not peacefully returned by Serb rebels until 1998. The Croats named it the Homeland War, while the Serbs called it the War in Croatia. At first, the Serbs of Croatia, with the active assistance of the Yugoslav People's Army (usually abbreviated to JNA for Jugoslavenska Narodna Armija), tried to prevent Croatia's secession. Once secession was declared and given international recognition, the new Croatian government, police, and military, had to fight the Serbs, who started a secession of their own, as they were unwilling to live in this new Croat state. The JNA first claimed that it was merely interjecting itself between the Croats and Serbs, but soon they openly sided with the local Serbs.

On March 16, 1991, Milošević, president of Serbia, declared that Yugoslavia was finished and Serbians would no longer accept decisions of the federal government. The four members of the presidency who represented Serbia, Montenegro, Kosovo, and Vojvodina departed. Violent incidents happened in ethnically mixed areas. In April 1991, Serb irregulars attacked Croat police in eastern Slavonia either on their own initiative or motivated by Milošević. On May 19, 1991, a referendum on independence took place in Croatia (boycotted by the Serbs) and 94.17 percent voted for independence, though an option of remaining in a more confederately arranged Yugoslavia was theoretically left open. On June 25, Croatia declared *razdruženje* (disassociation), namely, breaking the bonds. By this time approximately one-fourth of Croatia was under Serb control. Serbs forces—local, irregulars from Serbia, and the JNA—shelled cities such as Vukovar, Osijek, Dubrovnik, Šibenik, Karlovac, and others. By August it had become a full-scale war.

While the fighting was interconnected, one can discern four distinct areas where military confrontations took place—Krajina and central Dalmatia; western Slavonia; eastern Slavonia, Baranja, and western Srem; and Dubrovnik—as well as the so-called Battle of the Barracks, which took place throughout Croatia. While the Battle of the Barracks was not specifically for territory, it had much to do with the Croats' ability to fight the better armed

Serbs and ultimately win their goal of an independent country. The Yugoslav army was usually stationed in casernes or barracks in most large cities. It had been the aim to make the army a laboratory for interethnic cooperation, so the soldiers were almost always from other parts of Yugoslavia. When the hostilities broke out, Croat police forces carried out coordinated attacks against the JNA barracks, joined spontaneously by the local inhabitants. The army seems to have reacted with restraint, perhaps because it was weakened due to numerous desertions not only by Croats and Slovenes, but by Albanians, Macedonians, and others who were not motivated to fight—it was not their war. The predominantly Serb officer corps and soldiers seemingly preferred to extricate themselves and negotiate a withdrawal (usually to Bosnia or Serbia), and in that process, they surrendered a tremendous arsenal to the Croats.[2] All this took place during a short period of time, from September 14 to 19, 1991. The Croats had previously been successful in smuggling much weaponry from abroad, particularly from Hungary.

The bulk of the fighting in Krajina (consisting of Lika, Banija, and Kordun) was from August to December 1991. Economically speaking, the region was underdeveloped but had a favorable strategic position, dominating the major highways from Zagreb and the north part of the country to the Dalmatian coast. This region had the largest concentration of Serbs, who, with the assistance of the JNA, quickly overran Croat villages and expelled the Croat population by means of terror and threat. Hundreds of Croats were killed in the villages of Dubica, Baćin, Cerovljani, Lipovača, Poljanak, and others. Prolonged imprisonment was the fate of many captured Croats, while others were deported and their villages destroyed, including cultural and religious objects. The JNA prevented the Croatian government from sending forces to assist the local Croats and this region became the "heart" of the Serb autonomous areas in Croatia. There was a clear desire to remain part of the Serb-dominated Yugoslavia, and this region relied heavily on assistance from Belgrade. The presence of the JNA changed the dynamic of an insurrection into a well-organized secessionist movement.

The Battle for Dalmatia in 1991 and 1992 is misnamed, as only parts of Dalmatia were involved. Two coastal cities, Zadar and Šibenik, had a sizable Serbian hinterland. The forces of Krajina Serbs assisted by the JNA were unsuccessful in taking the two cities; nevertheless the Serbs continued to shell these cities for the next 100 days, causing material damage and casualties. The largest Dalmatian port city, Split, was shelled from the sea by the Yugoslav navy, but it did not fall. The three bloodiest events were the battle for the Maslenica bridge near Zadar, the Škabrnja massacre (a village near Zadar where about sixty Croat civilians and soldiers were killed), and the village of Kijevo near Šibenik, a town that had been 99 percent Croat, but which the JNA overran in a two-day assault and ethnically cleansed it. The Serbs were unable to capture any large cities on the coast, though they shelled several cities from their outskirts and caused death and destruction. By December 1991, the UN peacekeepers were inserted between the combatants, the battle lines stabilized, and the hostilities all but stopped. Occasional attacks and counterattacks continued, but now there was international pressure and monitoring. When the Croats led a counterattack at Medak, it caused such an uproar that by 1993, both sides had to lay low. (In the meantime, everyone's attention was on Bosnia, where the war was transferred.) Serbs continued to control the area until August 1995, when they lost it during the Croatian Operation Storm.

The case of Dubrovnik attracted international attention and condemnation. Dubrovnik is located in southernmost Dalmatia near Montenegro and is famous world wide for its well-preserved medieval walled port city, which once was an independent republic in the mold of Venice. Dubrovnik and its environs were attacked by JNA units consisting mostly of Montenegrins. The plunder and destruction of the surrounding area was matched by the shelling of the city (an estimated 1,000 shells hit the city), but the local defenders held their positions. The towns of Konavoski Dvori and Dabova weren't so lucky. There the destruction was total. Serbian and Montenegrin irregulars and Yugoslav army reservists went on a rampage, sparing nothing and no one. Resistance was out of the question; the predominantly Croat population in its entirety fled. Small villages and farms were plundered and everything from television sets to cows and chickens was carried off. The pillaged homes and farms were burned to the ground. Fires were set to fields and orchards, and livestock was killed in huge numbers. "[With] Dubrovnik the Croatian war entered a new stage, for which no rational explanation could be furnished. No apparent political or military gains for Serb forces could be discerned. The destruction of Dubrovnik placed the full irrationality and capriciousness of the fighting in the Balkans before the eyes of the world."[3] The siege of Dubrovnik resulted in a lot of Western sympathy for the Croat cause, as the Serbs presented themselves as utter barbarians.[4]

In western Slavonia, the Serb population lived almost entirely in villages in a fairly underdeveloped region. The Serb territorial paramilitary defense easily established control over these villages. Their leadership was inclined to negotiate with Zagreb and even signed a secret agreement moving toward a peaceful incorporation into an independent Croatia, but this was nixed by the Krajina leadership. In May of 1995, the Croatian army undertook an offensive named Operation Flash that retook western Slavonia, giving the Croats a morale boost, but this was an omen of things to come for the Serbs. The Croat army took 1,500 POWs and in a matter of days, about 30,000 Serbs were forced to flee into Bosnia or Serbia while some 250 Serbs perished. By this time, the Croatian army was far more disciplined and under control, and few reprisals took place.

It appears that the region of eastern Slavonia–Baranja–western Srem (or Srijem) was one of the bloodiest theaters of the war. The fighting began with Serb irregulars ambushing Croat police. It spread like a wildfire with both local populations quickly arming themselves and killing, burning, looting, beating, imprisoning, torturing, and deporting each other. Mass executions took place. One of the defining battles of the war took place over the city of Vukovar. The Croat forces defended Vukovar for eighty-seven days, but then it fell to the Serbs after they had reduced the city to ruins trough the JNA's constant shelling. Serbs carried out massacres of the remaining Croat population, the most deplorable being the Ovčara massacre where over 260 patients of the Vukovar hospital were killed and buried in a mass grave. While the number of the dead and wounded in the battles around Vukovar and its environs (especially Borovo Selo, Dalj, Erdut, Klisa, and Aljmaš) has not been accurately determined, it is claimed that 880 Croat defenders were killed, 770 were wounded, and another 1,000 in the surrounding villages were killed. About 1,500 Serb soldiers and volunteers lost their lives and another 2,500 were wounded. The largest regional city, Osijek, was shelled, allowing the Serb forces to reach the opposite bank of the Drava River, but they would not risk significant losses of their own forces in order to take the city.

Reports of Serb aggression reached the Western public, but very little was heard about the Croat ethnic cleansing.

> The Serb forces behaved according to Tudjman's [the president of Croatia] expectations, to the point of madness. This effectively concealed that Serb towns and villages throughout Croatia were being torched and razed too by the HDZ [Croatian Democratic Union] supporters and other right-wing paratroops; that scores of Serbs were massacred from Gospić, Daruvar, Karlovac, Virovitica, Sisak, Ogulin, and other towns; and that a half million Serb civilians had to abandon their homes to escape Croatian reprisals. . . .
> . . . Milošević indeed made it possible for flagrant human rights violations perpetrated by Tudjman's forces to be disregarded by the international community.[5]

The Serbs had established several autonomous regions—western Slavonia, Serbian Krajina, eastern Slavonia–Baranja–western Srem, and Dubrovnik— which were later consolidated into an internationally unrecognized entity called the Republic of Serbian Krajina. Some of the villages and towns in those areas were inhabited by Serbs, some by Croats, and some by both ethnicities. What ensued were the killings, flight, and deportation of Croats from areas under Serb control and the reverse from areas held by the Croats. The UN and the EU (European Union) politicians attempted to negotiate, as did Milošević and Franjo Tudjman, but negotiations frequently broke down as there was no real readiness for a cease-fire or armistice. More accurately, there was a willingness to *sign* agreements, since as many as twenty armistices were concluded, but not to *adhere* to them. They were signed and then promptly violated, sometimes by Serbs, sometimes by Croats. Finally under U.S. negotiator Cyrus Vance, an armistice cease-fire agreement was reached in November 1992 and then a more permanent armistice in January 1993. The UN armistice created the so-called UNPAs (UN protection areas), which separated the combatants. The UN also imposed an arms embargo, which all entities bypassed with various degrees of success. Gradually, the Western international communities assisted the Croat side, both actively and passively, in two separate attacks, so that by 1995 the Croat army had driven the Serb forces and population from western Croatia (Operation Bljesak [Flash]), and then from Krajina (Operation Oluja [Storm]). The active warfare in Croatia formally ended in August 1995, when the Croat army carried out Operation Oluja at Krajina (Lika, Kordun, and Banija). The assumption had been that the battle over Krajina would be very bloody and long, as both sides were well armed and experienced. Surprisingly, the Serbs were ordered by their command to withdraw, and an enormous exodus took place as approximately 200,000 Serbs left the entire Krajina region on short notice. Only a few people in their eighties and nineties were left behind. There appears to have been some secret agreement between Milošević and Tudjman for this to have been carried out. On the whole, the Croatian forces permitted this exodus; however, there had been shelling and sporadic attacks upon the fleeing Serbs. More atrocious was the behavior of some of the Croatian soldiers, who murdered the remaining old folks, burned and plundered the land, and killed the livestock. This was the single largest ethnic cleansing of the wars of the 1990s. It produced practically no Western outrage and relatively little journalistic and scholarly analysis, as people felt that the Serbs deserved it. By that point in the fighting, Western public opinion held that the Serbs were the perpetrators; so, how could they also be victims? Later some Croatian military commanders were indicted for war crimes (see chapter 13), and the International Criminal Tribunal for the Former Yugoslavia (ICTY) in The Hague was preparing an indictment against Croatia's President Tudjman when he died in 1999.

Only eastern Slavonia–Baranja–and Srem remained under local Serb control. With the urging of the UN, the Croatian government engaged in negotiations rather than armed re-conquest of the Serb-held UNPA. By 1998, Croatia was able to retake control of the entire territory, as most Serbs had departed. For all practical purposes, Croatia was no longer a pluralist society but was ethnically clean. It was independent, was recognized by the international community, joined the EU and NATO, and after Tudjman's death, became democratic in fact and not only in name. It reluctantly delivered some of the indicted generals to The Hague and carried out some war crime trials against Serbs and Croats. Even though Croatia's accession to the EU is conditioned on its prompt judicial dealing with war criminals, late in 2010 Amnesty International accused Croatia of delaying the prosecution of war crimes and of showing partiality by investigating fewer Croat than Serb perpetrators.[6] A very limited number of Serbs were allowed to return to their ancient homelands; however, few young people dared to accept this offer. The young men in particular worried that they might be accused of war crimes or treason and were afraid to visit or to resettle.

WAS IT GENOCIDE AND/OR ETHNIC CLEANSING?

The war in Croatia was preceded by the fear of genocide, more by the minority Serbs than by the majority Croats. The Serbian Orthodox Church had already claimed that in Kosovo, the Albanians carried out genocide (see chapter 12). This was followed, as stated previously, by a sharp rise in Croatian-Serbian conflict as each side did politically everything to rally their populace, including manipulatively appealing to ethnoreligiosity. Milošević emphasized the injustice done to the Serbs, real and imagined, to stir up emotions and linkages to the genocides of World War II. Granted, he exaggerated the threat and injustices, but where there is smoke, there is also fire. The claim of an impending genocide undergirded Milošević's strategy, and Tudjman complied by promoting policies that really did threaten Croatia's Serbs. Tudjman and Milošević were the "couple from hell," as they reinforced each other, since the policies of one worked to the advantage of the sinister policies of the other. They helped each other achieve their initial goals; for Tudjman, the international recognition of Croatia's independence regardless of cost, and for Milošević, battlefield victories in pursuit of expanding Serbia to incorporate all territories inhabited by Serbs. It is very likely that had different men been at the helm of these two states, war may have been avoided and thousands of lives may have been saved.

First there was a threat of genocide that caused real widespread fear among Serbs outside of Serbia and a feeling of solidarity among Serbia's Serbs. This fear was based on collective memory of the Ustaša genocides and was reinforced by a resurgence of policies resembling those promoted by the Ustaše. Then ethnic cleansing and perhaps genocide occurred, first primarily carried out by Serbs against Croats and then carried out by Croats against Serbs.

Croat genocide deniers, who appeared prior to the war—similar to Holocaust deniers—tried to refute or minimize the Jasenovac and other genocides. They called these massacres a Serbian anti-Croat myth. Most prominent of these deniers was Tudjman himself, who wrote a book between 1983 and 1987 called *Bespuća povijense zbiljnosti: Rasprava o povijesti i filozofiji zlosilja* (Wastelands of Historical Reality: Discussion on History and Philosophy of Aggressive Violence).[7] In it, this former general turned historian turned nationalist politician, claimed that only about 20,000 Serbs were killed in Jasenovac, contradicting the traditional estimate of 600,000. Prior to writing the book, Tudjman raised the anxiety of Serbs through his policies of reconciliation with the former Ustaše and Domobran and the fact that he permitted the reprinting of some writings of former leaders of the NDH (Nezavisna Država Hrvatska), such as Ante Pavelić. Tudjman's political party, Hrvatska Demokratska Zajednica (HDZ, or Croatian Democratic Union) united the vast majority of Croats and became the overwhelming tool for toppling the monopoly of the Communist Party. On July 25, 1990, under Tudjman's leadership, the Croatian parliament, Sabor, passed amendments to the constitution that promoted disengagement from Yugoslavia, adopted a Croatian flag that resembled the Ustaše's flag, changed the currency from *dinar* to *kuna* (again a return to World War II usage), declared the Serbian language and script no longer co-equal to the Croat language, and declared Serbs as a national minority rather than a part of the constitutive nation of Croatia. In other words, he declared Croatia to be the state of ethnic Croats! To many Croats, these were the natural affirmations of the distinctiveness of Croatia's traditions and identity. To Serbs, it was a threat to replay Ustaša genocides.

A rapid formation of a Croat army and police force followed, which was armed by secret purchases of weapons from the arsenals of former Eastern European satellite nations and some African states. Serbs were being sacked from their jobs not only in the police force, where they were overrepresented, but also as teachers, nurses and doctors, journalists, and secretaries. Vandalism by Croatian extremists against all things Serb ensued, including cars (even those of Serbian tourists on the Dalmatian coast) and homes. Anti-Serb graffiti escalated the tensions. Croat paramilitary groups were being formed and used kidnapped Serbs to train themselves in throat cutting.[8] In an alarming fashion, the Serbian TV stations and newspapers presented these incidents, forewarning genocide daily.

Serbs in Croatia and in Serbia responded vigorously. To them it was logical that if Croatians wanted to depart from Yugoslavia, they could not take the areas in which Serbs constituted the population majority with them.[9] The Krajina Serbs revolted angrily and impulsively, as they had a military tradition—nurtured by their conflicts with the Turks and the Hapsburgs—that conflicted with those of the Croats living around them. In August of 1990, the Serbs set up roadblocks around Knin, thus tying up a crucial strategic railroad juncture. Milan Martić, soon to become the official leader of the Krajina Serbs, organized Serb paramilitary groups named Martićevci. These groups began terrorizing not only non-Serbs from the vicinity but also Serbs who were known to favor cooperation with the Croats. These bands were joined by irregulars from Serbia who were led by Željko Ražnjatovic-Arkan and Vojislav Šešelj. They incited the troops with considerable ultranationalist propaganda, seemingly motivated by the desire to loot—which they did rather thoroughly in Croat villages.[10]

Much of the killing and destruction took place in the process of Yugoslavia's disintegration. The fighting had characteristics of both a civil war and a war of aggression, the latter of which was triggered by Croatia's international recognition as an independent country. The basic question was, if Croatia has the right to secede from Yugoslavia, do predominantly Serb regions of Croatia have the right to secede from Croatia? Could they either annex themselves to rump Yugoslavia (that is, other Serbian lands) or become an independent mini-state, Republika Srpska Krajina? Was there a process whereby the Serbs could extricate themselves from Croatia? No such process was initiated by bona fide negotiations or other nonviolent means, and therefore Serbs and Croats ended up killing each other. The fighting was so vicious that many units, especially the paramilitaries, were clearly guilty of murder; war crimes; crimes against humanity; persecution on political, racial, and religious grounds; violations of the laws and customs of war; breaches of the Geneva Convention of 1949; and unlawful confinement, imprisonment, torture, and inhumane acts—as the many indictments of the ICTY exemplified.

Some of the indictments specified the charge as extermination or, more rarely, genocide. Ethnic cleansing was in many instances not merely carried out but the declared intention of the commanders and the combatants. Sometimes neighbor killed neighbor; sometimes murder occurred within mixed marriages. On the Serb side, people either volunteered or were quasi-conscripted from the Serb population of Croatia, as well as from Serbia proper and Vojvodina. Particularly vicious were Arkan's Tigers, Šešelj's White Eagle Četniks, the volunteer battalion Dušan Silni, and the Martićevci organized by Milan Martić (who became minister of the interior and then prime minister of Krajina). They all engaged in orgies of murder, torture, and other indignities. These units were imbued with hatred and extreme Serb nationalism, but a powerful motive was enrichment; everything that could be moved—TVs and other electronic equipment, cars, tractors, livestock, jewelry, foreign hard currency, even window frames—was trucked to Serbia. Captured Croats were offered to members of their family for huge ransom, and if the family was unable to raise the money, the captive was killed.[11]

Croats also committed war crimes of various sorts, but for a long time the Croat press argued that since they were defending themselves against aggression, their actions were not morally or legally equivalent to the aggressor's. Yet Ante Gotovina, Janko Bobetko, Rahim Ademi, and Mirko Norac were indicted at the ICTY in The Hague. Many Croats argued that one cannot commit war crimes and crimes against humanity when one defends one's country from foreign aggression, but this argument has not been accepted by international jurists working for the ICTY.

Many international journalists wrote or filmed their war reports.[12] Domestic and foreign scholars provided analyses of war criminals and genocidaires, but for our purposes, here is a list of indictments against war criminals who survived to be tried (Arkan was assassinated in Belgrade prior to arrest).

Serbs in Croatia who had been indicted by ICTY for genocides, extermination, crimes against humanity, war crimes, grave breaches of the 1948 Geneva Convention, violations of laws and customs of war, and so on were as follows:

Slobodan Milošević, various posts as the supreme leader of Serbs. Trial lasted four years in which he defended himself. Died on March 11, 2006, during his trial in The Hague, shortly before sentencing was to take place.

Vojislav Šešelj, self-appointed leader of the modern-day Četniks, especially the "White Eagles"; head of the Radical Party; and deputy in the Serbian Parliament. Surrendered on February 24, 2003. Indicted on charges of crimes against humanity and joint criminal enterprise for activities in Vukovar and eastern Slavonia. ICTY trial in process at the time of writing.

Milan Babić, first president of the Krajina autonomous region in Knin. Pleaded guilty and was given thirteen years. Committed suicide in his prison cell at The Hague in 2006.

Milan Martić, minister of defense and the prime minister/president of the Republic of Serb Krajina, leader of the Martićevci irregulars and police. Indicted for crimes against humanity, violation of the laws and customs of war, persecutions, murder, torture, deportation, attacks on civilians, and wanton destruction of civilian areas. Participant in criminal enterprise to forcibly remove non-Serb population in order to create a unified Serb held-area; virtually all Croats and other non-Serbs were expelled in areas under his control.[13] Sentenced to thirty-nine years.

Željko Ražnjatović-Arkan, professional criminal, self-appointed leader of the paramilitary gang Serbian Volunteer Guard, named Arkan's Tigers. Indicted by ICTY for crimes against humanity in Knin, Erdut, Vukovar, eastern Slavonia, as well as in many locations in Bosnia. Assassinated in Belgrade in 2000 prior to his arrest.

Goran Hadžić, leader of the Serb autonomous region of eastern Slavonia, Baranja, and western Srijem. Indicted but was a fugitive until his capture on July 20, 2011.

Slavko Dokmanović, former mayor of Vukovar municipality. Accused of aiding and abetting the hospital massacre in Vukovar. Indicted and tried in The Hague but committed suicide (or was murdered) just prior to his sentencing in 1998.

Mile Mrkšić, general. Tried for not preventing the Vukovar hospital massacre. Sentenced to twenty years.

Miroslav Radić, general. Tried for not preventing the Vukovar hospital massacre. Sentenced to twenty years.

Veselin Šljivančanin, major of JNA, directly in charge of the Ovčara (near Vukovar) massacre of Croats. Sentenced after appeal to ten years for his role in the Vukovar massacre.

Croats who were indicted by ICTY were as follows:

Rahim Ademi, ethnic Albanian officer in the Croatian army. Charged with war crimes at the Medak Pocket. Released from The Hague to be tried in Croatia. Acquitted and released in 2008.

Janko Bobetko, the most senior Croatian general. Indicted for war crimes at the Medak Pocket. Died at the age of eighty-four before he could be surrendered to ICTY.

Ante Gotovina, general. Indicted in 2001 for responsibility for crimes in connection to Operation Storm; in hiding for many years with the active assistance of the Croatian government and immigrant community. Arrested in Spain in 2005. Trial was to begin in May 2007 but was postponed until March 2008. On April 15, 2011, sentenced to twenty-four years for war crimes and crimes against humanity. Sentence evoked mass protests of Croats and will be appealed.

Ivan Čermak, general. Case is conjoined with Ante Gotovina's on same charges. Acquitted on April 15, 2011.

Mladen Markač, general. Case is conjoined with Ante Gotovina's on same charges.[14] Sentenced to eighteen years for being part of a criminal enterprise to remove Serbs from the Krajina during Operation Storm.

Looking at the entire picture, a total of about 10,000 to 15,000 were killed[15] and, of course, many more were wounded and about 200,000 were displaced. The Croat losses were greater than the Serb's. Serb extremists committed more war crimes and crimes against humanity. The Croat extremists, as they were defending the territorial integrity of their new state, also committed war crimes and crimes against humanity. Both sides emptied many villages and drove out the enemy's population from various areas in the hope of establishing ethnically pure areas where they would not need to contend with the other. Both Serbs and Croatians carried out ethnic cleansing in a variety of areas of Croatia. Both sides charged the other with genocide. My conclusion is that they were mutual borderline genocides.

During Operation Storm at the end of the war, the Croatian government forces drove out nearly the entire Serb population of Croatia, numbering between 200,000 and 300,000. This effort was led by nationalist leaders and with the apparent complicity of the international community (in particular the United States, which provided military intelligence and know-how and facilitated the arming of Croats despite an official embargo). Fewer Serbs remained in Croatia after 1995 than after 1942. There were no longer significant communities, but only individual Serbs remained. When such a large community (about 12–15 percent of Croatia's population) is completely expelled from a country, even if not accompanied by a massive bloodbath—it is genocide. Tudjman and a few of his associates did not live long enough to be tried for genocide at the ICTY, although an indictment was being prepared.

Only in the last few years, Croatia started practicing real democracy, and steps are being made to rectify past genocide. In July 2010 the newly elected Croatian prime minister, Ivo Josipović, accompanied the Israeli president, Shimon Peres, to the Jasenovac camp site to honor the victims, expressing satisfaction that they could join together in bowing to the victims in an action of facing their past.[16] One hopes that it will take less than sixty-five years for Serbs and Croats to issue official apologies and pay respects to the victims of the wars of 1990s so that real reconciliation can take place. Serbian president Borislav Tadić, accompanied by Croatian president Ivo Josipović, already issued such apologies in person and condemned Serb wartime atrocities by going to Vukovar, to the Ovčara site of a mass grave.[17] These two men represent the democratic wing of their respective nations that has to contend with opposition by the nationalist elements in their countries. If the democratic wing can persuade the majorities in their countries that reconciliation is possible through apologies and dialogue, these two nations may avoid in the twenty-first century the cataclysms of the twentieth.

10

War in Bosnia and Herzegovina

Many Western observers and scholars maintain that the nationalities of Bosnia and Herzegovina (B&H) lived harmoniously and in peace until modern politicians, particularly Serb leaders such as Slobodan Milošević, Radovan Karadžić, and General Ratko Mladić, initiated a war of aggression. This assertion does not correspond to historical reality. As Aleksa Djilas writes, "Bosnia's history shows that although all three main groups have traditions of tolerance, extremism dominated in unstable periods. Tolerance, such as there was, was often the result of rule by a foreign power, which forcefully prevented groups from fighting each other."[1]

PROBLEMS LEADING TO THE WAR

During the 1990s, many people in the federal Yugoslav Republic of Bosnia and Herzegovina expected that they would avoid the war that raged in Croatia because people of all nationalities and religions lived more or less harmoniously with each other. Yet logically they could not have avoided the war. If the various ethnic groups in all of Yugoslavia were unable to resolve the contentious issues, why would this state—the most multiethnic and multireligious of all—escape the fate of others whose composition was seemingly simpler? Looking at an ethnographic map of B&H and seeing how intermingled the population was, it is clear that one could not separate the population by ethnoreligiosity without a war. Those who did hope, no matter how well meaning they might have been, lived in an illusion. If Serbs and Croats were unwilling to live peacefully next to each other in Croatia, why would they be willing to do so in B&H, where the composition of the population was 44 percent Muslims/Bosniaks, 33 percent Serbs, 18 percent Croats, and 5 percent Yugoslavs and others (mostly Muslims or mixed marriages)?

Although the war in Croatia started almost a year earlier, its development made war in B&H inevitable because the Croatian and Serbian authoritarian regimes engaged in criminal wartime activities and appealed to their sizable ethnic "sibling" communities in B&H. Both Franjo Tudjman and Milošević had designs on incorporating either all of B&H or at least their own ethnic communities into their statehood projects. Neither leader wanted B&H to survive. As early as March 1990, Tudjman and Milošević met secretly in Karadjordjevo to carve up B&H between themselves, leaving Alija Izetbegović, the leader of Bosniaks (Muslims)[2] and B&H's actual president, two equally bad options: either to be part of Milošević's rump Yugoslavia or to declare independence like Croatia, the result of which would inevitably be war. The "couple from hell" became a deadly trio, which was dangerous to the well-being of Bosnia, although Izetbegović was not nearly as sinister as the other two. The situation was greatly aggravated by the activities of local nationalist leaders (Karadžić stands out as the most extreme) who galvanized their respective groups into extreme chauvinism. In their milder forms, the national ideologies could have expressed the legitimate national aspirations of Serbs, Croats, and Bosniaks, but under the circumstances of a failing federation (which in reality functioned as a unitary Communist state as long as Josip Broz Tito was the unquestioned boss), the process developed into a vicious type of chauvinistic nationalism, which in turn led to ethnic cleansing, genocide, and ethnic war by each ethnoreligious group in order to prevent becoming an oppressed minority living in a state controlled by a rival nationality. This deadly conflict of ideologies caused a tragedy of epic proportions.

Seeing that Yugoslavia was disintegrating, each of the three ethnoreligious nationalisms had their own goals in B&H. Serbs claimed they had been threatened and victimized by the other two and therefore it was imperative to assure that all Serbs lived in one Serbian state. In Bosnia, this ideology was embodied by both Milošević and Karadžić. Their determination, combined with superior military strength, caused the greatest amount of human and material damage as they sought to take over a maximal amount of territory (they aimed for all of B&H and actually occupied as much as 70 percent of it at one point). All parties contributed to the carnage, but Serb armies and irregulars, which included Montenegrins (Montenegrins and Serbs were in the same state structure and largely identified themselves with the Serb cause), acted the most aggressively and mercilessly and inflicted the most horrendous damage in lives and property. They resurrected the Četnik movement's ideology, insignia, and tactics.

The Croat ideology, embodied in Tudjman, propagated the opposite goal. His strategy was to break away from the union with the Serbs and claim all of B&H or at least a sizable part of it, in order to annex it to Croatia. In the end, the Croats created a separate Croat-dominated entity of B&H called Herzeg-Bosna. They cooperated with Muslims as a tactic to fight the Serbs, but soon carried out their own vicious ethnic cleansing and genocidal massacres. Similar to the Serbs, the Croats resurrected many of the Ustaše symbols and methods. Both Serbs and Croats showed clear throwbacks to the conflict of World War II.

Whether or not the Muslim/Bosniak ideology sought to numerically dominate B&H and impose its own rule over the others (as their enemies maintained and as implied in Izetbegović's "Islamic Declaration") is a matter of debate. A clear answer to that is unlikely to surface. The Serbs and Croats aimed to partition the B&H state, and knowing just how intermixed the population was, the Muslim Bosniaks knew that if they did not strengthen their Muslim identity, they would either disappear or be reduced to insignificance. For Bosniaks, protecting the unity and independence of B&H was their means of survival. In 1993 during a very bleak period of the war, Izetbegović temporarily agreed to a partition of Bosnia that would have given them a small part—about 20 percent—of the state, but this would have been tantamount to losing the war. Under the great stress of being ethnically cleansed, many parts of B&H demonstrated an increasingly hard-line Islamic core, some of them becoming jihadist. Foreign mujahedeen were gladly welcomed to fight for the Muslim cause, and these militants strengthened the Islamic ideology among many Bosniaks. Paradoxically, Izetbegović was simultaneously the symbol of both the cooperative and flexible part of Muslim strategy and the more clearly ethnoreligious alternative for Bosniaks, who were backing away from their predominantly secular lifestyle to a more assertive Muslim identity.

The advent of the multiparty system spelled disaster for B&H. The three major parties defined themselves primarily by their ethnoreligious following: the *Croatian* Democratic Union (a spin-off of Tudjman's party in Croatia), the *Serbian* Democratic Party (as with the Croatian party, it was "democratic" in name only), and the Party for Democratic Action (without explicitly referring to the word *Muslim*, it was nevertheless clearly recognized as the party of Muslims). There were other parties with more inclusive platforms but, unfortunately, the population rallied around these three as people sought security among their compatriots and simultaneously instilled fear among other ethnoreligious communities. This development was foreseeable; in the transition to democracy, the establishment of each party with a predominantly ethnic component (as the Nazi Party was in Germany) should have been proscribed. Multiparty elections in and of themselves are *not* a prelude to democracy, but on the contrary, they are a prelude to civil strife that frequently leads to war. This surely was the case in B&H and also in Kosovo and Macedonia.

All three ethnoreligious communities prepared for war,[3] but the Muslims were the least well prepared. The war formally commenced on April 6, 1992, with the official recognition of the state's independence from Yugoslavia. The Muslims and Croats consented overwhelmingly by a referendum (February 1992), with the Serbs boycotting the vote. Serbs had earlier voted in a plebiscite (November 9–10, 1991) in which only Serbs participated. They decided overwhelmingly that they would prefer being in Yugoslavia along with all other Serbs, rather than being a minority in B&H. Karadžić, the Montenegrin psychiatrist, poet, and politician who became the undisputed leader of the Bosnian Serbs, threatened misery for Muslims if B&H opted to secede: "The Muslims had started down the path that led Croatia to hell, except the hell in Bosnia-Herzegovina will be one hundred times worse and will bring the disappearance of the Muslim nation."[4]

In an increasing hostile atmosphere, the violence started while parliamentary and political wrangling was still taking place. It began in Mostar, the main city of Herzegovina, in the fall of 1991. The Croats and Muslims of Mostar were, roughly speaking, equally numerous and the Serbs were a large minority. The fighting first broke out between Croats and Serbs and lasted for months, as these two ethnic groups were more ready for war. The Muslims were still hoping that the war would somehow bypass them as they were the least ready to fight.

Across the Sava River from Slavonski Brod in Bosanski Brod, fighting began in the spring of 1992. Bosanska Krajina, the area of northwest Bosnia with the largest city of Banja Luka, proclaimed Serb autonomy in the fall of 1991. This is the process that would eventually bring about the creation of the Republika Srpska (Serbian Republic). The JNA (Jugoslavenska Narodna Armija, or the Yugoslav People's Army) moved heavy artillery to the mountains on the outskirts of Sarajevo, having convinced Izetbegović that they were there to protect the city, when in fact they were preparing to lay siege to the capital. The siege lasted nearly four years. Most of the citizens of the cosmopolitan capital, Sarajevo, demonstrated peacefully in the streets, valiantly attempting to declare that they intended to live in unity and peace, only to be shot at by Serb extremists. Even though Sarajevo was targeted day and night by heavy artillery and snipers, many Serbs decided to stay in the city and share the awful destiny with their Muslim and Croat neighbors.

The local Serbs, with the assistance of the JNA, were militarily superior and by far the best prepared. A number of paramilitary bands—Arkan's Tigrovi (Tigers), Šešelj's Beli Orlovi (White Eagles), Red Berets[5] (crack forces of the Serbian Ministry of Interior)—crossed into Bosnia from Serbia and sowed terror with their unchecked cruelty toward the non-Serb population and those local Serbs who were for interethnic cooperation. Many irregular paramilitary bands were locals from Bosnia, such as the Osvetnici (Avengers) of Milan Lukić, the Srpska Dobrovoljačka Garda (Serbian Volunteer Guard), and the Žute Ose (Yellow Wasps) led by Dušan Vučković. They carried out atrocities in eastern Bosnia and elsewhere, committing monstrous war crimes that gave all Serbs a horrendous reputation. The Serb intention was to carve out a contiguous area that would either be united with Serbia or become an independent state. At the outbreak of the war, they sought to take over Bijeljina, Zvornik, Bratunac, Srebrenica, Žepa, Rogatica, Višegrad, Goražde, and Foča, all situated on the Drina River along the state line with Serbia.[6] There was no regard for the Muslim civilians living in these cities; they were murdered or deported if they did not flee. Fear that plans were being made to exterminate them had been spread in all communities. Weapons dealers did brisk business. First they convinced Serbs in one village that the Muslims in the next village were planning to attack. Having done a good business there, the dealers would visit the Muslim village the next day, saying that the Serbs had armed themselves and they better purchase weapons or else they would perish.

The most confusing element of the war in B&H is that it became an all-out war of everyone against everyone else, but it was mostly a three-way ethnic war between Serbs, Muslims, and the fairly well-prepared Croats, who had anticipated the outbreak of the war. The Serbs were the strongest and most brutal in exterminating their rivals; they soon had control of two-thirds of the land. The Muslims were handicapped by lack of preparation. They had hoped, as in the past, to appraise whether the Serbs or Croats would prevail and then side with the prospective winner. But the Serbs prevented this from taking place. They had an unrelenting belief that the Muslims were fundamentalists who planned to take over not only B&H but also the rest of the Balkans, exterminating the Serbs in the process. The Serbs were not going to allow this.

Milošević and Tudjman conducted the war from outside the combat zone, but they had their eager semiautonomous collaborators. On the Serb side, these leaders were Karadžić, General Mladić, Biljana Plavšić, Momčilo Krajišnik, and Nikola Koljević, and they were assisted from Serbia by Željko Ražnjatović-Arkan and Vojislav Šešelj with their bloodthirsty irregulars. Their aim was, as stated earlier, to conquer the entire territory of B&H and annex it to rump Yugoslavia. If that wasn't practical, they planned to take as much territory as possible, make it homogenously Serb, proclaim that they were unwilling to live in the same state with their enemies, and thus create their own state. The headquarters of this quasi-state was Pale, a suburb of Sarajevo, but eventually Banja Luka, a large city in the northwest became the administrative seat of the government of Republika Srpska.[7]

The Croats also aspired to control B&H. Some had declared that the border of Croatia was the Drina River, which demarcates the border with Serbia. The Croat plan would mean the end of Bosnian statehood. The largest number of Croats lived in Herzegovina. In 1992, Mate Boban, a Croat supermarket clerk turned politician, proclaimed an autonomous "Herzeg-Bosna" entity with Mostar as its center. As a result, the Croat forces, particularly the pro-Fascist and pro-Ustaša HVO (Hrvatsko Vijeće Obrane, or Croatian Defense Council), attempted to get rid of the Serbs and Muslims in the area. Many units of HVO wore Ustaša insignia and saluted with "Heil Hitler" and "Za dom—spremni" (for the homeland—ready)—all symbols of Ante Pavelić, who had been a Herzegovinian native.[8] In addition to HVO, there were also black-shirted soldiers wearing insignia of HOS (Hrvatske Obranbene Snage, or Croatian Defense Forces). These were the military units of the right-wing Croatian Party of Right.[9] Interestingly, they did not seek to partition B&H but fought for an undivided B&H with the ultimate hope of annexing the entire state to Croatia. Still other irregular bands were named Crna Legija (Black Legion), Jastrebovi (Falcons), Yellow Ants, and so forth. Among the most prominent Croat political and military leaders were Dario Kordić, Jadranko Prlić, and General Tihomir Blaškić. The HVO and Croat Territorial Defense Forces carried out war crimes and ethnic cleansing against both Serbs and Muslims. At first many Muslims who were savagely attacked by Serbs joined the Croat forces, but seeing that Croats had separatist aims, they then joined the Bosnian army under Izetbegović's control, which was multiethnic but predominantly Muslim. The Muslims were unwilling to be driven out of Mostar as they had been driven out of Gacko and several other Herzegovinian cities (while the Serbs took Trebinje), and by 1993, the erstwhile allies became enemies. Croats had carried out ethnic cleansing of the Neretva Valley.[10] Mostar became a divided city with the eastern shore of the Neretva River being Muslim controlled and the western part, Croat. A vicious long-lasting armed conflict destroyed much of this ancient city, with the Croats inflicting greater damage, destroying much of eastern Mostar, including the famous sixteenth-century bridge by which the city got its name. The city was still factually divided by the end of the first decade of the twenty-first century, despite the formal ending of the war.

Under pressure from President Bill Clinton, the war between the Muslims and Croats ended in 1993 and a Muslim-Croat Federation was forced upon unwilling rivals, so that they could be a counter-force to the Republika Srpska. They figured that only if these two forces collaborated, was there a chance that the Serbs could be defeated or forced to negotiate seriously. Yet from time to time, Serbs and Croats cooperated against the Muslims; Karadžić and Boban met in May 1992 in Graz, Austria, and signed a document to partition B&H, but that plan fell through.[11]

The Western press rarely reported Bosniak/Muslim, that is, Bosnian army war crimes and ethnic cleansing or even successes of the Army of B&H until late in the war. That was either because Westerners were not in that part of the country or because they pictured the Muslims as victims and the Serbs as perpetrators; Muslim victories were inconsistent with this image. Some Muslims engaged in unspeakable atrocities and some journalists thought that to report on these would be an expression of moral equivalencies, figuring that the Muslims (similar to the Croatians) were waging a defensive war. The best known and most feared by their enemies were the Green Berets (led by Jusuf Juka Prazina[12] and Ismet Bajramović-Ćelo[13]). The Green Berets consisted predominantly of about 35,000–40,000 religiously dedicated Muslims, organized as early as the fall of 1991.[14] In their ranks were Bosniaks with extremist Islamist leanings, as well as mujahideens from various Muslim countries who were dreaded because of their fanatical destructiveness. The Patriotska Liga (Patriotic League), the Seventeenth Krajina Brigade under Fikret Ćuskić, and the Crni Labudovi (Black Swans) from Kakanj were other Bosniak paramilitary units. The forces under the command of Naser Orić destroyed about fifty Serb villages near Srebrenica, where they carried out massacres and expelled thousands of Serbs from their homes,[15] all done from the "safe haven" Srebrenica, that was supposed to have been disarmed. This took place prior to General Mladić's mass murder of about 8,000 Muslim men who were captured when Srebrenica was overrun by Mladić's forces in summer 1995. Mladić's forces carried out the largest mass murder after World War II. The ICTY (International Criminal Tribunal for the Former Yugoslavia) released Orić for inadequate legal proof, but Dutch researchers and filmed evidence attest to his prior systematic killing of all Serbs he could lay hands on.[16]

MAJOR EVENTS OF THE WAR

Since the details of the war in B&H have been described in numerous reports, articles, and books, I provide only a short overview here. The course of the war is hard to describe. There was no single front, and many events overlapped or occurred simultaneously. Alliances changed; ethnic groups that had been allied sometimes turned against each other (e.g., Bosniaks and Croats) or vice versa (e.g., Serbs had fought Croats but occasionally assisted them in their war against the Bosniaks or supplied weapons to Bosniaks to help them fight the Croats more effectively). There were also intraethnic battles such as the HVO against the HOS or the Fifth Army of B&H against Fikret Abdić's Bosniaks in Bihać, who were willing to cooperate with both Serbs and Croats. Each of the three major ethnic groups had numerous paramilitary allies who sometimes acted independently and at other times placed themselves under unified command. Add into this mix the various international players, such as the negotiators on behalf of the UN and European community (Peter Carrington, Jose Castileiro, Cyrus Vance, David Owen, and Thorvald Stoltenberg) as well as the international military forces sent by the UN. Add the foreign volunteers (Russians and Greeks fighting on the Serb side; Germans, Austrians, and Western mercenaries fighting for the Croatians; and Iranian Revolutionary Guards and various Muslim mujahideens on the Bosniak side), and one gets a mild sense of the chaotic developments in B&H between 1992 and 1995.

On September 25, 1991, the UN Security Council passed Resolution 713 placing an arms embargo on all Yugoslavian territory. This had minimal impact on the Serbs, as they inherited the JNA's arsenal. The Croats successfully bought arms on the black market and smuggled them in. Initially, the Army of B&H was most negatively affected by the embargo, and Muslims pleaded that they should at least have weapons to fight back if they were attacked and threatened by extinction. Eventually, Muslim countries, with implicit U.S. consent, successfully smuggled in enough weapons to give the Army of B&H fighting capacity.

On October 21, 1991, the Serb deputies, having left the parliament of B&H, created the Assembly of Serb People of B&H and then on January 9, 1992, renamed it the Republika Srpska B&H. On November 18, 1991, the Croats made their move and established the Croatian Republic of Herzeg-Bosna. On April 6, 1992, Western countries recognized B&H's independence and the shooting in Sarajevo began. The first person to be killed in Sarajevo was a Serb.

In May 1992, mortar shells landed in Sarajevo killing sixteen people in a bread line. Shelling and sniper killings of Sarajevo civilians continued persistently. In the summer of 1992, after numerous Serb military victories leading to the takeover of about two-thirds of the country, Serbs began their massive ethnic cleansing of non-Serbs throughout B&H. Their activities included massacres, rapes, torture, and deportations to concentration camps and persisted into the fall and winter.

During the winter 1993, Serbs blockaded food and fuel; the UN declared "safe havens" but did not provide sufficient protection for them. International negotiators Vance and Owen proposed a plan for a cease-fire, but as with many other previous cease-fires, this one was accepted by both Milošević and Karadžić and rejected by the Republika Srpska parliament.

In the fall of 1993, the Army of B&H (three-fourth Muslims and one-fourth Croats and Serbs) started making advances against the Croats. There were reports of regular army units from Croatia and Serbia fighting in the war.

On February 4, 1994, the market-place massacre in Sarajevo by a mortar shell provoked massive revulsion in world public opinion. The government of B&H blamed the Serbs, who, in turn accused Muslims of inflicting it themselves for propaganda purposes. Sixty-eight died and 200 were wounded. In March 1994, President Clinton coerced both parties to end the Croat-Bosniak war and join together in a federation against the Serbs, with the intention of providing secret arms and tactical support.

During the summer of 1994, the Bosnian army had some success against the Serbs and success in the Bihać pocket. The Krajina Serbs from Croatia intervened on behalf of Abdić, but NATO bombed their airports. In February 1995, Serbs violated the cease-fire and blocked international relief efforts.

On February 13, 1995, the ICTY charged twenty-one Serb commanders of genocide and crimes against humanity. In March 1995, Karadžić ordered the isolation of Srebrenica and Žepa and on July 9, ordered the conquest of Srebrenica. General Mladić overran the inadequate Dutch UN garrison in Srebrenica. Women, children, and old Muslim men were transported to Tuzla, which was held by Bosniaks. The men were separated and then secretly massacred, making this the single largest European massacre since World War II with 7,000–8,000 men executed in a two- to three-day period.

In July 1995, Karadžić and Mladić were indicted for genocide in the siege of Sarajevo. On August 28, 1995, Serbs shelled the Markala open market, causing a massacre, and NATO ordered air strikes against Serb positions. Serbs retaliated by taking UN hostages and placing them in harm's way.

Once the Bosnian army started making military advances by fall 1995, great international pressure was placed on all sides. As a result, Milošević, Tudjman, and Izetbegović met at the Dayton Conference on November 1–21, 1995. After adroit negotiation by Richard Holbrooke and Warren Christopher, the three Balkan leaders signed the Dayton Peace Accords on November 21. The federation got 51 percent and the Serbs 49 percent of the territory, with B&H remaining a single state made up of three entities. On December 14, 1995, the Dayton Accords were confirmed by the signing of the Paris Peace Treaty. One of the results was the creation of IFOR (Implementation Force), with 66,000 NATO troops, including Americans for the first time.

In July 1996, the West forced Karadžić to resign as president of Republika Srpska. He later went into hiding, as did Mladić, and both became fugitives of justice. Karadžić was arrested in Belgrade on July 21, 2008, and was delivered to the ICTY. Mladić remained in hiding until May 27, 2011, when he was arrested and quickly brought to The Hague.

In September 1996, the first internationally observed free elections in B&H took place. The disturbing results were that the three political parties and their leaders who took B&H into war received massive support from their respective ethnic populations. This confirmed the ethnic division of B&H in the mind of the population. An international governor (high representative) had the right of veto and the right to remove officials and invalidate decisions that would potentially deepen the conflict. Over a decade later, there were still outbreaks of interethnic strife and intra-ethnic violence. On September 22, 2010, the president of B&H, Haris Silajdžić, declared that B&H was still threatened by forces wishing to partition it and that he resolved to fight them as in the previous war.[17]

THE HORRORS OF ETHNIC CLEANSING

The reason for the war in B&H was to make it impossible for people of various ethnic groups to continue to live together peacefully. The territories where Serbs lived were scattered; the only way to bring those Serbs together was to dislocate other populations by war. The alleged rationale for ethnic cleansing was that the land belongs to those who inhabit it, and in the minds of many ethnic cleansers, it was not enough to obtain numeric prevalence on that land. They sought to assure that in the future, the descendants of their enemies would not threaten the demographic domination of their own descendants. Hence, even babies were to be killed. All three sides carried out ethnic cleansing, but it is estimated that the Serbs did about 80–90 percent of it. Anthony Lewis points to its "military purpose: it is much easier to hold territory seized in the name of Serbian nationalism if all non-Serbs there are killed or terrorized."[18] Of course, the same logic applies to others.

Massacres took place in Ahatovići, Ahmići, Doljani, Foča, Grabovica, Korićanske Stijene, Lašva Valley, Mankale, Paklenik, Prijedor, Srebrenica, Sjeverin, Tuzla, and Višegrad. Concentration camps run by Serbs were located in Keraterm, Manjača, Omarska, Trnopolje, Uzamnica, Vilina Vlas, and Vojno. Concentration camps run by Croats were at Čelebići, Dretelj, Gabela, Heliodrom, Kaonik, Vitez, and Žepa. Concentration camps run by Bosniaks were at Čelebići, Musala Hall in Konjic, and Donje Selo (a camp for Serb women and children).

In eastern Bosnia, the very brutal ethnic cleansing of the non-Serb (mostly Muslim) population took place in towns such as Foča, Čajniče, Modriča, and especially Višegrad. Some of these towns changed hands more than once and each time, when the Serbs occupied them, another series of massacres, rapes, tortures, and deportations took place. Višegrad, famous for its Turkish bridge memorialized by Nobel Prize winner Ivo Andrić's *Bridge on the Drina*, became a place of numerous massacres, some carried out on the bridge itself in broad daylight to frighten the Muslim population, and some on the banks of the river Drina, on Pionirska Street and Bikavac. Serbs gathered Muslims into a house and set it on fire; then they lobbed grenades into it. Those who tried to escape the inferno were shot. The Spa Hotel Vilina Vlas was turned into a rape camp. After the JNA withdrew from Višegrad, the city was terrorized by Avengers, a relatively small group of Serb extremists led by a former waiter, Milan Lukić. Lukić and his relatives and friends killed thousands of Muslims. In his ICTY trial at The Hague, Lukić was found responsible for personally killing 132 people and received a life sentence on July 29, 2009. He was only the second person to be given a life sentence, while his cousin Sredoje received thirty years, and Mitar Vasiljević received fifteen years.[19]

The Serbs took over the city of Banja Luka and the vicinity in northwest Bosnia without fighting. Nevertheless, the municipal authorities ordered the expulsion of many Muslims and Croats, who also were terrorized by extremists.[20] Between June and August 1992, about 430 mosques, including the historic Ferhadija and Arnaudija, were dynamited.

In Trebinje, eastern Herzegovina, in January 1993, the Serb government ordered all Muslims out of the city within a few days. In Prijedor, Muslims and Croats were placed into concentration camps such as Trnopolje, Keraterm, and Omarska where killing, torture, and rape were the norm.[21] Western journalists' photos of the Omarska inmates became a horrifying reminder of the skeletal inmates of the Nazi camps, clarifying the extent to which the Serbs' extermination policies resembled the Nazis'.[22] It became clear that in most areas held by the Serb administration or irregulars, Karadžić's threat that Muslims would be extinct if war broke out[23] was being implemented. A Serb policeman, Darko Mrdja, separated over 200 men from a convoy of Trnopoje prisoners heading to Travnik on a supposed prisoner exchange. Mrdja took the men to a ravine at Korićanske Stijene where he and others shot them at point blank and pushed them off the cliff.[24]

On June 2, 1992, at Ahatovići, near Ilidža in the vicinity of Sarajevo, sixty-four Bosniaks were imprisoned in Rajkovac and tortured. On June 14, 1992, they were placed on buses that were then attacked by Serbs, who killed fifty-six of the prisoners.[25]

The public opinion in the West was that Serbs were the sole perpetrators of these heinous crimes and that the Croats and Muslims were helpless victims, similar to the Jews during the Holocaust. In 1992 I wrote that the Serbs were committing these crimes because they were more powerful and numerous, pointing out that if the Croats and Muslims were in a position of superiority, they would commit the same crimes. I was met with indignity by Croat and Muslim friends who saw the Serbs as barbarian perpetrators and the non-Serbs as exclusively victims. Regretfully, I was right. Not long afterward, Croats and Bosniaks engaged in a vicious mutual war that brought about its own massacres, tortures, ethnic cleansing, and concentration camps.

In the Lašva Valley on April 16, 1993, the biggest HVO (Croat) massacre of the Croat-Bosniak war took place. The Lašva Valley ethnic cleansing practically eliminated the Bosniaks from this area in central Bosnia. Particularly dreadful was the Ahmići massacre during which HVO forces killed as many as 120 Bosniaks—ranging in age from ninety-six years old to three months old—and destroyed their homes. Some were burned alive, but most were shot at point blank range. These were well-planned operations. Sometimes the Bosniaks were warned and some did evacuate the area, but in other cases they were suddenly surrounded and raped, killed, or driven out. The Fourth Battalion was a special military police unit named Jokeri (Jokers) that was particularly vicious and merciless in carrying out mass murder, camp imprisonment with severe torture, and rape. (Emaciated prisoners were filmed like those filmed at Omarska.) The Jokeri were assisted by other units such as the Vitezovi, a brigade from Vitez; the Nikola Šubic Zrinjski brigade from Busovača; the Domobran (Home Guard) local Croats from each of the villages; and even units of the regular army from Croatia. Dario Kordić, the military and political leader, and General Tihomir Blaškić received twenty-five and nine years, respectively (Blaškić's sentence was reduced from forty-five years to nine upon appeal for these crimes).[26]

Other villages and towns in Lašva Valley were ethnically cleansed by Croats. Dario Kordić instigated and planned the ethnic cleansing of Donja Večeriska, Gacice, Gomionica, Gromljak, Naodioci, Novaci, Pirići, Putiš, Rotilj, Šantići, Sivrino Selo, and Vitez. Up to 2,000 people were missing or killed. Bosniaks were used as hostages and human shields. At the Busovača massacre on January 25 and February 1993, forty-three Bosniaks were killed and seventy men were transported to Kaonik, where most of them were killed. On April 16, 1993, the Croat HVO—in alleged reprisals for attacks by the Army of B&H against HVO—surprised the Bosniaks, killing eight and burning many homes. Altogether in the Vitez region, 172 Bosniaks were killed, 1,200 were detained, and about 5,000 were expelled. The Croats tried to blame the Serbs and Muslims for these massacres but did not succeed. Sixteen Croats were indicted by ICTY, of whom eight were convicted. In addition, the Croats inflicted heavy shelling on the Gornji Vakuf and Zenica market places, and they also massacred Bosniaks in Bistrica, Dusa, and Hrasnići.[27]

Some of the heaviest fighting took place in and around Mostar, the main city of Herzegovina that was coveted by Croats, Muslims, and the minority Serbs. The Serbs briefly controlled the city but were driven out by Croats and Bosniaks, who cooperated against the Serbs. Then the two communities, which were roughly equal in size, turned against each other. The Neretva River divides Mostar into a predominantly Muslim eastern section and a predominantly Croat western section. When these two ethnic groups turned against each other, a bitter intra-urban war broke out as each side wanted to control the entire city. Apartheid and ethnic war became the reality of Mostar. While both parts of the city sustained heavy damage, the Bosniak or eastern part of Mostar was repeatedly pulverized. According to the British war correspondent Ed Vulliamy, eastern Mostar had far more destruction than Sarajevo. While it was impossible to ethnically cleanse the 380,000 inhabitants of the besieged Sarajevo, the Croats did intend to completely cleanse the 55,000 Bosniaks from Mostar.[28] One of the ironies of these wars is that the Croats, who had bitterly complained of the barbarism of the Serbs in destroying the cultural heritage of Dubrovnik and Vukovar, had no qualms about destroying the famous bridge over the Neretva. The Croats' destruction of this symbol, built in 1558, shows that cultural vandalism is the monopoly of no nation.

In one case, when the Army of B&H fought back, they became overwhelmed and had to surrender to the Croats; 75 soldiers and about 400 civilians were taken prisoners by commander Mladen Naletilić-Tuta's Punishment Squad. Captured Muslims from this and other operations were taken to the concentration camps at Heliodrom in Rodoc or Ljubuški. There they were subjected to dog attacks, beatings, sexual assaults, and deprivation of water and food, and they were forced to sing Croatian nationalistic songs.

There was a larger concentration camp at Dretelj near Medjugorje. It was first a Croat camp for the captured Serbs, but when the Croat-Bosniak war broke out, between 400 and 700 Bosniaks were incarcerated there. In July 1993, it held as many as 2,270 inmates. The inmates were subjected to ethnic insults and beatings, and they were forced to abuse or beat each other. At least four inmates were killed. Vulliamy, who was among the first to visit the Dretelj Camp, provided a truly nightmarish picture on par with Omarska (which he had also visited). This camp became the symbol of the worst conditions of human depravity of this war, matching the horrors of the Holocaust in Western perceptions. Dretelj was a former JNA encampment, and at first the Croat politicians claimed that if the barracks were good for Yugoslav soldiers, they would be good for the Muslim prisoners. But in truth, the metal hangars in which the prisoners were kept were previously garages for motor vehicles; they had bare cement floors, no windows, no toilet facilities, no water, and insufficient air. In these hangars, hundreds or thousands of prisoners died of suffocation, thirst, and hunger or by direct torture and killing.[29] At Gabela camp near Čapljina, the inmates were deprived of water, were frequently beaten, and at least one man was killed for hiding some bread.

The Muslims/Bosniaks were also capable of ethnic cleansing. Some of it was retaliatory. Norman Cigar describes the situation in the following manner:

Muslim retaliation against the Croatian community began to occur on a regular basis and, by the end of the summer of 1993, the Bosnian Army had eliminated thirty-three Catholic parishes in central Bosnia. In the process, the Muslim forces had also committed atrocities, such as the September 1993 massacre of the Croatian population of the village of Uzdol and similar attacks elsewhere in the Vareš area. These actions included the killings of civilians, deportation, rape, attacks on churches, and the burning and looting of villages.[30]

Cigar concluded that the radical elements among Muslims may have concluded "that ethnic cleansing may indeed be a rational alternative," since the international community was not likely to act effectively to save the Muslims. Furthermore, the policy would provide the Muslim community more territory without fear of international reprisal. Some of the attacks were carried out by Arab mujahedeens and native Islamic extremists who used stealth to kidnap or kill Croat officers.

There were also concentration camps under the joint command of Izetbegović's Bosnian government and the Croat HVO—for example, the Čelebići camp near Konjic for which there was evidence at ICTY that several leading commanding officers had "killed, tortured, sexually assaulted, beaten and otherwise subjected to cruel and inhuman treatment"[31] captured Serbs from the villages surrounding Konjic. Joint Bosniak and Croat forces sought to keep the road around Konjic, between Sarajevo and Mostar, out of Serb control and attacked a number of villages inhabited by Serbs between April and December 1992. Many of these villagers were elderly people. They were held in the former JNA barracks and were interrogated about weapons and responsibilities for attacks. Those deemed to have lesser culpability were taken to a sports hall named Musala in another camp at Konjic. Even there some fifteen Serbs were killed. More people were tortured and killed in Čelebići, where the inmates slept and defecated on the floor; where they were tortured, sometimes with wooden sticks and sometimes with electric prods; and where some Serbian women were raped (two had been repeatedly raped). The ICTY sentenced the Croat camp commander, Zdravko Mucić, to nine years for torture; Mucić's Muslim deputy, Hazim Delić, to eighteen years for murder, torture, and rape; and Esad Landžo, a guard at Čelebići, to fifteen years for murder. Zejmil Delalić, the military commander of the region, was released due to insufficient evidence of legal responsibility. The camp was dismantled at the end of December 1992.

In his scathing attack on the ICTY's judgment, Carl Savich, a Serb scholar, claims that there were additional concentration camps for Serbs established mostly by Muslims; for example, Torčin Silo in Hadžići near Sarajevo; Krupa near Pazarići, where about 800 Serbs were held; Livno, which held 950 Serbs; Bradina with 3,000; Tomislavgrad in Raščani with 1,000; Odžak with

1,000; the Tušanj stadium at Tuzla with 4,500; and the Zetra in Sarajevo with 500 Serb inmates, of whom 300 were murdered. Savich does not provide the source for these claims.[32] He also states that 20,000 Serbs from Mostar were ethnically cleansed, along with 7,000 from Bihać and 1,000 from Duvno. Savich also states that in an attack by the Army of B&H on Bradina, the Serb men were massacred while the women and children were held in a tunnel. To Savich, it is natural that each side in a civil war would try to completely homogenize its territory; he says that what happened in B&H was a regular occurrence in civil wars. But the United States and the European community decided to use the Bosniaks and Izetbegović as tools for Western designs; they maligned the Serbs and declared that the Muslims were the victims. Savich's views are just one instance of how each side attempted to interpret events advantageously for their own side.

As evident from the preceding, all three sides operated detention and/or collection camps or centers. Serbs ran most of them, thirteen large concentration camps, while the Croats operated four. About 200,000 inmates were located in Croat camps in Herzeg-Bosna. The Red Cross documented the existence of fifty-one camps, many of them spontaneously organized in schools, sports halls, factories, camping grounds, and military barracks.[33] It was in these camps that heinous crimes against humanity took place.

The war in B&H was full of inconsistencies and horrendous excesses, but from time to time acts of kindness across ethnoreligious lines occurred. Examples are presented in some detail by Svetlana Broz, Tito's granddaughter, who moved from Belgrade to Sarajevo during the war to show her solidarity with the victims. In her book, *Good People in Evil Times*, she provides nearly a hundred instances of people risking their own lives to save people's lives from the "enemy."[34] Opposite examples also abound, not only of extremists sometimes killing cooperationists in their own ranks, but also sacrificing their own co-ethnoreligionists. Particularly controversial is the charge that one or both Sarajevo Marakala open market massacres may have been caused, not by Serb artillery and mortar shells, but by Muslims targeting their own population in order to provoke the West to become involved in the war on their side. Steven Burg and Paul Shoup point out that no clear decision has been made regarding the pro and con of the Markala massacres, but they also point out several other instances where UNPROFOR (United Nations Protection Force) soldiers concluded that some Bosniak forces sacrificed members of their own community for a tactical or strategic aim.[35] Another problematic issue is that Bosniak attacks on surrounding Serb villages were sometimes preceded by reported Serb attacks on the so-called safe zones. Obviously these Bosniak raids do not justify the kind of killing that ensued in Srebrenica, for instance, but it helps one understand why the Serbs decided to attack.

THE SREBRENICA GENOCIDE

Juridically, the case has been settled: the massacre in Srebrenica, an industrial town in eastern Bosnia, between July 6 and 19, 2005, has been ruled as genocide by ICTY; and the International Court of Justice concurred, stating that it fell within article II (a) and (b) of the UN Genocide Convention.[36] The massacre was carried out under the supreme command of General Mladić, who was personally present when military and paramilitaries from Republika Srpska and Serbia killed approximately 8,000 Bosniaks (8,373 names), almost all males. They deported over 20,000, mostly women, children, and elderly, to Bosniak-held territory. It was the most extensive massacre in Europe after World War II, and has come to symbolize the evil of the Bosnian war in the same way that Jasenovac and Auschwitz are symbols of earlier genocides. The UN Security Council confirmed that it was genocide, and the vast majority of scholars have come to the same conclusion. By now, most honest Serbs also accept that what was done allegedly in their name was genocide.[37] Official Serb sources denied it for a long time, but in March 2010, Serbia's parliament passed a condemnation of the massacre by a slim majority and apologized that Serbia did not do more to prevent it—but they did not use the word *genocide* in conjunction with their official action.

The customary view of the Srebrenica massacre is that evil Serbs, without provocation, planned and carried out the genocide by overrunning a UN protected safe area, where they killed the unarmed Bosniak/Muslim civilians, as they had been doing throughout the war. Serbs bad guys, Bosniaks good guys; case closed.

This simplified scenario is inaccurate, though it was presented in one form or another by those who then justified greater international (including U.S.) involvement to bring the war to an end in about six months' time. The war, as it unfolded around Srebrenica, turned out to be lengthy and very complex, even if one does not look at it in the wider context of wars in the former Yugoslavia and the international interventions evoked by it. Our focus is on the micro level.

The starting point is the 1992 Serbian ethnic cleansing of many eastern Bosnian cities (Bijeljina, Višegrad, Zvornik, Bratunac, and Foča) at the beginning of the war; the goal was to create a contiguous Serb-controlled land having a common border with Serbia. The ethnic composition of both the town and the district of Srebrenica was about 75 percent Bosniak and 25 percent Serbs, with the towns being predominantly Muslim and the surrounding villages mostly Serb. In the first month of the war, April 1992, the Serbs were winning most of the battles throughout B&H. They occupied the predominantly Bosniak town of Bratunac near Srebrenica and killed several hundred Bosniaks, while

6,000–7,000 fled to nearby Srebrenica.[38] The Serbs then suffered a defeat in Srebrenica,[39] and in the subsequent months, Bosniak forces under Orić's leadership—functioning within the Army of B&H's command structure—occupied and destroyed many Serb villages surrounding Srebrenica and ethnically cleansed a large area of Serbs, matching the grizzly horrors done by the Serbs.

> Between May 1992 and January 1993 forces from Srebrenica attacked and destroyed scores of Serb villages. The attacks outraged the Serbs. A great deal of animosity towards the men of Srebrenica stems from this period. The Serbs put a lot of effort into collecting evidence of war crimes committed by Muslims in such villages as Brežani, Zalažje, Batkovići, Fakovići, and Glogova. Evidence indicated that Serbs had been tortured and mutilated and others were burned alive when their houses were torched. Over 1,300 people were reputedly killed during this period.[40]

By the end of 1992, the front lines had stabilized and stayed basically unchanged until the summer of 1995. But despite numerous cease-fires, there was no peace. In fact, the Serbs counterattacked and surrounded Srebrenica, and by March 1993, the huge number of Bosniak refugees and townspeople had run out of food and water. The Serbs only occasionally permitted humanitarian deliveries, which prompted the French general Phillippe Morrilon, then commander of the UN forces, to make a highly publicized visit to Srebrenica. For a period, he became the hostage in a desperate Bosniak attempt to secure protection from the UN.[41] The events of this visit were so dramatic that if they were on a film or in a novel, most would conclude that the filmmaker or author went way beyond what was believable. However, Mladić let in some humanitarian convoys and permitted several thousand refugees to leave. He then made an offer to allow the UN to send in any number of buses and trucks to evacuate all Bosniaks from Srebrenica. Had this offer been accepted, the subsequent extermination may not have taken place. But many in the U.S. government, the UN, and the Bosnian government refused, saying that such an evacuation would assist the process of ethnic cleansing. A high Bosnian army official, communicating the refusal to allow the evacuation to representatives of the international community, stated, "The convoy is not allowed to come in. We are ready to sacrifice these people." And his colleagues stated that such mass evacuation "is not in the interest of the Bosnians and contradictory to their military goal."[42] While the Serbs loosened their siege, the government of B&H wasted an opportunity to save the lives of thousands of people by blocking the evacuation. The evacuation would have contributed to ethnic cleansing, but the future would have unfolded less disastrously. Some Bosnian officials, like Haris Silajdžić, favored the evacuation but they were overruled by the hardliners in the government.

As a response, Mladić tightened the encirclement. Srebrenica was about to fall as Serb forces came to within about a mile of the town's center. The UN Security Council prevented the takeover by passing Resolution 819 on April 16, 1993. The Serb army backed off. The UN resolution provided for contradictory interpretation. While it enabled the negotiation of a cease-fire between the commanding officers Halilović and Mladić, it also demanded the demilitarization of Srebrenica. The Serbs assumed that this meant the demilitarization of the entire safe zone, while the Muslims interpreted it as the demilitarization of the town only; thus the Bosniaks avoided being demilitarized. Jan Willem Honig and Norbert Both conclude, "In fact the UN never tried systematically to disarm the Muslims of Srebrenica."[43] The Dutch UNPROFOR unit's reasoning seems to be that this would mean disarming the victims, but it led to some unwanted developments that contributed to the final tragedy.

A cease-fire initiated by former president Jimmy Carter lasted from January 1 to May 1, 1995. This time was used by Bosniaks and Croats to prepare for more fighting. The Army of B&H and the Croats had by then formed a federation under the pressure from Bill Clinton's government. It seems that they had also secretly received military assistance from the United States and were gaining momentum, while the Serbs suffered from attrition and sagging morale. The Serbs apparently concluded that they needed to consolidate the territories that they intended to hold for the Republika Srpska. They knew that they would not be able to hold eastern Bosnia until they defeated the Bosniaks in the enclaves of Srebrenica, Žepa, and Goražde.

The Bosniak army of about 3,000–4,000 fighters frequently raided the Serb villages. They fortified Srebrenica by digging trenches around the area. "Complaints from the Serbs appeared to confirm that the Muslims regularly mounted raids into Serb territory to terrorize the local Serb population and acquire booty."[44] Further, "Orić and his cronies were also responsible for much of the trouble with the Serbs, which stemmed from Muslim raids on Serb communities just outside the enclave. Also Orić's men had the disconcerting habit of taking positions close to the Dutch and then opening fire on the Serbs, hoping to entice them and the Dutch into a firefight."[45] The Dutch warrant officer, Piet Hein Both, wrote on June 11, 1995, "The Muslims are provoking the fighting."[46]

On June 24, General Mladić indicated to the UN that he would no longer tolerate the constant raids by the Bosniaks. He wrote to UNPROFOR Sarajevo headquarters: "The attacks against the territories controlled by R[epublika] S[rpska] Army . . . brutally violates the status of [the] Safe Area of Srebrenica. Due to that fact I strongly protest and warn you that we will not tolerate such cases in the future."[47] On June 26, a Bosniak unit foolishly attacked the Serb village of Višnjica, and that was the last straw for the Serbs; they decided that if the UN was unable to demilitarize the safe zones, they would. And they did. The decision does not seem surprising, yet it seems to have surprised both the Bosniaks of Srebrenica and the international community.

The Serb decision to overrun the Srebrenica enclave was very thoroughly planned by a disciplined military force. It was set on removing the presence of Bosniaks from the area not only in 1995, but in the future. Mladić and his commanders clearly had the cooperation of not only Karadžić and the leading politicians of Republika Srpska but also the general staff of JNA and Milošević and his government (despite some serious differences of opinion regarding the further developments of the conflict between Belgrade and Pale). The takeover began on July 6. Briefly, fierce fighting between the Bosniaks and the Serbs took place, but as the Serbs pressed on "the Bosnian army deserted their positions around Srebrenica."[48] The Dutch were forced to surrender after the Serbs threatened to destroy them and the people of Srebrenica if they didn't call off the requested air support, which UNPROFOR did. Mladić was now in complete control of the Srebrenica enclave. The Bosniak forces did not, as expected, resist, but decided to flee.[49] Some succeeded to reach Bosniak territory; others were captured by the Serbs.

What followed was cold-blooded slaughter of individuals, small groups, and large groups. Mladić at first acted reassuringly and even in a friendly manner, promising to evacuate all except the confirmed Bosniak war criminals. One of the proofs that the entire operation was preplanned is that forty to sixty trucks and buses appeared. Women, children, and elderly men beyond the age of fighting ability were separated from the able-bodied men; however, the selection was not very careful, and many who were certainly unable to fight were probably grouped with the men. About 20,000 to 22,000 women, children, and elderly were then trucked to the nearest Bosniak-controlled town, Kladanj. "The units carrying out the deportation and executions had to be efficient and experienced 'ethnic cleansers.' The cooperation of local militia and police, who would be able to identify and detain suspected Muslim 'war criminals,' was also a key. . . . Several thousand Serb troops were needed to mop up the enclave, to deport the women and children, and to arrest, detain, interrogate and execute the men."[50] The massacre of 8,000 men took several days, the Serb army being careful to destroy the evidence by burying the bodies in mass graves. Aerial photographs pointed to the locations of some of the mass graves, but the forensic search and subsequent exhumation and identification of the remnants has taken years of work and is not yet complete. In the case of General Radislav Krstić, the sentencing judgment by Trial Chamber I of ICTY, delivered by Presiding Judge Almiro

Rodriguez, details the events leading up to the Serbian conquest of Srebrenica, as well as the forcible transfer of the women, children, and aged men and
the sporadic but systematic mass executions of the captured men in groups of
1,000 to 1,500. All of this led the court to conclude beyond any reasonable
doubt, that genocide did take place in the Srebrenica enclave and that General
Krstić personally aided and abetted the genocide.[51]

The trial chamber and the appeals chamber unanimously affirmed that
genocide occurred in Srebrenica. By killing the males who were a part of
the protected group, namely, the victims, the Serbs intended to destroy *a
part, a substantial part* of the group. The approximately 8,000 who were
exterminated were numerically substantial, they were a prominent part of the
Muslims who were in Srebrenica at the time, and they were in the control of
the perpetrators. The ICTY also found that there was *intent* on the part of the
perpetrators to destroy this group; even though many of the men served in
the military, the group also included males who were clearly not capable of
fighting, and they were also murdered. The killing of all these males under
the command of the main staff of the Serb military had an impact on the ability of the group to survive in the future, and it included the forcible transfer
of the women and children.

However, the appeals chamber reduced the charge against General Krstić
to a charge more easily proven legally than genocide itself: being part of a
joint criminal enterprise to commit genocide thus guilty of aiding and abetting genocide. Further, the ICTY judgment in the Krstić case provided a
clear statement of genocidal intent by saying that the killing of Srebrenica's
males intended the destruction of the target group (that being Srebrenica's
Muslims), who in turn were part of the Bosnian Muslims and thus there was
a causal connection to their intended destruction.

In its preamble, the UN General Assembly Resolution 47/121 of December
18, 1992, deemed ethnic cleansing to be a form of genocide, stating

> Gravely concerned about the deterioration of the situation in the Republic of
> Bosnia and Herzegovina owing to intensified aggressive acts by the Serbian
> and Montenegrin forces to acquire more territories by force, characterized by a
> consistent pattern of gross and systematic violations of human rights, a burgeon-
> ing refugee population resulting from mass expulsions of defenceless civilians
> from their homes and the existence in Serbian and Montenegrin controlled areas
> of concentration camps and detention centres, in pursuit of the abhorrent policy
> of "ethnic cleansing", which is a form of genocide.[52]

In February 2007, the International Court of Justice deliberated a lawsuit
against the government of Serbia. The government of B&H charged Serbia's
government with the genocide of Bosnian citizens, but the court did not find

Serbia guilty of genocide. It did determine that the government of Serbia knew what was happening in Bosnia and specifically in Srebrenica, but did not take measures to prevent it.

An astonishingly large number of military and civilian personnel participated in this genocide. According to a Special Bosnian Serb Working Group, 25,083 people participated of which 19,473 were armed forces (17,074 known by name).[53] A detachment of Greek volunteers also participated in the massacre. By 2010, forty-two mass graves had been uncovered and another twenty-two are believed to exist. The Serb authorities had attempted to move the remains of the dead from one site to another in the hope of hiding the monstrous crime. And every year on the anniversary of the genocide, July 11, additionally identified bodies have been buried during memorial services.

GENOCIDAL RAPE

Issues surrounding genocidal rape are prone to ambiguity and are easily manipulated, misunderstood, and underestimated or overestimated; thus, I am going to state my position succinctly at first and then follow it up with details dealing with the various aspects of the issue. Every act of rape is a repulsive, tragic, and dehumanizing act that demeans the raped person's body and soul. In the war in B&H, Croatia, and possibly Kosovo, two types of rapes occurred. One is the nearly universal accompaniment of war in which troops or paramilitaries—out of a variety of motives, such as assertion of their power, terrorizing the population, denigrating the victims, or gratifying their sexual desires—rape young and old females (occasionally also males). A second, more recently recognized, type perpetrated in the Balkan wars of the 1990s was the systematic exploitation and terrorization of captured women, sometimes with the express purpose of impregnation, carried out for nationalist purposes related to ethnic cleansing and genocide. These rapes are usually called genocidal rapes (others call them systematic rapes or state rapes), because there is evidence that such rapes may have been ordered or encouraged by superiors. Upon the discovery of this type, some people sought to make genocidal rape known to the wider public. But soon such information was exploited for propaganda purposes by exaggerating the number of victims, blaming only one side in the war for perpetrating such crimes, and claiming that only the women of another ethnoreligious group were subject to this practice. A more detailed exposition of the issue follows.

Rapes have evidently been by-products of wars from time immemorial. By and large, commanding officers accepted the behavior of their troops ("boys will be boys") and rarely punished offenders. During some wars, rapes were carried out in mass, as was pointed out regarding the Balkan wars early in the century (see chapter 4) and certainly also during World War II. These rapes were categorized as individual crimes, however, and few soldiers were ever tried for them. Prior to concrete claims of genocidal rapes, it was assumed that instances of rape also occurred in the wars of the 1990s.

But in 1992 and even more so in 1993, reports began to arrive not only of frequent rapes but of mass rapes and rape camps where women were repeatedly raped, mostly by Serb rapists primarily targeting Muslim/Bosniak, but also Croat, girls and women. The phenomenon of genocidal rape was first reported by journalists who had evidence from one or two localities, and then based on that estimate, they extrapolated the figures to the entire territory of B&H, arriving at a shocking number of 10,000–12,000 genocidal rapes. Roy Gutman of *Newsday*[54] sent a series of dispatches based on his interviews with women who had been raped, especially in Foča and Brezovo Polje. Many of the women and the medical personnel who attended the survivors claimed that these rapes were often highly organized and that a number of the rapists told the women that they were ordered to do it by their superiors. Evidently, rape was to be an instrument of war for the purpose of ethnic cleansing.

Soon the charges grew exponentially to 20,000, 40,000 and 60,000. In a highly one-sided analysis, authors such as Beverly Allen[55] blamed genocidal rape entirely upon Serbs and their desire to father Serb offspring, to humiliate Muslim and Croat women, and to project shame on their entire community. Catharine McKinnon asserts that mass rape was a genocide specifically targeting women with the intent to destroy the group of which they are members. Both Allen and McKinnon seemed not to be interested in the fate of all women of Bosnia, since they focus almost exclusively on the victims of mass rape by Serbs. They show no concern for Serb women who had been raped by the others. Some of these authors are making a wider ideological argument regarding the "war of the sexes," patriarchy, the role of pornography, and an alleged primitive atavistic belief that a conceived child is of the ethnicity of the rapist while the woman is merely an incubator.[56]

A number of skeptics have contested the charges of systematic or genocidal rape as vastly exaggerated sensationalist claims based on very slim evidence. Diana Johnstone examined many of the claims and concluded that most of them were propagandist efforts to stigmatize the Serbs rather than fact-based investigations of the allegations.[57]

Legal scholar Karen Engle has provided the most thorough and nuanced analysis of all kinds of reasons for and implications of wartime rapes as dealt with by ICTY.[58] She notes the advances in jurisprudence by ICTY as they dealt with the approximately 20 percent of charges that contained elements of sexual assault and three cases (named by ICTY as *Čelebići, Furundžija, and*

Kunarac) that specifically dealt with rape. In the first case, *Čelebići*, Muslim soldiers had been found guilty of raping Serbian women; in the second, *Furundžija*, Croat soldiers had been found guilty of raping Muslim women; and in the last one, *Kunarac*, Serb soldiers and paramilitaries had been found guilty of systematic and widespread rape of Muslim women in Foča, Gacko, and Kalinovik—rape that amounted to torture and enslavement. Of great importance for the future is that ICTY decided that sexual assault may be considered as one means of genocidal war.

My own interpretation is that the large number of rapes had no single motive and varied from place to place and from perpetrator to perpetrator. I do not accept the argument that raping was the specific ethnic characteristic of one nation (usually ascribed to Serbs) or that somehow women of one ethnicity suffered more uniquely than others (usually ascribed to Bosniak women, because they are Muslims). In cases where rapes had been commanded, it was by lower military officers. One of the most powerful motives for many of the rapes was the notion of collective revenge—both for what may have happened recently, including during World War II, and in the more mytho-historical sense that the conquering Ottoman Turkish Muslims raped or forcibly married Serbian Christian women and that such behavior persisted into the nineteenth century. There were certainly popular songs about girls being forced to marry powerful overlords. In addition, there is a very famous epic song, "Smrt Smail Age Čengića" (Death of Smail Aga Chengich), by the nineteenth-century Croat poet Ivan Mažuranić that pictures a powerful Muslim overlord using a Christian girl sexually. In the mytho-historical view,[59] it is as if long-past events just happened yesterday or today. Therefore, to avenge one's people by raping a Muslim (or Croat) girl was to some Serb men a chance to even out the score and perhaps, as in sports, take the lead. Another overlooked factor is that soldiers often feel entitled to compensate for their individual and collective endangerment and distress by taking whatever they wish from the enemy—hence looting, pillaging, and raping.

That Serbian army officers, leaders of paramilitaries, and even politicians ordered systematic rape and participated in these acts was testified to by perpetrators during their trials at ICTY. A center under Muslim control had been established in Zenica, which started caring for these women and taking their testimonies. Many were then taken to Zagreb for further medical attention, where again attempts had been made to collect information about what was taking place.[60] The exact number of genocidal or mass rapes may never be known because many traumatized women never came forward to report, but even if the number is closer to 12,000, it is still horrendous. If the courts insist that the term *genocide* must be used sparingly, then the very concept of genocidal rape needs to be further examined. In the ICTY judgments, there were several men found guilty of raping women, but nearly always the number of women who had been raped according to the indictment was fairly small (though there were some instances of sustained raping over a longer period or of group rape).

According to a UN report, "Available information indicates that rape has been committed by all sides in the conflict. However, the largest number of reported victims have been Bosnian Muslims, and the largest number of perpetrators have been Bosnian Serbs. There are few reports of rape and sexual assault among members of the same ethnic group."[61] There were reports that Muslim women had been deliberately impregnated and kept so long in confinement that they would be forced to bear "Serb" children. Other women testified that as soon as they became pregnant, they were set free in exchanges of captured personnel and either had abortions or the resulting children were given up for adoption.[62]

The reference to "rape camps" conjures up notions of rows of barracks surrounded by barbed wire. It is not clear whether this terminology was deliberately chosen in order to evoke such images. Most rapes did take place in concentration camps (e.g., Trnopolj and Omarska), but that was not the major purpose of such camps; calling them "rape camps" thus seems misleading. The rapes often took place in locations such as motels, cafes, school buildings, storage halls, or private homes. Other rapes took place on the front lines, in the person's home, or even in some public place. Obviously, these locations (as opposed to concentration camps) did not make the rapes any less horrendous or devastating. Often the rapes were intentionally humiliating in that they took place in front of mothers, children, fathers, husbands, and other onlookers. The women ranged from young children to older women, though most frequently they were between the ages of fourteen and thirty-five. Women testified that sometimes they were selected at the very outset of being captured when their captors divided the groups into men of fighting ability, older women and men and children, and then younger women, particularly good-looking ones. A particularly grizzly case involves a young Muslim girl of about fourteen who had been raped, tied to the tank turret, and then driven around well after she died and was reduced to a skeleton.[63]

The vast majority of the cases seem to be Serb men raping Bosniak and (less frequently) Croatian women; later in Kosovo, it was Serb men raping ethnic Albanian women. In other cases, Croat men raped Bosniak women and Serb women were raped by Croat or Muslim men. The most infamous rape places were Motel Kod Sonje in Vogošća near Sarajevo; Hotel Vilina Vlas near Višegrad; school buildings in Foča, Rogatica, and Kalinovik; a saw mill at Kozarac; and motels in Brčko and Doboj. Serbian women reported being raped in the camp at Čelebići.

There were also reports of homosexual rape and sexual assaults, not only by members of the group in charge of a situation, such as a concentration camp, but also coerced sexual assaults among inmates.

ICTY did decide that genocidal rape took place in B&H—the first instance in international jurisprudence of charging not merely rape in a war situation but genocidal rape. Vulliamy viewed such rapes as "a programme integral to the genocidal violation of one people of another."[64] Eric Weitz points out that genocidal rape is "a social act that involves large numbers of men. . . . The rapists seem never to have been disciplined by higher Serbian authorities, which the men could only have understood as approval of their actions. At the same time, the tribunal [ICTY] specifically stated that the men were not following orders to rape and doubted that such orders existed. 'The evidence shows free will on their part.'"[65]

DID GENOCIDE OCCUR IN BOSNIA AND HERZEGOVINA?

While numbers are not essential to the evidence of genocide, nevertheless an astonishingly high number of people were killed, usually estimated at 100,000–200,000, but according to ICTY's prosecutorial office, the number was between 25,000 and 329,000 people.[66] The number of wounded had to be larger than the number of dead. Approximately 50 percent were Muslims, 30–35 percent were Serbs, and 15–20 percent were Croats, which fairly closely corresponds to the composition of the population. The UN Human Rights Commission estimated that about 12,000 women were raped, the majority by Serbs. Of a B&H population numbering about 4 million, approximately 900,000 to 1.2 million Bosnians of all three ethnicities became refugees abroad, while up to 1.5 million were displaced within their country. About half of the refugees were Bosniaks, about 500,000 were Serbs, and 150,000 were Croats.[67]

If ethnic cleansing is a form of genocide, then what happened in B&H was undoubtedly genocide because not only was ethnic cleansing documented by nearly all observers and by the changed ethnographic statistics, but the perpetrators often openly declared it was their aim. But if ethnic cleansing is a crime lesser than genocide, then opinions may be divided as to whether genocide took place in B&H (and by extension in Croatia and Kosovo). I have argued that every genocide includes ethnic cleansing but not every ethnic cleansing is genocide.[68] Ethnic cleansing could be considered a subcategory of genocide or a milder mass crime than genocide, but it is doubtful that such fine distinction would matter to the victims of ethnic cleansing.

Helen Fein provided a seemingly clear-cut distinction between the two: "Ethnic cleansing requires either a protected reservation within a state or a free exit for the victims to escape; genocide precludes both protection and exit."[69] In some situations Helen Fein's distinction would be very useful, such as when there is a government in charge that persecutes a minority. However in B&H, there were three ethnoreligious groups, each of which had governmental structures. Plus, there were two neighboring countries, Serbia and Croatia, which directly meddled and promoted radical polarization as they planned to create different state entities. Under these circumstances, it is hard to say if a victim group had the chance to flee or if there existed in the group's own territory a place to which people of their ethnicity could be deported or places where captives can be swapped. For many people there seemed to be no way out but to die. While in some genocides many victims are unarmed civilians, in B&H many civilians took steps to arm themselves, no matter how inadequately, knowing what was about to happen to them. Thus, it was not a classic genocide of a people being taken to slaughter like lambs, though certainly many specific instances fit that description. The killing of one group of civilians was often later avenged by the killing of civilians of the perpetrators. Thus members of each ethnoreligious group could be both perpetrators and victims.

Norman Cigar, the author of *Genocide in Bosnia*,[70] has no doubt that genocide took place in B&H, as he equates it with ethnic cleansing. He provides plenty of data regarding the horrors of the war and specifically of ethnic cleansing; to him, this is sufficient proof that genocide took place. In his opinion, only Serbs carried out the genocide and did so in a planned effort to produce an ethnically pure Serbia, led by the centralized political leadership of Milošević and supported by underling Karadžić.[71] Cigar describes Croat, Croatian, and even Bosniak war crimes, but does not elevate them to the same level as Serb and Serbian actions.

Approximately one-third to two-thirds of B&H's population was displaced by the war, which harmed the civilian population more than the combatants. People of all three ethnic groups had been displaced, but not all in equal numbers or for the same motivation. Extremists and militaries of all three groups carried out ethnic cleansing.[72] The government of B&H did not urge the Bosniaks or the others to voluntarily move, while the Serb and Croat administrations urged their own populations to move, often frightening them with the possible consequences, such as retribution, if they did not move.[73] Hence there was also some self–ethnic cleansing. In many instances the perpetrators came from outside of the local community. They immediately took steps against the leaders of the community. They killed, arrested, or incarcerated in concentration camps those leaders in what some call eliticide. Thus, politicians, educators, legal professionals, religious leaders, and municipal administrators were targeted first, with the goal of depriving the community of effective leadership and making it less able to resist whatever befell them in the attack. Later, members of the local community of the same background as the perpetrators were required to show solidarity with them and often joined and justified the carnage.

The UN ICTY was very cautious in leveling the charge of genocide in its indictments. There are a very large number of indictments for war crimes, crimes against humanity, and violations of the Geneva Convention of 1949, but out of about 180 indicted who were tried by ICTY, only 10–15 were accused of genocide.[74]

A minority of legal experts argue that what happened in B&H was genocide. On August 2, 2001, in *Prosecutor vs. Radislav Krstić*, the ICTY ruled that "customary international law limits the notion of genocide to those acts seeking the physical or biological destruction of all or part of the group. Hence, an enterprise attacking only the cultural or sociological characteristics of a human group in order to annihilate these elements which give that group its own identity distinct from the rest of the community would not fall under the definition of genocide."[75]

On April 14, 2004, the trial chamber confirmed the January 14, 2000, ICTY decision in *Prosecutor vs. Kupreškić and Others*by agreeing that the Lašva Valley ethnic cleansing of Muslims by Croats was persecution but not genocide. So, the ICTY does not consider ethnic cleansing genocide. Yet the ICTY did conclude that some of the ethnic cleansing was genocidal.

The European Court of Human Rights tried Nikola Jorgić, a Serb paramilitary who killed many Muslims in the Doboj area in 1992. He had been apprehended in Germany, so a German court tried him. They decided that he was guilty of genocide, based upon the definition of genocide in German legislation. In September 1997, the European Court of Human Rights (ECHR) convicted Jorgić of genocide and sentenced him to four life sentences. On July 12, 2007, the ECHR reviewed the German court's judgment and ruled that it was consistent with the 1948 convention.

From this it is clear that some courts have a broader definition of genocide than others. The ICTY is eager to protect the notion of genocide for the truly most horrendous instances, lest it become a meaningless, commonplace term and consequently uses the indictment and the decisions about genocide sparingly. Of course, there is also a danger of interpreting the UN Genocide Convention too narrowly.

During the ethnic cleansing in B&H, a small number of people were urged to change their religion or culture; in other respects, the differences between Bosnian Croats, Muslims, and Serbs are minimal. It was exactly because of these two distinctions that many people were killed, tortured, maimed, raped, deported, or had to flee. While genocide did not mean that all people of a victim group on earth would have become physically extinct, they did became physically and biologically extinct (or nearly extinct) in certain areas of B&H where they and their ancestors had resided for centuries. If several of the major leaders accused were guilty of genocide, then surely many of the lesser perpetrators who were carrying out their orders were also guilty of genocide or assisting in genocide, and a conclusion must be reached that surely *genocide occurred!*

Because of what happened in B&H—namely, the mass killings, torture, deportation, concentration camps, arson, and extermination of all three ethnic groups, with the Bosniak Muslims being the most victimized—entire areas that had once supported mixed populations had become ethnically homogenous, or nearly so. That would appear to indicate that genocide had taken place in certain areas of B&H, if we can determine a crucial element of the definition, namely, the intent of the perpetrators. Such intention is more difficult to prove legally because most genocidaires are careful enough to cover their trail. Yet, those involved in ethnic cleansing felt they had a clear task, that is, to carve out a territory where they would have undisputed control, without the presence of a "foreign" element, so that the area would be theirs now and in the future. Such was the case of Radoslav Brdjanin, president of the Crisis Staff of the Autonomous Region of Krajina of Republika Srpska, who was indicted in connection with persecutions, deportations, murders, torture, and destruction in the autonomous region of Krajina. He was sentenced to thirty years. Others, like Vojislav Šešelj, who was not a government official at the time, propagated chauvinistic ideas and threatened others with extermination if they did not leave. Željko Ražnjatović-Arkan was a career criminal who became the leader of the paramilitary force named Tigers; he was indicted with crimes against humanity and violating the laws of war in a number of municipalities in B&H prior to his assassination in Belgrade in 2000. But vastly more influential was Karadžić, who clearly threatened the Muslims with extermination if they persisted with their intention to seek B&H independence, as quoted previously. Karadžić acted impetuously, and occasionally Milošević attempted to curb both Karadžić's and Mladić's aggressiveness against Muslims and Croats,[76] usually unsuccessfully. My overall conclusion goes against the grain of the general opinion that Milošević was the worst culprit of the Balkan wars. In my opinion, Karadžić and Mladić were more chauvinistic and destructive; ultimately the two of them contributed more to Bosnian genocides than Milošević.

Milošević died toward the end of his trial and thus no judgment was issued, though it is likely that he would have been found guilty on many counts, including genocide in Bosnia. Šešelj, Karadžić, and Mladić were being tried at the time of this writing. The trial of Šešelj was frequently delayed, though

Šešelj surrendered himself voluntarily to ICTY, expecting to be vindicated. He had already been in detention since February 2003 and had tried to make a mockery of the trial, for which he was held in contempt of court. Karadžić went into hiding and lived as a fugitive until July 2008, when he was sensationally arrested by the Serbian police, having artfully disguised himself as a holistic medicine guru.[77] He and his many followers in Belgrade, sought to prevent extradition, but the Serbian government speedily delivered him to ICTY. Karadžić is following Milošević's and Šešelj's example of defending himself with a likely lengthy trial. General Mladić eluded justice for sixteen years, both in the open and in hiding, even though the Serbian newspapers and politicians predicted often that he would be captured in the near future. ICTY chief prosecutors, including the current one, Serge Brammertz, urged the Serbian government to increase their efforts to capture Mladić.[78] On May 27, 2011, the drama ended when Mladić was arrested at the home of a relative in the village of Lazarevo in Vojvodina, looking as a shadow of his former self after apparently having suffered several strokes.[79] The Serbian government of Borislav Tadić expeditiously delivered him to ICTY, where he is likely to be tried either jointly or parallel with Karadžić on nearly identical indictments. The main charges are the siege of Sarajevo, the mistreatment of UNPROFOR hostages, and, most importantly, the Srebrenica genocide.

There are also arguments *against* considering ethnic cleansing in B&H as genocidal. A case in point is that Serbs and Croats frequently satisfied themselves with the expulsion of Muslims rather than their extermination, in order to create a Great Serbia or Great Croatia. Another frequently made point is that the Serb or Croat army would capture and intern the men, but deport the women, children, and older men, thereby showing it wasn't their intention to destroy them all. In the war on B&H, various sides focused on interning or exterminating men aged sixteen to sixty. This "gendercide," as one scholar has called it—that is, killing those of the male gender, specifically men able for military service—seems to have the military objective of preventing such men from becoming soldiers or irregulars for the enemy who inflict future damage to one's own forces. One can classify gendercide as a war crime or crime against humanity, but one would probably have to indicate that there was no intention to bring about the physical or biological extermination of the other ethnic group.

One of the most confusing issues of the UN Genocide Convention's formulation is that one can carry out genocide over a "part" of the target group. How large or small can the part be? Some say that even a single person, if killed with the intent to destroy the group, would suffice as a part. I consider this as reductio ad absurdum. Since so many civilians of all three ethnicities were killed in this war, one might argue that the part should be large enough to reasonably qualify as a significant part. The ICTY has specified that the leadership of a group is a big enough part; if leadership is exterminated, that suffices in considering the act genocidal. Is it genocide when a great loss of population (two-thirds to three-fourths)—due to defeats in battles or through peace negotiations in which they surrender an area—occurs in an area where the group used to be a majority (such as the Serb losses at Mt. Ozren in the vicinity of Sarajevo)?

French scholar Jacques Semlin points out that there is a great range of scholarly definitions of genocide, from very broad ones, like the one in the *Encyclopedia of Genocide*,[80] to very narrow ones. Semlin completely by-passes the decision of whether to call the Bosnian massacres genocide, but instead settles for "mass crime," which for him is a more comprehensive term than mass murder. Mass crime "is characterized by the destruction of large segments of civilian population, often accompanied by atrocities, which would first appear to be random and without purpose. Yet, beyond the mur-derous frenzy of men, which we often hold responsible for such crimes, 'mass crime' follows a 'rationality,' albeit a delirious one."[81] Semlin argues that a collective psychosis developed in the Balkans that was based on fear that had its roots in the memory of massacres, mutual and foreign, that occurred during the last two centuries, first based on religion and later on nationality. The perceived threat led to a radical polarization of society; fearing real or imagined annihilation, the groups became increasingly willing to be manipu-lated to annihilate the "enemy." According to Semelin most people, including the Balkan leaders, did not talk about it but simply acted out, perpetrating mass crime preemptively. Receptivity to the message of threat leads to ethnic cleansing "that is not only premeditated but long and carefully prepared."[82] The murderous frenzy was supported by high governmental officials, police, the military, and various militias. The ultranationalist speeches of leaders of one group were matched by similar speeches of the other. Semelin thinks that such speeches by Tudjman were used as a pretext for Milošević's actions, but I think that the causal relationship is not so clear; Tudjman's speeches may have been the reason for increased Serb anxiety, feeding Milošević's determi-nation to provide the Serbs with the borders that they believed they deserved.

Semelin also raises the question why such atrocities were committed in the process of ethnic cleansing. He provides two alternatives: One is that such atrocities have a functional role; they contribute to a more efficient expulsion of the unwanted population, who are so frightened that they not only run for their lives but never wish to come back. Atrocities will make it impossible for good neighborly relations with one another for a long time. The other is that such extreme violence, according to Wolfgang Sofsky, "has no other goal than itself."[83] In other words, it is meaningless, except that it is the universal way people behave in such extreme situations. Semelin leaves the option open, saying that much more research is needed in order to determine the correct answer. My own response, consistent with my previous avoidance of the either-or options in favor of a both-and approach, is that in Croatia, B&H, and Kosovo, the circumstances differed from place to place and time to time. In certain situations, the intoxication with violence, each person feeding on the brutality by others, may have simply been part of a meaningless orgy of destruction, whereas in other situations the perpetrators were quite aware that brutal actions do have a useful function in defeating and expelling the enemy, breaking their will to resist.

In comparison to many classical genocides, the Yugoslav case both during World War II and in the wars of the 1990s were much more complex. As Henry Huttenbach states,

> the wars in Bosnia-Herzegovina were characterized as genocidal but with differences. There were three antagonists and three victims; in the conflict each ethno-group—Bosnian Muslim, Croat, and Serb—was both perpetrator and victim in some degree. Genocidal and anti-genocidal stratagems and tactics can be ascribed to all three combatants.
>
> Depending on the circumstances, each group was either on the defensive or on the attack. When it went on the offensive it engaged in genocidal violence if circumstances permitted. Three-way polarization guaranteed a psychology of extermination. . . . Out of the ruins has come a new dynamic, namely genocide/ethnic cleansing and counter-genocide/counter ethnic cleansing.[84]

Huttenbach proceeds by saying that for political reasons, the Western countries, including scholars and journalists, simplified issues by proclaiming Serbia as the villain and the others as victims. "So, while the bulk of the onus of war crimes, of violations of human rights, of genocide, were put on Serbian shoulders, the equally serious crimes of Croats and Bosnian Muslims were generally, at least initially, overlooked and, at least, ranked distant second to the crimes of ethnic cleansing associated with Serbia. The results are a distortion of reality, and justice seriously compromised."[85]

APPENDIX

In order to provide a vivid picture of the situation in the early years of the Bosnian war, a translation of a segment of the book *Ubijanje smrti* [The Killing of Death] by Jasmin Imamović, a deputy mayor of Tuzla, is provided for the reader.[86] These were eyewitness accounts provided to Imamović by people who had succeeded in escaping to Tuzla from areas conquered by the Serbs.

I am from the vicinity of Bratunac . . . the village of Suha. Serbian Četniks came, "White Eagles." They surrounded the settlement, divided us into groups, took golden jewelry, money, watches. . . . At the stadion they separated us. Women, children, old people to the right, and we, able men, left. . . . They took 600 of us to the sport hall of the Elementary School "Vuk Karadžić" in Bratunac. While we were entering the hall I looked through the open door of the locker room. In it were about twenty bloody, butchered corpses. I recognized only Osman Halilović. Both of his eyes had been dug out. After that the commander of the "White Eagles," Bane and several Četniks, my neighbors, entered.

Did you recognize anyone?

Yes, Milan Tršić, Ratko Živanović, Milisav Simić. . . . In the middle was a table, and on the table iron rods, handles for hoes, ropes, some wires, large scissors, hooks with which they later dug out eyes. . . . In one part of the hall were lying bloody, but still living people.

They started calling one by one. They were beating with all implements from the table, and then turned them facing the floor and killed them. Some they took out of the hall and there cut their throats.

How do you know that they cut their throats?

When a Četnik who took him out returned, he would say, "I bandaged his neck."

Did they select people on some account, accusing them of something?

They called the imam of Bratunac, Mustafa Mujukanović, and some others. To the imam they ordered to sing Četnik songs and raise three fingers. He refused. They stripped him to the waist and pushed him face down to the floor. They beat him with wooden and iron pipes until they got tired and until he stopped showing signs of life. During this they tried to force him to drink beer. Then they took him out of the hall.

We bandaged efendi's neck, they said when they returned.

You said they called only a few? What about the others that they tortured and killed?

The selection of the unfortunate whom they carried out by a ball or rope which hangs from the ceiling and serves for sport exercises.

How?

They would throw the ball on the ceiling, it bounces and whoever it hits is taken to be liquidated. The rope they swung and they'll kill the one who had the bad luck to be touched.

Do you remember anything else?

Well, Džemo Hodžić they first beat up, and then they shot him in the neck thrice. I was among those who carried him to the truck. I saw he was still alive. They also saw him. They returned him to the hall and a Četnik from Milić killed him with an axe handle. In the hall they killed many in front of us, Mehthat Medalia Delić and his two sons and many others. Twice I was in the group that put the dead on trucks. In just these two trucks we loaded 120 corpses.

After the arson of my village Glogovo, Četniks took all of us, men, women, children to the Orthodox church in the village of Kravica. There were already a lot of us Muslims. Around three hundred. They separated able men from the others. Us men they beat with rifle butts and wooden handles.

Did any of the Serb Četniks stand out?

Yes, Momir Nikolić, son of Vasa. Our neighbor from Hranča. With the tool for sharpening knives he first took out Šaban Salkić's right eye and let it hang down his face. Then he took out the left. Then they took him away, saying. "You are going so they can see you."

Was there raping?

Raping of women, girls and little girls they carried out on the road to Kravica and after they locked us in their church. G.B. was 15 years old, A.H. 13, and Ibro's daughter seventeen. While one raped, the other four held the girl by the hands and feet. They were forcing us to watch.

Did you recognize anyone among the Četniks who carried out the rapes?

Zoran Mladenović who was employed in Bratunac, and among these barbarians was also Golub Erić, Četnik and criminal already in World War II.

Where did Četniks carry out all the killings of Bošnjaks?

In the Orthodox church, in front of the church, and on the way while they were leading us to the Serb village of Kravica. Most of us from Glogovo were killed by a female teacher from the Elementary School in Kravica. They called her Bela [White] and I know she is the wife of Ljubisav Jovanović from Kravica. . . . She killed Šaban Gerović with a knife. Nuria Rizvanović she hit with a rifle butt in the head so that both of his eyes dropped out. . . . Then she finished him with a pistol. Salih Junuzović she cut open his belly so that his intestines fell out. One Četnik asked her, "Bela, do you have a heart?" She answered, "I don't have a heart" and continued to kill with a pistol. She killed about thirty men.

Do you have all the names of the murdered?

How would I not know? They were all my relatives and neighbors.

Those who were killing were also your neighbors?

Yes, I know their names. Here, I have a list of both . . . here . .

Good. Thanks. Quiet down now. . . .

11

Protracted Conflict and War in Kosovo

Of all the regions of former Yugoslavia, Kosovo (its formal name was Kosovo and Metohija, sometimes abbreviated to Kosmet; Albanians call it Kosova) was doubtlessly the most difficult to untangle; people often referred to it as the Kosovo knot. In the post–World War II period, Kosovo was the very first crisis, and it was also the last crisis of the twentieth century, occurring in 1998–1999 and resulting in the creation of the seventh independent state rising out of the ruins of Yugoslavia. Kosovo received international recognition in 2007, though many countries have withheld recognition. In July 2010 the International Court of Justice in The Hague confirmed the legality of Kosovo's declaration of independence from Serbia.[1]

OVERVIEW OF SERBIAN-KOSOVAR ALBANIAN RELATIONSHIPS, 1945–1999

Almost anything the Serbs say about the history of Kosovo is contested by Albanians and vice versa. The Serbs maintain Kosovo was the cradle of their earliest medieval state in the eleventh century and the site of its holiest monasteries, a kind of Serbian Holy Land or Jerusalem. Albanians claim they were there earlier, prior to the arrival of Serb tribes, since they believe themselves to be the descendants of the aboriginal Illyrians. Serbian mytho-history regards the Battle at the Kosovo Field[2] in 1389 as a confrontation between Christian princes led by the Serbian Prince Lazar and Ottoman Turks and their Muslim allies (which would include Albanians). Albanians say that their fighters were allies of the Serbs jointly resisting Ottoman advances. Some

197

historians say that actually there were Serb and Albanian knights and warriors in the Ottoman army as well as in Prince Lazar's. In all these contested
claims, it is probably fair to say that the Serbs were a dominant, state-creating
entity in Kosovo from 1169 until the battle at Kosovo, and that the outcome
of that battle did not spell the immediate termination of the Serbian state.

After the Turkish conquest, when part of the Balkan population converted
to Islam, Albanians converted in much larger numbers than their Balkan
neighbors (70 percent of Albania's population converted to Islam; however,
the percentage of Kosovo Albanian converts rises to over 90). As Muslims,
Albanians, along with ethnic Turks, received a privileged position in ruling
the "masses." Thus from the fourteenth century until the early twentieth century, Albanians were dominant over the Serbs.

Coexistence between Albanians and Serbs was always a zero-sum game;
one dominated while the other was subjugated. Then the tables would turn
and the formerly subjugated would exact terrible revenge when they became
dominant. In Kosovo, as is the case elsewhere in the Balkans, fear and desire
for revenge are probably the single most important factors for ethnic cleansing and genocide. The Serb revenge against the Albanian villages and people,
whom they considered allies of the Turks in the Balkan wars of 1912–1913,
is described in chapter 3. Also described briefly in chapter 3 is the Albanians'
hostility toward the retreating Serbs during World War I. When the Serb army
was fleeing the advance of the Austro-Hungarian and German troops and had
no alternative but to reach the Adriatic Sea via Albania, the Albanian population attacked the troops and many Serbian soldiers lost their lives.

After World War I, Kosovo was incorporated into the newly formed Kingdom of Serbs, Croats, and Slovenes. Now the Serbs were in control, and they
avenged themselves against the Albanians. During World War II the Italian
army occupied Kosovo and annexed it to Italian-controlled Albania, providing the Albanians with the opportunity to terrorize and expel Serbs. After
Italy surrendered to the Allies, the German army quickly occupied Kosovo,
and the Albanians continued to have the upper hand (see chapter 5).

From 1945 to 1967

After the end of World War II, the pendulum continued to swing (and it has
continued to the present) despite some contradictory policies implemented
in Kosovo during Josip Broz Tito's regime. Tito's aim was to stop the pendulum, but ultimately he was not successful. Seeing the very large presence
of Albanians in a land so crucial to Serbia's identity, Tito reincorporated
Kosovo into Serbia but accorded it the status of an autonomous region,[3] similar to the status granted to Vojvodina due to the latter's diverse ethnic com-

position. The Yugoslav Communist Party nurtured some ambitions (fueled by Stalin between 1945 and 1947) that Yugoslavia should incorporate Albania as one of its federal states. During that time, Tito gave fairly substantial aid to the Albanian Communists. All this came to an abrupt end in 1948 when the Soviets expelled Yugoslavia from the Communist block of nations. From that point onward, Yugoslavia and Albania became "mortal" enemies. Prior to that, Aleksandar Ranković, the Serb Communist head of the Ministry of Interior, which included the state security service (OZNA, or Odeljenje za Zaštitu Naroda, later renamed UDBA, or Uprava Državne Bezbednosti), had free reign in terrorizing the Kosovo Albanians, some of whom continued to fight the incorporation of Kosovo into Yugoslavia. The oppression was described as bloody. But then matters improved gradually.

After 1953, Yugoslavia began a gradual policy of liberalization, while the Communist leader Enver Hoxha of Albania moved in exactly the opposite direction, hardening his dictatorship more and more. For many Albanians, survival meant escaping to Yugoslavia over the rugged border. Yugoslavia accepted these refugees, as it provided visible proof that the Yugoslav form of Communism was superior to the hard-line Stalinist version. With Ranković's forced retirement in 1966, the activities of the secret services were considerably relaxed, and gradually Kosovo Albanians received more rights. "Over the next twenty years, and especially after 1974, ethnic Albanians ruled the roost, holding most positions of power in the province."[4]

From 1968 to 1986

From 1968 to 1981, the ethnic Albanian Communists and police dominated the political, economic, and cultural life of the province. Their presence in the federal government was also manifested by two Kosovar Albanians—Fadil Hodža, who was president of Yugoslavia in 1978–1979, and Sinan Hasani, who was president from 1985–1987. Kosovo's representative in the collective presidency had the right to veto, as did all the other members. None of that would suffice, however; ethnic Albanians demanded a republic, saying they were dissatisfied with their status as a national minority within Yugoslavia[5] since they were more numerous than the Slovenes and Montenegrins, who had their own republic. The Albanian language was used in public schools and cultural institutions, and the University of Priština was the only university in the world outside of Albania to provide instruction in the Albanian language.

One might expect that the see-saw of domination and subjugation would finally end and that the two nations would settle into equality, though not necessarily into friendship. However, during one of my visits to Yugoslavia around

1965, as we drove from Macedonia to Montenegro through Kosovo, I was astonished to see that local Albanians were flying the Albanian national flag, which might hint at loyalty to the neighboring country rather than to the one in which they lived. Later I heard stories (from a Serbian professor who taught at the University of Priština) of Albanian students consistently disrupting Serbian professors' classes and making life miserable for them merely because they were Serbs. Non-Albanian soldiers who served the army in Kosovo complained of being discriminated against in various ways, including not being served in Albanian bars and restaurants. Charges were made that Albanians were carrying out genocide against the Serbian and Montenegrin population in Kosovo with non-Albanians being both induced and pressured to leave Kosovo. A demographic explosion of the Albanian population and the increasing number of refugees from Albania dramatically altered the structure of the population, with the Serbs dwindling to the ratio of 1:9. To the average Serbs it seemed that the predominantly ethnic Albanian administration and population was making a deliberate and organized attempt to drive out the Serbs.[6] The Serbian Communists, however, did not dare to criticize this development, as they might have been accused of Serbian nationalism by Tito. It was the Serbian Orthodox Church that first issued a pastoral letter on this issue.[7] At first the letter was not given publicity in Yugoslavia. In it were allegations of murder, rape (including rapes of nuns), forcible migration, and destruction of Serbia's most sacred sites and monasteries, the majority of which are located in Kosovo. An Orthodox priest, Žarko Gavrilović, wrote, for instance, that Serbs were being assailed by both external and internal enemies and that Kosovo was the negative example of these attacks "as there they rape 9 and 13 year old girls, old women and nuns of 70 and older, girls and women, they beat and murder people, burn down monastic residences, dig-over graves and destroy historical monuments, forcibly appropriate arable land and forests. But Serbs don't even have the right to complain against the oppression and injustice. And when they do complain they are proclaimed to be national enemies."[8] The same author, along with other religious and secular writers, wrote of the "biological and spiritual peril of the Serbs" and indicated that Serbs "in a variety of places suffer national humiliation, religious, national, and political discrimination."[9]

Serbian newspapers started printing ever more sensational stories of crimes, including rapes of Orthodox nuns and murders of Serbians by Albanians. Even if the claims of the Serbian Orthodox Church and the media were exaggerated and overdramatized, something was going on that was deeply worrisome to Serbs, yet it was not officially being recognized by the Communist Party, which has always feared the rise of national chauvinism and sought to repress and silence it. But Serbians of Kosovo and Serbs throughout Yugoslavia were increasingly troubled and felt that no one was helping them.

They claimed that a form of ethnic cleansing and perhaps even genocide (in the popular usage of the term) was taking place against Serbs. They did not go to courts, feeling it would be useless, as the courts were controlled by the Communist Party. So, they tried to publicize their grievances. Not many people other than Serbs listened or believed them.

The 1974 constitution granted the two autonomous provinces prerogatives that practically matched those of the six republics, with the exception of the right to secede from the federation. The empowerment of Vojvodina and Kosovo reduced the role of the government of Serbia in these two provinces. Unsurprisingly this would become an issue once Tito died. As long as Tito lived, these legal formulations were basically theoretical in nature since Tito *actually* made all major decisions. During Tito's lifetime, his decisions were loyally implemented by the Communist Party (later called League of Communists) bureaucracy.[10] Only after Tito's death, when the various Communist leaders could no longer reach consensus on which policies to follow and were torn by their regional interest, did they begin agreeing or disagreeing with some of the 1974 constitutional provisions.

A year after Tito's death, many Kosovar Albanians went to the streets to demand that Kosovo be given the status of a republic. The 1974 constitution defined the federation practically as a confederation, and enshrined the freedom of each republic to secede from the federation. If Kosovo became a republic, it would give the more numerous Kosovar Albanians the ability to annex themselves to Albania. The 1974 constitutional provisions spelled the death-knell to Yugoslavia, although people did not realize it at the time. Ignorance can be bliss, and for quite a long time Yugoslavs celebrated the considerable freedoms and prosperity that the country enjoyed in the 1970s and 1980s.

The situation in Kosovo again became a zero-sum game; Albanians gained (though they were far from satisfied and still considered themselves unequal), and Serbians lost. Serbians felt throughout the 1970s and 1980s that the Albanians' ultimate goal was secession and either annexation to Albania (the project Great Albania) or independence for Kosovo. These ambitions were as unacceptable to Serbians as they were attractive to most Albanians. The Kosovar Albanians continued to feel that the Serbians were oppressing them and discriminating against them, while the Serbians felt the Kosovar Albanians were victimizing them and crowding them out of the cradle of their civilization. The Serbs regarded the Albanians as intruders who were now taking over a land that had given them hospitality and more rights than they had in their mother country, from which perhaps 200,000 Albanians had escaped and relocated in Kosovo and beyond.

Kosovo was not Bosnia and Herzegovina (B&H), though some abroad have attempted to draw parallels. The three peoples of B&H shared almost everything in common except religion and to some degree culture. In Kosovo, the two peoples had totally unrelated languages, very different cultures and traditions, and different religions—Serbs are Orthodox, Kosovar Albanians are Muslims. They were divided by rather different clan and family traditions, the Albanians adhering generally to older, stricter customs and mores, while the Serbs yielded more rapidly to modernizing tendencies. For the Serbs this meant smaller families, especially after 1961 (2.8 children per woman); Albanians continued having many children and closely knit large, extended families (6.16 children per woman).[11] A very large number of Serbs were prejudiced against Albanians. Serbs (and most Yugoslavs) used the term *Šiptar* to describe someone backward and ignorant, yet Šiptar was the very name that Albanians proudly used for themselves because Shquipetar in their language means "sons of eagles." Albanians in turn nurtured resentment and disdain toward Serbs. The two did not interact much socially, and intermarriage was rare; however, when free from the manipulation from others, some did have relatively good neighborly relations. Both peoples tended to give preferential treatment to members of their own ethnic group. In general, the groups did not like each other; many hated each other.

The first signs of unrest among the Albanians manifested themselves in the late 1970s but did not erupt in much violence. It was becoming clear that Albanians were organizing themselves, but it was not clear to outsiders what their aim was. Many Serbs feared the worst. Student demonstrations at the University of Priština indicated that Albanians sought greater cultural autonomy and a separate school system. Serbs counterdemonstrated, and the police were given orders to break them up, as the Communists of Serbia still aimed to prevent the rise of nationalism among both groups. However, when Ranković died in 1983, his funeral was attended by tens of thousands of Serbians in clear protest of what they considered unacceptable treatment of their co-nationals in Kosovo.

Increasing reports appeared in the Serbian press and media of Albanians doing ethnic cleansing (often using the term *genocide* instead) by rapes, violence, and pressure tactics, for example, forcing Serbs to sell their properties to Albanians. Subsequent sociological research by Serb civil rights activists[12] proved that Kosovo actually had fewer rapes than the other republics and that most of the rapes were Albanian on Albanian and Serbian on Serbian. Events were heading to a boiling point and proved also to be a turning point in Slobodan Milošević's career and in Yugoslavia's history.

From 1987 to 1999

Many domestic and international delegations made their way to Kosovo to have a firsthand look at the situation. A previously little known Communist bureaucrat, Milošević was sent to Kosovo on such a fact-finding journey on April 24, 1987, and "a happening" took place at Kosovo Polje, near Priština. Heading to a public meeting, Milošević was met by local Serbs complaining that they were being abused by the police when they wanted to express their grievances. Milošević's spontaneous response, "No one has the right to beat you in your own country," exploded like a bombshell. The former inconspicuous banker was transformed into an instant folk hero, a legend in his own time. "Slobo" (abbreviation of Slobodan) gave rise to the *maspok* (*masovni pokret*, or mass movement) that was not only a wake-up call to Serbian pride but also an "antibureaucratic revolution" in which Milošević and his followers would go from town to town and topple the entrenched Communist bureaucrats and replace them with people who enthusiastically followed his every word. In an incredibly short time, Milošević became the undisputed leader of Serbs, not merely in Kosovo or in Serbia, but throughout Yugoslavia. To many of his followers, Milošević was a new Tito—a new mythic Kosovo liberator replacing the mythical Tito father figure.[13] Milošević's genius was that he was the first Communist leader to understand that Tito was *really* dead and that there was a power vacuum that he could fill. This he intended to do—except that the Communist leaders of the other republics already had cushy jobs that they were not willing to relinquish, thinking that it was better to be a big fish in a small pond rather than a small fish in a big one, never knowing when the bigger fish might decide to gobble them up.

Kosovo played a crucial role in stimulating Serbian nationalism. The 600th anniversary of the legendary Battle of Kosovo took place on Vidovdan (St. Vid's Day) on June 28, 1989. Being an exceptionally important date, it was preceded with great pomp and ceremony by a highly publicized procession of the relics of Prince Lazar from Belgrade through much of the territory where Serbs lived in Yugoslavia—many of which were never part of Lazar's fiefdom. The emotional pitch increased to a fever point at Kosovo Polje, where between 300,000 and 2 million Serbs had gathered on St. Vid's Day. Milošević descended in a helicopter and in the presence of a large number of Orthodox bishops, priests, and political dignitaries delivered a speech that brought the crowd to exultation. It was not a demagogic speech but reminded the Serbs of all the sacrifices they had made so that all could live in a common country; Milošević pledged not to allow Yugoslavia to be broken up. He reminded the enthralled crowd that "six centuries later, we are again in battles and before battles. They are not armed [battles] though those may not be excluded. But, regardless of what kind they are, they cannot be won without decisiveness, courage, sacrifice."[14] The animosity and hatred between Serbs and Albanians would not relent from that point onward.

Three years before, in 1986, several members of the Serbian Academy of Sciences and Arts (SANU for Srpska Akademija Nauka i Umetnosti) wrote a draft of a "Memorandum"—inaccurately attributed to the writer Dobrica Ćosić, who soon would become rump Yugoslavia's prime minister—in which the predicament of the Serbs in Yugoslavia, especially in regard to Kosovo, was analyzed. Recommendation was made that Serbs should no longer shoulder the main responsibility for governing and policing Yugoslavia only to receive accusations of hegemony rather than acknowledgment or gratefulness. Instead, they argued, Serbia should demand corrections to the 1974 constitution, which had deprived it of equal status in the federation. The "Memorandum" stated that genocide was being carried out on the Serbians by Kosovo Albanians, thereby seconding the claim made by the Serbian Orthodox Church a few years earlier. In short, they saw themselves as victims— exactly at the same time when some of the other nationalities perceived themselves as victims of Serbian domination. Comparative victimology is a recipe for disaster, as each side sees itself as aggrieved and as having to assert its right to rectify the suffering as best it can. This "Memorandum" was the work of only a few authors. It was never discussed or adopted by SANU and it was leaked out to the press without SANU's authorization; hence, it was never an official document.[15]

Milošević was able to use the never-approved SANU "Memorandum" as a directional signpost. He was not a Serbian nationalist, and never became one, but he was politically astute and realized that nationalism was the card to play as Socialism and Marxism lost their power over the masses and even over the bureaucrats. Communists in the entire country were now quickly morphing into respective nationalists. First the conflict was between national Communist bureaucracies, though it soon became a conflict between nationalists, that is, national chauvinists, as others emerged to join the feverish drive to discover their people's true identity, as quickly as a chameleon changes colors.

Milošević rapidly moved to assure the Kosovo Serbians' primacy in all areas of political and economic life. Albanians struck back with massive demonstrations that resulted in violent police repression in which about 100 died and 900 were wounded. The September 1987 mass murder of fellow soldiers by an apparently mentally disturbed ethnic Albanian soldier (among his victims were also Bosnian Muslims) was interpreted both by the police and the press as a well-planned attack meant to destabilize Yugoslavia with the backing of the regime in Tirana. Simultaneously, Milošević skillfully took control of all Serbia's governmental and party structures while alienating the other republics. In 1989 Serbia's parliament adopted constitutional amendments that revoked the autonomy of both Kosovo and Vojvodina and reintegrated the entire territory of the Republic of Serbia into a single governmental unit. Serbs celebrated; the minorities responded generally with passive resistance and occasionally with violence.[16] Yugoslavia was rapidly heading toward its demise.

The power relationships in Kosovo had changed dramatically in 1985. Serbs started repressing Albanians, who lost their leadership positions in the Communist Party, the government, police, state corporations, schools, and universities. The Albanian language was marginalized in public communications, and the government of Serbia utilized a brutal repressive mechanism to elevate the Serbian population at the expense of the Albanian. Incidents of violence took place, especially when the Albanian population organized strikes and demonstrations to protest the changes. Albanians generally avoided armed violence because they were aware of the power of the police and the army. The ethnic Albanian leaders and population formed a parallel unofficial system of self-government, organizing their own schools and economic activities with the financial assistance of émigrés, and they successfully appealed to the international community, gaining the sympathies of Western politicians and intellectuals. This was the beginning of a fairly deeply ingrained perception in the West: "Kosovar Albanians, good; Serbians, bad." Milošević briskly moved to clamp down on Albanian resistance, including a week-long hunger strike by Albanian miners in the Trepča mines in March 1989. This hunger strike gained them the sympathy of many in Slovenia, Croatia, and Bosnia (some of it humanitarian but some politically motivated), who sensed that Albanians were capable of weakening Serbia and thereby giving more elbow room for their own independence movement.

Many expected the Kosovar Albanians to rise in an insurrection during the wars in Croatia and Bosnia, but that did not happen. Milošević's policies to secure monopoly of power for Serbs in Kosovo were met with Gandhian peaceful resistance led by the writer Ibrahim Rugova. From 1987 to 1998, the Kosovar Albanians peacefully resisted and Milošević had plenty of chances to work out some sort of expanded autonomy with the flexible Rugova, but Milošević was convinced that only an iron fist policy would keep the Albanians docile. Milošević's acts of repression strengthened the solidarity and resistance of the Kosovar Albanians, and from time to time they too responded violently, which in turn brought more police repression, particularly against students, consisting of mass arrests, interrogations, beatings, internment, closing of schools, and so on. When the Krajina Serbs were driven out of Croatia by Croat forces with American assistance, creating the largest ethnic cleansing in the Balkans up to that point, the stage was set for a change in the Kosovar Albanian stance. Many concluded that Rugova's stance wasn't producing the desired results, and they became convinced that only a military confrontation with the Serbs would do so.[17] A vicious cycle of Albanian insurrection and Serb repression, with ineffective police measures and policy miscalculations, culminated in the war of 1999. During the 1980s and most of the 1990s, however, there appeared to be alternatives to war, but Milošević did not pursue them.

European governments felt that the situation in the lands of former Yugoslavia was normalizing and that it was time to repatriate the large number of refugees from the previous Yugoslav wars. This may have contributed to the determination by the more radical elements of the Kosovar resistance to take more violent measures. The two communities seemed to be locked in an irreconcilable conflict. Kosovo Serbians lived with siege mentality; Kosovar Albanians were suffering harassment and persecution. The practice of nonviolent civil resistance,[18] which had the support of conflict resolution activists in the West, was weakening. Increasingly, Kosovar Albanians were no longer willing to settle for greater autonomy within Serbia; they sought self-determination with an eye toward independence or annexation to Albania.[19]

From 1989 to 1995 the situation in Kosovo was frozen, stuck on "bad." The Albanian community was being remarkably disciplined in nonviolent resistance and noncooperation while Serbia was preoccupied with the wars in Croatia and B&H. The Serbs began losing both of these wars in 1995, and Milošević was not in the mood to lose Kosovo as well—and his policies assured that he would lose it a few years later.

The older Kosovar Albanians were willing to continue Rugova's tactics and strategy, but many young Kosovars were losing patience and were amenable to the call to arms by a small band of rebels that called themselves Kosovo Liberation Army (KLA in English; UÇK in Albanian), that was becoming increasingly active in 1996. Beginning in March of 1998, Isaak Musliu, Adem Jashari, Agim Çeku, Ramush Haradinaj, Fatmir Limaj, and others began attacking, killing, and kidnapping Serbian police and civilians and claiming control of Drenica, an area of central Kosovo in which the resistance to Serbs was habitual. The Serbians immediately labeled the KLA a criminal terrorist band, an assessment shared by the CIA and other Western intelligence agencies.[20] Many people in these bands had been common criminals who had engaged in the lucrative trade of transporting drugs from the Near East into Western Europe; they also engaged in white slavery, black market sale of weapons, and other criminal activities. Younger Kosovars no longer cared about the immoral and criminal character of these bands. As long as they were for Albanian independence and against the Serbs they were acceptable. KLA's numbers and popularity grew. Their first infusion of sophisticated arms came from the 1997 looting of the armories of the Albanian army in Albania proper, when many of the weapons found their way into Kosovo; the second infusion was made possible through the financial support of the Albanian immigrants in the West who financed and helped to smuggle arms. The U.S. government, being fed up with Milošević, figured that any enemy of Milošević and of Serbia should be supported in order to weaken Serbia and hopefully topple Milošević. A large number of sources reported that most of the violence was caused by the KLA, the successes of which provoked Serbian counterinsurgency measures, and those, in turn, eventually resulted in covert and overt U.S. support of the KLA.[21] "The KLA had a record of viciousness and racism that differed little from that of Milošević's forces. Attacking Serb civilians through terrorist acts was always a central feature of the KLA's military strategy."[22] In 1998 the KLA established the clandestine Lapusnik prison camp in which they mistreated and murdered Serbs and Albanian collaborators.[23]

Needless to say, no government, including the government of Serbia, could allow such terrorist and insurrectional activities in their territory. The KLA's aim was clearly not just more autonomy—that was Rugova's aim—but secession. Milošević and his advisors felt that the only way to deal with the KLA threat was ruthless suppression. One of the results was a series of massacres in Drenica, the region of the birthplace and stronghold of KLA, at the end of February and early March 1998, during which both innocent people and insurrectionists were tortured and executed. In the summer of 1998, mass protests of Albanians led to a Serbian response of sending army and police reinforcements, which led to a "week of terror in Drenica." The KLA did not sustain many losses, but civilians suffered. The greater the police brutality, the more Albanians joined the KLA. Many Kosovar Albanians came to believe that the time for passive resistance was over; it was time for armed combat, reflected in the slogan "We are all UÇK." And, indeed, the insurrection had the active or passive support of most Albanian civilians. The vicious circle of violence soon led to ever-increasing killings, torture, beatings, arson, arrests, and human rights abuses on the part of both sides—many innocents suffered along with the guilty. In mid-July 1998, about 2,000 Albanians (and a much smaller number of Serbs) were killed, over 40,000 homes were burned down, and upwards of 300,000–400,000 people were internally displaced.[24] Then the KLA seized the initiative, and according to British defense minister Lord Robertson, up until January 1999, "the KLA were responsible for more deaths in Kosovo than the Yugoslav authorities had been."[25]

In September 1998, the Organization for the Security and Cooperation in Europe (OSCE) decided to send a large number of unarmed monitors (around 2,000) in the Kosovo Verification Mission—but according to Howard Clark, the monitors came too late and were too poorly prepared. The OSCE concluded that they were unable to monitor or prevent the escalating violence and withdrew in late March 1999. The OSCE had previously confirmed a combined Serbian police and army massacre of forty-five Albanian men at Račak and additional killings in Rogovo, Ragovina, Vučitrn, and Kačanik,[26] as well as Bela Crkva, Mala and Velika Krusa, Dubrava, Meja, and Suva Reka. The massacre at Račak provoked a NATO military response, just as the market massacres in Sarajevo and Srebrenica did in Bosnia. The Serbians denied the massacre and claimed the Albanians were trying to provoke Western attacks by staging the massacre using bodies of KLA people previously killed in armed combat.[27]

OVERVIEW OF THE WAR OF 1999

The international community, especially the Contact Group (United States, United Kingdom, France, Germany, and Russia) attempted to resolve the conflict but did not have great success, especially since the Russians tended to give greater credence to the Serbian version of events than the Western allies did. Fearing a huge influx of refugees, as happened in the Bosnian conflict, the West decided to become proactive rather than reactive. Bill Clinton thought he had learned a lesson in Bosnia: don't wait until the tragedy strikes; instead intervene preemptively. Milošević was being pressured into accepting Western military presence in Kosovo, which he steadfastly refused, but he did allow unarmed inspection.

After the massacre at Račak, Madeline Albright, Clinton's secretary of state, and other members of the contact group convened a meeting at Rambouillet, France, in February 1999. On the surface it was to be a negotiation between the representatives of the Serbian government and the KLA rebels and Kosovar politicians in the presence of the diplomats of the great powers, but that was not the case. Diana Johnstone rightly called the meeting a farce.[28] The conditions consisted of a list of nonnegotiable points presented to the two parties with a take-it-or-leave-it attitude. The Kosovar rebels at first refused to accept the deal but were convinced to accept it when they realized that at least one of the conditions imposed by the West could not be accepted by *any* sovereign state, including Yugoslavia, namely, that NATO troops would not merely control Kosovo, but would have unlimited access to any part of Serbia without Serbia's permission. The "agreement" that was proposed by the West required only symbolic concessions from the Albanians and a humiliation for the Serbians (according to Clark, a "defeat—a defeat brought on by their own maltreatment of the Albanians"[29]). One cannot argue with Clark's conclusion that "Rambouillet was a diktat to Serbia. . . . Now the West wanted a showdown . . . NATO embarked on a campaign not to protect Kosovo but rather to defeat and punish Serbia."[30] Milošević naturally refused. Neither he nor any head of a sovereign state would or could accept such a demeaning condition. It was a condition calculated to enable NATO to declare war on Serbia—the first (unauthorized by the UN) attack by NATO on a country that had not militarily intervened against another country. Richard Holbrooke, Clinton's point man for the Balkans, did go to Belgrade to impress upon Milošević the seriousness of the situation, but he refused to budge, and the NATO air force began a systematic bombing not only of military targets in Kosovo and throughout Serbia and Montenegro but of civilians, transportation (buses, trains, etc.), the electric grid, oil refineries, water processing plants, and other targets. The bombing lasted seventy-eight days before Milošević succumbed. Massive destruction resulted but, curiously, relatively little damage was incurred by Serbia's army. However, during the bombardment a far larger expulsion and flight of Kosovar Albanians took place than in the pre-attack days.

The air campaign that was allegedly fought to prevent the ethnic cleansing of Albanians and protect the multinational composition of Kosovo achieved the exact opposite. First, it led to an ethnic cleansing of Albanians of massive proportions, allegedly resulting in over 200,000 refugees. Later, when Serbia yielded and NATO ground forces entered Kosovo, leading to a massive and rapid return of the Kosovar Albanians, the KLA in turn carried out a reverse ethnic cleansing, killing and driving out most of the Serbs, as well as Roma, Turks, Bosniaks, Montenegrins, and others. In a relatively short time Kosovo ceased to be a multiethnic community and became a nearly homogenous Albanian province protected by the very forces that were to ensure its multiethnicity.

In the prelude to the war, NATO claimed that the Serbs had carried out genocide in Kosovo. U.S. Secretary of Defense William Cohen justified the impending war as being fought to stop genocide. He stated that 100,000 Albanian men of military age were missing.[31] President Bill Clinton also claimed that tens of thousands had been killed by the Serbs and, later, at a June 25, 1999, press conference, stated that "NATO stopped deliberate, systematic efforts at ethnic cleansing and genocide."[32] He compared Kosovo to the Holocaust. The U.S. State Department likewise stated that there was evidence of genocide, claiming that up to 500,000 Kosovars were dead or missing. These charges were vastly exaggerated.

While the media presented the seventy-eight-day bombing of Serbia (March 24–June 11, 1999)—which in itself caused 495 dead,[33] most of them Serbians, and many of them hundreds of miles away from Kosovo—as an attempt to *prevent* Milošević's ethnic cleansing (some immediately called it genocide), my contention is that it actually greatly *intensified* the ethnic cleansing. Of course, the Serbians would have been happy to see all Albanians vacate Kosovo, but they knew this was not practical so they opted for extreme brutality that might either pacify the rebellion or induce many Kosovars to leave the province. But the exodus became massive only *after* the bombing began on March 24, 1999. In contrast to the situation in Bosnia, where NATO acted too cautiously and slowly, Steven L. Burg argues that NATO too quickly abandoned its mediation between the Serbian government and the representatives of the Albanian insurrectionists, saying that "mediation rapidly gave way to coercive bombing, which triggered a Serbian plan to expel much of the ethnic Albanian population, carried out with great violence against the innocent civilians."[34] According to Tim Judah, just before the onset of NATO bombing there were hardly any refugees in Albania; a week later there were 300,000.[35] Instead of finding evidence of a careful Serb plan of ethnic cleansing, Judah reports that there were many inconsistencies in the apparently quickly devised plan to destroy the KLA and hopefully embroil neighboring Albania, Macedonia, Montenegro, Bosnia, and possibly Greece and Turkey in a regional war over the sudden influx of refugees that would complicate NATO's mission. The plan did not work; it boomeranged on Milošević. At first people of the world may have had sympathy for Serbia when they saw a small country being attacked by the mightiest military pact, but the sympathy was lost when they watched cable TV and repeatedly saw pictures of miserable Albanians fleeing across the borders. Western propaganda attempted to portray a Holocaust-like forced deportation of the mass of humanity, but while no clear picture emerges of what happened there during these weeks, some of the refugees most likely fled out of fear, having heard rumors of massacres and being afraid of NATO bombing. Other Albanians were rounded up by the Serbs and expelled, and still others were threatened by the KLA to leave in order to aggravate the situation, employing the Leninist principle of making things worse in order to make them better. And lastly there were contradictory orders by local commanders who themselves did not know exactly what to do. Judging from reports, the Serbian army was reasonably careful in their treatment of Albanians, but the Serbian police were not, particularly police units composed of local Serbs. As always, by far the most brutal were the paramilitaries both from Kosovo and from Serbia who were intent on murdering, looting, raping, burning, and committing other atrocities.[36] Charges of organized rapes, some of which were called "town square mass rapes," were launched by some Western politicians and mass media. These charges were never substantiated and are considered "imaginary" by Johnstone.[37]

In an article, David Gibbs shows that "in fact, the Serbs implemented the Holbrooke agreement, and it was the *Albanians* who caused the agreement to break down"[38] and thus made a war inevitable. Moreover "the record suggests that the Clinton administration was seeking a pretext for war with Serbia,"[39] and the collapse of peace talks at Rambouillet offered this pretext. John

Gilbert, former British defense minister, stated at a later parliamentary hearing "that key negotiators were in fact seeking to sabotage the conference."[40] Thus, it was not unreasonable for Serbia to later object to the American and European demands that NATO peacekeepers enjoy "unrestricted passage and unimpeded access" throughout Yugoslavia—in effect, that Serbia consent to being an occupied country.

Americans were told that the Serbs in that war were oppressors while Albanians were victims—an oversimplification that bears a strong resemblance to later American reports of the guilty Sunnis and innocent Shiites of Iraq. But the KLA, Gibbs recounts, "had a record of viciousness and racism that differed little from that of [Serbian leader Slobodan] Milošević's forces." And far from preventing mass killings, the "surgical strikes" by NATO only increased them. The total number killed on both sides before the war was about 2,000. After the bombing, which resulted in fewer than 500 dead, mostly civilians and including many Albanians, and in the Serb revenge for the bombing, between 9,000 and 12,100 people were killed by Serb security forces.[41] ICTY's (International Criminal Tribunal for the Former Yugoslavia) prosecutor's office also estimates that after the bombing, 3,000 people were missing, of whom about 2,500 were Albanians, 400 were Serbs, and 100 were Roma.

A great wave of Kosovar Albanians was either expelled or fled. According to the UN High Commission for Refugees, the total number was 848,100 of which 444,600 fled into Albania; 244,500 fled into Macedonia; 69,900 fled into Montenegro;[42] and 91,000 either fled into Bosnia or were airlifted to other countries. More than 500,000 were displaced inside Kosovo. Over half of Kosovo's 2 million inhabitants were uprooted. Clark states that the Serbians had no need to kill, as Albanians were ready to flee, but the Serbians killed, raped, burned, looted, and carried out war crimes and crimes against humanity—all in the desire to punish the Albanians for all the misery they thought Albanians caused the Serbians over the decades. Both sides visualized themselves as victims—but in the early stages of the conflict and during the war, Albanians suffered enormously. If escaping Serbian control was the goal, the suffering may have paid off.

In May 1999 Slobodan Milošević was indicted by the ICTY for crimes against humanity for deporting 750,000 Kosovars and for the deaths of 600 individually identified Albanians, specifying massacres in Srbica, Djakova, and Velika Kruša. Since Milošević died in The Hague prior to the completion of his trial, the ICTY was not able to legally establish what happened in Kosovo.

A team of scholars led by Patrick Ball of the American Association for the Advancing of Science issued a report to ICTY entitled "Killings and Refugees Flow in Kosovo March–June 1999."[43] The report states that the killings and migrations occurred early in NATO's attack, mostly late March and early April 1999. The report's authors reject the hypothesis that the NATO attacks caused the killings or that the KLA's fighting with the Serbs was the cause; instead, they conclude that the actions of the Yugoslav armed forces are to blame, as the population flights were not random and sporadic but were caused by a common, systematic activity. They estimate that 10,356 Kosovars were killed, a computation based on a sample, and provided the range of 9,002 to 12,122. The report's authors also conclude that 850,000 Kosovars were forced out of their homes. Many of them had their Yugoslav IDs taken and the men were often separated from the women and taken away. From this they conclude that the exodus was due to Serbian policy rather than Albanian panic.

A report on the flight of refugees to Macedonia[44] states that 344,500 refugees entered Macedonia with an unusual pattern; there was a sudden increase after the beginning of the NATO campaign and a sudden decrease in the later stages.

From these reports I conclude that as horrendous as the police, military, and paramilitary massacres of Albanians had been in 1998 and 1999, there was no great flight and/or expulsion of Albanians from Kosovo until the NATO bombing. The bombardment of NATO may not have directly caused the flight and expulsion, but indirectly it led to both a spontaneous flight and a wave of ethnic cleansing carried out by the Serbian police and military, accompanied by repulsive war crimes. I concur that "while massive violations of human rights occurred in Kosovo, however, genocidal atrocities did not occur, at least as defined under the Genocide Conventions."[45] Kosovar Albanians had been expecting that the international community would resolve their dilemma and bring about liberation from the Serbs. A tragic mixture of Albanian flight, upon seeing that NATO was not undertaking a land invasion but only aerial bombing, and the Serb police administering as much destruction as they could to their hated enemy brought about this catastrophic exodus.

Both sides inflicted severe human losses upon each other, but the more organized Serbian government carried out massacres and caused a massive disappearance of Kosovars, many of whom had been arrested and imprisoned. Subsequently, the Serbian press discovered that many of the Albanians had been cruelly slaughtered by Serbia's authorities, who, in order to avoid the discovery of bodies in mass graves, transported them in refrigerated trucks to the north of Serbia where many of them were dumped into the Danube or buried in mass graves at the huge air force base at Batajnica, Vojvodina.[46] Serbian authorities attempted to hide the mass graves, so that the number of murdered may never be accurately known. The round figure of 10,000 killed is probably much more on target than the initial U.S. claim of 500,000 dead.

More accurate yet is the ICTY figure of 11,334 dead, though only 2,108 bodies had been excavated by 1999.[47]

From 1999–2003

Fortunately the exodus was of relatively short duration. After Milošević caved under Russian pressure and NATO's widespread bombing, 808,913 out of 848,100 Albanians returned within weeks or months,[48] making it one of the quickest refugee returns in history. However, as a result of their return, between 100,000 and 247,391[49] non-Albanians (about 50 percent of all Serbs living in Kosovo) fled. Enraged Albanians carried out a reverse ethnic cleansing not only of Serbs and Montenegrins but also of Roma, Turks, Goranci, Bosniaks, and Croats. According to Macedonian sources, after August 1999 a wave of about 2,000 Roma arrived in Macedonia from Kosovo, fleeing the returning Albanians, and about 8,000 Serbs, Roma, and Albanians who had been unregistered in Macedonia decided not to return to Kosovo.

UN Resolution 1244 states that no legal changes would be made to the borders of Federal Republic of Yugoslavia (Serbia and Montenegro still carried the old name), but Kosovo was handed over to a temporary UN administration and to KFOR (Kosovo Force) consisting mostly of NATO but also Russian troops. Serbia, in fact, lost Kosovo permanently, as the United States and its allies did not allow (and probably never intended to) Kosovo to return to Serbian administration. The NATO intervention was allegedly to preserve a multiethnic Kosovo, but Kosovo had never been more ethnically homogenous than under the UN administration. Only small Serbian enclaves and a handful of Serbians living in big cities remained, daring not to leave their homes without KFOR protection.

THE DESTRUCTION OF SERBIAN ORTHODOX HOLY PLACES

Mass communal violence in Kosovo during mid-March 2004 seems to have surprised many in the West, including UN civilian and military authorities.[50] But it did not surprise those who have some sense of the long-range relationships between ethnic Albanians and Serbs living in Kosovo. For some of us, this was a "we told you so" case. In October 2003 a Russian (of Jewish rather than Orthodox affiliation) who served several years in Kosovo as an UNMIK (UN Mission in Kosovo) policeman informed me that NATO-led UN forces were not protecting the province's Serbs, who were rarely able to leave their homes. In his opinion, the ability of Kosovo's Serbs to survive over the long term was questionable.[51]

In mid-March 2004, mob violence in Kosovo left twenty-eight dead (of whom eight were Serbs), perhaps a thousand wounded, and the destruction of several Serbian villages, including the torching of over 400 homes, the destruction of thirty churches, and damage to another eleven churches.[52] The mayhem resembled old-style anti-Jewish pogroms involving pillage, destruction, and death. This devastation took place in a province "controlled" by some 18,000 UN KFOR soldiers and several thousand UNMIK policemen. UN forces themselves came under attack by Albanian mobs, with several soldiers killed, some injured, and seventy-two UN vehicles destroyed. The UN forces did save some lives, but on the whole they could not stem the violence.

The drowning on March 16, 2004, of three Albanian children near Kosovska Mitrovica, a Serbian enclave in northern Kosovo, sparked mob action. Albanians assumed that Serbs were responsible because the sole surviving thirteen-year-old stated that Serbs had chased them and unleashed a dog against them. Albanian language press and media coverage inflamed emotions. Near Kosovska Mitrovica, stone-throwing Albanian mobs attacked Serbs. The fighting quickly escalated to the use of firearms. Almost instantly the rest of Kosovo exploded as Albanians attacked everything Serbian that was in their way, especially monasteries, cloisters, and churches, many of which were centuries-old treasures of Orthodox spiritual creativity.[53] Serbian Orthodox bishop Artemije (Radosavljević) of Raška-Prizren and Kosovo-Metohija described the attacks as another Kristalnacht, the infamous 1938 Nazi pogrom against Jews in Germany, while UN governor of Kosovo, Harri Holkeri, called them "a crime against humanity." For a senior NATO commander, the attacks in Kosovo were "not far from ethnic cleansing."[54]

According to *Forum 18*, 112 Orthodox churches and monasteries have been destroyed since 1990 without adequate UN protection.[55] Nor has anyone been apprehended for these crimes since the beginning of UN control. However, during the riots of 2004 events were more dramatic in that hundreds if not thousands of Albanians participated. At first it seemed that the actions were spontaneous, but some UN authorities later claimed that events were well-organized. Later some Albanian politicians and former KLA commanders were finally arrested and charged with orchestrating the destruction.[56] In the end an international prosecutor cleared Serbs of any involvement in the drowning of the children.[57]

ETHNIC CLEANSING IN REVERSE

The Albanian process of reverse ethnic cleansing against Serbs in Kosovo continued to take place.[58] What happens in Kosovo has an almost immediate impact in the region, not only on Albanian-Serb relations, but on Muslim-Christian relations across the Balkans. Some Serbs view the events in Kosovo as the criminal activity of organized Albanian bands who are intent on wiping out the remnants of Serbian life and culture in a region that Serbs see as the cradle of their nationhood. Indeed, as soon as violence broke out in Kosovo in the spring of 2004, it was answered by mob violence that broke out in other parts of Serbia, where the sole mosque in Belgrade was set on fire,[59] as was one in Niš and Novi Pazar and an Islamic center in Novi Sad. In other places, lacking Muslim targets, Protestant centers were attacked. In neighboring Macedonia, Molotov cocktails were thrown at a mosque in Kumanovo, while, presumably in retaliation, two small Orthodox churches in that vicinity were attacked. In Bosnia, Orthodox churches as well as mosques were reciprocally attacked, while in Montenegro mosques had to be protected.

Sacred objects, no matter how precious, historic, and important, were immediate targets of interethnic violence. Some Albanians wrote, "Death to Serbs" and "Down with UNMIK" on church walls of Prizren, just as Serbs used to write on mosques, "This is Serbia," or as Macedonians once erected a cross on a Muslim building in Bitola. Even though a small number of religious fanatics may have been involved in these attacks, I still remain convinced of the fundamental correctness of my conclusion from the early 1990s that the Balkans are engulfed in religious wars fought by irreligious people.[60] The most immediate cause of these events is the radically different goals of Albanians and Serbs regarding Kosovo and the incredibly naïve expectation of Western politicians that where others failed over the span of centuries, they can create a multiethnic democratic community out of Kosovo in a short time.

But local aspirations are not multiethnic. Most Albanians want an independent state of Kosovo, ideally without any non-Albanians, especially with no Serbs. Many aspire in the long run to unite with Albania and wish to annex Albanian populated areas in Macedonia, southern Serbia, Montenegro, and Greece. They fancy that the United States is tacitly supportive of at least some aspects of a Great Albania project.

On the other hand, Serb appetites for a Great Serbia have been severely cramped, and a much more realistic view prevails in Belgrade that an international supervision of Kosovo is a necessity. Belgrade would settle for a partition of Kosovo even as Kosova has declared independence, which the Serbs vow they will never accept. Neither Albanians nor Serbs believe peaceful coexistence in Kosovo is possible, making the Western dream of a multiethnic democracy in Kosovo unrealistic. The allegedly "preventive" and "humanitarian" NATO attack on Serbia in 1999 has only made matters worse.[61] Instead of contributing to the solution, the resulting UN administration of Kosovo has continued to be a tremendously destabilizing factor because none of the presently available solutions are acceptable to both Albanians and Serbs. In the meantime the UN and European politicians still delude themselves with notions of a multiethnic Kosovo democracy.

Pictures of the destroyed churches and monasteries in Belo Polje, Čaglavica, Devic, Djakovica, Gnjilane, Kosovo Polje, Kosovska Mitrovica, Lipljan, Obilić, Peć, Podujevo, Prizren, Priština, and Svinjare are a testimony to the barbaric nature of conflict between Albanians and their Slavic neighbors.[62] At the same time, it is doubtful that Albanian attacks on Orthodox Serbian sacred places are primarily religious in motivation. Probably only small groups are inspired by Wahabism, a radical militant sect of Islam, from Saudi Arabia. It seems that the primary motive is the primal instinct of ethnic cleansing—Albanians' desire to expel all non-Albanians and to appropriate real estate, legally or illegally. To that end most Albanians want to remove *everything* that is Serbian from their midst. Churches, monasteries, and graveyards are symbols of a people's presence and identity and even hooligans instinctively know that by attacking these symbols, one sends the unmistakable signal that the enemy is to vanish.

While ethnic cleansing seems to be primarily a secular process, it does carry embedded religious overtones. Deep in the Balkan subconscious is the ethnoreligious identity marking people with the stamp *Orthodox, Catholic, Christian,* or *Muslim.* All of these labels figure in the fabric of many centuries of enduring conflict. The antidote would be tolerance, human rights, and interreligious dialogue. But all three are in woefully short supply in the Balkans.

Kosova's Independence

In 2007 Kosova declared itself an independent country. It was very quickly recognized by the United States and some of its allies—over sixty countries so far. However, some NATO countries and many other countries, and of course Serbia, have not recognized it. It is too early to know whether Kosova's independence will in the long run bring regional reconciliation or whether it will continue to be the main bone of contention, unsettling relations among countries. I see little reason to be optimistic.

Ironically, the United States and the international community intervened in Croatia and Kosovo against Serbs to prevent ethnic cleansing of non-Serbs and preserve the multiethnic nature of these two countries; instead, they became complicit in the reverse ethnic cleansing of Serbs from both of those countries. Now only a very tiny Serb community of mostly very elderly people remains in Croatia and Kosova, living in fear; yet the West proclaimed the victory of pluralistic democracy. A dose of sarcasm is well justified. It is encouraging that Balkan political and military leaders were hauled to ICTY to answer for their misdeeds. It is a shame that more of them were not tried and a pity that the judicial net cannot yet be cast wider to include others from the international community whose decisions caused untold suffering; doing so would allow the Balkan war criminals to enjoy the company of their more powerful "neighbors," who also contributed to the carnage.

As for Kosovo, one wonders when the pendulum will swing again.

DID GENOCIDES AND/OR ETHNIC CLEANSING OCCUR IN KOSOVO?

Four accusations need to be answered regarding whether genocide and/or ethnic cleansing occurred in Kosovo after World War II. It seems too obvious that massacres, various war crimes, and crimes against humanity have occurred much of the time from 1945 to the present.

The first accusation is that the Albanians were carrying out genocide against the Serbian population by steadily pushing them out of Kosovo. This charge was made by the Serbian Orthodox Church and later by the "Memorandum" of the Serbian Academy of Arts and Sciences as well as the Serbian media in the 1970s and 1980s.

The second accusation is that the government of Slobodan Milošević carried out genocide in 1998 and 1999 just prior to and during NATO's war against Serbia over Kosovo.

The third is that NATO's bombing of Serbia constituted genocide.

And the fourth is the countercharge that the KLA and the Albanian Kosovar authorities carried out a reverse genocide of the Serbs after the end of the fighting, doing so with the complicity of NATO's KFOR and the international community's governing authorities.

With regard to the first accusation, there is no evidence of intentional genocide, but Albanians persistently pressured Serbians and Montenegrins to move out of Kosovo, amounting to low level ethnic cleansing.

Regarding the second accusation, very obvious ethnic cleansing of Kosovar Albanians took place in 1999 (at least); it was witnessed on TVs worldwide, with hundreds of thousands of ethnic Albanians fleeing, being deported, or being internally displaced by actions of military and police forces (regular as well as paramilitary) commanded by Milošević and his government. These flights were accompanied by killing and rape (there is no evidence of genocidal rape, though some people quickly wanted to add the charge to make the Serbs look more monstrous). The question of intent needs to be explored by courts to see whether the Serbs intended to cleanse Kosovo of all or most Albanians. It seems more likely that the aggressive meddling of the international community (specifically the United States and NATO) through concentrated and widespread aerial attacks on all of Serbia and Montenegro led to a typical Balkan explosion of blind rage, with Serbs intent on inflicting as much harm as possible to others even at the cost of one's own survival. There does not seem to be enough proof for the accusation of genocide. No charges of genocide were raised in ICTY's Kosovo indictment against Milošević.[63] However, accusations of war crimes and crimes against humanity were leveled against not only the forces of Serbia but also those of the KLA. Entire villages had been ethnically cleansed and for a short time it seemed as if most Albanians or Serbs in some regions of the province were being driven out.

The third case—NATO's bombing of Serbia, including Kosovar Albanians on whose behalf the bombing allegedly took place—did not start ethnic cleansing but contributed to the speedier expulsion and killing of Albanians, even if it happened only as an unintended consequence. But the killing of many innocents (more civilians died than soldiers) constitutes war crimes on the part of NATO forces; however, no one will be tried for these crimes. The ICTY prosecutor's office intended to try those who were guilty of these crimes because they were convinced that war crimes had been committed on the part of NATO's forces, but they had to drop the investigation, since NATO refused to cooperate and possibly would have obstructed other ICTY investigations.[64] The powerful have ways to protect themselves!

The fourth case—namely, the near emptying of Kosovo of all of its former Slavic inhabitants—is a case of reverse ethnic cleansing. There seemed to be intent to get rid of the Serbs and Montenegrins and even other non-Serbs. Very few émigrés of these ethnic groups dare to return even ten years after the end of the war, despite the presence of international police and military. The conclusion is that genocide had taken place, parallel to the disappearance of Serbs from Croatia. There seems to be no political will at the UN or in the European community to try such cases, as most leaders seem focused on moving beyond these events to build a future with less conflict. Many Serbs are still grumbling, particularly the national chauvinists; the moderate mainstream wants to be accepted into the European community and NATO and is willing to cooperate. The slogan, "no peace without justice" is put on hold in the Balkans in favor of "peace is possible only by bypassing justice."

The ICTY disproportionately punished Serbian civil, army, and police officials who were in command posts trying to quell the KLA rebellion but did not punish the commanders of the KLA who engaged in comparable violence.

ICTY tried and passed the following sentences:

Serbian officials, in addition to Milošević, all sentenced in 2009:

Milan Milutinović, former Serbian President. Acquitted.

Nikola Šainović, Yugoslav deputy prime minister. Twenty-two-year imprisonment.

Dragoljub Ojdanić, Yugoslav army chief of staff. Fifteen-year imprisonment.

Nebojša Pavković, Yugoslav army general. Twenty-two-year imprisonment.

Vladimir Lazarević, Yugoslav army general. Fifteen-year imprisonment.

Sreten Lukić, Serbian police general. Twenty-two-year imprisonment.

Vlastimir Djordjević, former assistant minister of the Serbian Ministry of Internal Affairs, chief of its Public Security Department. Fugitive from justice until his arrest in 2007. Trial commenced at the tribunal in January 2009. In February 2011 he was sentenced to twenty-seven years in prison for murdering at least 724 Kosovar Albanians and controlling the expulsion of 200,000.[65]

Vlajko Stojiljković, Serbian Interior Minister. Shot himself on the steps of the Parliament in 2002.

Kosovar Albanians:

Isaak Musliu, former KLA commander. Acquitted in 2007.

Ramush Haradinaj, former leader of the KLA and former prime minister of Kosova. Acquitted in 2008 but partial retrial ordered in 2010 on suspicion of threats against witnesses.

Idriz Balaj, commander of the "Black Eagles" of KLA. Acquitted in 2008 but partial retrial ordered in 2010.

Lahi Brahimaj, commander of KLA and deputy to Haradinaj. Six years imprisonment in 2008, confirmed in 2010.

Fatmir Limaj, member of KLA. Acquitted in 2007.

Haradin Bala, commander of KLA. Thirteen-year imprisonment in 2007 for murders of Serbs and alleged Albanian collaborators in the Lapušnik KLA concentration camp.

Hashim Thaçi, prime minister of Kosova. Avoided indictment at ICTY but accusations were raised against him in 2010 that he participated in drug trafficking and the forcible organ transplants of captured Serbs during the Kosovo conflict.[66] Allegedly welcomed a judicial investigation declaring that he was innocent.

Beqe Beqaj, gang-style "enforcer." Guilty of contempt of court. Charged that he attempted to intimidate KLA trial protected witnesses, asking them to retract their statements.

It is hard to be optimistic that the manner in which the "Kosovo knot" has been cut by the international community and the politics of intimidation prevailing in Kosova will bring a lasting peace and reconciliation to the Balkans.

12

International Criminal Tribunal for Yugoslavia

There are two widely held truisms. One is that one nation's terrorists are another nation's freedom fighters and heroes and vice versa. The other is that all is fair in war and love. These truisms were widely asserted in the wars of the 1990s in the former Yugoslavia. The International Criminal Tribunal for the Former Yugoslavia invalidated both of them. During the wars of Yugoslavia's dismemberment, a heroic liberator of the Albanians was perceived as a terrorist by the Serbs, a legendary defender of Serbian rights was regarded as a war criminal by the Bosnians or Croats, a popular defender of the homeland for the Croats was a detested ethnic cleanser to the Serbs. Many Americans considered Slobodan Milošević the new Hitler; many Serbs retaliated by picturing Clinton as Hitler. These drastically different perceptions of the leading protagonists in the wars of disintegration of Yugoslavia stood in the way of accountability for the almost unimaginable destruction that took place during the 1990s. It is most unlikely that the nations on whose behalf they violated international norms and conventions would have tried them. War crime trials of the past were almost entirely trials of the defeated by the winners, such as at Nurenberg and Tokyo. The wars in the Balkans did not result in clear winners or losers, at least in the sense that one side had to unconditionally surrender to the other. Not having lost decisively made it possible to assert the second truism, namely, what was done had to be done as it was a struggle for survival. People reasoned that one may resort to any means in self-defense. Of course, people had a general awareness of both the Geneva Conventions and the UN Genocide Convention, but these were viewed as abstractions, whereas the defeat of the enemy was seen as a necessity to be pursued by all available means. Hence, few people, if any, would have faced trials by courts of their own state, had a new device not been created by the UN. The device, the International Criminal Tribunal for the Former Yugoslavia (ICTY), was (and remains) controversial. At first it was perceived as ineffective, but ultimately ICTY produced a fairly impressive record of convictions of *individuals* accused of a wide range of crimes, which may in the long run remove the taint of collective guilt from the participating nations. In her statement to the court about the Slobodan Milošević case, Chief Prosecutor Carla Del Ponte addressed this cardinal point:

> I bring the accused, Milošević, before you to face the charges against him. I do so on behalf of the international community and in the name of all member states of the United Nations, including the states of the former Yugoslavia. The accused in this case, as in all cases before this Tribunal, is charged as an individual. He is prosecuted on the basis of his individual criminal responsibility. No state or organization is on trial here today. The indictments do not accuse an entire people of being collectively guilty of the crimes, even the crime of genocide. It may be tempting to generalize when dealing with the conduct of the leaders at the highest level, but that is an error that must be avoided. Collective guilt forms no part of the prosecution case. It is not the law of the Tribunal.[1]

On May 25, 1993, while the fighting and destruction was still going on, the UN Security Council established in Resolution 827 a tribunal with a long awkward name, International Tribunal for the Prosecution of Persons Responsible for Serious Violations of International Humanitarian Law Committed in the Territory of the Former Yugoslavia since 1991. Soon it was renamed to the more practical International Criminal Tribunal for the Former Yugoslavia, which was still further abbreviated to its acronym ICTY. This court was going to prosecute only the higher level decision makers rather than the thousands of individuals who implemented the policies and decisions of their superiors. At first the expectations and the support for this tribunal were quite low, with most people hoping that it would serve as a deterrent against committing the most egregious violations of the 1949 Geneva Convention, which provided humanitarian protections for civilians. The immediate scope of ICTY's responsibility was the serious violations of the 1949 Geneva Convention, violations of the laws or customs of war, crimes against humanity, and genocide. Its mission was to dispense justice to individuals who were deemed responsible for violations of international humanitarian law, to deter further crimes, to provide justice to victims, and to assist in the process of peacemaking, thereby contributing to the process of reconciliation among the peoples of former Yugoslavia.

The maximum sentence that the court can dispense is imprisonment for life. During the trial the accused is held at The Hague, unless they are granted temporary release. Upon sentencing, they are assigned to serve their term in the prison system of a country willing to take them. Over 1,200 people from over eighty countries on staff manage this very costly system (over $275 million in 2001–2007). The chief prosecutor decides which investigations are to commence, but a judge must confirm the indictments in order to proceed. A trial cannot take place unless the accused is physically present. The internationally recognized principles of a fair trial are applied, for example, the accused is considered innocent until proven guilty and defendants are provided legal counsel if they are unable to hire their own lawyers. In theory, the accused has the right to be tried without delay, but in practice it takes time for both the prosecution and defense to obtain all the necessary evidence, so many of the accused wait years before their trial begins. Defendants have the right to examine witnesses, though the identity of many witnesses is protected so that they are not intimidated or killed (as some of them were). In some cases the defendants have published the names of protected witnesses or threatened them even prior to appearing on the witness stand.

From its very inception, the court was deemed to be a political tool in the hand of Western countries, primarily the United States, to punish Serb leaders. It became obvious fairly soon that the other new ex-Yugoslav states felt that their civilian and military leaders must not face prosecution at ICTY. Western political leaders seemed surprised not to receive the cooperation of the various Balkan states, clearly not understanding that "justice" is not a uniformly or universally agreed upon concept. Mass demonstrations against the indictment and arrest of certain accused "heroes" were a fairly common sight, as were press and media attacks on both the institution and its representatives, particularly the chief prosecutor, for what was perceived as political persecution and punishment. There were prominent citizens, including a head of state, who instructed their governments to obstruct the investigations, despite superficial verbal promises of cooperation to arrest the accused, to protect the witnesses, and to provide the material evidence needed for the trials.

At first there were few results. The first sentence was issued on November 29, 1996, to Dražen Erdemović, an ethnic Croat who had been forced to serve in the Bosnian Serb Army and participate, under duress, in the execution of about seventy Bosniaks. He confessed voluntarily, submitted himself to ICTY, and pleaded guilty. At first he was given a ten-year prison sentence, but in 1998 it was reduced to five. This sentencing may not seem like a major achievement for ICTY, but it was the first step toward significant accomplishments.

By early 2011, about fourteen years later, ICTY had issued 161 indictments, of which 124 had been completed and 37 were ongoing. The last fugitive, Goran Hadžić, former premier of the "Republic of Serbian Krajina" (a temporary, unrecognized Serb-dominated region of Croatia), was delivered to ICTY on July 22, 2011. ICTY has tried major political and military leaders, including Milan Babić, Tihomir Blaškić, Ramush Haradinaj, Radovan Karadžić, Danilo Kordić, Radislav Krstić, Momčilo Krajišnik, Milan Martić, Slobodan Milošević, Ratko Mladić, Dragoljub Ojdanić, Naser Orić, Nebojša Pavković, Momčilo Perišić, Biljana Plavšić, and Vojislav Šešelj. Some were sentenced to life imprisonment; some were acquitted; some, after appeal, had their longer sentences shortened (e.g., Tihomir Blaškić) or extended! (e.g., Veselin Šljivančanin); some died in prison (Slobodan Milošević) or committed suicide (e.g., Milan Babić); and others died prior to their arrests (e.g., Gojko Šušak and Janko Bobetko), some by assassination (e.g., Željko Ražnjatović-Arkan). Slobodan Milošević, the former president of Yugoslavia and Serbia, whose trial lasted four years, died in March 2006, a week or so prior to finishing the defense arguments, thereby preventing the completion of the trial. His trial was significant in that he was the first head of state to face charges of genocide, crimes against humanity, grave breaches of the Geneva Conventions, and violations of the laws and customs of war for Kosovo, Croatia, and Bosnia.[2] He insisted on defending himself, a tactic used by several other prominent accused (Karadžić and Šešelj) in order to (fairly successfully) politicize the defense and obstruct the normal flow of the trial. The prosecution was collecting evidence for trials against Franjo Tudjman, the president of Croatia, and Alija Izetbegović, the president of B&H, but both died (on December 10, 1999, and October 19, 2003, respectively) prior to the issuance of an indictment. Otherwise, they may have joined the "Yugoslav community" at Scheveningen prison in The Hague.[3] Since ICTY used all the judicially recognized protections for the accused, as well as for the victims, those who awaited trials and sentencing were relatively free. Being locked up next to each other, regardless of their ethnicity, they often seemed to get along fairly well despite having been until recently "irreconcilable" enemies.

The number of indicted and arrested increased at first very slowly, there being only one in 1997, four in 1998, and two in 1999. In 2000 the number and rank of the indicted started increasing dramatically.[4] From 2004 on there was a veritable explosion of voluntary surrenders to The Hague. Most of them entered not guilty pleas. Nineteen or twenty pleaded guilty to specific crimes, publicly expressed remorse, and recognized the suffering of the victims. In many cases they entered into a plea agreement, receiving reduced sentences, but were often willing to become witnesses in the trials of higher level perpetrators.[5] Thirteen accused requested or were directed to transfer their cases to courts of national jurisdiction (mostly to B&H, and a few to Croatia and Serbia), though for nine of them the decision was reversed and they were tried by ICTY.[6]

Three major factors contributed to making the court so successful in arresting and trying such a large number of defendants. One of them was the tenacity and skill of the chief prosecutors, the first being Richard Goldstone of South Africa; the second, Louise Arbor of Canada; the third, Carla Del Ponte of Switzerland; and the fourth, Serge Brammertz of Belgium. These lawyers, who often did not receive much assistance from the UN or from Western governments, faced the anticipated duplicity and noncooperation from the governments of successor states of Yugoslavia. They used their prosecutorial know-how and the power of their will to apprehend as many of the accused as they could, despite the fact that several were fugitives for many years (e.g., Radovan Karadžić for thirteen years, Ratko Mladić for sixteen years, and Ante Gotovina for four). The second factor, aside from Kosovo, was that the international community, including the interventions of the public prosecutor, was successful in bringing pressure on the other governments to cooperate with ICTY. They did so because the successor regimes in the Balkan states had an overwhelming desire to become members of the EU and NATO. The benefits of that membership for young democracies outweighed the reluctance to turn their own heroes over to a process that would clearly disclose them as war criminals, ethnic cleansers, or even the genocidaires that they were. As the new government officials showed willingness to cooperate, they were doing so at considerable political risk: the many "patriotic" nationalists in their country might vote them out of office or, worse, assassinate them.

The third factor was the ICTY's transparency. The court slowly confronted the populations of the various states with the undeniable truth of what was secretly or under false pretenses done in their name—that, indeed, many of their heroes had innocent blood on their hands. The voluminous documentation that runs into the hundreds of thousands of pages and videos, as well as the televised transmission of the trials, have convinced many that it was not merely "an evil time" but that "evil people" were in charge and that events could have been very different had these individuals made better choices.

The response to these pressures was that the number of those who were surrendered to ICTY increased substantially. Some of the accused surrendered on their own—some, like Vojislav Šešelj, mistakenly hoping that this would bring them fame. A small number of the accused surrendered hoping to clear their names and, indeed, some were acquitted. A number of sentence reductions and acquittals were not deserved but were based on inadequate evidence because of noncooperation by the defendant's government. For example, in March 2003 Tihomir Blaškić, commander of the Croat army, was given a forty-five-year sentence for the massacres committed by his troops in the Lašva Valley. That sentence was reduced to nine years in July 2004 for lack of detailed evidence, which was withheld by the Croatian government. Subsequently, Croatia's president, Stjepan Mesić, provided that evidence, which, in the opinion of Carla Del Ponte, would have been of "significant evidentiary value" in regard to Blaškić's role in the Massacre at Ahmići.[7]

Two other successful obstructions were in regard to alleged war crimes of NATO's (North Atlantic Treaty Organization) air war against Serbia in 1999 and against the leaders of the Kosovo Liberation Army commanders for the period of 1991–2004. Carla Del Ponte received requests that she investigate charges that NATO deliberately attacked civilian targets and was guilty of war crimes. She explored whether a full-fledged investigation could be mounted. "But I quickly concluded that it is impossible to investigate NATO, because NATO and its member states would not cooperate with us. . . . I had collided with the edge of the political universe in which the tribunal would not be allowed to function."[8] In other words, she would not have been successful in her attempts to investigate the case, but she would have damaged her ability to investigate the local Balkan war crimes because she would not have received cooperation from NATO member governments. This clearly shows that international justice is still to a significant degree the 'justice' by those who have more power over those who have less.

There were plenty of indications that a number of Kosovar Albanians had committed various war crimes in their effort to get rid of the Serb administration and citizens. But here the problem was almost the opposite of NATO's organized stonewalling. In 1998 and 1999, "KLA [Kosovo Liberation Army] soldiers abducted hundreds of Serbs, Roma, Albanians, and members of other ethnic groups" who were beaten, tortured, raped, executed, or made to disappear. After Milošević surrendered to NATO on June 12, 1999, 593 Serbs, Slavic Muslims, Montenegrins, Roma, and over "1,500 Albanians disappeared after KLA had taken them into custody during the bombing" and an additional 300 disappeared by 2000.[9] The identity of the commanders of KLA was known, but not the chain of command. In Kosovo, the investigation was stymied by lack of governmental structures and valid evidence, unwillingness of witnesses to come forward because of fear (based on the ancient blood feud customs), ignorance, poverty, and other criminal activity of some of the culprits before they became known as freedom fighters. Not only did potential witnesses fear to step forward, but KFOR (Kosovo Force) officials and UNMIK (UN Mission in Kosovo) police force likewise feared for their own safety and those of their families. Carla Del Ponte stated that "some judges at the Yugoslavia tribunal feared the Albanians' reach. Swiss compatriots warned me to be careful of retaliation. (Some Swiss officials even cautioned against discussing certain Albanian-related issues in this memoir, and I am discussing them here only with extreme care.)"[10] Intimidation was so real that witnesses "were so terrified to speak about the KLA that they would not even discuss its presence in specific areas."[11] It is not surprising that there was insufficient evidence and that the Kosovar Albanian leaders (with one or two minor exceptions) escaped punishment by being acquitted. KFOR and international representatives were so eager to bring some control and semblance of peace and order that they were willing to sacrifice justice.

The trials at ICTY proved, with the exception of the above mentioned Kosova Albanians, what all good law seeks to assert—that no person is above the law and that the culture of impunity (which is displayed from mafia-sponsored killings to dictatorial silencing of "enemies of the people," from terrorist plots to white-collar crimes, and particularly by powerful political and military leaders in times of war) must be opposed by fair judicial processes that give the best opportunity to cut the vicious cycle of revenge and mass murder. Evidence is harder to produce at a trial than it is under normal circumstances, but once it is done, it stands up to scrutiny better in cases of attempted denials.

Under circumstances of conflict, especially during war, there is not merely a war of weapons but also a war of words, a propaganda war. Propaganda creates a reality not as it is but as we want it to be. Therefore, we blame the evil on our enemies and appropriate the virtues to ourselves. Consequently, it is hard to persuade us that our own heroes engaged in horrendous war crimes and crimes against humanity—even to the extent of genocide. Interestingly, in the Balkans people were less reluctant to acknowledge the existence of ethnic cleansing—some even boasted about it—because each ethnic group was utterly convinced that the land the enemy held was rightfully theirs. The enemy came and unjustly settled it. Now their "welcome" had expired, and it was time for them to leave, either of their own free will or by force.

A complicating problem for the implementation of justice was the transition from authoritarianism to real democracy. During this transition, democratic elections provide legitimacy to authoritarian figures to get and stay in power. After the fragmentation of Yugoslavia, for example, the authoritarian figures who led the people into war were still popular enough to be reelected. Even after more truly democratic leaders were elected, they were rarely secure in their positions because the state security, police, army, and government bureaucracy were still in the hands of their authoritarian foes. A wolf in sheep's clothing is still a wolf. As long as Milošević, Tudjman, Karadžić, Šešelj, Gotovina, Mladić, and the like were in the corridors of power, there was great resistance to let the truth, all the truth, and nothing but the truth come to light.

The pros and cons of ICTY, and the other war crimes tribunals that were spawned off ICTY (e.g., Rwanda), will be discussed for a long time. An internal problem is that the judges and attorneys come from different nations with different civil law and common law judicial traditions. This leads to conflicts as to which evidence may be considered sufficient for an indictment or which appeal by a defendant is justified. Such issues are not likely to disappear altogether, but over the years some convergence in theory and practice is likely to occur.

More serious are external conflicts regarding the court. Some regard ICTY as merely an imperialist instrument for the subduing of inconvenient localized opponents to Western influence. To others, the ICTY personnel were inept, slow-moving bureaucracies that allowed themselves to be toyed with by unscrupulous, self-absorbed war criminals. Still others are aware that many perpetrators continue to live with or near the victims and that the court considers these individuals "small fry" for which there is neither money nor political will to bring them to justice, regardless of the monstrous things they have done. Among the bloodiest perpetrators were the Red Berets. Zoran Djindjić, the former prime minister of Serbia, was assassinated by the Red Berets before they were apprehended. Before being assassinated, Djindjić made this insightful statement:

> The killing was not systematic, like during Hitler's wars. Thousands of people, psychopaths, were willing to kill one for one thousand German marks. . . . Milošević wanted to clear the Albanians from Kosovo. There was no specific order to kill, but orders to do what needs to be done. After two years the minds have changed. People don't want to recall. And they've started believing their own lies. All we can hope for is for you to get the main ones. We can get sixty or seventy executioners. And we'll leave ten thousand killers to go free. But this is all we can do. Milošević loosed the accumulated hatred of five hundred years. Very negative energy is still around.[12]

If the chief prosecutors and their teams only follow evidence of direct commands or orders for extermination, murder, rape, deportation, and ethnic cleansing, a number of the accused might escape punishment (as happened with the Kosovar Albanian leaders). Two other tools are more successful. One is to trace the evidence up the chain of command, holding superiors accountable for the crimes of their followers or for not having punished the culprits after they committed the crime. The other one is to link a number of the war criminals into a "joint criminal enterprise," those who were intertwined in planning and executing actions such as the Srebrenica massacres, the Lašva Valley massacres, the Vukovar Hospital massacre, or the Drenica Kosovo massacres.

Genocide and assisting and abetting genocide are the most difficult crimes to prove in court because one must prove intent. Very few leaders leave conscious verbal or written traces of their genocidal intent, but the court is able to conclude from the scope of the crime that an entire or a part of a religious, ethnic, or racial group was going to be eradicated. Thus, ICTY has produced a number of genocide verdicts based on the UN Genocide Convention, and beyond that, it has given further legal clarification to the convention itself, as seen in chapter 1.

ICTY has also clarified the application of the Geneva Conventions, decided on the category of genocidal rape as a form of crime against humanity, and expanded on the command responsibility doctrine. It has also provided extensive documentation in the local languages to the courts of B&H, Croatia, and Serbia, which will make it easier for them to prosecute the lesser perpetrators in their jurisdictions so that many additional suspects have and may yet receive their day in court.[13] Their number is in the thousands.

Some of the accused have charged that ICTY is not a properly constituted court and that it does not have legal standing to try them. They were not successful. Others have said they were not legally arrested but were kidnapped. That didn't help them either. Others have deliberately disrupted the proceedings, demeaned the court and its personnel, ridiculed the institution (e.g., laughed at the wigs of the judges, or made shameful remarks regarding female justices or attorneys, or used sordid, obscene references and swear words aimed at the judges or prosecuting team to such a degree that they were sentenced for contempt of court). Some of their followers at home seem to delight in the antics of their idol (which can be viewed on YouTube). Without legal relevance, still others have used the proceedings, aimed at the audience at home, to make political speeches, or have tried to give history lessons to the judges—of course, always justifying their nation's "defensive" role in the war.

It is also gratifying that ICTY's judgment of genocide has brought solace, satisfaction, and even a measure of closure to the grieving. Verdicts of genocide, in the Srebrenica case, for example, cannot bring back to life the murdered or repay for the suffering of the survivors; nevertheless, it helps knowing that an international court concluded that, indeed, genocide had taken place and some individuals have been found guilty of this greatest of all crimes.

Finally, it is gratifying to realize the the ICTY has been successful in apprehending and judging all of the main accused. It is of even greater consequence that the various national courts of Balkan countries have also successfully prosecuted alleged war criminals, though, of course, it would be too much to expect that those courts will get all the guilty ones and that justice will be evenhanded. The 2011 apprehension and trial of the ninety-seven-year-old Sándor Kepiro in Budapest, a former Hungarian police officer accused of killing civilians during the 1942 Ratsiya in Novi Sad[14] confirms that crimes against humanity, war crimes, and participating in genocidal massacres do not "expire." The perpetrators are liable to judgment in international or domestic courts no matter how long they hide, whenever and where ever they are caught—till the end of their days.

13

Onward into the Twenty-first Century

A Postscript

For Europe, the twentieth century began with a genocidal conflict in the Balkans; it also ended with one in the Balkans. This troubled history almost repeated itself at the beginning of the twenty-first century with an ethnically based conflict in Macedonia.

THREAT OF GENOCIDE AVERTED IN MACEDONIA

At first Macedonia avoided being directly embroiled in the wars of disintegration of the former Yugoslavia. Not being in the forefront of secessionism, Macedonia benefited by becoming an independent nation without firing a single shot. For a while it seemed that this small country of about 2 million might avoid the kind of interethnic warfare that marked the destruction of the Yugoslav federation.

With the inevitability of the downward pouring of sand in an hourglass, the violence finally moved from the north into the southernmost part of the former Yugoslavia. Although most Macedonians were probably puzzled why this was happening to them, since they perceive themselves as tolerant and good-natured, it would have been a miracle had they not been dragged into war. Both external and internal factors worked in that direction. Collective insecurity and fear almost always lead to violence. Macedonia is surrounded and suffused by insecurity and fear, mainly because the country is surrounded by neighbors who are not only hostile to it but in many ways deny its very right to exist. Greeks to the south consider Macedonia as being northern Greece and refuse to acknowledge the new state's name. They wanted it to be called the Former Yugoslav Republic of Macedonia and enforced an embargo that lasted several years. Bulgarians consider Macedonians western Bulgarians and would like to absorb them into their state. Serbians used to consider them southern Serbs, but have not made any threatening moves, rather acquiescing to Josip Broz Tito's decision to recognize Macedonia's right to nationhood, statehood, and a separate language. However, the Serbian Orthodox Church still has not conceded autonomy and autocephaly to the Orthodox Church in Macedonia, a step boldly asserted by the Macedonian Church. And there have never been friendly relations with Albania to the west, due to Macedonia's ethnic Albanians' secessionist aspirations.

In recent years, NATO added to Macedonia's external insecurity. At the time of NATO's bombing of Serbia in 1999, based on actions in Kosovo, Macedonia was coerced into allowing NATO troops to stage the entry into Kosovo by crossing its territory from Greece. Many Macedonians demonstrated against NATO's use of their roads and facilities. The sudden influx of some 250,000 (some claim up to 600,000) ethnic Albanian refugees from Kosovo completely unbalanced the small country. Not only was it an enormous strain on Macedonia's meager economic resources, but when the international community started providing aid, it seemed that most of it was going to ethnic Albanians and very little or none to the Macedonians. Far more disconcerting was an implied message that NATO (and particularly the United States) sided with the Albanians, which encouraged them to think the time had come to seek autonomy or independence in all areas where they were numerous. The delicate coexistence of Macedonians and Albanians was thus undermined, and Macedonia became a time bomb.

Internal threats are as serious as external ones. Macedonia is economically a poor country with few resources. Their aim is to become democratic, but they have little democratic experiences. Its population is multiethnic. There are Turks, Roma, and Vlachs, in addition to the ethnic minorities of neighboring countries, but two ethnic groups predominate: Macedonians (a Slavic people), who make between two-thirds to three-fourths of the population, and ethnic Albanians, who make up one-fourth to one-third of the population. The number of Albanians is growing significantly faster than the Macedonians because of migration from Albania and Kosovo and a much higher birthrate. That growth is perceived as a grave threat by Macedonians; they know that in Kosovo, Serbs lost ground to Albanians to the point of near extinction. Parallels between Kosovo and adjacent western Macedonia are ominous.

The two groups do not mix much—less and less in the post-Tito era.[1] In the post-Communist period, the notion of Albanians living in a single Albanian state has become an attraction. Seeing what happened in Kosovo, Macedonia's Albanians began boldly claiming autonomous prerogatives, aiming at either a federal structure in the tiny country or a constitutional arrangement whereby the Albanians would have additional constitutional prerogatives.

Kiro Gligorov, a respected former Communist, was elected as the first president of Macedonia. The eight years of his presidency were relatively stable, though he barely survived the head wounds caused by an assassination attempt in the middle of Skopje. In 2000, a small sensation was caused when an opposition party, the Internal Macedonian Revolutionary Organization-Democratic Party for Macedonian National Unity, won by the tiniest of majorities. Even more surprising was the little known presidential candidate who won the office—Boris Trajkovski,[2] a lawyer and a licensed local preacher of the United Methodist Church. He was elected with the help of Albanian voters who probably considered him a lesser evil than an Orthodox Macedonian. Trajkovski gained great prominence as the crisis progressed and international politicians increasingly turned to him as their partner in negotiations.

Late in 2000, a small group of armed ethnic Albanians occupied a few ethnic Albanian mountain villages on the Macedonian border with Kosovo. Attempts to dislodge them by the police (and the barely existing army of Macedonia) resulted in more casualties to the Macedonians than to the well-equipped and well-trained insurrectionists. The commanders of these forces presented themselves adroitly to the Western press as the National Liberation Army (NLA)—with the same initials (UÇK) in Albanian as the Kosovo Liberation Army. They wanted to be perceived as fighters for greater political rights for Albanians. To the Macedonians, the picture looked entirely different: they saw criminal elements of the Kosovo Liberation Army wanting to protect their extremely lucrative routes for smuggling drugs, white slaves, and arms. Their ultimate aim was to partition Macedonia and create a Great Albania in which they would hold sway. So the Macedonians considered them terrorists and contended that they should be dealt with as terrorists elsewhere. The militants hoped that the Macedonian forces would use extreme repression, which would then alienate the Albanian population into a popular uprising. Most Macedonians reacted with blind rage and hatred to the military successes of the rebels, who at one point held Arachinovo, a suburb of the capital Skopje about five miles from center city. All Albanians were being equated with the terrorists. Ugly ethnic slurs and stereotypes surfaced on both sides, even among intellectuals and in the press; extremists wrote graffiti "death to Albanians" with swastikas, even on mosques. They shouted "Albanians to the gas chambers," and their rivals answered with anti-Christian slogans. Macedonian citizens demanded weapons to personally "take care" of the terrorists and very likely many innocents—responding in kind to the indiscriminate threats and violence made by the terrorists against Macedonian civilian targets.

Macedonians and Albanians are divided by language, customs, history, and culture, but religion is also a distinguishing factor; the vast majority of Albanians are Muslims (with a small Catholic minority) while the Macedonians are predominantly Orthodox Christians. Religion played a role in this conflict. It frequently manifested itself not in what was done but what was not done, that is, in withholding from each other acts of justice, caring, and acceptance that both religions formally uphold. Each side pointed to omissions and even commissions by the other side, but no criticism was raised against even the most atrocious behavior of people in one's own camp.

Communism did bring about a massive secularization of the population. Yet a fair number of younger people began to attend worship, weddings are held with religious ritual, churches and mosques are being built, and a decisively larger number of young people receive theological education. The Orthodox Church, in cooperation with many politicians, aspired to make the Macedonian Orthodox Church the state church. The Macedonian constitution used to single out the Orthodox Church's unique place in Macedonian history. The Muslims do not seem opposed to this, but they would like to have Islam mentioned as a historic religion as well. Leaders of both religions demand mandatory religious education in schools, each to their own constituencies. Smaller religious communities fear the impact of such an arrangement on the children of their members.

Both Slavic Macedonians and ethnic Albanians feel threatened, fearing for their safety and expressing similar belligerence and hatred. The NLA terrorists took over several villages, threatened to poison the drinking water for the capital Skopje, drove out numerous Macedonian families from majority populated Albanian towns, and desecrated some churches. The Macedonian militia and vigilantes retorted by burning down some mosques, beating up Albanians, and acting as if they were accepting the fight that would lead the country into civil war. Over a hundred people were killed in these unrests and about 170,000 people were displaced, 74,000 internally—it was a low-intensity war that could have erupted into a full-scale ethnic war.[3]

Fortunately they had a wise leader in Boris Trajkovski, who availed himself of the help from the international community—both military peacekeepers and diplomatic intervention. He organized, with the help of some outsiders like myself, interreligious dialogues so as to at least neutralize the animosities between the religions or, as actually happened, guiding these dialogues into instruments of mutual understanding and cooperation. The hardest concession was the rewriting of parts of the constitution, giving more rights to the Albanians, including an expanded use of minority languages in public institutions, and recognizing five historic religions. U.S. and Western diplomatic and financial aid was crucial in these negotiations. The leaders of the rebels organized themselves into a third Albanian political party to pursue their aims politically rather than militarily, and they eventually entered into the government. The insurrection ended in 2002, and by 2004, when Trajkovski died in an airplane crash,[4] the country was reasonably stable, though still crisis prone. Smaller outbursts by other Albanian insurrection groups continued into 2010, indicating that the instability persisted despite concessions and efforts to address a variety of issues. Genocide and ethnic cleansing were knocking at Macedonia's door; thus far they have avoided welcoming the deadly visitor.

PROSPECTS FOR THE BALKANS

In meteorological terms, the situation in the Balkans could be described as partly cloudy, with scattered rain and the possibility of severe storms. The enticement to become part of Europe (as if they weren't situated in the *oldest* part of civilized Europe!) is very strong. Greece, Turkey, Bulgaria, Albania, Slovenia, and Croatia are members of NATO, and several other countries are candidates. Greece, Bulgaria, and Slovenia are members of the European Union with Macedonia and Croatia being candidate countries. Membership conditions place a great deal of pressure on countries to follow democratic and human rights principles. The International Criminal Tribunal for the Former Yugoslavia, European Union, and other members of the international community have encouraged the states in which genocides and ethnic cleansing took place to continue uncovering mass graves;[5] to try the large number of lesser perpetrators of war crimes in the courts of Bosnia and Herzegovina, Croatia,[6] and Serbia; and to pursue the suspects wherever they may be hiding.[7] Pursuing all these issues does not guarantee political, social, economic, and financial success; even countries that seem reasonably stable, experience crises (e.g., Greece) or erupt into violence.[8] On the surface it would seem that Slovenia, Croatia, and Bulgaria have less internal turbulence. The neuralgic areas where there are many unresolved problems are Bosnia and Herzegovina, Kosovo (and by extension Serbia, Albania, and Montenegro), and Macedonia (and thereby its neighbors). Neither the Albanians nor the Serbs have yet accepted the fact that their ethnic nationals are living in different states. On the surface, it appears that if they all became members of the European Union, reasons for fighting would cease,[9] but that is doubtful. Should some of the ethnic groups, for example, Albanians and Bosniaks, continue their rapid demographic growth, they will still tend to expand at the expense of their less fertile neighbors. Before too long there will be pressure for some to move out and new threats of ethnic cleansing will emerge.

Economic discrepancies will drive the poorer to seek employment in richer parts of Europe. New economic, social, cultural, and religious tensions will emerge. Unless conscious and timely steps for intercultural and interreligious dialogue are undertaken, fear, tension, and hatred may follow and bloodshed won't be far behind. If the processes of reconciliation to deal with the recent genocidal wars and ethnic cleansing are not pursued vigorously, there won't be enough determination to prevent another outbreak of massacres, just as happened after Tito's promise of "brotherhood and unity." The new slogan of "democracy, civil society, and human rights" may prove to be a superficially thin new skin that does not affect real healing but merely covers the wounds that are left to fester and then resurface with vengeance. Right-wing, neo-Nazi, and anti-immigrant politicians, journalists, and others are already exploiting fears and suspicions and are manipulating European masses into contemplating new rounds of forcible removals of populations (as is happening to the Roma). Concern about Islamic fundamentalism is quite real but is prone to manipulation by other types of fundamentalists. The Islamophobia of secularized Christians in Europe entices anti-modernist and anti-globalist fanaticism on the part of some extreme Islamists.

The alternative to such a pessimistic scenario is to prosecute steadfastly alleged perpetrators of war crimes, ethnic cleansing, and genocide; to continue to organize conferences and museums at which investigations of these crimes are carried out; and to encourage individual research of various aspects of Balkan genocides in order to settle even more precisely what took place and who is responsible for the atrocities. Most important of all is the need to promote genuine humanitarian dialogue and cooperation that can lead to a more successful neighborliness among the peoples of the Balkans, Europe, and the world. One should not bet that it is going to happen on its own. Dedicated efforts toward reconciliation, dialogue, and cooperation are indispensable.[10]

Time Line

1908   Austria-Hungary annexes Bosnia and Herzegovina, pushing out Turkey.
1912   First Balkan war: Bulgaria, Greece, Montenegro, and Serbia form the Balkan League and go to war against Turkey. Unrecognized mutual genocides take place.
1913   Second Balkan war: Bulgaria wages war against Greece and Serbia. Turkey and Romania also attack Bulgaria, which loses the war. Genocidal activities continue.
1914   World War I breaks out, sparked by the assassination of Hapsburg Archduke Ferdinand in Sarajevo by a young Serb nationalist.
1918   World War I ends. Kingdom of Serbs, Croats, and Slovenes is created. It is renamed Yugoslavia in 1929.
1939   Italy occupies Albania and turns it into their protectorate.
1940   Italy attacks Greece but is rebuffed.
1941   Germany, Italy, Hungary, and Bulgaria defeat and partition Yugoslavia and conquer Greece. Independent State of Croatia is formed as a Nazi puppet regime under Pavelić. Tito's Partisans and Mihajlović's Četniks begin a war of resistance that turns into an all-out civil war and a war against occupying forces. Holocaust, genocides, and ethnic cleansing take place from 1941 to 1945.
1945   World War II ends. Communist Party headed by Tito takes power, establishing the Federal Republic of Yugoslavia. Retaliatory genocides and ethnic cleansing are carried out against ethnic minorities related to the occupiers, as well as politicide against collaborators and anti-Partisan forces.

1948   Tito breaks with Stalin, which marks gradual shift toward a milder dictatorship.
1980   Tito dies, leaving no heir apparent. Power struggle slowly emerges.
1987   Increasing unrest in Kosovo leads to rise of Milošević.
1990   Bulgaria and Albania topple their Communist governments.
1991   Slovenia and Croatia declare independence. War breaks out, leading to Yugoslavia's disintegration. War in Croatia includes ethnic cleansing and genocide. It ends in 1995, with all territories recouped in 1998.
1992   War in Bosnia and Herzegovina breaks out, characterized by ethnic cleansing and genocide.
1993   International Criminal Tribunal for Yugoslavia is established in The Hague.
1995   War in Bosnia and Herzegovina ends based on the Dayton Peace Accords.
1999   War starts in and over Kosovo. NATO bombards Serbia and Montenegro.
2001   Rebellion of ethnic Albanians in Macedonia ends peacefully with international mediation.
2008   Kosova declares independence. Partition of Yugoslavia ends with seven independent countries.

Notes

PREFACE

1. Miroslav Volf, "Exclusion and Embrace: Theological Reflection and 'Ethnic Cleansing,'" *Religion in Eastern Europe* 13, no. 6 (December 1993): 1.

2. Steven Leonard Jacobs, ed. *Confronting Genocide: Judaism, Christianity, Islam* (Lanham, MD: Lexington Books, 2009), 151–81.

3. International Commission to Inquire into the Causes and Conduct of the Balkan Wars, *The Other Balkan Wars: A 1913 Carnegie Endowment Inquiry in Retrospect* (Washington, DC: A Carnegie Endowment Book, 1993), 7.

CHAPTER 1 DEFINITIONS OF GENOCIDE AND ETHNIC CLEANSING

1. Raphael Lemkin invented the word *genocide*. See the more recent edition of his seminal work, Raphael Lemkin and Samantha Power, *Axis Rule in Occupied Europe: Laws of Occupation, Analysis of Government, Proposals for Redress* (Clark, NJ: Lawbook Exchange, 2005). Also see R. J. Rummel, *Death by Government* (New Brunswick, NJ: Transaction, 1994). Rummel has written pioneer volumes on cases of genocide; see also his volumes on China (*China's Bloody Century* [New Brunswick, NJ: Transaction, 1991]) and Soviet Russia (*Lethal Politics* [New Brunswick, NJ: Transaction, 1996]), and *Statistics of Democide: Genocide and Mass Murder* (New Brunswick, NJ: Transaction, 1997). Irving L. Horowitz, *Taking Lives: Genocide and State Power*, 4th ed. (New Brunswick, NJ: Transaction, 1997). Leni Yahil, *The Holocaust* (New York: Oxford University Press, 1990).

2. Daniel Jonah Goldhagen, *Worse Than War: Genocide, Eliminationism, and the Ongoing Assault on Humanity* (New York: Public Affairs, 2009), 74–84, asserts

that political leaders or the like are always the prime movers, not only of genocides but also of a more inclusive "eliminationalist" context.

3. Norman M. Naimark, *Fires of Hatred: Ethnic Cleansing in Twentieth-Century Europe* (Cambridge, MA: Harvard University Press, 2001), 6.

4. Quoted in Naimark, *Fires of Hatred*, 7.

5. Naimark, *Fires of Hatred*, 6.

6. Ben Kiernan, *Blood and Soil: A World History of Genocide and Extermination from Sparta to Darfur* (New Haven, CT: Yale University Press, 2007).

7. Paul Mojzes, *Yugoslavian Inferno: Ethnoreligious Warfare in the Balkans* (New York: Continuum, 2005), 111–12.

8. Henry R. Huttenbach, "The Genocide Factor in the Yugoslav Wars of Dismemberment," in *Reflections on the Balkan Wars: Ten Years after the Break-Up of Yugoslavia*, ed. Jeffrey S. Morton, R. Craig Nation, Paul C. Forage, and Stefano Bianchini (New York: Palgrave Macmillan, 2004), 23.

9. Huttenbach, "The Genocide Factor," 24.

10. Huttenbach, "The Genocide Factor," 32.

11. Huttenbach, "The Genocide Factor," 32.

12. Mojzes, *Yugoslavian Inferno*, 170–72.

13. Benjamin Lieberman, *Terrible Fate: Ethnic Cleansing in the Making of Modern Europe* (Chicago: Ivan R. Dee, 2006).

14. For example, Paul Mojzes, "Ethnic Cleansing in the Balkans," in *Will Genocide Ever End?* ed. Carol Rittner, John K. Roth, and James M. Smith (St. Paul, MN: Paragon House, 2002), 52–54.

15. Lieberman, *Terrible Fate*, 10.

16. The poem celebrates Bishop Danilo's ethnic cleansing of Montenegro (the so-called "Christmas Eve Massacre") in the early eighteenth century. In the poem, the Muslim converts implore for coexistence:

> Small enough is this our land,
> Yet two faiths there still may be
> As in one bowl soups may agree
> Let us still as brothers live.

Bishop Danilo rejects the appeals as temptations. He states, "Our land is foul; it reeks of this false religion." And, following his command,

> No single seeing eye, no tongue of Turk
> escaped to tell his tale another day.
> We put them all unto the sword
> All those who would not be baptised.
> But who paid homage to the Holy Child,
> were all baptised with sign of Christian cross.
> And as brother each was hail'd and greeted.
> We put to fire the Turkish houses,
> That there might be no stick nor trace
> Of these true servants of the devil!

Source: Michael Sells, *The Bridge Betrayed: Religion and Genocide in Bosnia* (Berkeley: University of California Press, 1996), 15.

17. Quoted in Smilja Avramov, *Genocide in Yugoslavia* (Belgrade: BIGZ, 1995), 298. Italics are mine for emphasis.

18. Quoted in Avramov, *Genocide in Yugoslavia*, 327.

19. Huttenbach, "The Genocide Factor," 23.

20. Huttenbach, "The Genocide Factor," 24.

21. Robert Gellately and Ben Kiernan, "The Study of Mass Murder and Genocide," in *Specter of Genocide: Mass Murder in Historical Perspective*, ed. Robert Gellately and Ben Kiernan (Cambridge: Cambridge University Press, 2006), 15.

22. Gellately and Kiernan, "The Study of Mass Murder," 15–16.

23. Gellately and Kiernan, "The Study of Mass Murder," 25.

24. Sells, *The Bridge Betrayed*, 55–58.

25. See the disagreement over that issue by the two authors, Steven L. Burg and Paul S. Shoup, *War in Bosnia-Herzegovina: Ethnic Conflict and International Intervention* (Armonk, NY: M.E. Sharpe, 1999), 14, without informing the readers who supports which position.

26. Lieberman, *Terrible Fate*, 4.

27. Lieberman, *Terrible Fate*, 4.

28. Mojzes, *Yugoslavian Inferno*, 154–70.

29. Lieberman, *Terrible Fate*, 10.

30. Lieberman, *Terrible Fate*, 17.

31. Lieberman, *Terrible Fate*, 29–30.

32. Lieberman, *Terrible Fate*, 50.

33. Lieberman, *Terrible Fate*, 52.

34. I have been intrigued by American scholars' tendency to see the times of empires as benevolent compared to the rise of modern nationalism, contrary to scholars from Eastern Europe. I wonder whether being part of a modern American "empire" tends to make American scholars less aware of the evils of imperial behavior and the tragic legacy that liberation from such imperial grasp brings for the future of former colonial or neocolonial territories.

35. Jacques Semelin, *Purify and Destroy: The Political Uses of Massacre and Genocide*, trans. Cynthia Schoch from the French (New York: Columbia University Press, 2007).

36. Semelin, *Purify and Destroy*, 266–70.

37. Michael Mann, "Explaining Ethnic Cleansing," in *The Genocide Studies Reader*, ed. Samuel Totten and Paul R. Bartrop (New York: Routledge, 2009), 64. The quote is italicized in the original. The rest of Mann's seven points are from pp. 67–69.

38. Based on Payam Akhavan and Mora Johnson, "International Criminal Tribunal for the Former Yugoslavia," in *The Genocide Studies Reader* (see note 37), 442–51.

39. Quoted in Akhavan and Johnson, "International Criminal Tribunal," 450.

40. Quoted in Akhavan and Johnson, "International Criminal Tribunal," 450–51.

CHAPTER 2 THE HERITAGE OF HORRORS

1. I will use the word *Bosniak* (they pronounce it Boshnyak, while the Bosnian spelling is Bošnjak) for Bosnian Muslims because they have opted for it during and after the wars of the 1990s, although the Croats and Serbs of Bosnia may also occasionally use the term for themselves. For the latter two, I will use the term *Bosnian* and often include Herzegovinians in this term for brevity's sake, though the Herzegovinians would never call themselves Bosnians. In this book I will use Bosnia or the abbreviation B&H for Bosnia and Herzegovina interchangeably.

2. Četnik is a generic term for Serbian paramilitary volunteers (it comes from the word *četa* designating a small military unit). In the wars of the 1990s the word became a generally derogatory term for Serbs used by the Croats and Bosniaks.

3. Partisan (or in the Yugoslav original, *partizan*) was the name of the Communist-led national liberation movement that fought guerilla warfare against the occupying forces during World War II but also against various other militaries and paramilitaries operating in the country at the time.

4. Tim Judah, *Kosovo: War and Revenge*, 2nd ed. (New Haven, CT: Yale University Press, 2000), 1–3.

5. The conventional and Serbian pronunciation of the province is Kosovo; the Albanians call it Kosova.

6. Ustaše was the militant Croat nationalist movement that allied itself with the Nazis and Fascists and came to rule the so-called Independent State of Croatia from 1941 to 1945. Ustaše were also military forces akin to the German SS. Serbs sometimes derisively call all Croats Ustaše.

7. Ustaša is singular; Ustaše is plural.

8. Milan Bulajić, *Jasenovac na sudu: Sudjenje Dinku Šakicu* [Jasenovac on Trial: Judging Dinko Šakic] (Belgrade: Muzej žrtava genocida; Stručna knjiga, 2001), 331–43, esp. 334.

9. Bulajić, *Jasenovac na sudu*, 8.

10. Frederick F. Anscombe, "Albanian and 'Mountain Bandits,'" in *The Ottoman Balkans: 1750–1830*, ed. Frederick F. Anscombe (Princeton, NJ: Marcus Wiener Publishers, 2006), 87–107.

11. Anscombe, "Albanian and 'Mountain Bandits,'" 89–92.

12. People of those ethnic groups may have lived there subjugated by the Ottomans.

CHAPTER 3 BALKAN WARS 1912–1913: AN UNRECOGNIZED GENOCIDE

1. Silvija Djurić, ed., *Dnevnik pobeda: Srbija u balkanskim ratovima 1912–1913* (Belgrade: IRO, n.d.) is a recent reprint of journalistic reports written by Serbian and Western correspondents from the battlefields concurrent with the events, plus material from some military diaries. Many of these reports have been published in contemporary book accounts of these wars.

2. André Gerolymatos, *The Balkan Wars: Conquest, Revolution and Retribution from the Ottoman Era to the Twentieth Century and Beyond* (New York: Basic Books, 2002), 211–32.

3. Misha Glenny, *The Balkans: Nationalism, War and the Great Powers, 1804–1999* (New York: Penguin Books, 2001), 228–48.

4. Glenny, *The Balkans*, 236.

5. According to the information at the website of the Armenian National Institute, the 1894–1896 Hamidian massacres were "near-genocidal atrocities" and the 1909 Adana massacres also fell short of that definition. See Rouben Paul Adalian, "Hamidian (Armenian) Massacres," Armenian National Institute, www.armenian-genocide.org/hamidian.html (accessed July 12, 2006) and Rouben Paul Adalian, "Adana Massacre," Armenian National Institute, www.armenian-genocide.org/adana.html (accessed July 12, 2006).

6. The text of the convention may be found in many sources. One of them is in Carol Rittner, John R. Roth, and James M. Smith, eds., *Will Genocide Ever End?* (St. Paul, MN: Paragon House, 2002), 209–11.

7. International Commission to Inquire into the Causes and Conduct of the Balkan Wars, *The Other Balkan Wars: A 1913 Carnegie Endowment Inquiry in Retrospect* (Washington, DC: A Carnegie Endowment Book, 1993) (hereafter cited as *The Other Balkan Wars*). The report was written by the Balkan commission of inquiry headed by Baron d'Estournelles de Constant of France with Professor Josef Redlich of Austria, Professor Walther Schuecking of Germany, Dr. H. N. Brailsford of England, Professor Samuel Dutton of the United States, Professor Pavel Miliukov of Russia, and M. Justin Godard, Esq., of France. Different chapters of the book were penned by the various members of the committee but received unanimous approval by the entire committee. The authors endeavored to be evenhanded and objective in their reporting but did not receive the cooperation of the government of all the belligerent states. Much of the data provided in this section of my book is based on this report as it appears the Carnegie Commission made an earnest effort to base its narrative on the reports by eyewitnesses; letters of soldiers; interviews with officials, military, and civilians; statistical and financial reports; maps; photos (the most gruesome having been deliberately excluded out of consideration for the sensibilities of the viewers); and so on. Despite the effort to present a balanced view, the report was rejected as prejudicial by the various participants in the conflict.

8. *The Other Balkan Wars*, 208–35 (chapter 5, "The War and International Law").

9. *The Other Balkan Wars*, 13. The ellipses are in the original.

10. *The Other Balkan Wars*. Italics are in the original.

11. *The Other Balkan Wars*, 15.

12. *The Other Balkan Wars*, 16.

13. *The Other Balkan Wars*, 19.

14. Benjamin Lieberman, *Terrible Fate: Ethnic Cleansing in the Making of Modern Europe* (Chicago: Ivan R. Dee, 2006), 58.

15. *The Other Balkan Wars*, 148. In a footnote the authors explain that the term *Bashi-Bazouk* no longer applies only to Turkish irregulars but to all the belligerent na-

tions; the different belligerent nations have their own words for the paramilitary bands such as *Komitadji* for the Bulgarian and *Andarte* for the Greek. The parallels to the Srebrenica massacre of 1995, which ICTY ruled was genocide, are all too obvious.

16. *The Other Balkan Wars*, 149.

17. *The Other Balkan Wars*, 149 (italics in the original).

18. *The Other Balkan Wars*, 149.

19. *The Other Balkan Wars*, 149.

20. *The Other Balkan Wars*, 154–55. Throughout the report, Serbia and Serbians are called Servia and Servians, as was fairly common in the nineteenth century.

21. *The Other Balkan Wars*, 287–88, 306.

22. *The Other Balkan Wars*, 155–56.

23. *The Other Balkan Wars*, 72.

24. Reported by Lieberman, *Terrible Fate*, 59.

25. Tim Judah, *Kosovo: War and Revenge,* 2nd ed. (New Haven, CT: Yale Nota Bene, Yale University Press, 2002), 18.

26. Reported in Judah, *Kosovo*, 19, based on Leon Trotsky, *War Correspondence of Leon Trotsky: The Balkan Wars, 1912–1913* (New York: Monad Press, 1991), 120.

27. Kastriot Dervishi, ed., *Massacres in Chameria*, trans. Etleva Sakajeva from Albanian (Tirana, Albania: Publishing House "55", 2010), 9.

28. *The Other Balkan Wars*, 73.

29. *The Other Balkan Wars*, 89.

30. *The Other Balkan Wars*, 197.

31. *The Other Balkan Wars*, 113.

32. *The Other Balkan Wars*, 326–28.

33. *The Other Balkan Wars*, 130. This seems incomprehensible in the light of Greek-Turkish enmity in the second half of the twentieth century, but one should remember that in the meantime, during the 1920s, Greeks and Turks fought a bitter war in Anatolia.

34. *The Other Balkan Wars*, 124.

35. *The Other Balkan Wars*, 132. It is interesting that the Greek sources accused the Bulgarians of these crimes but the Carnegie Commission concluded that they were perpetrated by the Ottoman army.

36. Lieberman, *Terrible Fate*, 62.

37. Lieberman, *Terrible Fate*, 63.

38. Lieberman, *Terrible Fate*, 70–71.

39. Lieberman, *Terrible Fate*, 70.

40. *The Other Balkan Wars*, 79–80.

41. *The Other Balkan Wars*, 106–7.

42. *The Other Balkan Wars*, 93.

43. *The Other Balkan Wars*, 94.

44. *The Other Balkan Wars*, 106–7, 277–78.

45. *The Other Balkan Wars*, 327.

46. *The Other Balkan Wars*, 280.

47. *The Other Balkan Wars*, 187–93.

48. *The Other Balkan Wars*, 197.

49. *The Other Balkan Wars*, 199.
50. During the Holocaust some Christians—regretfully too few—hid Jews trying to escape the Nazis. In the Balkan wars, there was a case of a Bulgarian finding refuge in a Jewish home as he was sought by the Greeks in Serres. See *The Other Balkan Wars*, 321. Jews, who constituted the largest single ethnic group in Salonika, were more tolerated by the Turks, to whom they did not seem to be an occupational threat, than by the Greeks. This lack of Greek tolerance eventually led to a mass exodus of Jews as Salonika became an increasingly homogeneous Greek city.
51. Similar accusations against the Greek treatment of the Cham Albanians in contested territories have been leveled by Bequir Meta, *The Cam Tragedy* (Tirana, Albania: Sejko, 2007), 22–29.
52. *The Other Balkan Wars*, 137.
53. *The Other Balkan Wars*, 165.
54. *The Other Balkan Wars*, 165–69.
55. *The Other Balkan Wars*, 272.
56. *The Other Balkan Wars*, 181.
57. *The Other Balkan Wars*, 181.
58. *The Other Balkan Wars*, 265.
59. *The Other Balkan Wars*, 265.
60. *The Other Balkan Wars*, 267.
61. *The Other Balkan Wars*, 215.
62. *The Other Balkan Wars*, 277–398.
63. Four hundred thousand is the figure of deported Turks according to Katrin Boeckh, *Von den Balkankriegen zum Ersten Weltkrieg: Kleinstatenpolitik und ethnische Selbstbestimmung auf dem Balkan,* Südosteuropäische Arbeiten Bd. 97 (München, Germany: Südoesteuropaische Arbeiten, 1996) as per book review of Frano Prcela in *Crkva u svijetu* (Split, Croatia) 33, no. 4 (198): 435.
64. *The Other Balkan Wars,* 267–68.
65. *The Other Balkan Wars,* 271–72.
66. *The Other Balkan Wars,* 267; italics are mine.
67. Isidor Djuković, "Genocid nad Srbima u austrougarskim logorima" [Genocide of Serbs in Austro-Hungarian Camps] in *Genocid u 20. veku na prostorima jugoslovenskih zemalja*, 49–58.
68. Dušan Bogdanović, "Through Facts to the Truth," in *Šušnjar 1941: Proceedings—Papers, Testimonies and Documents* (Oštra Luka, RS, Bosnia and Herzegovina, 2008), 158.
69. Lieberman, *Terrible Fate*, 75.
70. Silvija Djurić and Vidoslav Stefanović, eds., *Golgota i vaskrs Srbije 1915–1918* [Golgotha and Resurrection of Serbia 1915–1918] , vol. 3 (Čakovec, Croatia: TIZ Zrinski, IRO "Beograd," 1990). There are seventeen unnumbered pages of photographs located between pages 440 and 473.
71. Djurić and Stefanović, *Golgota i vaskrs Srbije*, vol. 3, "Uvodni deo dokumentacije medjunarodne komisije o Bugarskim zločinima u Srbiji" [Introductory Part of the Documentation of the International Commission about Bulgarian Crimes in Serbia], 624–60, originally from Aleksandar Trajković, *Vreme bezumlja: Dokumenti o*

bugarskim zločinima u vranjskom kraju 1915–1918 [Insane Times: Documents about Bulgarian Crimes in the Region of Vranje 1915–1918] (Belgrade, 1981), pp. 75–90. Document from the Hague Conventions: *Documents relatifs aux violations des Conventions de la Haye et du Droit international en general, comises da 1915–1918 par les Bulgares en Serbie ocupee* (Paris, 1919) vol. 1 (hereafter cited as *Documents relatifs*).

72. *Golgota i vaskrs Srbije*, vol. 3, "Izveštaj američkog novinara Vilijama Drajtona" [The Report of the American Journalist William Drayton], 661–74, taken from Trajković, *Vreme bezumlja*, 116–26. This report was also cited from *Documents relatifs*, vol. 2.

73. "Izveštaj američkog novinara Vilijama Drajtona," trans. P. Mojzes from Serbian, 674.

74. Lieberman, *Terrible Fate*, 82.

75. Judah, *Kosovo*, 22.

76. Meta, *The Cham Tragedy*, 35–43.

CHAPTER 4 MULTIPLE GENOCIDES
OF WORLD WAR II: WESTERN BALKANS

1. Istvan Deak, "The One and the Many," in *The Black Book of Bosnia: The Consequences of Appeasement*, ed. Nader Mousavizadeh (Washington, DC: Basic-Books, 1996), 17.

2. Benjamin Lieberman, *Terrible Fate: Ethnic Cleansing in the Making of Modern Europe* (Chicago: Ivan R. Dee, 2006), 187.

3. Quoted in Lieberman, *Terrible Fate*, 188.

4. Vuk Drašković, *Nož*, 6th ed. (Belgrade: Nova knjiga, 1986). Translated by Milo Yelesiyevich as *Knife* (New York: Serbian Classics Press, 2000). The book was written between 1979 and 1982 and could have been regarded prophetic if it had not contributed to the enticement of the desire for revenge, despite the author's attempt to both fire up and cool down such destructive impulses between related peoples. Another of his books, *Molitva* [Prayer], 2 vols. (Belgrade: Nova knjiga, 1985, 1986) had a similar disquieting impact. These books are examples of literature and other intellectual explorations of the genocides of World War II that could have had a powerful inducement for the outbreak of the next round of genocides of the 1990s.

5. The proceedings are gathered into five books, which are bilingual English and Serbian. The first book, on the New York conference of 1997, is *Jasenovac: Proceedings of the First International Conference and Exhibit about Jasenovac Concentration Camps* (Banja Luka, Bosnia and Herzegovina: Public Institution Memorial Area Donja Gradina and Association Jasenovac-Donja Gradina, 2007); the second, on the Banja Luka conference of 2000, is *Jasenovac: Proceedings of the Second International Conference on Jasenovac* (Banja Luka, Bosnia and Herzegovina: Public Institution Memorial Area Donja Gradina and Association Jasenovac-Donja Gradina, 2007); the third, on the Jerusalem conference of 2002, is *Jasenovac: Proceedings of the 11th International Conference on Holocaust and 3rd International Conference on*

Jasenovac (Banja Luka, Bosnia and Herzegovina: Public Institution Memorial Area Donja Gradina and Association Jasenovac-Donja Gradina, 2007); the fourth, on the Banja Luka Conference of 2007, is *Jasenovac: Proceedings of the 4th International Conference on Jasenovac* (Banja Luka, Bosnia and Herzegovina: Public Institution Memorial Area Donja Gradina and Association Jasenovac-Donja Gradina, 2007); *Jasenovac: The Systems of Concentration Camps and Execution Sites of the Croatian State for the Extermination of Serbs, Jews and Gypsies in WWII* (Banja Luka, 2011) (hereafter cited as *Jasenovac 1, 2, 3, 4*, and *5*, respectively). I participated in the 2007 and 2011 conferences. Another book about the first conference in New York was compiled by Barry M. Lituchy, ed., *Jasenovac and the Holocaust in Yugoslavia* (New York: Jasenovac Research Institute, 2006).

6. Paul Mojzes, "Ethnic Cleansing," in *Will Genocide Ever End?* ed. Carol Rittner, John K. Roth, and James M. Smith (St. Paul, MN: Paragon House, 2002), 51–56.

7. Mojzes, "Ethnic Cleansing," 54.

8. Peter Brock, *Media Cleansing, Dirty Reporting: Journalism and Tragedy of Yugoslavia*, 2nd ed. (Los Angeles: GM Books, 2005), 311.

9. Velimir Terzić, *Jugoslavija u aprilskom ratu 1941* (Titograd: n.p., 1963).

10. Franjo Tudjman, *Horrors of War: Historical Reality and Philosophy*, rev. ed., trans. Katarina Mijatović from Croatian (New York: M. Evans, 1996), 268. Tudjman does not provide his own estimate, though he wrote that the figure could range between twenty and forty thousand.

11. Damir Mirković, "Victims and Perpetrators in the Yugoslav Genocide 1941–1945: Some Preliminary Observations," *Holocaust and Genocide Studies* 7, no. 3 (Winter 1993), 320.

12. Mirković, "Victims and Perpetrators," 319.

13. For example, R. J. Rummel, *Death by Government* (New Brunswick, NJ: Transaction Publishers, 2007), 340–43.

14. "God with us," "God protects the Serbs," and "God protects the Croats," respectively.

15. An excellent example of a clergyman's and scholar's application of religious principles to the challenge of reconciliation is by Donald W. Shriver Jr., *An Ethic for Enemies: Forgiveness in Politics* (New York: Oxford University Press, 1997). To my knowledge, no similar work has as yet been written by clergy and scholars of the Balkans to provide a similar prophetic witness for overcoming genocidal tragedies.

16. Among the many other publications printed in the West are Martha Minow, *Between Vengeance and Forgiveness: Facing History after Genocide and Mass Violence* (Boston: Beacon Press, 1998); William Bole, Drew Christiansen, S.J., and Robert T. Hennemeyer, *Forgiveness in International Politics: An Alternative Road to Peace* (Washington, DC: United States Conference of Catholic Bishops, 2004); and Lucia Ann McSpadden, ed., *Reaching Reconciliation: Churches in Transition to Democracy in Eastern and Central Europe* (Uppsala, Sweden: Life & Peace Institute, 2000).

17. Quoted in Paul Mojzes, "Examination of Genocide: Truth and Justice Instead of Political and Economic Gain," in *Jasenovac 4*, 90.

18. Slavko Goldštajn, in *Politika* (Belgrade), July 22, 2008. Translated by Paul Mojzes.

19. Quoted by Dušan Bogdanović, "Through Facts to the Truth," in *Šušnjar 1941: Proceedings—Papers, Testimonies and Documents* (Oštra Luka, RS, Bosnia and Herzegovina, 2008), 159.

20. Bogdanović, "Through Facts to the Truth," 160.

21. Bogdanović, "Through Facts to the Truth," 160.

22. Bogdanović, "Through Facts to the Truth," 161.

23. Nada Kisić Kolanović, "Podržavljenje imovine Židova u NDH" [The Nationalization of Jewish Property in the Independent State of Croatia], *Časopis za suvremenu povijest* (Zagreb), no. 3 (1998): 431.

24. Smilja Avramov, *Genocide in Yugoslavia* (Belgrade: BIGZ, 1995), 300.

25. Quoted in Kolanović, "Podržavljenje imovine," 433. Translated from Croatian by Paul Mojzes.

26. Vladimir Dedijer is one of the rare authors who contradicts that the camps were under the exclusive control of the Ustaše, claiming that "Jasenovac and all other concentration camps stood directly under the control of the Gestapo and the German military defense." See his *The Yugoslav Auschwitz and the Vatican: The Croation* [sic] *Massacre of the Serbs During World War II*, trans. Harvey L. Kendall from German (Buffalo, NY: Prometheus Books, 1992), 54.

27. This discussion is based on the presentation of Slavko Goldstein (or Goldštajn), a Croatian Jewish activist and journalist at the Third International Conference on Jasenovac in Jerusalem, December 29–30, 2002, in *Jasenovac 3*, 83. Map on p. 318.

28. "Zemaljska komisija Hrvatske za utvrdjivanje zločina okupatora i njihovih pomagača," in *Zločini u logoru Jasenovac* [Croatian State Commission for Establishing Crimes of Occupying Forces and Their Assistants, *Crimes in the Jasenovac Camp*], trans. Dragica Banjac from Croatian (Banja Luka: Besjeda, 2000), 4.

29. *Zločini u Jasenovcu*, 62–65.

30. For a concise summary of the range of victims by different authors, see David Bruce MacDonald, *Balkan Holocausts? Serbian and Croatian Victim-Centered Propaganda and the War in Yugoslavia* (Manchester, UK: Manchester University Press, 2002), 161–62.

31. D. Mirković, "Victims and Perpetrators," 322.

32. D. Mirković, "Victims and Perpetrators," 98. Also Goldštajn's educated estimate.

33. Dragan Cvetković, "Jasenovac in the System of Suffering of the Civilians in the Independent State of Croatia—A Quantitative Analysis (Or Numbers Once more Revisited)," in *Jasenovac 4*, 69.

34. Cvetković, "Jasenovac in the System of Suffering," 76–77.

35. Goldstein, *Jasenovac 3*, 83–84.

36. Goldstein, *Jasenovac 3*, 83.

37. *Zločini u logoru Jasenovac* (see note 28), 40–65.

38. Srboljub Živanović, "Forensic Observations on the Efficiency of the Catholic and Muslim Croatian Murderers' Way of Killing and Torturing of their Serbian, Jewish, and Roma Victims," in *Jasenovac 4*, 43–45.

39. Cadik I. Danon Braco, *The Smell of Human Flesh: A Witness of the Holocaust Memories of Jasenovac* (Belgrade: Dosije, 2006), 97.

40. Danon Braco, *The Smell of Human Flesh*, 97.

41. Barry M. Lituchy, "Introduction," *Jasenovac and the Holocaust in Yugoslavia* (New York: Jasenovac Research Institute, 2006), xxv.

42. Damir Mirković's review of Djuro Zatezalo, *Jadovno: Kompleks ustaških logora 1941* [Jadovno: A Complex of Ustaša Camps, 1941] in *South Slav Journal* 29, nos. 1–2 (2010), 148.

43. Milorad Bajić, "David u jamama Golijata" [David in the pits of Goliath], *Srpsko nasledje: istorijske sveske* 13 (January 1999) in www.srpsko-nasledje.co.yu/sr-1/1999/01/article-7.html (accessed November 24, 2003). Bajić's numbers of victims are considerably higher than Zatezalo's (previous footnote).

44. *Zločini fašističkih okupatora i njihovih pomagača protiv Jevreja u Jugoslaviji* [Crimes of Fascist Occupiers and their Assistants against Jews in Yugoslavia] (Belgrade: Association of Jewish Communities in FPR Yugoslavia, 1952), 58–59 (hereafter cited as *Zločini*).

45. (Bishop) Atanasije Jevtić, "Od Kosova do Jadovna" [From Kosovo to Jadovno], initially published in *Pravoslavlje*, nos. 400 (November 15, 1983), 404 (January 15, 1984), and 405 (February 1, 1984); electronic version www.kosovo.com/sk/rastko-kosovo/istorija/kosovo-jadovno.html (accessed December 1, 2003).

46. *Zločini*, 59.

47. *Zločini*, 125.

48. From the testimony of a local islander who was present at the exhumation; *Zločini*, 125–26.

49. *Zločini*, 127–30.

50. *Zločini*, 75–76.

51. *Zločini*, 76–79.

52. *Zločini*, 79–80.

53. www.pavelicpapers.com/ (accessed September 24, 2003).

54. Marko Attila Hoare, "The Ustaša Genocide," *The South Slav Journal* 25, nos. 1–2 (Spring–Summer, 2004): 35.

55. Vladimir Umeljić, *Srbi i genocidni XX vek* [Serbs and Genocidal Twentieth Century] (Belgrade: Magna plus, n.d.), 151, quoting Sarajevo Catholic Archbishop Ivan Šarić from May 11, 1941.

56. MacDonald, *Balkan Holocausts?*, 134.

57. Dedijer, *The Yugoslav Auschwitz*, 28. "Already for centuries Papal hatred has been levied loudly against the Orthodox Serbs" (p. 28). This is the theme of the book. While much evidence is amassed to support his indictment of the Roman Catholic Church, it is my conviction that he leaves out all evidence contrary to his conviction that the Catholic Church is still evil and inquisitorial.

58. Jure Krišto, "Vjerski prijelazi u NDH—primjer šibeničke biskupije" [Religious Transfer in ISC—Example of the Šibenik Bishopric], *Časopis za suvremenu povijest* (Zagreb) 29, no. 2 (1997): 235–48. Krišto claims historical objectivity but he too strenuously interprets the data as to deny the huge number of forced conversions, whatever their actual number, in order to declare his Catholic Church innocent

of any wrongdoing. Krišto's findings leave unanswered why such large numbers of applicants for conversion from Serbian Orthodoxy to Catholicism did not also happen before or after World War II.

59. Umeljić, *Srbi i genocidni XX vek*, 141.

60. Umeljić, *Srbi i genocidni XX vek*, 140–45. In one particularly revolting account from the concentration camp Koprivnica, the Ustaše ordered about a hundred young Jewish inmates to masturbate and then brought in about fifty Orthodox priests, ordering them to uncover their behinds; the Ustaše then tried forcing the Jews to rape the priests (p. 146, based on "Saopštenje o zločinima okupatora i njihovih pomagača u Vojvodini 1941–1945, Zločini okupatora u Sremu, 1941–1945" [Novi Sad, 1946], 102–03).

61. Marko Oršolić, *Zlodusima nasuprot* [Contra Evil Spritis], 2nd rev. ed. (Sarajevo: MAUNA-Fe, 2008), 20.

62. Umeljić, *Srbi i genocidni XX vek*, 169–80. Also Dedijer, *The Yugoslav Auschwitz*, 176–230. One such example is Friar Dr. Srećko Perić, who preached in his church in Gorica, "Brothers Croats, go and slaughter all Serbs; first cut the throat of my sister who married a Serb, and then all Serbs. When you are finished with the work, come to me to the church, and I will accept your confessions and then forgive all your sins." In that area, 5,600 Serb men, women, and children were killed. Umeljić states that the information is gathered from the State Archives for the Investigation of War Crimes in Belgrade.

63. See Umeljić's photocopy in *Srbi i genocidni XX vek*, 265 of an article in *Nova Hrvatska* no. 11, January 13, 1942.

64. Umeljić, *Srbi i genocidni XX vek*, 167, based on "Dokumenti nedavne prošlosti," *Dobri pastir, vjesnik zagrebačkih župa* (Zagreb), no. 8 (1945): 5.

65. Oršolić, *Zlodusima nasuprot,* 18–19.

66. Danon Braco, *The Smell of Human Flesh*, 16.

67. Jacques Sabille, "Attitude of Italians to the Persecuted Jews in Croatia," in *Jews under the Italian Occupation*, Leon Poliakov and Jacques Sabille (New York: H. Fertig, 1983), 132.

68. Sabille, "Attitude of Italians," 149–50.

69. *Zločini*, 123.

70. Davide Rodogno, *Fascism's European Empire: Italian Occupation during the Second World War*, trans. Adrian Belton (Cambridge: Cambridge University Press, 2006), 362.

71. Rodogno, *Fascism's European Empire*, 364.

72. Rodogno, *Fascism's European Empire*, 372.

73. Rodogno, *Fascism's European Empire*, 185–86.

74. Rodogno, *Fascism's European Empire*, 187. At first there were 4,000 inmates in Pag (Pago in Italian), of which 900 were Zagreb Jews. The number increased to 6,000. In September 1941 the Italian garrison discovered 1,500 bodies, but the Italians estimated that about 9,000 were killed, the bodies of most having been thrown into the sea.

75. Rodogno, *Fascism's European Empire*, 187.

76. Rodogno, *Fascism's European Empire*, 188.

77. Rodogno, *Fascism's European Empire*, 191.
78. Rodogno, *Fascism's European Empire*, 192.
79. Rodogno, *Fascism's European Empire*, 364.
80. Rodogno, *Fascism's European Empire*, 365.
81. Rodogno, *Fascism's European Empire*, 367.
82. Rodogno, *Fascism's European Empire*, 385.
83. Quoted in Rodogno, *Fascism's European Empire*, 392–93.
84. Quoted in Frank P. Verna, *Yugoslavia under Italian Rule, 1941–1943: Civil and Military Aspects of the Italian Occupation* (PhD diss., University of California, Santa Barbara, 1985), 114. Italics in the original.
85. Arriggo Petacco, *A Tragedy Revealed: The Story of Italians from Istria, Dalmatia, and Venezia Giulia, 1943–1956*. Trans. Konrad Eisenbichler from Italian (Toronto: University of Toronto Press, 2005), 34.
86. Verna, *Yugoslavia under Italian Rule*, 115–16.
87. Verna, *Yugoslavia under Italian Rule*, 120.
88. Quoted in Verna, *Yugoslavia under Italian Rule*, 123–24.
89. Verna, *Yugoslavia under Italian Rule*, 124.
90. Verna, *Yugoslavia under Italian Rule*, 348.
91. The information on the camps is incomplete. There were twenty-four camps in Slovenia alone. Additionally, there were camps at Gonars, Monigo, Chiesanuova, Renicci, Fiume, Visco, Fraschette di Alatri, Cairo Montenotte, Pisticci, Ferramonti Tarsia, Ancona, Lipari, Uštica, Fossalon di Grado, Tavernelle, Molat, Forte Mamula, Prevlaka, Bakar, Scoglio Calogera, Ugliano, Vodice, Laurana, San Martino di Brazza, Lesina, and Kraljevica (Porto Re). The latter three were specifically for Jews. In Montenegro and Albania, the camps were at Durazzo, Kotor, Klos, Preza, Kavaje, Bar (Antivari). In Greece the camps were on the island of Paxos, Othoni, Lazarati, Fanos, Acronaupia, Kalavryta, Trikala, and Larissa. See Verna, *Yugoslavia under Italian Rule*, 355–59.
92. Verna, *Yugoslavia under Italian Rule*, 351.
93. *Zločini*, 123.
94. *Zločini*, 133.
95. Rodogno, *Fascism's European Empire*, 335.
96. About three hundred elderly and sickly Jews who remained on Rab were rounded up by the Germans and were together with Istrian Jews taken to Auschwitz. None returned. *Zločini*, 132–33.
97. Rodogno, *Fascism's European Empire*, 400.
98. Joachim A. Hösler, "Konfliktreiche Vergangenheit" [Conflict Rich Past], *Glaube in der 2. Welt* (Zurich), no. 6 (2008): 18.
99. Hoesler, "Konfliktreiche Vergangenheit," 18.
100. Quoted in Fouad Ajami, "In Europe's Shadows" in *The Black Book of Bosnia* (see note 1), 49.
101. Aleksa Djilas, "The Nation That Wasn't," in *The Black Book of Bosnia* (see note 1), 24.
102. Sofija Praća-Veljović, "Genocide in Sanski Most," in *Šušnjar 1941* (see note 19), 83.

103. Praća-Veljović, "Genocide in Sanski Most," 75–82.
104. See Milan Crnomarković, "Crimes in Sanski Most," in *Šušnjar 1941* (see note 19), 149, and Drago Trninić, "Šušnjar in 1941," in *Šušnjar 1941* (see note 19), 155.
105. Praća-Veljović, "Genocide in Sanski Most," 88–89 and Milan Bulajić, "Šušnjar Near Sanski Most" (1941–1944); "Genocide over Serbs and Jews on St. Elijah's Day 1941," in *Šušnjar 1941* (see note 19), 122–24.
106. *Zločini*, 66.
107. *Zločini*, 68.
108. *Zločini*, 69–70.
109. *Zločini*, 71–72.
110. *Zločini*, 71.

CHAPTER 5 MULTIPLE GENOCIDES IN WORLD WAR II: NORTHEASTERN AND CENTRAL BALKANS

1. *Zločini fašističkih okupatora i njihovih pomagača protiv Jevreja u Jugoslaviji* [Crimes of Fascist Occupiers and Their Assistants against Jews in Yugoslavia] (Belgrade: Association of Jewish Communities in FPR Yugoslavia, 1952), 9–12 (hereafter cited as *Zločini*).
2. *Zločini*, 14–15.
3. Ženi Lebl, *Do "konačnog rešenja": Jevreji u Beogradu 1521–1942* [To "The Final Solution": Jews in Belgrade 1521–1942] (Belgrade: Cigoja, 2001), 299–304 (hereafter, title abbreviated as *DKR: Beogradu*).
4. Milan Ristović, "The Persecuted and Their Abettors: Solidarity and Help for the Jews in Serbia 1941–1945," in *Izraelsko-srpska naučna razmena u proučavanju Holokausta/Israeli-Serbian Academic Exchange in Holocaust Research*, bilingual edition, ed. Jovan Mirković (Belgrade: Muzej žrtava genocida, 2008), 215–16.
5. Lebl, *DKR: Beogradu*, 311–12.
6. Lebl, *DKR: Beogradu*, 312–13.
7. Lebl, *DKR: Beogradu*, 319–20.
8. *Zločini*, 24.
9. The German name for the vehicle was Saurer and was apparently one of a small fleet of these super large vehicles manufactured specifically for the gassing of victims. The truck was returned to Germany for repair in June 1942 and was not brought back for use in the Balkans.
10. Ristović, "The Persecuted," 216–17.
11. Damir Mirković, "Victims and Perpetrators in the Yugoslav Genocide 1941–1945: Some Preliminary Observations," in *Holocaust and Genocide Studies*. Vol. 7, No. 3 (Winter 1993), 325.
12. Jennie Lebl was personally saved by Jelena Glavaški, who was subsequently executed and was posthumously awarded this recognition. See Zheni Lebl, *Do "konačnog rešenja": Jevreji u Srbiji* [To the "Final Solution": Jews in Serbia] (Belgrade, Serbia: Cigoja, 2002), 117 (hereafter, title abbreviated as *DKR: Srbiji*).
13. *Zločini*, 37.

14. *Zločini*, 40–42.

15. *Zločini*, 43–45.

16. *Vernichtungskrieg: Verbrechen der Wehrmacht 1941–1944* (Hamburg: Hamburger Edition HIS Verlag, 1996); pages 21–58 deal with the war crimes of the German Army in Serbia.

17. *Vernichtungskrieg*, 23. All illustrated with numerous photos of the killings by German army photographers.

18. *Vernichtungskrieg*, 50.

19. Zheni Lebl, *Plima i slom* [High Tide and Breakdown] (Gornji Milanovac, Serbia: Dečje novine, 1990), 347.

20. Lebl, *Plima i slom*, 355 and 360.

21. Barry Lituchy, "Introduction," in *Jasenovac and the Holocaust in Yugoslavia*, ed. Barry Lituchy (New York: Jasenovac Research Institute, 2006), xxxi.

22. *Zločini*, 137.

23. Excerpts of their testimonies are found in *Zločini*, 158–63.

24. *Zločini*, 149–54. Also Pavle Šosberger, *Novosadski jevreji* [Jews of Novi Sad], 2nd ed. (Novi Sad: Prometej, 2001), 39–45.

25. For instance, Aleksandar Veljić, *Racija: Zaboravljen Genocid* (Belgrade: Metphysica, 2007), 277–78.

26. For instance, Drago Njegovan, ed., Pokrajinska komisija *Zločini okupatora i njihovih pomagača u Vojvodini protiv Jevreja* [Crimes of the Occupiers and their Assistants in Vojvodina against the Jews], (Novi Sad: Prometej, 2011), 97 (hereafter, title abbreviated as *Zločini u Vojvodini protiv Jevreja*).

27. *Zločini*, 164.

28. Njegovan, *Zločini u Vojvodini protiv Jevreja, 105.*

29. *Zločini*, 172–73.

30. Šosberger, *Novosadski Jevreji*, 50.

31. *Zločini*, 179–82.

32. Their death march is described in *Zločini*, 182–88.

33. Jennie Lebel, ed., *A Memorial of Yugoslavian Jewish Prisoners of War: Half a Century after Liberation, 1945–1995* (Tel Aviv, Israel: Udruženje veterana drugog svetskog rata u Israelu, Jugoslavenska grupa, 1995). The text is in Hebrew, Serbian, and English.

34. *Zločini*, 131.

35. Lebl, *Plima i slom,* 383–85.

36. Nenad Antonijević, "Holocaust in the Area of Kosovo and the Metohija during World War II and Its Context," in *Izraelsko-srpska naučna razmena u proučavanju Holokausta* (see note 4), 411.

37. Lebl, *Plima i slom*, 384–85.

38. *Zločini*, 131–32.

39. Davide Rodogno, *Fascism's European Empire: Italian Occupation during the Second World War*, trans. Adrian Belton (Cambridge: Cambridge University Press, 2006), 386.

40. Wolf Oschlies, "Im Kosovo: Juden unerwünscht," *Glaube in der 2. Welt* 35, no. 3 (2007): 16–17.

41. Tim Judah, *Kosovo: War and Revenge.* 2nd ed. (New Haven, CT: Yale University Press, 2002), 28.

42. Judah, *Kosovo*, 27.

43. Quoted in Judah, *Kosovo*, 27.

44. Milan D. Lazić, "Zločini i genocid Šiptara nad kosmetskim Srbima od 1941. do 1945. godine [Crimes and Genocide of Shiptars over Serbs of Kosmet from 1941 to 1945] and Nenad Antonijević, "Albanski zločini nad Srbima u italijanskoj okupacionoj zoni na Kosovu i Metohiji u Drugom svetskom ratu" [Albanian Crimes over Serbs in the Italian Occupational Zone in Kosovo and Metohija in World War II], in *Genocid u 20. Veku na prostorima Jugoslovenskih zemalja* [Genocide in the twentieth Century on Territories of Yugoslav Lands], ed. Jovan Mirković (Belgrade: Muzej žrtava genocida, 2005), 145–55 and 157–66, respectively.

45. David Bruce MacDonald, *Balkan Holocausts? Serbian and Croatian Victim-Centered Propaganda and the War in Yugoslavia* (Manchester, UK: Manchester University Press, 2002), 142.

46. See Serbian War Crimes in *Wikipedia*, s.v. "Chetniks," en.wikipedia.org/wiki/Chetniks (accessed July 6, 2010).

47. Quoted in Benjamin Lieberman, *Terrible Fate: Ethnic Cleansing in the Making of Modern Europe* (Chicago: Ivan R. Dee, 2006), 190.

48. Jennie Lebel, *The Mufti of Jerusalem Haj-Amin el-Husseini and National Socialism*, trans. Paul Münch from Serbian (Belgrade: Cigoja, 2007), 190–209.

49. "Genocide against Bosniaks in Višegrad 1941–1945," genocideinvisegrad .worldpress.com/2009/12/29/genocide-against-bosniaks-in-visegrad (accessed July 6, 2010). See also genocideinvisegrad.wordpress.com/2008/11/ (accessed June 4, 2011).

50. D. Mirković, "Victims and Perpetrators," 321.

51. Dragan Cvetković, "Bosna i Hercegovina—numeričko odredjivanje ljudskih gubitaka u drugom svetskom ratu" [Bosnia and Herzegovina: Numerical Determination of Human Losses during World War II] in *Prilozi istraživanju zločina genocida i ratnih zločina* [Contributions to Research of Genocide and War Crimes], ed. Jovan Mirković (Belgrade: Muzej žrtava genocida, 2009), 108.

52. Cvetković, "Bosna i Hercegovina," 118. Translated from Serbian by Paul Mojzes.

53. Cvetković, "Bosna i Hercegovina," 142.

54. Cvetković, "Bosna i Hercegovina," 134.

55. It is ironic that to the best of our knowledge their ancestry is India, from which the term *Indo-Aryan* connotes the race that Germans called Aryan.

56. Dragoljub Acković, "Licitiranje o broju romskih žrtava u Jasenovcu u Nezavisnoj Državi Hrvatskoj" [Auction of the Number of Roma Victims in Jasenovac and Independent State of Croatia], in *Genocid u 20. Veku na prostorima jugoslovenskih zemalja, 471.*

57. vrlika.free.fr/jasenovac.htm, p. 5 (accessed December 1, 2003).

58. Jovan Mirković, "Hronologija zločina (April-Avgust 1941. godine)-Prilog dokazima o genocidnostnom karakteru Nezavisne Države Hrvatske" [Chronology of Crime: Contribution of Evidence about the Genocidal Character of the Independent State of Croatia] in *Prilozi istraživanju zločina genocida i ratnih zločina* (Belgrade: Muzej žrtava genocida, 2009), 66–67.

59. D. Mirković, "Victims and Perpetrators," 325.

CHAPTER 6 MULTIPLE GENOCIDES IN
WORLD WAR II: SOUTHEASTERN BALKANS

1. *Holocaust Encyclopedia*, s.v. "Bulgaria," www.ushmm.org/wlc/en/article .php?ModuleId=10005355 (accessed July 7, 2010).

2. "The Virtual Jewish History Tour: Bulgaria," www.jewishvirtuallibrary.org/ jsource/vjw/bulgaria.html (accessed July 7, 2010).

3. Pavel Stefanov, "The Bulgarian Orthodox Church and the Holocaust: Addressing Common Misperceptions,"*Religion in Eastern Europe* 26, no. 2 (May 2006): 12, 15–16.

4. Currently Greece is trying to block the international use of the name Republic of Macedonia by insisting it be called The Former Republic of Yugoslavia Macedonia. The United States recognizes the country's name as the Republic of Macedonia.

5. Zhamila Kolonomos and Vera Veskoviḱ-Vangeli, *Evreite vo Makedonija vo vtorata svetska vojna, 1941–1945* [Jews in Macedonia during the Second World War, 1941–1945], vol. 1 (Skopje: Makedonska akademija na naukite i umetnosti, 1986), 84–85. See also Žheni Lebl, *Plima i slom* [High Tide and Breakdown] (Gornji Milanovac, Serbia: Dečje novine, 1990), 325–47.

6. Kolonomos and Veskoviḱ-Vangeli, *Evreite vo Makedonija*, 87.

7. Vera Veskoviḱ-Vangeli, "Antisemitskoto zakonodavstvo na fashistichka Bugariya—faktor za demografskite promeni vo Makedonija" [Antisemitic Legislation in Fascist Bulgaria—Factor for Demographic Changes in Macedonia], in *Evreite vo Makedonija* (see note 5), 108.

8. Belev's fate at the end of the war was somewhat unclear. Some believed that he succeeded to escape in unknown directions, while others stated that he was summarily executed by the police upon having been captured at the end of the war (Lebl, *Plima i slom*, 374).

9. Kolomonos and Veskoviḱ-Vangeli, *Evreite vo Makedonija*, 118.

10. Kolomonos and Veskoviḱ-Vangeli, *Evreite vo Makedonija*, 119, 123–24. The number of deported from Macedonia varies between 7,056; 7,122; 7,162; and 7,240.

11. Lebl, *Plima i slom*, 374.

12. Kolomonos and Veskoviḱ-Vangeli, *Evreite vo Makedonija*, 122.

13. Lebl, *Plima i slom*, 375, 377.

14. Lebl, *Plima i slom*, 372.

15. Nora Levin, *The Holocaust: The Destruction of European Jewry, 1933–1945* (New York: Thomas Y. Crowell, 1968), 521.

16. David Rodogno, *Fascism's European Empire: Italian Occupation during the Second World War*, trans. Adrian Belton (Cambridge: Cambridge University Press, 2006), 391–92.

17. Kolomonos and Veskoviḱ-Vangeli, *Evreite vo Makedonija*, 124.

18. Levin, *The Holocaust*, 523.

19. Levin, *The Holocaust*, 524.

20. "Jewish Holocaust Victims of Thessaloniki (Salonika)," Foundation for the Advancement of Sephardic Studies and Culture, www.sephardicstudies.org/thess .html (accessed June 25, 2010).

21. "Massacres and Atrocities of WWII," members.iinet.net.au/~gduncan/ massacres.html (accessed June 25, 2010).

22. "Massacres and Atrocities."

23. Beqir Meta, *The Cham Tragedy* (Tirana, Albania: Sejko, 2007), 73–82.

CHAPTER 7 RETALIATORY GENOCIDES AGAINST WARTIME ENEMIES

1. Either of their own will or that of various governments, the identity of many people living in Macedonia was very fluid. Many who had been previously regarded as Bulgarians could now declare themselves Macedonians.

2. In this chapter, no differentiation is made among German speakers regardless whether they originated from Austrian or German lands.

3. Arbeitskreis Dokumentation, *Verbrechen an den Deutschen in Jugoslawien 1944–1948* (Munich: Donauschwäbische Kulturstiftung, 2000) (hereafter cited as *VDJ*).

4. Radna grupa za dokumentaciju, *Genocid nad nemačkom manjinom u Jugoslaviji 1944–1948* [translated from *Genocide of the Ethnic Germans in Yugoslavia 1944–1948* into Serbian by Dragutin Janjetović] (Belgrade, Serbia: Premis, 2004), 40–41 (hereafter cited as *GNMJ*).

5. Due to their prevalence, *all* Germans were nicknamed "Švabe." The word *Švabe* was used both descriptively (even by themselves) but also pejoratively by the Slavic population.

6. *GNMJ*, 239–40.

7. Dieter Blumenwitz, *Rechtsgutachter über die verbrechen an die Deutschen in Jugoslawien 1944–1948* (Munich: Juristische Studien, 2002), 14.

8. While most of the German survivors energetically reject this, viewing themselves as merely accepting the status quo brought about by the outbreak of the war, the view that some Germans were not merely pro-Nazi but spied for Germany and undermined anti-Nazi resistance was common knowledge in Yugoslavia. See Tomo Šalić, *Židovi u Vinkovicma i okolici* [Jews in Vinkovci and the Environs] (Osijek, Croatia: Židovska općina Osijek, 2002), 422–23.

9. In "Bericht von Superintendent Sebele uber das Werk in Jugoslawien an Bischof Gerber," confidential typescript of January 11, 1946, this ethnic German Methodist pastor mentions that a few of his colleagues and deaconesses became admirers of Hitler. A relative of mine by marriage was a German Lutheran pastor who became active in pro-Nazi propaganda in Osijek during the war. He was captured by the Partisans at the end of the war and was never seen again.

10. Branko Pavlica, "Sudbina Nemaca u Srbiji" [Destiny of Germans in Serbia], in *Teme* (Niš, Serbia) 29, no. 3 (July–September 2005), 380. Local Germans claimed that the division was conceptualized for self-defense of German dwellings but that the German High Command had other plans and utilized the division on other battlefronts.

11. Pavlica, "Sudbina Nemaca u Srbiji," 381. The order to evacuate all Germans was postponed to avoid the impression that Germany was losing the war. By the time the order did arrive, it was too late for many of them to withdraw. Thus very large numbers fell into the hands of the Partisans and the Red Army. Among those, a large number had no intention of evacuating because they considered themselves innocent of any wrongdoing.

12. *VDJ*, 276.

13. Blumenwitz, *Rechtsgutachter über die verbrechen*, 16.

14. *GNMJ*, 196. Since there are statistical inconsistencies in the book, I have opted to provide a range of the numbers cited in various places in the book.

15. Pavlica, "Sudbina Nemaca u Srbiji," 382, and Duško Dimitrijević, "Restitucija 'stečenih prava' pripadnika nemačke manjine u bivšoj Jugoslaviji" [Restitution of the "Acquired Rights" of Members of the German Minority in the Former Yugoslavia], *Teme* 29, no. 3 (2005): 400. There is some disagreement about the loss of citizenship, as *de iure* no such decision was made but de facto they had no rights.

16. Blumenwitz, *Rechtsgutachter über die verbrechen*, 19.

17. *GNMJ*, 220.

18. *GNMJ*, 196.

19. *GNMJ*, 196.

20. The lower figure is from Pavlica, "Sudbina Nemaca u Srbiji," 383. The higher figure is *GNMJ*, 232.

21. *GNMJ*, 6.

22. *GNMJ*, 130.

23. Pavlica, "Sudbina Nemaca u Srbiji," 384–85.

24. *GNMJ*, 160.

25. *GNMJ*, 161.

26. The liquidation camps are italicized with the approximate number of killed in parenthesis. *GNMJ*, 130.

27. The totals in this list are based on a list in *VDJ*, 320.

28. *VDJ*, 196.

29. *VDJ*. There is a significant discrepancy in numbers offered by various sources.

30. *VDJ*, 171–76.

31. A rather detailed camp-by-camp narrative based on eyewitness reports is provided in *VDJ*, which is a summary volume of a four-volume, 4,034 page series entitled *Leidensweg der Deutschen im kommunistischen Jugoslawien* published in Munich between 1991 and 1995. See *VDJ*, 336.

32. *VDJ*, 187–92.

33. *VDJ*, 129.

34. Pavlica, "Sudbina Nemaca u Srbiji," 385–87.

35. *GMNJ*, 63–64.

36. Women commanders or guards were uniformly singled out as being more cruel than the men.

37. Zoran Janjetović, "Da li su Srbi počinili genocid na Podunavskim Švabama?" [Did Serbs Commit Genocide over Danubian Swabians?], in *Genocid u 20.veku na prostorima jugoslovenskih zemalja* (Belgrade: Muzej žrtava genocida, 2005),

231–38. He seems defensive in regard to Serbs stating that the policies originated and were carried out not by Serbs alone, but also by other Yugoslavs.

38. Blumenwitz, *Rechtsgutachter über die verbrechen*, 30–32.

39. Carl K. Savich, "Holocaust in the Vojvodina, 1941–44," www.serbianna .com/columns/savich/062.shtml (accessed June 9, 2011).

40. The ethnic cleansing of Germans took place not only in Yugoslavia but also in Poland, Czechoslovakia, and Hungary. A total of about 12 to 15 million Germans were driven out from lands in which they had lived for generations or centuries while about 2 million perished.

41. *VDJ*, 132, based on Tibor Cseres, *Vebosszu Bácskában* [Blood Vendetta in Bachka] (Budapest, 1991), 246. Croatian historian Zdravko Dizdar, basing his figure on archival material, states that in Srem, which was not under Hungarian control during World War II, 1,776 Hungarians were "liquidated"; hence, more would have been killed in Bačka, but probably fewer than 10,000. See Zdravko Dizdar, "Prilog istraživanju Bleiburga i križnih putova (u povodu 60.te obljetnice), Semj. Zb" (2005), 179. en.wikipedia.org/wiki/Bleiburg_massacre (accessed July 4, 2010).

42. Tibor Cseres, *Serbian Vendetta in Bacska*, www.hungarianhistory.com/lib/ cseres/cseres02.htm (accessed June 9, 2011).

43. See "Methods of Holocaust," Hunsor, www.hunsor.se/freezingweeks/ frsecond.html (accessed July 6, 2010). When one tallies the figures given for each locality where killings were taking place, the number seems to be 15,391, but clearly the figures are also approximations because for a number of villages, the round figure of 2,000 victims is reported.

44. "Bericht von Superintendent Sebele uber das Werk in Jugoslawien an Bischof Gerber," confidential typescript of January 11, 1946.

45. Arrigo Petacco, *A Tragedy Revealed: The Story of Italians from Istria, Dalmatia, and Venezia Giulia.* Trans. Konrad Eisenbichler from Italian (Toronto, Buffalo, and London: University of Toronto Press, 2005), ix, 133.

46. Petacco, *A Tragedy Revealed*, 43–47.

47. Petacco, *A Tragedy Revealed*, 112 and 133.

48. All these numbers are contested as will be seen later.

49. The Partisans formally renamed themselves as the Yugoslav People's Army during the last months of the war.

50. As it became increasingly obvious that the Allies were going to win the war, many Četniks, Domobrans, and others deserted and joined the Partisans.

51. Dizdar, "Prilog istraživanju Bleiburga," presents an extensive description and analysis based on recently available archival material. Much of his findings are quite reliable, though I do not agree with some of his more nationalistic conclusions, which are, as far as nationalism goes, fairly moderate.

52. Nigel Nicholson, "The Witness," *The South Slav Journal* (London) 22, nos. 1–2 (83–84) (Spring–Summer 2001): 77–88. Nicholson, one of the few surviving British officers, ascribed the turnover to the Fifth Corps of the British Army, and stated that on May 17, 1945, they received an order, "All Yugoslav nationals at present in the Corps area will be handed over to Tito forces as soon as possible. They will not be told of their destination" (p. 80). There is much legal and histori-

cal wrangling as to who among the politicians or military leaders issued this and similar orders.

53. David Bruce MacDonald, *Balkan Holocausts? Serbian and Croatian Victim-Centered Propaganda and the War in Yugoslavia* (Manchester, UK: Manchester University Press, 2002), 170.

54. My cousin, as a sixteen- or seventeen-year-old Domobran, was captured near Dravograd and either escaped or was released and came to stay with us for some months, fearing to return to his hometown where he might have been more easily recognized and perhaps killed.

55. Damir Mirković, "Victims and Perpetrators in the Yugoslav Genocide 1941–1945: Some Preliminary Observations," *Holocaust and Genocide Studies* 7, no. 3 (Winter 1993), 321.

56. MacDonald, *Balkan Holocausts?* 172–73.

57. MacDonald, *Balkan Holocausts?* 172.

58. Dizdar, "Prilog istraživanju Bleiburga," 146.

59. Dizdar, "Prilog istraživanju Bleiburga," 137.

60. Dizdar, "Prilog istraživanju Bleiburga," 151.

61. Ali Zerdin, "45 Mass Graves Found in Slovenia," *The Philadelphia Inquirer*, September 8, 2010.

62. Sometimes the term *križni put* is used to describe the entire journey from leaving their home base to fleeing the Partisans to the return home—for those who survived—many years later.

63. Dizdar, "Prilog istraživanju Bleiburga," 162.

64. Ivica Radoš, "Jama tisuću smrti" [The Pit of a Thousand Deaths] and Sanja Zegnal-Epeha, "I u Hrvatskoj iskopane kosti žrtava iz 1945" [In Croatia Also Dug Out Bones from 1945], in *Jutarnji list* (Zagreb), March 6, 2009, 9.

65. Cadik I. Danon Braco, *The Smell of Human Flesh: A Witness of the Holocaust Memories of Jasenovac* (Belgrade: Dosije, 2006), 163–64.

CHAPTER 8 ETHNIC CLEANSING DURING YUGOSLAVIA'S WARS OF DISINTEGRATION IN THE 1990S

1. James Ridgeway and Jasminka Udovički, "Introduction," in *Yugoslavia's Ethnic Nightmare: The Inside Story of Europe's Ongoing Ordeal*, ed. Jasminka Udovički and James Ridgeway (New York: Lawrence Hill Books, 1995), 3.

2. Henry Huttenbach erroneously attributes the phrase to a journalist who noticed the link of these wars to ethnicity and to the attempts to purge certain territories of unwanted population. See Henry R. Huttenbach, "The Genocide Factor in the Yugoslav Wars of Dismemberment," in *Reflections on the Balkan Wars: Ten Years after the Break-Up of Yugoslavia*, ed. Jeffrey S. Morton, R. Craig Nation, Paul C. Forage, and Stefano Bianchini (New York: Palgrave Macmillan, 2004), 24.

3. Most authors who analyzed the wars of Yugoslavia's disintegration claim that Kosovo's status as an autonomous province of Serbia was established by the constitution of 1974. This is simply not true. Vojvodina became an autonomous province in

1945 while Kosovo and Metohija (the official name of Kosovo after World War II) was legally proclaimed an autonomous area also in 1945 and upgraded to equal status with Vojvodina in 1963.

4. The term was either *narod* or *narodnosti*. *Narod* can mean people or folk (similar to the Germanic *Das Volk*) and corresponds to ethnicity or nationality of the majority. *Narodnosti* was used to indicate national minorities.

5. For a more thorough analysis of that process see my *Yugoslavian Inferno: Ethnoreligious Warfare in the Balkans* (New York: Continuum, 1994), 152–75. Many books were written on this topic.

6. For my interview of President Milan Kučan on September 1, 1993, in Ljubljana, see Mojzes, *Yugoslavian Inferno*, 94.

7. One of Tito's nicknames was *Stari* (Old Man), connoting not age but respect.

8. Serbs and Croats tend to offer entirely different narratives of specific battles and the nature and casualties of this war.

9. For instance Norman M. Naimark, *Fires of Hatred: Ethnic Cleansing in Twentieth Century Europe* (Cambridge, MA: Harvard University Press, 2001), 139.

10. For example, Smail Balić, for many years the leader of the Bosnian Muslim community in Vienna, made that statement at the Jewish-Christian-Muslim trialogue in Graz, Austria in 1993.

11. Matija Mažuranić, "An 'Illyrian' Croat's 1839–40 Vision of Bosnia," *South Slav Journal* 28, nos. 3–4 (109–110) (Autumn–Winter, 2007): 43–49.

12. Mažuranić, "An 'Illyrian' Croat's 1839–40 Vision," 47.

13. Aleksandar S. Jovanović, *Poraz: Koreni poraza* [Defeat: Roots of Defeat] (Veternik, Serbia: Idij, 2001), 29, maintains that the JNA actions actually harmed the Serbs, as they would have defeated the Croats had the Army not intervened.

14. Svetlana Broz, *Good People in Evil Times: Portraits of Complicity and Resistance in the Bosnian War*, ed. Laurie Kain Hart, trans. Ellen Elias Bursać from Serbian (New York: Other Press, 2005); also, interview with Mehmed and Hana Kalabić from the vicinity of Maglaj, B&H, at Palm Beach Gardens, Florida, June 20, 2009. Both had been interned in Serb and Croat concentration camps at Branković and Žepče, yet bear no ill will or resentment toward Croats or Serbs.

15. David Owen, *Balkan Odyssey* (New York: Harcourt Brace, 1995).

16. Warren Zimmerman, *Origins of a Catastrophe* (New York: Times Books, Random House, 1996), 130–40.

17. Lenard Cohen, "Bosnia's 'Tribal Gods': The Role of Religion in Nationalist Politics," in *Religion and War in Bosnia*, ed. Paul Mojzes (Atlanta, GA: Scholars' Press, 1998), 43–73.

18. Ridgeway and Udovički, "Introduction," 12–13.

19. Ridgeway and Udovički, "Introduction," 12.

20. Misha Glenny, *The Fall of Yugoslavia* (London & Baltimore: Penguin Books, 1992).

21. Michael Sells, *The Bridge Betrayed: Religion and Genocide in Bosnia* (Berkeley: University of California Press, 1996). Sells is a colleague in the field with whom I cooperated on a number of issues.

22. The term, of course, is inaccurate, because in that case it would be applicable to all Slavs, including Croats, Macedonians, and Slovenes. If the term is appropriate—which I contest—it would be more accurate as *Christoserbianism*.

23. Mitja Velikonja, *Religious Separation & Political Intolerance in Bosnia-Herzegovina*, trans. Rang'ichi Ng'inja from Slovenian (College Station, TX: Texas A&M University Press, 2003). Velikonja is a personal friend.

24. Garry A. Phillips, "More Than the Jews . . . His Blood Be upon All the Children: Biblical Violence, Genocide, and a Responsible Reading," in *Confronting Genocide: Judaism, Christianity, and Islam*, ed. Steven Leonard Jacobs (Lanham, MD: Lexington Books, 2009), 82–85.

25. I have described some of the details in *Yugoslavian Inferno*, ch. 7; in "The Camouflaged Role of Religion in the War in Bosnia & Herzegovina," in *Religion and the War in Bosnia* (Atlanta, GA: Scholars Press, 1998), 74–98; and in "The Role of Religious Communities in the War in the Former Yugoslavia," *Religion in Eastern Europe* 13, no. 3 (June 1993): 13–31.

26. Paul Mojzes, "The Religiosity of Radovan Karadzic," *Religion in Eastern Europe* 15, no. 4 (August 1995): 17–22.

27. As a spoof some in Vojvodina raise four fingers as a double *V* for "Velika Vojvodina" (Great Vojvodina).

28. Paul Mojzes, "The Camouflaged Role of Religion in Bosnia," in *Religion and War in Bosnia* (see note 17), 77–81.

29. Mehmet Kalabić told me about the arrival of a Muslim *hodža* to his military unit during the war in Bosnia, who urged them to defend the faith and become *šehid* (martyrs), which most of them sarcastically refused saying if the *hodža* sees such glory in martyrdom, why doesn't he take the gun and fight. Interview with author, Palm Beach Gardens, Florida, June 20, 2009.

30. Richard B. Myers and Albert C. Pierce, "On Strategic Leadership," *JFQ/Joint Force Quarterly* (Washington, DC), no 34 (3rd quarter, 2009): 13.

31. Peter Brock, *Media Cleansing: Dirty Reporting. Journalism and Tragedy in Yugoslavia* (Los Angeles: GM Books, 2005). In the interest of disclosure, Brock is an acquaintance whom I respect, but with whom I do not always agree. However, his bitter criticism of Western "pack journalism" and the biases of much of the media are basically correct.

CHAPTER 9 WAR IN CROATIA

1. One of the legacies of World War II was that a larger number of Serbs joined the Communist Party and hence were "rewarded" disproportionately with leadership positions throughout Yugoslavia, including Croatia. By the 1980s, Croats expressed their resentment of this favoritism and began to unilaterally redress the situation by firing Serbs based on their ethnicity.

2. This arsenal consisted of approximately 200–250 tanks, 150–180 armored personnel carriers, 400 heavy artillery, eighteen ships, and a huge amount of smaller guns.

3. Ejub Štitkovac, "Croatia: The First War," in *Yugoslavia's Ethnic Nightmare: The Inside Story of Europe's Unfolding Ordeal*, ed. Jasminka Udovički and James Ridgeway (New York: Lawrence Hill Books, 1995), 162.

4. According to an anecdote when someone warned the commander of the JNA that they were destroying Dubrovnik, one of the oldest cultural landmarks, he re-

sponded by saying, "Don't worry. When we take it we'll rebuild it to be even older." The siege of Dubrovnik was a clear Croat victory in the propaganda war in that the claims of the destruction of the city were exaggerated, as I was able to see for myself several years after the end of the war.

5. Štitkovac, "Croatia," 163.

6. Arnaud Kurze, "Bringing Back War Crimes Issues: Croatia and the EU Enlargement Process," *The South Slav Journal* 29, nos. 3–4 (113–114) (Autumn 2010): 140–47. Amnesty International, "Croatia 'Failing' in War-Crime Probe," *Philadelphia Inquirer*, December 9, 2010, A8.

7. The American edition was entitled *Horrors of War: Historical Reality and Philosophy*, rev. ed., trans. Katarina Mijatović from Croatian (New York: M. Evans, 1996). The English translation muted some of the pro-Fascist and anti-Semitic passages.

8. Information obtained in the summer of 1993 from Professor Zdenko Roter, sociologist from Ljubljana, who told me of a Croat worker in his orchard in Slovenia who shared with him that he had been recruited to such a unit. Their commander told him to practice cutting the throat of a captured Serb. Allegedly, all the draftees stated that they already knew how to cut throats so that they did not have to practice this skill on this captive.

9. Štitkovac, "Croatia," 152.

10. Štitkovac, "Croatia," 159–60.

11. My former classmate Milan Budak, a journalist for the Novi Sad daily *Dnevnik*, recounted such stories to me during a conversation in the summer of 1993. He had gone as a reporter to eastern Slavonia and was an eyewitness to many horrendous events. He had intended to write about them when it would be safe, but premature death due to a heart attack prevented him from carrying out his intention.

12. For example, Misha Glenny, *The Fall of Yugoslavia: The Third Balkan War*, rev. ed. (New York: Penguin Books, 1993).

13. www.icty.org/x/cases/martic/cis/en/cis_martic_en.pdf (accessed June 13, 2011).

14. For additional information on ICTY trials and judgments, see chapter 12.

15. Carla Del Ponte with Chuck Sudetic, *Madame Prosecutor* (New York: Other Press, 2009), 39.

16. "Presidents Peres and Josipovic visit Jasenovac Memorial Site," daily .tportal.hr/79051/Presidents-Peres-and-Josipovic-visit-Jasenovac-Memorial-Site. html (accessed June 13, 2011).

17. Associated Press, "Serb Leader Gives Wartime Apology," *Philadelphia Inquirer*, November 5, 2010.

CHAPTER 10 WAR IN BOSNIA AND HERZEGOVINA

1. Aleksa Djilas, "The Nation That Wasn't" in *The Black Book of Bosnia: The Consequences of Appeasement*, ed. Nader Mousavizadeh (New York: Basic Books, 1996), 24.

2. Prior to the war it was customary to refer to this group as Muslims, but increasingly they opted to use the more secular term *Bosniak* as many of them were not religiously affiliated to Islam.

3. Steven L. Burg and Paul S. Shoup, *The War in Bosnia-Herzegovina: Ethnic Conflict and International Intervention* (Aemonk, NY: M.E. Sharpe, 1999), 130.

4. A somewhat modified version of the statement is in Burg and Shoup, *The War in Bosnia-Herzegovina*, 65 and 78.

5. Years later, some members of the Red Berets carried out the assassination of Zoran Djindjić, the prime minister of Serbia after the ouster of Milošević.

6. Ejub Štitkovac and Jasminka Udovički, "Bosnia and Hercegovina: The Second War," in *Yugoslavia's Ethnic Nightmare: The Inside Story of Europe's Unfolding Ordeal*, ed. Jasminka Udovički and James Ridegway (New York: Lawrence Hill Books, 1995), 178.

7. During my visit to Banja Luka in May 2011, I could see that efforts continued to be made to disassociate Republika Srpska from B&H. Ethnic cleansing succeeded as Serb dominance was easily observable.

8. In Croatia, Franjo Tudjman was surrounded by Herzegovinian Croats, such as Gojko Šušak, who were encouraging him to be inflexible regarding B&H.

9. The shorter lived HOS (Hrvatske Obranbene Snage) sought to retain a unified B&H but collided with HVO and upon its commander's assassination by HVO, HOS gradually disintegrated.

10. Burg and Shoup, *The War in Bosnia-Herzegovina*, 135.

11. Štitkovac & Udovički, "Bosnia and Hercegovina," 190.

12. He was later released on account of excessive violence and then assassinated when he left the country.

13. A Sarajevo criminal, who along with similar shady types organized the first resistance to the attacks upon Sarajevo and therefore became romanticized in popular Muslim lore.

14. Burg and Shoup, *The War in Bosnia-Herzegovina*, 130.

15. www.un.org/icty/indictment/english/ori-3ai50630e.htm, www.icty.org/x/cases/oric/ind/en/ori-3ai050630e.pdf (accessed June 14, 2011).

16. Jan Willem Honig and Norbert Both, *Srebrenica: Record of a War Crime* (New York: Penguin, 2007), 133, and the documentary film *Ethnic Cleansers and the Cleansed: The Unforgiving* (Films for the Humanities and Sciences, 1994).

17. Silajdžić did not explicitly name the source of the threat but stated they were those who had been defeated in the war of the 1990s, thereby alluding to Serb nationalists. The speech, delivered in English, was made at the Balkan Leaders' Summit 2010 in New York, on September 22, at which the author was present.

18. Anthony Lewis, "War Crimes," in *The Black Book of Bosnia* (see note 1), 56.

19. See lengthy judgment against Vasiljević at www.un.org/icty/vasiljevic/trial/judgment/index.htm (accessed July 23, 2009). For Milan Lukić see "Judgement Summary for Milan Lukić and Sredoje Lukić," ICTY, www.icty.org/x/cases/milan_lukic_sredoje_lukic/tjug/en/090720_judg_summary_en.pdf (accessed July 24, 2009).

20. Kemal and Izeta Omerhodžić, a physician and teacher, were expelled with their two daughters. Izeta was first fired for allegedly not following the curricular requirement that one day the instructor was to use the Latin and the next day the Cyrillic alphabet. Milan and Mira Barić, a Croat-Serb mixed marriage, and their two daughters were likewise pressured to leave (after she was first individually pressured

to divorce her husband). Both couples are my friends, and the information was obtained in conversations.

21. Štitkovac and Udovički, "Bosnia and Hercegovina," 185. The fate of two women held and raped at Omarska has been the theme of the film *Calling the Ghosts*, a 1996 documentary directed by Mandy Jacobson and Karmen Jelinčić, distributed by Women Make Movies. The camp commander, Željko Mejakić was delivered first to ICTY but they sent him to Sarajevo to be tried by the B&H courts for war crimes for which he received a sentence of twenty-one years.

22. Peter Brock, *Media Cleansing, Dirty Reporting: Journalism and Tragedy in Yugoslavia*, 2nd ed. (Los Angeles: GM Books, 2005), 245–56, contends that the photos and the attending vilification of Serbs was staged by Western journalists in a search for sensationalism and fame.

23. Štitkovac and Udovički, "Bosnia and Hercegovina," 170 and 178.

24. "Korićani Cliffs Massacre," in *Massacres in Bosnia and Herzegovina* (Memphis, TN: Books LLC, 2010), 27–31. For crimes against humanity and war crimes, Mrdja received a sentence of seventeen years upon entering a plea agreement at the ICTY. See www.un.org/icty/mrdja/trial/judgment/index.htm (accessed July 24, 2009).

25. www.iwpr.net/index.php?apc_state=hen$s=o&o=p=tri&J=EN&s=f8o=1633 84 (accessed July 23, 2009).

26. "Lalva [sic] Valley Ethnic Cleansing," in *Massacres in Bosnia and Herzegovina* (see note 24), 35–46.

27. "Lalva [sic] Valley Ethnic Cleansing," 35–46.

28. Ed Vulliamy, *Seasons in Hell: Understanding Bosnia's War* (New York: St. Martin's Press, 1994), 331–41, esp. 333.

29. Vulliamy, *Seasons in Hell*, 324–29.

30. Norman Cigar, *Genocide in Bosnia: The Policy of "Ethnic Cleansing"* (College Station, TX: Texas A&M Press, 1995), 137.

31. www.un.org/icty/pressreal/p364-e.htm (accessed July 24, 2009).

32. Carl Savich, "Celebici," Serbianica.com, www.serbianna.com/columns/savich/047.shtml (accessed July 24, 2009),

33. David Bruce MacDonald, *Balkan Holocausts? Serbian and Croatian Victim-Centered Propaganda and the War in Yugoslavia* (Manchester, UK: Manchester University Press, 2002), 241.

34. Svetlana Broz, *Good People in Evil Times: Portraits of Complicity and Resistance in the Bosnian War*, ed. Laurie Kain Hart, trans. Ellen Elias Bursač from Serbian (New York: Other Press, 2005).

35. Burg and Shoup, *The War in Bosnia-Herzegovina*, 164–65.

36. "Srebrenica Massacre," in *Massacres in Bosnia and Herzegovina* (see note 23), 92.

37. For example, Serbia's "Women in Black" organizes annual commemorations of the Srebrenica genocide; Christina M. Morus, e-mail on behalf of the organization, June 19, 2010. Serbia's Parliament adopted a Declaration on Srebrenica on March 31, 2010, which moves toward accountability but falls short of calling the event genocide.

38. Charles Lane, "Dateline Zagreb: The Fall of Srebrenica," in the *Black Book of Bosnia: The Consequences of Appeasement*, ed. Nader Mousavizadeh (New York: BasicBooks, 1996), 117.

39. Honig and Both, *Srebrenica*, 78. Most of the information of the Srebrenica events come from this book written by two Dutch journalists who set out to investigate in great detail these particular war crimes because it was the Dutch battalion that was supposed to protect the Srebrenica "safe area" at the time when the genocide occurred.

40. Honig and Both, *Srebrenica*, 79. Other sources contest this figure saying that only 600–1,000 Serbs had been killed. See *Massacres in Bosnia and Herzegovina*, 133–34.

41. Honig and Both, *Srebrenica*, 85ff.

42. Quoted in Honig and Both, *Srebrenica*, 92.

43. Honig and Both, *Srebrenica*, 106.

44. Honig and Both, *Srebrenica*, 130.

45. Honig and Both, *Srebrenica*, 133.

46. Honig and Both, *Srebrenica*, 136.

47. Quoted in Honig and Both, *Srebrenica*, 173.

48. Honig and Both, *Srebrenica*, 23.

49. Lane, "Dateline Zagreb," 121.

50. Honig and Both, *Srebrenica*, 30.

51. "Radislav Krstić Becomes the First Person to Be Convicted of Genocide at the ICTY and Is Sentenced to 46 Years Imprisonment," in *The Genocide Studies Reader*, ed. Samuel Totten and Paul R. Bartrop (New York and London: Routledge, 2009), 452–62. This is one of the concise yet sufficiently detailed accounts of the tragic events of July 1995.

52. *Wikipedia*, s.v. "Bosnian Genocide," en.wikipedia.org/wiki/Bosnian_Genocide (accessed June 14, 2011).

53. *Massacre in Bosnia and Herzegovina*, 125.

54. For example, Roy Gutman, "Muslims Recall Serb attacks" (August 23, 1992); "A Daily Ritual of Sex Abuse" and "Rape Camps: Evidence of Serb leaders in Bosnia OKd attacks" (April 19, 1993) from www.haverford.edu/relg/sells/rape2.html (accessed November 19, 2003).

55. Beverly Allen, *Rape Warfare: The Hidden Genocide in Bosnia-Herzegovina and Croatia* (Minneapolis: University of Minnesota Press, 1996). Allen's radically feminist account displays, however, no concern for Serbian women that had been raped as she considers only Serbian men capable of carrying out such revolting acts. See also Catherine A. MacKinnon, *Are Women Human? And Other International Dialogues* (Cambridge, MA: Belknap Press of Harvard University Press, 2006). Alexandra Stiglemayer, ed. *Mass Rape: The War Against Women in Bosnia-Herzegovina* (Lincoln, NE: University of Nebraska Press, 1994) includes more moderate accounts.

56. A more inclusive exploration of the possible motives for genocidal rape, or what Sharlach calls "state rape," can be found in Lisa Sharlach, "State Rape: Sexual Violence as Genocide," in *The Genocide Studies Reader* (see note 50), 180–92. How-

ever, she also bypasses rapes of Serb women by Croats and Muslims. I am deeply suspicious of motives of those who deliberately overlook the pain and losses of one ethnic group in order to vilify it.

57. Diana Johnstone, *Fools' Crusade: Yugoslavia, NATO, and Western Delusions* (New York: Monthly Review Press, 2002), 78–90. Brock, *Media Cleansing*, 59–72, came to similar conclusions. I share their misgivings without wishing to minimize the agony of the thousands of women who were raped.

58. Karen Engle, "Feminism and Its (Dis)Contents: Criminalizing Rape in Bosnia and Herzegovina," *The American Journal of International Law* 99, no. 778 (2005): 778–816, esp. 800; www.utexas.edu/law/centers/humanrights/about/engle_publications/Feminism_and_Its_DisContents.pdf (accessed July 26, 2010).

59. Paul Mojzes, *Yugoslavian Inferno: Ethnoreligious Warfare in the Balkans* (New York: Continuum, 1994), 40.

60. The semi-documentary film *Calling the Ghosts* provides a particularly powerful testimony of the experience of two middle-aged professional women, one a Croat and the other a Bosniak, who took their case to ICTY in The Hague.

61. UN Document A/50/329 (August 4, 1995), 17, as cited by Burg and Shoup, *The War in Bosnia-Herzegovina*, 171.

62. Vulliamy, *Seasons in Hell*, 198.

63. I heard this story in the summer of 1993 from a Serbian Orthodox priest, (the late) Reverend Jovan Nikolić, who decided to remain in Zagreb rather than flee. He was bitterly critical of the behavior of Serbian and Serb politicians and armies but even more so of the leadership of the Serbian Orthodox Church whom he charged with moral bankruptcy.

64. Vulliamy, *Seasons in Hell*, 196.

65. Eric D. Weitz, *A Century of Genocide: Utopias of Race and Nation* (Princeton, NJ: Princeton University Press, 2006), 228, quoting ICTY, "Judgment of Trial Chamber II in the Kunarac, Kovač and Vuković Case" (press release JL/P.I.S./566-e 22, February 2001), www.un.org/icty/TrialC2/judgment/index.htm (accessed August 29, 2002).

66. Carla Del Ponte with Chuck Sudetic, *Madame Prosecutor: Confrontation with Humanity's Worst Criminals and the Culture of Impunity* (New York: Other Press, 2009), 39.

67. Burg and Shoup, *The War in Bosnia-Herzegovina*, 170–71.

68. Paul Mojzes, "Ethnic Cleansing in the Balkans," in *Will Genocide Ever End?* ed. Carol Rittner, John K. Roth, and James M. Smith (St. Paul, MN: Paragon House, 2002), 54.

69. Helen Fein, "Ethnic Cleansing and Genocide: Definitional Evasion, Fog, Morass or Opportunity" (paper presented at the Association of Genocide Scholars, Minneapolis, June 10–12, 2001) is quoted in Robert Gellately and Ben Kiernan, "The Study of Mass Murder and Genocide" in *Specter of Genocide: Mass Murder in Historical Perspective*, ed. Robert Gellately and Ben Kiernan (Cambridge and New York: Cambridge University Press, 2006), 20.

70. Cigar, *Genocide in Bosnia*, 4.

71. Cigar, *Genocide in Bosnia*, 4. The assertion that the aim was for an ethnically pure and homogenous Serbia flies in the face of the fact that Serbia itself had a

rather heterogeneous population and that no organized government efforts had been made to expel Hungarians, Slovaks, Muslims, Ruthenians, Romanians, and others from Serbia. A large number of Muslims, including Albanians, continued to live in Belgrade during these wars.

72. Burg and Shoup, *The War in Bosnia-Herzegovina*, 176. The authors provide numerous instances of ethnic cleansing by all three communities.

73. Burg and Shoup, *The War in Bosnia-Herzegovina*, 172.

74. Among them were Slobodan Milošević, Radovan Karadžić, Ratko Mladić, Radislav Krstić, Dragan Jokić, Vidoje Blagojević, Vujadin Popović, Milenko Trifunović, Brano Džimić, Aleksandar Radovanović, Miloš Stupar, Slobodan Jakovljević, Branislav Medan, Petar Mitrović, Milorad Trbić, Nikola Jorgica, and Ljubiša Beara. For a more complete list of indictees, including those who committed crimes on the territory of B&H see www.icty.org/sections/TheCases/JudgmentList, en.wikipedia.org/wiki/List_of_ICTY_indictees, and *Wikipedia*, s.v., "Individuals Prosecuted for Genocide during the Bosnian War," en.wikipedia.org/wiki/Bosnian_Genocide#Individuals_prosecuted_for_genocide_during_the_Bosnian_war (accessed June 14, 2011).

75. Prosecutor vs. Radislav Krstić (Trial Judgment), #580, p. 204 in *Refworld*, updated July 27, 2010, www.unhcr.org/refworld/type,CASELAW,BIH,414810d94,0.html.

76. Mirha Dedić, "Sjednica Vrhovnog Saveta Odbrane: Kako je Slobodan Milošević vodio rat u BiH" [Session of the Supreme Defense Council: How Slobodan Milošević Conducted the War in B&H], *Slobodna Bosna* (Sarajevo), May 19, 2011, 46–51. The article contains transcripts of the session.

77. His capture and extradition was reported in most newspapers of the world. One example: "Karadzic Delivered for Eventual U.N. War Crimes Trial," *Palm Beach Post*, July 31, 2008, 3A. See also Dan Bilefsky, "Karadzic Arrest Is Big Step for a Land Tired of Being Europe's Pariah," *New York Times*, www.nytimes.com/2008/07/23/world/europe/23serbia.html (accessed January 21, 2011).

78. "Prosecutor: Serbs Need to Do More," *Philadelphia Inquirer*, September 23, 2010.

79. The news broke on May 27, 2011, the day of my arrival in Sarajevo. All TV and radio stations, magazines, and newspapers covered the story in great detail. While Muslims, Croats, and most of the international public jubilantly welcomed the news, many interviewed Serbs were bitter, feeling that a hero for the Serb cause was betrayed. Nevertheless, officials in Serbia and Republika Srpska gravely commented about the arrest being their legal obligation and a precondition for joining the European Union and/or NATO. Among the special editions devoted entirely to the arrest and analysis of General Mladić were *Slobodna Bosna* (Sarajevo), no. 759, May 27, 2011, and *NIN* (Belgrade) of May 28, 2011.

80. Israel W. Charny, ed., *The Encyclopedia of Genocide*, 2 vols. (Santa Barbara, CA: ABC-CLIO, 1999), 6–20.

81. Jacques Semelin, "Analysis of a Mass Crime: Ethnic Cleansing in the Former Yugoslavia, 1991–1999" in the *Specter of Genocide: Mass Murder in Historical Perspective*. Eds. Robert Gellately and Ben Kiernan (Cambridge and New York: Cambridge University Press, 2006), 354–55.

82. Semelin, "Analysis of a Mass Crime," 361.
83. Semelin, "Analysis of a Mass Crime," 369.
84. Henry R. Huttenbach, "The Genocide Factors in the Yugoslav Wars of Dismemberment," in *Reflections on the Balkan Wars: Ten Years after the Break-Up of Yugoslavia*, ed. Jeffery S. Morton, R. Craig Nation, Paul C. Forage, and Stefano Bianchini (New York: Palgrave Macmillan, 2004), 31.
85. Huttenbach, "The Genocide Factors," 31.
86. Jasmin Imamović, *Ubijanje smrti* [Killing of Death] (Tuzla, Bosnia: Radio Kameleon, 1995), 35–38. Translation from Bosnian/Serbian/Croat by Paul Mojzes.

CHAPTER 11 PROTRACTED CONFLICT AND WAR IN KOSOVO

1. Dan Bilefsky, "World Court Rules Kosovo Declaration Was Legal," *New York Times*, July 23, 2010, A4, www.nytimes.com/2010/07/23/world/europe/23kosovo .html (accessed June 15, 2011).
2. English language speakers call it the Field of Black Birds as *kos* is the Serbian word for black birds.
3. The statement by many writers (e.g., Norman M. Naimark, *Fires of Hatred: Ethnic Cleansing in Twentieth-Century Europe* [Cambridge, MA: Harvard University Press, 2001], 176) that Kosovo received its autonomous province status in the 1974 constitution is wrong. While I still lived in Yugoslavia until 1957, both Vojvodina and Kosovo were autonomous provinces within Serbia.
4. Laura Silber and Allan Little, *Yugoslavia: Death of a Nation* (New York: Penguin Books, 1997), 34.
5. A status given to them and to other ethnicities that had national states of their own outside of Yugoslavia.
6. Blagojević, "Iseljavanje Srba sa Kosova," 251.
7. "The Declaration of the Bishops of the Serbian Orthodox Church against the Genocide Inflicted by Albanians on the Indigenous Serbian Population, Together with the Sacrilege of Their Cultural Monuments in Their Own Country" (photocopied typescript signed by five Serbian Orthodox bishops of Western countries, September 14, 1988); see Paul Mojzes, *Yugoslavian Inferno: Ethnoreligious Warfare in the Balkans* (New York: Continuum, 1994), 136.
8. From a speech delivered on April 7, 1986, by Žarko Gavrilović, in *Na braniku vere i nacije* [For the Defense of Faith and Nation] (Belgrade: Štamparija "Solidarnost," 1986), 166. Translated from Serbian by Mojzes.
9. Gavrilović, *Na braniku vere i nacije*, 293 and 312 respectively. Trans. by Mojzes.
10. The Marxist notion of constitutions was that they are supposed to reflect rather than determine the sociopolitical and economic realities of the times. Thus there were frequent rewritings and adopting of constitutions, almost always by unanimous vote in the Narodna Skupština [People's Assembly].
11. Marina Blagojević, "Iseljavanje Srba sa Kosova: Trauma i/ili katarza" [Exodus of Serbs from Kosovo: Trauma and/or Catharsis], in *Srpska strana rata* [Serbian Side of the War], ed. Nebojša Popov (Belgrade: Republika, 1996), 235.

12. Srdja Popović, Dejan Janča and Tanja Petovar, *Kosovski čvor: Drešiti ili seći?* [Kosovo Knot: Unravel or Cut?] (Belgrade: Biblioteka Hronos, 1990), 31–47.

13. Olga Zirojević, "Kosovo u kolektivnom pamćenju" [Kosovo in Collective Memory] in *Srpska strana rata* (see note 11), 230.

14. Quoted in Zirojević, "Kosovo u kolektivnom pamćenju," 229. Translated from Serbian by Mojzes.

15. Svetozar Stojanović, *The Fall of Yugoslavia: Why Communism Failed* (Amherst, NY: Prometheus Press, 1997), 119–20.

16. Silber and Little, *Yugoslavia*, 69.

17. A very detailed description of this process is provided by Tim Judah in *Kosovo: War and Revenge*, 2nd ed. (New Haven, CT: Yale University Press, 2002) that is one the most astute reports and analyses of the Kosovo events.

18. Howard Clark, *Civil Resistance in Kosovo* (London: Pluto Press, 2000), 66–69.

19. Veton Suroi, "Kosova: A Case for Self-Determination" in *Kosova Watch* (Prishtina) 1, no. 2 (August 1992): 24–27.

20. Clark, *Civil Resistance*, 172–73. The KLA may have been secretly organized as early as 1990 with a few prominent Albanian politicians involved in it. Both Madeleine Albright—no friend of Serbs—and Robert Gelbard, U.S. special envoy, declared it at first to be a terrorist organization, but later Germany, the United States, and other Western governments started seeing the KLA as an instrument for weakening Milošević's government, and they began to actively train and support it.

21. David H. Gibbs *First Do No Harm: Humanitarian Intervention and the Destruction of Yugoslavia* (Nashville: Vanderbilt University Press, 2009), 180–82 and 185–87.

22. David H. Gibbs, "Was Kosovo a Good War?" *Tikkun*, tikkun.org/article.php/jul_09_gibbs (accessed July 30, 2010).

23. Hajredin Bala, one of the KLA prison guards at Lapušnik, was sentenced to thirteen years in prison by ICTY.

24. Clark, *Civil Resistance*, 178. Also www.hrw.org/legagcy/reports/1999/kosovo/Obrinje6.htm#TopOfPage (accessed September 7, 1999).

25. Quoted in Gibbs, *First Do No Harm,* 181.

26. Clarke, *Civil Resistance*, 180–81.

27. Slobodan Vuković, "Ulica Vase Miskina, Markale, Račak: Dogadjaji s Obaračem" [Vase Miskina Street, Markale, Rachak: Trigger Events], in *Teme* (Niš, Serbia) 33, no. 1 (January–March 2009): 201–14. This Serbian scholar argues—unconvincingly—that the three massacres in Bosnia and the one in Kosovo for which the Serbs were accused had all been planned and carried out by the Muslims themselves with Western knowledge in order to justify the subsequent Western military attacks upon the Serbs.

28. Diana Johnstone, *Fools' Crusade: Yugoslavia, NATO and Western Delusions* (New York: Monthly Review Press, 2002), 244.

29. Clark, *Civil Resistance*, 182.

30. Clark, *Civil Resistance*, 183.

31. Gibbs, *First Do Not Harm*, 199.

32. Press release, June 25, 1999, clinton6.nara.gov/1999/06/1999–06–25-press
-conference-by-the-president.html (accessed October 10, 2010).

33. Carla Del Ponte with Chuck Sudetic, *Madame Prosecutor: Confrontation
with Humanity's Worst Criminals and the Culture of Impunity* (New York: Other
Press, 2009), 39.

34. Steven L. Burg, "Intractability and Third-Party Mediation in the Balkans," in
Grasping the Nettle: Analyzing Cases of Intractable Conflict, ed. Chester A. Crocker,
Fen Osler Hampson, and Pamela All (Washington, DC: United States Institute of
Peace Press, 2005), 204.

35. Judah, *Kosovo*, 240.

36. Judah, *Kosovo*, 241–49.

37. Johnstone, *Fools' Crusade*, 88–90,

38. Gibbs, "Was Kosovo a Good War?"

39. Gibbs, "Was Kosovo a Good War?"

40. Gibbs, "Was Kosovo a Good War?"

41. Del Ponte, *Madame Prosecutor*, 39.

42. Del Ponte, *Madame Prosecutor*, 250.

43. Patrick Ball, Wendy Betz, Fritz Scheuner, Jana Dudukovich, and Jane Asher,
"Killings and Refugee Flow in Kosovo, March-June 1999," in shr.aaas.org/kosovo/
icty_report.pdf and shr.aaas.org/Kosovo/corrigendum-021115.pdf (accessed September 7, 2009).

44. Doncho Donev, Silvana Oncheva, and Ilija Gligorov, "Refugee Crisis in
Macedonia During the Kosovo Crisis in 1999," www.cmj.hr/2002/43/1/2/11885045
.pdf (accessed September 7, 2009).

45. Christopher C. Joyner and Anthony Clark Arend, "Rethinking the Legal
Nuances of Kosovo: Toward an Emerging Norm of Anticipatory Humanitarian Intervention?" in *Reflections on the Balkan Wars: Ten Years after the Break-Up of Yugoslavia*, ed. Jeffrey C. Morton, R. Craig Nation, Paul C. Forage, and Stefano Bianchini
(New York: Palgrave Macmillan, 2004), 175.

46. Jovana Gec, "Mass Grave of Kosovo Victims Is Found," *Philadelphia Inquirer*, May 11, 2010.

47. Joyner, Oncheva, and Gligorov, "Refugee Crisis," 310.

48. Judah, *Kosovo*, 286.

49. Judah, *Kosovo*, 287.

50. According to Lieutenant Colonel Jerzy Szesytynski of the Polish Special
Police Unit, "It was a big surprise to all of us"; Nicholas Wood, "Kosovo Smolders
after Mob Violence," *New York Times*, March 24, 2004.

51. Interview in Ekaterinburg, Russia, October 15, 2003.

52. For an early report see Associated Press, "6 Dead, Hundreds Wounded in Serbia Clash," *New York Times*, March 17, 2004. See: www.nytimes.com/aponlin.../AP-
Kosovo-Clashes.html?hp=&pagewanted=print&position (accessed March 17, 2004).
Several days later a more complete report was printed, Nicholas Wood, "Kosovo
Smolders after Mob Violence," *New York Times,* March 24, 2004. See www.nytimes

.com/2004/03/24/world/kosovo-smolders-after-mob-violence.html (accessed March 24, 2004).

53. Branko Bjelajac, "Kosovo & Serbia: Destruction Worse than Initially Believed, and Violence Sparks Incidents in Montenegro, Bosnia and Macedonia," *Forum 18*, March 24, 2004, www.forum18.org.

54. B-92 News Service Headlines (Belgrade), March 19, 2004, www.b92.net/english/news/index.php?nav_id=25794&dd=02&mm=12&yyyy=2003 (accessed April 2004).

55. B-92 News Service Headlines (Belgrade), March 19, 2004. For a specific case in Uroševac, see Branko Bjelajac, "Kosovo: Hand Grenade Attack on an Orthodox Church," *Forum 18*, December 19, 2003.

56. B-92 News Service Headlines (Belgrade), March 19, 2004 (see note 53).

57. Associated Press, "Probe: Serbs Not Tied to Drownings," *Philadelphia Inquirer*, April 29, 2004, based on an Associated Press report.

58. There had been plenty of early warnings. One of them was issued by Bishop Artemije during his presentation, "Multiethnic Kosovo: Diplomatic Dream or Balkan Reality," presented at the Western Policy Center, Washington, DC, January 29, 2004. Both a concise address and a full-text version were made available to author in typescript version, sent by Mark Elliott, editor of *East-West Ministry Report*.

59. The Serbian government allocated funds sufficient to repair the Belgrade Bajrakli mosque, taking responsibility for repairing the damage.

60. Mojzes, *Yugoslavian Inferno*, 125.

61. Paul Mojzes, "Religion and Armed Humanitarian Intervention in the Former Yugoslavia," in *Religion, Law, and the Role of Force: A Study of Their Influence on Conflict and on Conflict Resolution*, ed. J. I. Coffey and Charles T. Matthews (Ardsley, NY: Transnational Publications, 2002), 129–44.

62. serbianna.com and www.kosovo.net/?q=node/view/6.

63. Gibbs, *First Do No Harm*, 192.

64. Del Ponte, *Madame Prosecutor*, 58–61.

65. Mike Corder, "In final trial, war-crimes court sentences Serbia," *Philadelphia Inquirer*, February 24, 2011, A-20.

66. Paul Lewis, "Kosovo PM Is Head of Human Organ and Arms Ring, Council of Europe Reports," Guardian.uk, December 14, 2010, www.guardian.co.uk/world/2010/dec/14/kosovo-prime-minister-like-mafia-boss (accessed January 17, 2011).

CHAPTER 12 INTERNATIONAL CRIMINAL TRIBUNAL FOR YUGOSLAVIA

1. Carla Del Ponte, with Chuck Sudetic, *Madame Prosecutor: Confrontation with Humanity's Worst Criminals and the Culture of Impunity* (New York: Other Press, 2009), 144.

2. Milošević's indictment downloaded from www.un.org/icty/indictment/english/mil-ii011122e.htm (accessed November 19, 2003).

3. Slavenka Drakulić, *They Would Never Hurt a Fly: War Criminals on Trial in The Hague* (New York: Viking Adult, 2004). The well-known novelist provided her perceptive nonfictional observations of the ex-Yugoslav war criminals on trial.

4. For a well organized list see "Judgment List," ICTY, www.icty.org/sections/ TheCases/JudgementList (accessed January 18, 2011).

5. "Statements of Guilt," ICTY, www.icty.org/sections/Outreach/ StatementsofGuilt (accessed August 4, 2010).

6. "Status of Transferred Cases," ICTY, www.icty.org/sid/8934 (accessed August 4, 2010).

7. Del Ponte, *Madame Prosecutor*, 247–49, 253.

8. Del Ponte, *Madame Prosecutor*, 60.

9. Del Ponte, *Madame Prosecutor*, 276.

10. Del Ponte, *Madame Prosecutor*, 279–80.

11. Del Ponte, *Madame Prosecutor*, 283.

12. Quoted in Del Ponte, *Madame Prosecutor*, 159–60.

13. "ICTY Delivers New Set of Transcripts to Bosnia and Herzegovina, Croatia and Serbia," www.icty.org/sid/10585 (accessed January 21, 2011).

14. Pablo Gorondi, "Man, 97, Is on Trial for War Crimes," *Philadelphia Inquirer*, May 6, 2011, A21.

CHAPTER 13 ONWARD INTO
THE TWENTY-FIRST CENTURY: A POSTSCRIPT

1. Vividly portrayed in the Macedonian film *Before the Rain* (1994).

2. In the interest of transparency, I was a personal friend of Boris Trajkovski and at his request became involved in promoting dialogue and understanding in the Republic of Macedonia in 2001.

3. ICTY tried two accused Macedonian government officials of war crimes against the ethnic Albanians. Jovan Tarčulovski was sentenced to twelve years, while Ljube Boškovski was acquitted. See "Judgement List," ICTY, www.icty.org/sections/ TheCases/JudgementList (accessed January 18, 2011).

4. There are seemingly unfounded suspicions that the crash was an act of assassination. Trajkovski himself told me of three attempts on his life.

5. "Remains Found at Bosnia-Serb Lake," *Philadelphia Inquirer*, October 28, 2010.

6. "Prosecutor: Serbs Need to Do More," *Philadelphia Inquirer*, September 23, 2010, and "Croatia 'Failing' in War-Crime Probe," *Philadelphia Inquirer*, December 9, 2010.

7. Josh Lederman, "Bosnian Serb War-Crimes Suspect Held in Israel," *Philadelphia Inquirer*, January 19, 2011, A3.

8. Llazar Semini, "Albanian Violence Flares," *Philadelphia Inquirer*, January 22, 2011, A2.

9. A theme strongly expressed at the Balkan Leaders' Summit 2010. Making Europe Whole: Completing the Balkans' Euro-Atlantic Integration in New York,

September 22, 2010, at which presidents, prime ministers, and ministers of foreign affairs of Bosnia-Herzegovina, Bulgaria, Croatia, Kosovo, Macedonia, Montenegro, Slovenia, and Turkey spoke, all urging European integration.

10. Such as Boris Tadić, the president of Serbia, who has traveled to Bosnia and Herzegovina and Croatia to express regret for the war crimes committed at sites like Srebrenica and Vukovar, thereby contributing to reconciliation. "Serb Leader Gives Wartime Apology," *Philadelphia Inquirer,* November 5, 2010.

Bibliography

This bibliography contains sources cited in writing this book as well as a multilingual selection of sources that may be of use to future researchers. The bibliography is not meant to be comprehensive but to indicate the type of resources available to scholars and other readers. The most pertinent chapters in a book follow the main entry in an indented format. At the end of the formal bibliography is a list of journals that also tend to provide information about the subject matter.

BOOKS, CHAPTERS, AND ARTICLES

Adrović, Braho. *Rat u kući* [War in the House]. Berane: NIP "Nirvana" and Bijelo Polje, Montenegro: Libertas, 1999.

Akhavan, Payam, and Robert Howse, eds. *Yugoslavia the Former and Future: Reflections by Scholars from the Region.* Washington, DC: The Brookings Institution and Geneva: The U.N. Research Institute for Social Development, 1995.

Allen, Beverly. *Rape Warfare: The Hidden Genocide in Bosnia-Herzegovina and Croatia.* Minneapolis: University of Minnesota Press, 1996.

Ali, Rabia, and Lawrence Lifschultz, eds. *Why Bosnia? Writings on the Balkan War.* Stony Creek, CT: Pamphleteer's Press, 1993.

Anscombe, Frederick F. "Albanian and 'Mountain Bandits.'" In *The Ottoman Balkans: 1750–1830,* edited by Frederick F. Anscombe, 87–107. Princeton, NJ: Marcus Wiener Publishers, 2006.

Antisemitizam, holokaust, antifašizam. Zagreb: Židovska općina, 1996 (zbornik).

    Benyovski, Lucija. "Fašiticki logor Kampor na Rabu," 214–23.

    Kečkemet, Duško. "Židovski sabirni logori na području pod talijanskom okupacijom," 120–32.

Lengel-Križman, Narcisa. "Logori za Židove u NDH," 91–103.
————. "Sudbina preživjelih Židova iz logora na Rabu, 1943–1945."
Sobolevski, Mihael. "Židovi u kompleksu koncentracijskog logora Jasenovac,"
   104–19.
Arbeitskreis Dokumentation. *Verbrechen an den Deutschen in Jugoslawien 1944–
   1948.* Munich: Donauschwäbische Kulturstiftung, 2000.
Assa, Aaron. *Macedonia and the Jewish People.* Skopje: Macedonia Review, 1994.
Avramov, Smilja. *Genocide in Yugoslavia.* Belgrade: BIGZ, 1995.
Babić, Dušan. *Zločin ustaša.* Prepared for publication by Ivan Babić. Novi Sad: Polet
   Pres, 2003.
Bamberg, Sebastian, Kiersten Beckmann, and Thomas Meinhardt, eds. *Der Krieg auf
   dem Balkan.* Bad Vilbel, Germany: Pax Christi Bewegung-Deutsches Sekretariat,
   1992.
Banac, Ivo. *The National Question in Yugoslavia: Origins, History, Politics.* Ithaca
   and London: Cornell University Press, 1992.
Blumenwitz, Dieter. *Rechtsgutachten über die verbrechen an den Deutschen in Jugo-
   slawien 1944–1948.* Munich: Vorstand der Donauschwäbischen Kulturstiftung—
   Stiftung des Bürgerlichen Rechts, 2002.
Bole, William, Drew Christiansen, S.J., and Robert T. Hennemeyer. *Forgiveness in
   International Politics: An Alternative Road to Peace.* Washington, DC: U.S. Conference of Catholic Bishops, 2004.
Braham, Randolph L. *The Politics of Genocide: The Holocaust in Hungary.* Con-
   densed ed. Detroit, MI: Wayne State University Press, 2000. Published in association with the U.S. Holocaust Memorial Museum.
Brock, Peter. *Media Cleansing, Dirty Reporting: Journalism and Tragedy in Yugoslavia.* 2nd ed. Los Angeles: GM Books, 2005.
Broz, Svetlana. *Good People in an Evil Time: Portraits of Complicity and Resistance
   in the Bosnian War.* Edited by Laurie Kain Hart. Translated by Ellen Elias Bursač
   from Serbian. New York: Other Press, 2005. (Expanded version of the book originally published in English at Sarajevo, Bosnia: Grafičar promet, 2002.)
Bulajić, Milan. *Jasenovac na sudu: Sudjenje Dinku Šakiću.* Belgrade, Serbia: Muzej
   žrtava genocida and IS Stručna knjiga, n.d.
Burg, Steven L., and Paul S. Shoup. *The War in Bosnia-Herzegovina: Ethnic Conflict
   and International Intervention.* Armonk, NY: M.E. Sharpe, 1999.
Chalk, Frank, and Kurt Jonassohn. *The History and Sociology of Genocide: Analyses
   and Case Studies.* New Haven, CT: Yale University Press, in cooperation with the
   Montreal Institute for Genocide Studies, 1990.
Charny, Israel W., ed. *The Encyclopedia of Genocide.* 2 vols. Santa Barbara, CA:
   ABC-CLIO, 1999.
Cigar, Norman. *Genocide in Bosnia: The Policy of "Ethnic Cleansing."* College Sta-
   tion, TX: Texas A&M Press, 1995.
Clark, Howard. *Civil Resistance in Kosovo.* London: Pluto Press, 2000.
Colon, Michael. *Media Lies and the Conquest of Kosovo.* Translated by Milo Yele-
   siyevich, Terrence McGee, and Mick Collins from French. New York: Unwritten
   History, 2007.

Croatian State Commission for Establishing Crimes of Occupying Forces and Their Assistants. *Crimes in the Jasenovac Camp.* [bilingual Croatian title: *Zločini u logoru Jasenovac*]. Banja Luka, Bosnia: Besjeda, 2000.

Crocker, Chester A., Fen Osler Hamson, and Pamela Aall, eds. *Grasping the Nettle: Analyzing Cases of Intractable Conflict.* Washington, DC: United States Institute of Peace Press, 2005.

Burg, Stephen L. "Intractability and Third Party Mediation in the Balkans," 183–207.

Cseres, Tibor. *Serbian Vendetta in Bacska.* Online at www.hungarianhistory.com/lib/cseres/cseres00.htm.

———. *Vebosszu Bácskában* [Blood Vendetta in Bachka]. Budapest: Hunyadi Publisher, 1991.

Cviic, Christopher. *Remaking the Balkans.* Rev. ed. London: Royal Institute of International Affairs/Pinter, 1995.

Danon Braco, Cadik I. *The Smell of Human Flesh: A Witness of the Holocaust Memories of Jasenovac.* Belgrade: Dosije, 2006.

Davis, G. Scott. *Religion and Justice in the War over Bosnia.* New York: Routledge, 1996.

Dedijer, Vladimir. *The Yugoslav Auschwitz and the Vatican.* Translated by Harvey L. Kendall from German. Buffalo, NY: Prometheus Books, and Freiburg, Germany: Ahriman-Verlag, 1992.

Del Ponte, Carla, with Chuck Sudetic. *Madame Prosecutor: Confrontation with Humanity's Worst Criminals and the Culture of Impunity.* New York: Other Press, 2009.

Denitch, Bogdan. *Ethnic Nationalism: The Tragic Death of Yugoslavia.* Minneapolis: University of Minnesota Press, 1994.

Dervishi, Kastriot, ed. *Massacres in Chameria.* Translated by Etleva Sakajeva from Albanian. Tirana, Albania: Publishing House "55", 2010.

Dizdar, Zdravko. "Prilog istraživanju Bleiburga i križnih putova (u povodu 60.objetnice)" [Contribution Toward Research on Bleiburg and Paths of the Cross] (Senj. Zb. 32, 117–196, 2005). en.wikipedia.org/wiki/Bleiburg.massacre (accessed July 4, 2010).

Djilas, Aleksa. *The Contested Country: Yugoslav Unity and Communist Revolution 1919–1953.* Cambridge, MA: Harvard University Press, 1991.

Djurić, Silvija, ed. *Dnevnik pobeda: Srbija u balkanskim ratovima 1912–1913* [Diary of Victories: Serbia in Balkan Wars 1912–1913]. 2nd ed. Belgrade: IRO, 1990.

Djurić, Silvija, and Vidosav Stefanović, eds. *Golgota i vaskrs Srbije 1914–1915* [Golgotha and Resurrection of Serbia 1914–1915]. Vol. 1, 3rd ed. *Golgota i vaskrs Srbije 1915–1918.* Vol. 2. Belgrade: IRO "Beograd," and Čakovec, Croatia: TIZ "Zrinski", 1990.

Djurović, Bogdan, ed. *Etno-religijski odnosi na Balkanu* [Ethno Religious Relations in the Balkans]. Niš, Serbia: Jugoslovensko udruženje za naučno istraživanje religije, 1997.

Drakulić, Slavenka. *They Would Never Hurt a Fly: War Criminals on Trial in The Hague.* New York: Viking Adult, 2004.

Dva stoljeća povijesti i kulture Židova u Zagrebu i Hrvatskoj [Two Centuries of History and Culture of Jews in Zagreb and Croatia]. Edited by Narcisa Lengel-Krizman, Božidar Feldbauer, and Snješka Knežević. Zagreb: Židovska općina, 1998.

Fišer, Darko. "Židovi u Osijeku," 425–27.

Goldstein, Ivo. "Zagrebačka židovska općina od osnutka do 1941," 12–18.

Kovač, Vlasta. "Židovi Vukovara," 448–64.

Engle, Karen. "Feminism and Its (Dis)Contents: Criminalizing Rape in Bosnia and Herzegovina." *American Journal of International Law* 99, no. 778 (2005): 778–816; www.utexas.edu/law/centers/humanrights/about/engle_publications/ Feminism_and_Its_DisContents.pdf (accessed January 10, 2011).

Eventov, Yakir. *A History of Yugoslav Jews*. Tel Aviv: Hitahdut Olej Yugoslavia, 1971.

Faber, Mient Jan, ed. *The Balkans: A Religious Backyard of Europe*. Ravena, Italy: Longo Editore, 1996.

Finlan, Alistair. *The Collapse of Yugoslavia, 1991–1999*. Oxford, UK: Osprey Publishing, 2004.

Gavrilović, Žarko. *Na braniku vere i nacije* [For the Defense of Faith and Nation]. Belgrade: Štamparija solidarnost, 1986.

Gellately, Robert, and Ben Kierman, eds. *The Specter of Genocide: Mass Murder in Historical Perspective*. Cambridge: Cambridge University Press, 2006.

Gellately, Robert, and Ben Kierman. "The Study of Mass Murder and Genocide," 3–26.

Semelin, Jacques. "Analysis of a Mass Crime: Ethnic Cleansing in the Former Yugoslavia, 1991–1999," 353–70.

Gerolymatos, André. *The Balkan Wars: Conquest, Revolution and Retribution from the Ottoman Era to the Twentieth Century and Beyond*. New York: Basic Books, 2002.

Gibbs, David N. *First Do No Harm: Humanitarian Intervention and the Destruction of Yugoslavia*. Nashville, TN: Vanderbilt University Press, 2009.

Glenny, Misha. *The Balkans: Nationalism, War, and the Great Powers, 1804–1999*. New York: Penguin Books, 1999.

———. *The Fall of Yugoslavia: The Third Balkan War*. Rev. ed. New York: Penguin Books, 1993.

Goldhagen, Daniel Jonah. *Worse Than War: Genocide, Eliminationism, and the On-going Assault on Humanity*. New York: Public Affairs, 2009.

Goldstein, Ivo. *Holokaust u Zagrebu*. Zagreb: Novi Liber i Židovska općina Zagreb, 2001.

Grubišić, Ivan. *Konfesije i rat* [Confessions and War]. Split, Croatia: Knjižnica Dijalog, 1993.

Gutman, Roy. *A Witness to Genocide: The 1993 Pulitzer Prize–Winning Dispatches on the "Ethnic Cleansing" of Bosnia*. New York: Macmillan Publishing Company, 1993.

Hadžifejzović, Senad. *Rat uživo: War: Live on Air*. [Bilingual] Sarajevo, Bosnia and Herzegovina, 2002. (Printed in Ljubljana, Slovenia: Mladinska knjiga.)

Hall, Brian. *The Impossible Country: A Journey through the Last Days of Yugoslavia*. Boston: David R. Godine, 1994.

Heer, Hannes, and Birgit Otte. *Vernichtungskrieg: Verbrechen der Wehrmach 1941 bis 1944* [Extermination War: Crimes of the German Army 1941–1944]. Hamburg: Hamburger Institut für Sozialforschung, 1996.

Hewitt, William L., ed. *Defining the Horrific: Readings on Genocide and Holocaust in the Twentieth Century*. Upper Saddle River, NJ: Pearson, Prentice Hall, 2004.

Hartman, Florence. "Bosnia," 297–301.

Knox, Kathleen. "Bosnia: First Genocide Verdict May Bolster Other Cases," 306–7.

Parenti, Michael. "The Rational Destruction of Yugoslavia," 308–18.

Vulliamy, Ed. "Middle Managers of Genocide," 301–5.

Hoare, Marko Attila. "The Ustaša Genocide." *South Slav Journal* 25, nos. 1–2 (Spring–Summer 2004): 2–38.

Honig, Jan Willem, and Norbert Both. *Srebrenica: Record of a War Crime*. New York: Penguin Books, 1997.

Horowitz, Irving L. *Taking Lives: Genocide and State Power*. 4th ed. New Brunswick, NJ: Transaction, 1997.

Hösler, Joachim A. "Konfliktreiche Vergangenheit" [Conflict Rich Past]. *Glaube in der 2. Welt* (Zurich), no. 6 (2008): 18.

Imamović, Jasmin. *Ubijanje smrti* [Killing of Death]. Tuzla, Bosnia: Radio Kameleon, 1995.

International Commission to Inquire into the Causes and Conduct of the Balkan Wars. *The Other Balkan Wars: A 1913 Carnegie Endowment Inquiry in Retrospect*. Washington, DC: A Carnegie Endowment Book, 1993.

Ivanković, Željko. *Tetoviranje identiteta* [Tatooing of Identity]. Sarajevo: Rabić, 2007.

Izetbegović, Alija. *Islamska deklaracija* [Islamic Declaration]. Sarajevo: Bosna, 1990.

Jacobs, Steven Leonard. *Confronting Genocide: Judaism, Christianity, Islam*. Lanham, MD: Lexington Books, 2009.

Mojzes, Paul. "The Genocidal Twentieth Century in the Balkans," 151–81.

Phillips, Garry A. "More Than the Jews . . . His Blood Be upon All the Children: Biblical Violence, Genocide, and Responsible Reading," 77–91.

Jasenovac: Proceedings of the 11th International Conference on Holocaust and 3rd International Conference on Jasenovac. Banja Luka, Bosnia & Herzegovina: Public Institution Memorial Area Donja Gradina and Association Jasenovac–Donja Gradina, 2007.

Jasenovac: Proceedings of the 5th International Conference on Jasenovac. Banja Luka, Republika Srpska, Bosnia and Herzegovina: Public Institution Memorial Area Donja Gradina and Association Jasenovac—Donja Gradina, 2011.

Jasenovac: Proceedings of the 4th International Conference on Jasenovac. Banja Luka, Republika Srpska, Bosnia & Herzegovina: Public Institution Memorial Area Donja Gradina and Association Jasenovac—Donja Gradina, 2007.

Cvetković, Dragan. "Jasenovac in the System of Suffering of the Civilians in the Independent State of Croatia—A Quantitative Analysis (Or Numbers Once More Revisited)."

Mojzes, Paul. "Examination of Genocide: Truth and Justice Instead of Political and Economic Gain," 83–90.

Živanović, Srboljub. "Forensic Observations on the Efficiency of the Catholic and Muslim Croatian Murderers' Way of Killing and Torturing of their Serbian, Jewish, and Roma Victims," 43–45.

Jasenovac: Proceeding of Speeches 4th International Conference on Jasenovac. Banja Luka, Republika Srpska, Bosnia and Herzegovina: Association Jasenovac—Donja Gradina, 2008.

Jasenovac: Proceeding of the First International Conference and Exhibit about Jasenovac Concentration Camps [Jasenovac: Zbornik radova prve medjunarodne konferencije i izložbe o Jasenovačkim koncentracionim logorim]. Banja Luka, Bosnia & Herzegovina: Public Institution Memorial Area Donja Gradina and Association Jasenovac—Donja Gradina, 2007.

Jasenovac: Žrtve rata prema podatcima Statističkog zavoda Jugoslavije [Victims of War According to the Data of the Statistical Institute of Yugoslavia]. Sarajevo: Bošnjački Institut Zürich-Sarajevo, 1998.

Johnstone, Diana. *Fools' Crusade: Yugoslavia, NATO and Western Delusions.* New York: Monthly Review Press, 2002.

Jovanović, Aleksandar S. *Poraz: Koreni poraza* [Defeat: Roots of Defeat]. Veternik, Serbia: Idij, 2001.

Jovanović, Živadin. *Ukidanje države* [Terminating the State]. Veternik, Serbia: Dijam-M Pres, 2003.

Judah, Tim. *Kosovo: War and Revenge.* 2nd ed. New Haven, CT: Yale University Press, 2002.

———. "The Serbs: The Sweet and Rotten Smell of History." *South Slav Journal* (London) 19, nos. 1–2 (71–72) (Spring–Summer, 1998).

Karahasan, Dževad. *Sarajevo: Exodus of a City.* Translated by Slobodan Drakulić from Serbo-Croatian-Bosnian. New York: Kodansha International, 1994.

Karan, Vasilije. *Kako sam dobio pismo od Hitlera* [How I Got a Letter from Hitler]. 2nd ed. Laktaši: GrafoMark, n.d.

Kiernan, Ben. *Blood and Soil: A World History of Genocide and Extermination from Sparta to Darfur.* New Haven, CT: Yale University Press, 2007.

Kitanoski, Mišo, ed. *Skopskite Evrei* [Jews of Skopje]. Skopje, Macedonia: Globus-Kitano, 2002.

Klein, Dennis B., Richard Liebowitz, Marcia Sachs Littell, and Sharon B. Steeley, eds. *The Genocidal Mind.* St. Paul, MN: Paragon House, 2005.

Kolanović, Nada Kisić. "Podržavljenje imovine Židova u NDH" [The Nationalization of Jewish Property in the Independent State of Croatia]. *Časopis za suvremenu povijest* (Zagreb), no. 3 (1998): 429–53.

Kolonomos, Žamila, and Vera Vesković-Vangeli. *Evreite vo Makedonija vo vtorata svetska vojna, 1941–1945* [Jews in Macedonia During the Second World War]. Vols. 1 and 2. Skopje, Macedonia: Makedonska akademija na naukite i umetnostite, 1986.

Vesković-Vangeli, Vera. "Antisemitskoto zakonodavstvo na fashistichka Bugarija-faktor za demografskite promeni vo Makedonija" [Antisemitic Legislation of Fascist Bulgaria—A Factor for Demographic Changes in Macedonia], 107–24.

Korda, Josip, and Slavka Puškar. *Vinkovački kraj na putu u slobodu i socijalizam, 1895–1945.* Vinkovci, Croatia: Izdanje skupštine općine, OK SKH & SUBNOR, 1976.

Krestić, Vasilije. *Through Genocide to a Greater Croatia.* Belgrade: BIGZ, 1998.

Krišto, Jure. "Vjerski prijelazi u NDH—primjer šibeničke biskupije" [Religious Transfer in ISC—Example of the Šibenik Bishopric]. *Časopis za suvremenu povijest* (Zagreb) 29, no. 2 (1997): 235–48.

Kuper, Leo. *Genocide: Its Political Use in the Twentieth Century*. New Haven, CT: Yale University Press, 1981.

Kurze, Arnaud. "Bringing Back War Crimes Issues: Croatia and the EU Enlargement Process." *South Slav Journal* 29, nos. 3–4 (113–114) (Autumn, 2010): 140–47.

Kuzmanič, Tonči, and Truger, Arno, eds. *Yugoslavia War*. Ljubljana, Slovenia, and Schleining, Austria: Peace Institute Ljubljana and Austrian Study Centre for Peace and Conflict Resolution, 1992.

Lastavica, Dane. *Genocid nad srpskim narodom sreza Perušić, (Lika) 1941–1945 i 1991–?* [Genocide on Serbian People of the County of Perushich (Lika)], 1941–1945 and 1991–?]. Belgrade: Muzej žrtava genocida, 2002.

Lebel, Jennie. *A Memorial of Yugoslavian Jewish Prisoners of War: Half a Century after Liberation 1945–1995*. Tel Aviv, Israel: Udruženje veterana drugog svetskog rata u Israelu, Jugoslavenska grupa, 1995.

———. *The Mufti of Jerusalem Haj-Amin el-Husseini and National Socialism*. Translated by Paul Munch from Serbian. Belgrade, Serbia, Cigoja, 2007.

Lebl, Zheni. *Do "konačnog rešenja": Jevreji u Beogradu 1521–1942*. [To the "Final Solution": Jews in Belgrade 1521–1942]. Belgrade, Serbia: Cigoja, 2001.

———. *Do "konačnog rešenja": Jevreji u Srbiji* [To the "Final Solution": Jews in Serbia]. Belgrade, Serbia: Cigoja, 2002.

———. "Kindertransport iz NDH." *Bilten Udruženja Jevreja iz bivše Jugoslavije u Israelu* 42, no. 4 (1994): 15–18.

———. *Plima i slom* [High Tide and Breakdown]. Gornji Milanovac, Serbia: Dečje novine, 1990.

Levin, Nora. *The Holocaust: The Destruction of European Jewry 1933–1945*. New York: Thomas Y. Crowell Company, 1968.

Lieberman, Benjamin. *Terrible Fate: Ethnic Cleansing in the Making of Modern Europe*. Chicago: Ivan R. Dee, 2006.

Lituchy, Barry M., ed. *Jasenovac and the Holocaust in Yugoslavia: Analysis and Survivor Stories*. New York: Jasenovac Research Institute, 2006.

Maas, Peter. *Love Thy Neighbor: A Story of War*. New York: Alfred A. Knopf, 1996.

MacDonald, David Bruce. *Balkan Holocausts? Serbian and Croatian Victim-Centered Propaganda and the War in Yugoslavia*. Manchester, UK: Manchester University Press, 2002.

MacKinnon, Catherine A. *Are Women Human? And Other International Dialogues*. Cambridge, MA: Belknap Press of Harvard University Press, 2006.

Magaš, Branka, ed. *The Destruction of Yugoslavia: Tracking the Break-Up 1980–1992*. London, New York: Verso, 1993.

Malcolm, Noel. *Bosnia: A Short History*. New York: New York University Press, 1994.

Massacres in Bosnia and Herzegovina: Srebrenica Massacre, Lasva Valley Ethnic Cleansing, Prijedor Massacre. Memphis, TN: Books LLC, 2010.

Mažuranić, Matija. "An 'Illyrian' Croat's 1839–40 Vision of Bosnia." *South Slav Journal* 28, nos. 3–4 (109–110) (Autumn–Winter, 2007): 43–49.

McSpadden, Lucia Ann, ed. *Reaching Reconciliation: Churches in Transition to Democracy in Eastern and Central Europe*. Uppsala, Sweden: Life & Peace Institute, 2000.
Merrill, Christopher. *The Old Bridge: The Third Balkan War and the Age of the Refugee*. Minneapolis, MN: Milkweed Editions, 1995.
Mertus, Julie, Jasmina Tešanović, Habiba Metikoš, and Rada Borić, eds. *The Suitcase: Refugee Voices from Bosnia and Croatia*. Berkeley: University of California Press, 1997.
Meštrović, Stjepan, with Slaven Letica and Miroslav Goreta. *Habits of the Balkan Heart: Social Character and the Fall of Communism*. College, TX: Texas A&M University Press, 1993.
Meta, Beqir. *The Cham Tragedy*. Tirana, Albania: Sejko, 2007.
Minow, Martha. *Between Vengeance and Forgiveness: Facing History after Genocide and Mass Violence*. Boston, MA: Beacon Press, 1998.
Mirković, Damir. "Victims and Perpetrators in the Yugoslav Genocide 1941–1945: Some Preliminary Observations." *Holocaust and Genocide Studies* 7, no. 3 (Winter 1993): 317–32.
———. Book review of Zatezalo, Djuro. *Jadovno: Kompleks ustaških logora 1941* [Jadovno: A Complex of Ustaša Camps, 1941]. *South Slav Journal* 29, nos. 1–2 (2010): 147–51.
Mirković, Jovan, ed. *Genocid u 20. Veku na prostorima jugoslovenskih zemalja* [Genocide in the 20th Century on the Territory of Yugoslav Lands]. Belgrade: Muzej žrtava genocida, 2005.
Acković, Dragoljub. "Licitiranje o broju romskih žrtava u Jasenovcu i Nezavisnoj Državi Hrvatskoj" [Auction of the Number of Roma Victims in Jasenovac and Independent State of Croatia.], 468–76.
Janjetović, Zoran. "Da li su Srbi počinili genocid na Podunavskim Švabama?" [Did Serbs Commit Genocide Over Danubian Swabians?], 231–38.
———, ed. *Izraelsko-Srpska naučna razmena u proučavanju Holokausta/Israeli-Serbian Academic Exchange in Holocaust Research*. Bilingual ed. Belgrade: Muzej žrtava genocida, 2008.
Antonijević, Nenad. "Holocaust in the Area of Kosovo and the Metohija during World War II and Its Context," 409–24.
Ristović, Milan. "The Persecuted and Their Abettors: Solidarity and Help for the Jews in Serbia 1941–1945," 209–50.
———, ed. *Prilozi istraživanju genocida i ratnih zločina* [Contributions to the Research of Genocide and War Crimes]. Belgrade: Muzej žrtava genocida, 2009.
Mirković, Jovan. "Hronologija zločina (April–Avgust 1941. godine) Prilog dokazima o genocidnostnom karakteru Nezavsine Države Hrvatske" [Chronology of Crime: Contribution of Evidence about the Genocidal Character of the Independent State of Croatia], 11–78.
Cvetković, Dragan. "Bosna i Hercegovina—numeričko odredjivanje ljudskih gubitaka u drugom svetskom ratu" [Bosnia and Herzegovina: Numerical Determination of Human Losses during World War II], 79–156.
Mišina, Veljko Djurić. *Srpska pravoslavna crkva u Nezavisnoj Državi Hrvatskoj 1941–1945 godine* [The Serbian Orthodox Church in the Independent State of Croatia 1941–1945]. Veternik, Serbia: DIJAM-M-pres, 2002.

Mlakar, Boris, "Still a Burning Dilemma: Was There Also a Civil War Going in Slovenia during World War II?" *South Slav Journal* (London) 28, nos. 3–4 (109–110), (2009): 62–83.

Mojzes, Paul. "Religion and Armed Humanitarian Intervention in the Former Yugoslavia." In *Religion, Law, and the Role of Force: A Study of Their Influence on Conflict and on Conflict Resolution*, ed. J. I. Coffey and Charles T. Matthews. Ardsley, NY: Transnational Publications, 2002, 129–44.

———, ed. *Religion and the War in Bosnia*. Atlanta, GA: Scholars Press, 1998.

Cohen, Lenard. "Bosnia's 'Tribal Gods': The Role of Religion in Nationalist Politics," 43–73.

Mojzes, Paul. "The Camouflaged Role of Religion in Bosnia," 77–81.

———. "The Religiosity of Radovan Karadzic." *Religion in Eastern Europe* 15, no. 4 (August 1995): 17–22.

———. "The Role of Religious Communities in the War in the Former Yugoslavia." *Religion in Eastern Europe* 13, no. 3 (June 1993): 13–31.

———. *Yugoslavian Inferno: Ethnoreligious Warfare in the Balkans*. New York: Continuum, 1994.

Morton, Jeffery S., R. Craig Nation, Paul C. Forage, and Stefano Bianchini, eds. *Reflections on the Balkan Wars: Ten Years after the Break-Up of Yugoslavia*. New York: Palgrave Macmillan, 2004.

Huttenbach, Henry R. "The Genocide Factor in the Yugoslav Wars of Dismemberment," 23–34.

Joyner, Christopher C., and Anthony Clark Arend. "Rethinking the Legal Nuances of Kosovo: Toward an Emerging Norm of Anticipatory Humanitarian Intervention?" 165–86.

Mousavizadeh, Nader, ed. *The Black Book of Bosnia: The Consequences of Appeasement*. Washington, DC: BasicBooks, 1996.

Ajami, Fouad. "In Europe's Shadows," 37–54.

Deak, Istvan. "The One and the Many," 5–19.

Djilas, Aleksa. "The Nation That Wasn't," 19–27.

Lane, Charles. "Dateline Zagreb: The Fall of Srebrenica," 116–24.

Lewis, Anthony. "War Crimes," 55–64.

Myers, Richard B., and Albert C. Pierce, "On Strategic Leadership." *JFQ/Joint Force Quarterly* (Washington, DC), no. 34 (3rd Quarter, 2009): 12–13.

Naimark, Norman M. *Fires of Hatred: Ethnic Cleansing in Twentieth Century Europe*. Cambridge, MA: Harvard University Press, 2001.

Novaković, Nenad, ed. Zemaljska Komisija Hrvatske za utvrdjivanje zločina okupatora i njihovih pomagača [State Commission of Croatia for the Determination of Crimes of Occupiers and Their Assistants]. *Zločini u logoru Jasenovac*. [Crimes in the Jasenovac Camp]. Banja Luka, Bosnia: Besjeda, 2000.

Oršolić, Marko, *Zlodusima nasuprot* [Contra Evil Spirits], 2nd rev. ed. Sarajevo: MAUNA-Fe, 2008.

Owen, David. *Balkan Odyssey*. New York: Harcourt Brace, 1995.

Pavlica, Branko. "Sudbina Nemaca u Srbiji" [Destiny of Germans in Serbia]. *Teme* (Niš, Serbia) 29, no. 3 (July–September 2005).

Petacco, Arrigo. *A Tragedy Revealed: The Story of Italians from Istria, Dalmatia, and Venezia Giulia, 1943–1956*. Translated byKonrad Eisenbichler from Italian. Toronto: University of Toronto Press, 2005.

Petersen, Roger D. *Understanding Ethnic Violence: Fear, Hatred, and Resentment in Twentieth-Century Eastern Europe*. Cambridge: Cambridge University Press, 2002.

Pokrajinska komisija Vojvodine. *Zločini okupatora i njihovih pomagača u Vojvodini protiv Jevreja* (Crimes of the Occupators and Their Assistants in Vojvodina against Jews). Drago Njegovan, ed. Novi Sad, Serbia: Prometej, 2011.

Poliakov, Leon, and Jacques Sabille. *Jews under Italian Occupation*. New York: H. Fertig, 1983. (Reprint of a 1955 work.)

Sabille, Jacques. "The Attitude of the Italians to the Persecuted Jews in Croatia," 131–50.

Popov, Nebojša, ed. *Srpska strana rata: Trauma i katarza u istorijskom pamćenju* [Serbian Side of the War: Trauma and Catharsis in Historical Memory]. Belgrade: Republika, 1996.

Blagojević, Marina. "Iseljavanje Srba sa Kosova: trauma i/ili katarza [Exodus of Serbs from Kosovo: Trauma and/or Catharsis], 232–64.

Zirojević, Olga. "Kosovo u kolektivnom pamćenju" [Kosovo in Collective Memory], 201–31.

Popović, Srdja, Dejan Janča, and Tanja Petovar, eds. *Kosovski čvor: Drešiti ili seći?* [Kosovo Knot: Unravel or Cut?]. Belgrade: Biblioteka Chronos, 1990.

Portmann, Michael. *Kommunistische Abrechnung mit Kriegsverbrechern, Kollaborateuren, "Volksfeinden" und "Verrätern" in Jugoslawien während des Zweiten Weltkriegs und unmittelbar danach*. Unpublished master's thesis, Wien, 2002.

Radna grupa za dokumentaciju. *Genocid nad nemačkom manjiom u Jugoslaviji 1944–1948*. [Translated from *Genocide of the Ethnic Germans in Yugoslavia 1944–1948* into Serbian by Dragutin Janjetović]. Belgrade: Društvo za srpsko-nemačku saradnju, Beograd, Srbija i Crna Gora, and Donauschwäbische Kulturstiftung, München, 2004.

Ramet, Sabrina P. *Nationalism and Federalism in Yugoslavia 1962–1991*. 2nd ed. Bloomington: Indiana University Press, 1992.

———. *Balkan Babel: The Disintegration of Yugoslavia from the Death of Tito to the Fall of Milošević*. 4th ed. Boulder, CO: Westview Press, 2002.

Ristović, Milan. *U potrazi za utočištem: Jugoslovenski Jevreji u bekstvu od holokausta 1941–45* [In Search for a Safe Haven: Yugoslav Jews in Flight from the Holocaust, 1941–45]. Belgrade: Javno preduzeće Službeni List SRJ, 1998.

Rittner, Carol, John R. Roth, and James M. Smith, eds. *Will Genocide Ever End?* St. Paul, MN: Paragon House, 2002.

Mojzes, Paul. "Ethnic Cleansing," 51–56.

Rodogno, Davide. *Fascism's European Empire: Italian Occupation during the Second World War*. Translated by Adrian Belton. Cambridge: Cambridge University Press, 2006.

Romano, Jaša. *Jevreji Jugoslavije 1941–1945 žrtve genocida i učesnici NOB-a.* [Jews of Yugoslavia 1941–1945 Victims of Genocide and Participants of the People's

Liberation Struggle]. Belgrade: Jevrejski istorijski muzej Saveza Jevrejskih opština Jugoslavije, 1980.

Ručnov, Marko. *Zašto Jasenovac* [Why Jasenovac]. Belgrade: IKP "Nikola Pašić," 2001.

———. *Zašto Jasenovac*. Separat no. 1. Belgrade: Nikola Pašić, 2004.

Rummel, R. J. *Death by Government*. New Brunswick, NJ: Transaction Publishers, 2007.

———. *Lethal Politics*. New Brunswick, NJ: Transaction, 1996.

———. *Statistics of Democide: Genocide and Mass Murder*. New Brunswick, NJ: Transaction, 1997.

Šalić, Tomo. *Židovi u Vinkovcima i okolici* [Jews in Vinkovci and Surroundings]. Osijek, Croatia: Židovska općina Osijek, and Zagreb: Kuturno društvo "Miroslav Šalom Freiberger," 2002.

Samary, Catherine. *Yugoslavia Dismembered*. Translated by Peter Drucker from French. New York: Monthly Review Press, 1995.

Šaroviќ, Liljana, ed. *Štipskite Evrei* [Jews of Shtip]. Skopje, Macedonia: Evrejska zaednica vo Makedonija, 1999.

Sećanje Jevreja na logor Jasenovac [Memory of Jews of the Camp at Jasenovac]. Belgrade: Savez jevrejskih opština, 1972.

Sekulić, Tomislav. *Seobe kao sudbina* [Migrations as Destiny]. Veternik, Serbia: DIJAM-M-pres, 2002.

Sells, Michael A. *The Bridge Betrayed: Religion and Genocide in Bosnia*. Berkeley: University of California Press, 1996.

Semelin, Jacques. *Purify and Destroy: The Political Uses of Massacre and Genocide*. Translated by Cynthia Schoch from French. New York: Columbia University Press, 2007.

Shkreli, Azem, ed. *Knocking on Europe's Conscience: Kosova, Evidence & Documents*. Prishtine: Council for the Defense of Human Rights and Freedoms in Prishtina, 1992.

Shriver, Donald W., Jr. *An Ethic for Enemies: Forgiveness in Politics*. New York: Oxford University Press, 1997.

Silber, Laura, and Allan Little. *Yugoslavia: Death of a Nation*. New York: Penguin Books, 1997.

Šosberger, Pavle. *Novosadski Jevreji* [Jews of Novi Sad]. 2nd ed. Novi Sad: Prometej, 2001

Stanišić, Mihailo. *Projekti "Velika Srbija"* [Projects "Great Serbia"]. Belgrade: Javno preduzeće Službeni list SRJ, 2000.

Stefanov, Pavel. "The Bulgarian Orthodox Church and the Holocaust: Addressing Common Misperceptions." *Religion in Eastern Europe* 26, no. 2 (May 2006): 10–19.

Stefanović, Zoran, ed. *Crucified Kosovo: Destroyed and Desecrated Serbian Orthodox Churches in Kosovo and Metohija (June-October 1999)* [bilingual English and Serbian]. N.p.: "The Voice of Kosovo and Metohija," 1999.

Stiglemayer, Alexandra, ed. *Mass Rape: The War against Women in Bosnia-Herzegovina*. Lincoln: University of Nebraska Press, 1994.

Stojanović, Svetozar. *Propast komunizma i razbijanje Jugoslavije* [The Demise of Communism and the Breaking Up of Yugoslavia]. Belgrade: "Filip Višnjić" Institut za filozofiju i društvenu teoriju, 1995.

———. *The Fall of Yugoslavia: Why Communism Failed.* Amherst, NY: Prometheus Press, 1997.

Suroi, Veton. "Kosova: A Case for Self-Determination." *Kosova Watch* (Prishtina) 1, no. 2 (August 1992): 24–27.

Šušnjar 1941: Proceedings—Papers, Testimonies and Documents. Oštra Luka, RS, Bosnia and Herzegovina: 2008.

Bogdanović, Dušan. "Through Facts to the Truth," 157–64.

Bulajić, Milan. "Šušnjar Near Sanski Most (1941–1944); Genocide over Serbs and Jews on St. Elijah's Day 1941," 101–24.

Crnomarković, Milan. "Crimes in Sanski Most," 141–52.

Praća-Veljović, Sofija. "Genocide in Sanski Most," 69–93.

Trninić, Drago. "Šušnjar in 1941," 153–56.

Terzić, Velimir. *Jugoslavija u aprilskom ratu 1941* (Titograd, 1963).

Totten, Samuel. "Witnessing the Making of History: The Trial of Slobodan Milosevic." *Social Education* 67, no. 5 (September 2003): 267–72.

Totten, Samuel, and Paul R. Bartrop, eds. *The Genocide Studies Reader.* New York and London, Routledge, 2009.

Akhavan, Payam, and Mora Johnson, "International Criminal Tribunal for the Former Yugoslavia," 442–51.

Mann, Michael. "Explaining Ethnic Cleansing."

Sharlach, Lisa. "State Rape: Sexual Violence as Genocide," 180–92.

Totten, Samuel, William S. Parsons, and Israel W. Charny, eds. *Century of Genocide: Critical Essays and Eyewitness Accounts.* 2nd ed. New York: Routledge, 2004.

Tudjman, Franjo. *Horrors of War: Historical Reality and Philosophy.* Rev. ed. Translated by Katarina Mijatović from Croatian. New York: M. Evans, 1996.

Udovički, Jasminka, and James Ridgeway, eds. *Yugoslavia's Ethnic Nightmare: The Inside Story of Europe's Unfolding Ordeal.* New York: Lawrence Hill Books, 1995.

Štitkovac, Ejub. "Croatia: The First War."

Štitkovac, Ejub, and Jasminka Udovički. "Bosnia and Hercegovina: The Second War."

Umeljić, Vladimir. *Srbi i genocidni XX vek: Počinioci i žrtve, krivica i odgovornost* [Serbs and Genocidal Twentieth Century]. Belgrade: Magna plus, n.d. (Original title: *Die Besatzungszeit: Das genozid in Jugoslawien 1941–1945.* Los Angeles: Graphics High Publishing, 1994.)

———. *Srbi i genocidni XX vek: Komentari, prilozi, dokumenta.* Belgrade, Magna plus, n.d.

Vasiljević, Zoran. *Sabirni logor Djakovo* [Transit Camp Djakovo] Slavonski Brod: Centar za povijest Slavonije i Baranje and Spomen-područje Jasenovac, 1988.

Velikonja, Mitja. *Religious Separation & Political Intolerance in Bosnia-Herzegovina.* Translated by Rang'ichi Ng'inja from Slovenian. College Station, TX: Texas A&M University Press, 2003.

Veljić, Aleksandar, *Racija: Zaboravljeni genocid* [Ratsiya: Forgotten Genocide]. Belgrade, Serbia: Metaphysica, 2007.

Verdery, Katherine. *The Political Lives of Dead Bodies: Reburial and Postsocialist Change.* New York: Columbia University Press, 1999.

Verna, Frank Philip. *Yugoslavia under Italian Rule 1941–1943: Civil and Military Aspects of the Italian Occupation.* Ph.D. dissertation, University of California, Santa Barbara, 1985. Ann Arbor, MI: University Microfilms International.

Vernichtungskrieg: Verbrechen der Wehrmacht 1941–1944. Hamburg: Hamburger Edition HIS Verlag, 1996.

Vetlesen, Arne Johan. *Evil and Human Agency: Understanding Collective Evildoing.* Cambridge: Cambridge University Press, 2005.

Volf, Miroslav. "Exclusion and Embrace: Theological Reflection and 'Ethnic Cleansing.'" *Religion in Eastern Europe* 13, no. 6 (December 1993).

Vuković, Slobodan. "Ulica Vase Miskina, Markale, Račak: Dogadjaji s obaračem," [Vase Miskina Street, Markale, Račak: Events with a Trigger]. *Teme* (Niš, Serbia) 33, no. 1 (January–March, 2009): 201–14.

Vulliamy, Ed. *Seasons in Hell: Understanding Bosnia's War.* New York: St. Martin's Press, 1994.

Weitz, Eric D. *A Century of Genocide: Utopias of Race and Nation.* Princeton and Oxford: Princeton University Press, 2006.

Wildman, Georg, with Hans Sonnleitner and Karl Weber. *Verbrechen an den deutschen in Jugoslawien 1944–1948: Die Stationen eines Völkermords.* Munich: Donauschwäbische Kulturstiftung and Stiftung des privaten Rechts, 2000.

Yahil, Leni. *The Holocaust.* New York: Oxford University Press, 1990.

Zemaljska komisija Hrvatske za utvrdjivanje zločina okupatora i njihovih pomagača. *Zločini u logoru Jasenovac* [on same cover, the English translation: Croatian State Commission for Establishing Crimes of Occupying Forces and Their Assistants, *Crimes in the Jasenovac Camp*]. Translated by Dragica Banjac from Croatian. Banja Luka: Besjeda, 2000.

Žerjavić, Vladimir. *Gubitci stanovništva Jugoslavije u drugom svjetskom ratu* [Population Losses of Yugoslavia in the Second World War]. Zagreb: Jugoslavensko viktimološko društvo, 1980.

Zimmermann, Warren. *Origins of a Catastrophe.* New York: Random House, 1996.

Živić, Dražen. "Izravni demografski gubitci (ratne žrtve) Hrvatske (1990–1998.) uzrokovani velikosrpskom agresijom i neke njihove posljedice [Direct Demographic Losses (War Victims) of Croatia (1990–1998) Caused by the Greater Serbian Aggression and Some of Their Consequences]. *Društvena istraživanja* (Zagreb) 10, no. 3 (2001), 451–84.

Živkovic, Nikola, ed. *Srbi u ratnom dnevniku Vermahta* [Serbs in the War Diary of the German Army]. 2nd ed. Belgrade: Javno preduzeće Službeni list SCR, 2004.

Zločini fašističkih okupatora i njihovih pomagača protiv Jevreja u Jugoslaviji [Crimes of Fascist Occupiers and Their Assistants against Jews in Yugoslavia]. Belgrade: Association of Jewish Communities in FPR Yugoslavia, 1952.

PERIODICAL LITERATURE

Bilten—11-ti mart 1943 (Skopje, Macedonia).

Genocide and Holocaust Studies (Oxford University Press and U.S. Holocaust Memorial Museum).

Genocide Studies and Prevention (Virginia Commonwealth University and University of Toronto).

Journal of Genocide Research (Routledge, UK).

Kosova Watch (Prishtina: Kosova Helsinki Committee).

Prism Journal for Holocaust Educators (Yeshiva University, New York).

Probleme des Friedens, Pax Christi—Deutsches Sekretariat: "Bosnien-Herzegowina: Die Chances einer gerechten Lösung," no. 4 (1994).

Religion in Eastern Europe. Ed. Paul Mojzes and Walter Sawatsky (Elkhart, IN: Christians Associated for Relationships with Eastern Europe; quarterly).

The South Slav Journal. Formerly published in London, UK, but as of vol. 29, nos. 1–2 (Spring 2010), published in Budapest, Hungary.

Index

About the Author

Paul Mojzes is professor of religious studies and former provost and academic dean at Rosemont College in Pennsylvania and was the Ida E. King Distinguished Visiting Professor of Holocaust and Genocide Studies at Richard Stockton College of New Jersey. He is a native of Yugoslavia who came to the United States in 1957, having studied at Belgrade University Law School for two years. He received his A.B. degree from Florida Southern College, graduating summa cum laude, and earned his Ph.D. in church history from Boston University in 1965. Among the books he has authored and edited are *Christian-Marxist Dialogue in Eastern Europe, Religious Liberty in Eastern Europe and the USSR, Yugoslavian Inferno: Ethnoreligious Warfare in the Balkans,* and *Religion and War in Bosnia.* He is the coeditor of *The Journal of Ecumenical Studies* and founder and coeditor of *Religion in Eastern Europe.* He is a former president of Christians Associated for Relationships with Eastern Europe and is a participant in numerous interreligious dialogues and scholars conferences on the Holocaust and genocides, both in the United States and abroad.

CPSIA information can be obtained at www.ICGtesting.com
Printed in the USA
BVOW071536101011

273265BV00001B/5/P